CHRISTIANE FLORIANI BRUHN

The Procedure of Evidence Taking in the Brazilian Criminal Trial

Beiträge zum Internationalen und
Europäischen Strafrecht

Studies in International and
European Criminal Law and Procedure

Herausgegeben von / Edited by
Prof. Dr. Dr. h.c. Kai Ambos, Richter am Kosovo Sondertribunal
Berater (amicus curiae) Sondergerichtsbarkeit für den Frieden, Bogotá, Kolumbien

Band / Volume 55

The Procedure of Evidence Taking in the Brazilian Criminal Trial

An Analysis Inspired by Selected Features
of the German Criminal Procedure and the US-American
Criminal Procedure and Evidence Law

By

Christiane Floriani Bruhn

Duncker & Humblot · Berlin

The Faculty of Law of the Albert-Ludwigs-Universität Freiburg
accepted this work as thesis in the year 2021

Bibliographic information of the German national library

The German national library registers this publication in
the German national bibliography; specified bibliographic data
are retrievable on the Internet about http://dnb.d-nb.de.

All rights reserved.
© 2023 Duncker & Humblot GmbH, Berlin
Typesetting: 3w+p GmbH, Rimpar
Printing: CPI books GmbH, Leck
Printed in Germany

ISSN 1867-5271
ISBN 978-3-428-18819-2 (Print)
ISBN 978-3-428-58819-0 (E-Book)

Gedruckt auf alterungsbeständigem (säurefreiem) Papier
entsprechend ISO 9706 ♾

Internet: http://www.duncker-humblot.de

To my Parents

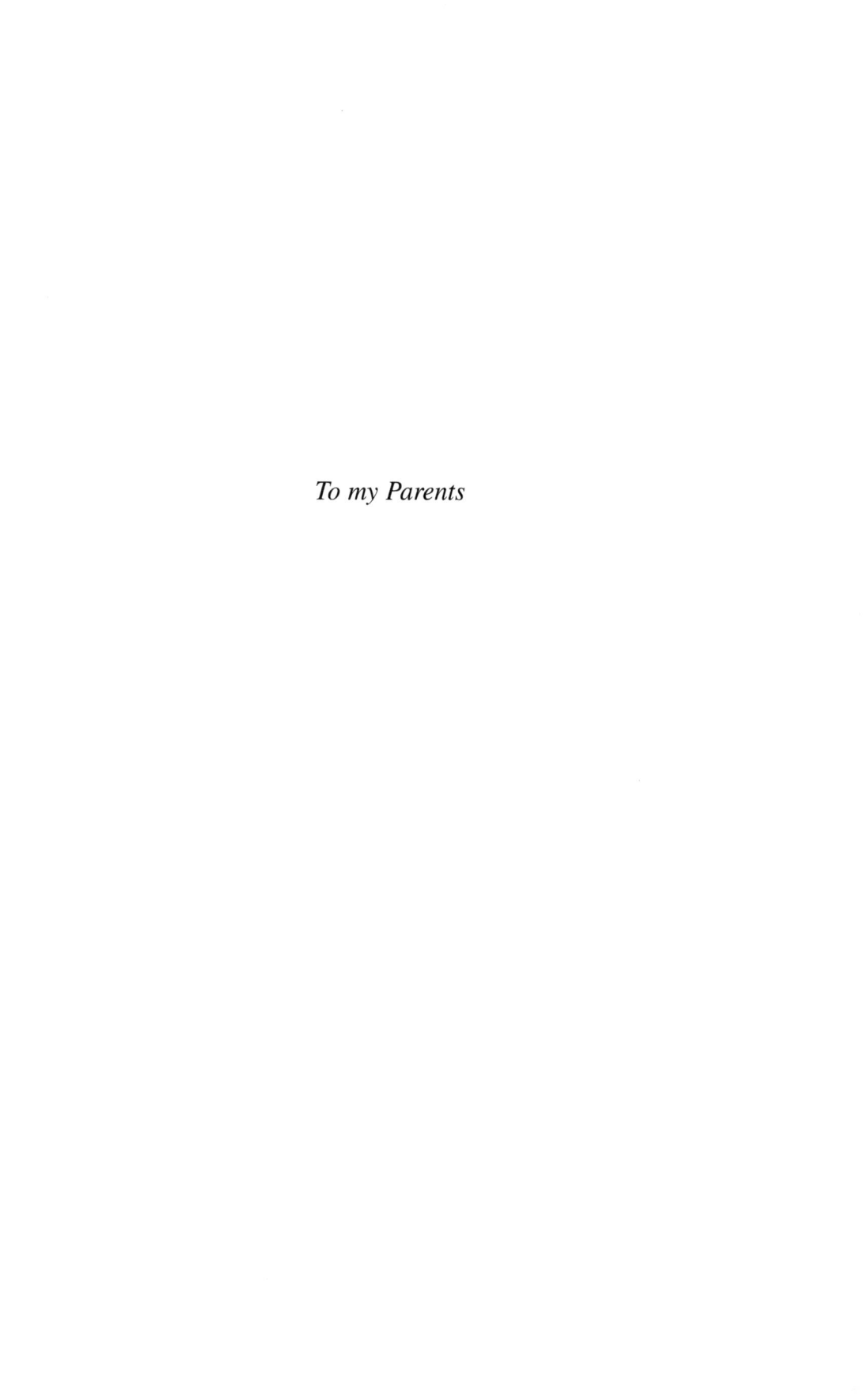

Foreword

I would like to start by thanking my doctoral supervisor Prof. Dr. Walter Perron for his constant availability and guidance throughout the years. Without his serenity, depth of knowledge and clarity of thought, this work would not have been the same!

I am grateful to Prof. Dr. Kai Ambos for giving me the opportunity to publish my dissertation in this series.

I would like to express my gratitude to Prof. Dr. Ulrich Sieber for having welcomed me as a master's student in 2013 and for having enabled me the unique experience of conducting research at the Max Planck Institute for seven years. I have grown tremendously as a person and as a researcher from that experience, and for that I will always be extremely grateful.

I would like to thank Prof. Dr. Ana Lucia Sabadell for without her great support and guidance, none of this would have been possible.

To the wonderful friends that I made during my master's and doctorate, I thank them for their support; they have played a vital part in making this period a very joyful and rewarding experience.

I would also like to thank my sister for her love and support over the years.

Finally, I would like to thank my parents for their constant encouragement and unwavering faith in me. It is a privilege to be their daughter.

Freiburg, May 2023 *Christiane Floriani Bruhn*

Table of Contents

Introduction 21
   I. Research Subject 21
   II. Research Objectives 22
   III. Research Method and Scope of Analysis 22
   IV. Structure of the Study 25

Part 1

The Development of the Normative Framework of the Brazilian Criminal Procedure   27

A. Historical Background 27
B. The Current Code of Criminal Procedure 30
   I. The Enactment of the Federal Constitution 31
   II. Modifications to the Code of Criminal Procedure 32
      1. Legislative Reforms 33
      2. Outcome of the Previous Reforms 35
      3. Latest Statutory Modifications 37

Part 2

Country Reports   40

Chapter 1

Germany   40

A. Introduction 40
B. Overview of the Criminal Procedure 41
   I. Legal Sources 41
   II. Court System 43
   III. Main Procedural Actors 45
      1. Judges 46
      2. Prosecutors 47

Table of Contents

    3. Defense Counsel 48
  IV. Procedural Phases 49
    1. Investigatory Phase 49
      a) Evidence Gathering by the State 49
      b) Rights of the Defense in the Investigatory Phase 51
    2. Intermediate Proceedings: Evidentiary Standard of hinreichender Tatverdacht 52
    3. Main Proceedings 53
      a) Preparation for the Main Hearing 53
      b) Main Hearing 54
        aa) Determining Attendance of the Procedural Actors and that Evidence is Present 54
        bb) Defendant's Examination 54
        cc) Evidence Taking and Closing Arguments 55
        dd) Deliberations, Voting and Pronouncement of Judgment 56
C. Evidence Law 57
  I. Introduction 57
    1. Finder of Fact: Professional and Lay Judges 57
    2. Trial Setting 58
      a) Officialized Factfinding 58
      b) Rights of the Prosecution and Defense in Participating in the Presentation of Evidence 59
  II. Methods of Proving Facts 60
    1. Exceptions to the Need of Proof 60
    2. Strict and Discretionary Forms of Proof 61
  III. Means of Evidence 62
    1. Defendant 62
    2. Witnesses 65
      a) Rights and Duties 66
      b) Particularities of the Examination of Witnesses 68
    3. Experts 69
    4. Documentary Evidence 70
    5. Inspection 72
  IV. Admissibility of Evidence 74
    1. Admissibility of Evidence and Rationale Behind Limiting or Excluding Evidence 74
    2. Statutory and Constitutional Rules Excluding or Limiting Evidence 75
      a) Protection of the Defendant's Right of Personality 75
      b) Nemo Tenetur Se Ipsum Accusare 76
      c) Prohibited Methods of Examining the Accused 79

	d) Witnesses' Rights and Duties to Refuse to Testify	80
	aa) Right to Refuse to Testify	80
	bb) Duty to Refuse to Testify	81
D. Evidentiary Principles and Procedural Safeguards		82
I. Principle of Ascertainment of the Truth		83
II. The Defendant's Right to Request the Court to Take Evidence		83
III. Principle of Free Evaluation of Evidence		86

Chapter 2

The United States of America — 87

A. Introduction 87
B. Overview of the Criminal Procedure 89
   I. Legal Sources 89
   II. Court System 90
   III. Main Procedural Actors 91
      1. Judges 91
      2. Prosecutors 92
      3. Defense Counsel 93
   IV. Procedural Phases 94
      1. Investigatory Phase 94
         a) Evidence Gathering by the State 94
         b) Rights of the Defense Prior to Trial 95
      2. Adjudicatory Phase 96
         a) Issuance of a Complaint and Initial Appearance 96
         b) Grand Jury or Preliminary Hearing: Evidentiary Standard of Probable Cause 97
         c) Arraignment and Pretrial Motions 99
         d) Trial 100
            aa) Jury Selection 100
            bb) Opening Statements, Evidence Taking, and Closing Arguments 101
            cc) Jury Instructions, Jury Deliberation, and Announcement of the Verdict   103
         e) Sentencing Phase 103
C. Evidence Law 104
   I. Introduction 104
      1. Finder of Fact: Jury and Bench Trials 105
      2. Trial Setting 106
         a) Party-Controlled Presentation of Evidence 106
         b) The Role of the Trial Judge 107
            aa) Role as an Umpire 107

bb) Judicial Discretion in Presenting Evidence 109
II. Methods of Proving Facts 110
   1. Evidence: Direct and Circumstantial Evidence 110
   2. Alternatives to Formal Proof 110
III. Types of Evidence 112
   1. Testimonial Evidence: Defendant, Witnesses and Expert Witnesses 112
      a) Witness Competency 112
      b) Examination of Witnesses 114
         aa) Credibility and Rehabilitation of Witnesses 115
         bb) Impeachment of Witnesses 115
   2. Real Evidence: Documentary and Demonstrative Evidence 118
IV. Admissibility of Evidence 120
   1. Admissibility of Evidence and Rationale Behind Limiting or Excluding Evidence 120
   2. Statutory and Constitutional Rules Excluding or Limiting Evidence 121
      a) Probative Value v. Prejudicial Effects 121
      b) Privilege Against Compulsory Self-Incrimination 123
      c) Search and Seizure 124
      d) Privilege 125
      e) Hearsay 127

D. Procedural Safeguards 129
  I. Safeguards to the Adversarial Trial Setting 129
   1. Discovery Rights of the Defense 129
   2. Compulsory Process Clause 132
   3. Confrontation Clause 133
  II. Safeguards to Lay Factfinding 135
   1. (Strict) Rules as to the Admissibility and Exclusion of Evidence 136
   2. Jury Instructions 136

Chapter 3

Brazil 137

A. Introduction 137
B. Overview of the Criminal Procedure 139
  I. Legal Sources 139
  II. Court System 142
  III. Main Procedural Actors 142
   1. Judges 143
   2. Prosecutors 144

3. Defense Counsel	145
IV. Procedural Phases	146
1. Investigatory Phase	146
a) Evidence Gathering by the State	146
b) Rights of the Defense in the Investigatory Phase	147
2. Adjudicatory Phase	149
a) Filing a Bill of Indictment and the Evidentiary Standard of Justa Causa	149
b) Filling a Written Reply to the Bill of Indictment and Setting a Date for Trial	150
c) Procedure of Evidence Taking	151
d) Closing Arguments and Sentencing	152
C. Evidence Law	153
I. Introduction	153
1. Finder of Fact: Professional Judges	153
2. Trial Setting	154
a) Elements of Officialized Fact-Finding	154
b) Elements of Party-Controlled Presentation of Evidence	156
II. Methods of Proving Facts	157
1. Information Gathered in the Investigatory Stage and Evidence Sensu Stricto	157
2. Direct and Circumstantial Evidence	158
III. Means of Evidence	159
1. Defendant	159
a) Examining the Defendant	160
b) Duty to Attend Trial and Exception to the Defendant's Examination at Court	163
2. Witnesses	163
a) Summoning Witnesses	165
b) Examining Witnesses	166
3. Victim	169
4. Experts	170
5. Documentary Evidence	171
IV. Admissibility of Evidence	172
1. Admissibility of Evidence and Rationale for Limiting or Excluding Evidence	172
2. Statutory and Constitutional Rules for Excluding or Limiting Evidence	173
a) Nemo Tenetur Se Ipsum Detegere	173
aa) Right to Silence	174
bb) Right Not to Be Compelled to do Something Except by Virtue of Law	175
b) Inadmissibility of Illegally Obtained Evidence	177
c) The Witnesses' Rights and Duties to Refuse Testimony	179
d) Hearsay	180
D. Evidentiary Principles	181
I. Principles Associated to the Officialized Factfinding	181

II. Principles Associated to the Party-Controlled Presentation of Evidence 183
   1. Principles of Audiatur et Altera Pars and (the Right) to a Full Defense 183
   2. Principle of Equality of Arms 184

Part 3
Key Concepts of Comparative Law, Comparative Study, and (Possible) Solutions to the Brazilian Criminal Procedure   186

Chapter 4
Terminology in Comparative Law   187

A. Introduction: Misapprehension of Legal Definitions 187
B. Theoretical Framework: Procedural Models 188
   I. Definitions 188
   II. Main Features 191
      1. Inquisitorial System 192
        a) Historical Approach 192
        b) Analytical Approach 193
      2. Adversarial System 195
        a) Historical Approach 195
        b) Analytical Approach 196
   III. Differences in the Concept of Truth and Justice 197
   IV. Structural Strengths and Weaknesses 200
      1. Inquisitorial System 200
      2. Adversarial System 202
   V. Definition of "Accusatorial" 202
C. Legal Definitions in the Brazilian Criminal Procedure 203
   I. Misdiagnosis of its Features as a Hinderance in Finding Effective Solutions 203
   II. Defining the Predominant Evidentiary Arrangement of the Brazilian Criminal Procedure 205

Chapter 5
The Importance of Identifying both a Country's Normative Framework and its Legal Culture in Comparative Law   209

A. Introduction 209
B. Legal Translations 211
   I. Procedural Culture 211

II. Importance of Understanding the Receiving Country's Institutional Context 213
　　III. The Introduction of Legal Ideas Conducted in Disregard to a Country's Normative
　　　　Framework and Procedural Culture 214
　　　　1. Example in the German Criminal Procedure 215
　　　　2. Example in the Brazilian Criminal Procedure 216
C. Identifying the Brazilian Legal Culture 217
　　I. The Influence of the Historical Background 218
　　II. The Role of the Procedural Actors: The Gap Between the Normative Framework
　　　　and the Legal Culture 219

Chapter 6
Comparative Study and (Possible) Solutions to the Brazilian Criminal Procedure 　222

A. Identifying the Main Problematic Features 222
　　I. Alleged Reason: "Inquisitorial" Features 222
　　II. Possible Reasons 224
　　　　1. Unawareness of the Indispensability of Procedural Safeguards 224
　　　　　　a) Sample of Lack of Procedural Safeguards in a Setting of Party-Controlled
　　　　　　　 Presentation of Evidence 226
　　　　　　b) Consequences of the Lack of Procedural Safeguards in a Setting of Officia-
　　　　　　　 lized Factfinding 227
　　　　2. Features Unrelated to the Inquisitorial Evidentiary Arrangement that Increase
　　　　　　the Risk of Judicial Bias 229
　　　　　　a) Mostly Partisan Character of the Criminal Investigation 229
　　　　　　b) Lack of Division of Judicial Roles 230
B. (Possible) Solutions to Selected Features of the Brazilian Criminal Procedure 231
　　I. Lack of Effective Procedural Safeguards 231
　　　　1. Initial Assessment 232
　　　　2. Countering the Structural Weaknesses Stemming from the Features of the Ad-
　　　　　 versarial Evidentiary Arrangement 234
　　　　　　a) Rights Afforded to the Defense in Gathering Evidence Prior to Trial 235
　　　　　　b) Rights Afforded to the Defense in Presenting Evidence at Trial 238
　　　　　　　 aa) The Extent of the Right to Subpoena 238
　　　　　　　 bb) As to the Desirability of Employing Cross-Examination in Examining
　　　　　　　　　 Witnesses 240
　　　　　　c) Suggestions 241
　　　　3. Countering the Structural Weaknesses Stemming from the Features of the In-
　　　　　 quisitorial Evidentiary Arrangement 243

II. The Trial Judge's Access to Information that was Gathered in the Investigatory
      Phase and its Use in Basing a Conviction 248
      1. Comparative Study 251
         a) Germany 251
         b) The United States 252
      2. Suggestions 253
C. Silver Lining: A Case for the Benefits of a Trial Setting with Both Inquisitorial and
   Adversarial Elements 254

Conclusion 257

Bibliography 261

Subject Index 272

List of Abbreviations

§, §§	Section, Sections
ABA	American Bar Association
ABA Model Rules	ABA Model Rules of Professional Conduct
ACHR	American Convention on Human Rights
ADI	Ação Direta de Inconstitucionalidade
ADCT	Ato das Disposições Constitucionais Transitórias
AG	Amtsgericht
AIIJ	Audiência de Instrução, Interrogatório e Julgamento
AJUFE	Associação dos Juízes Federais do Brasil
AMB	Associação dos Magistrados Brasileiros
Am. J. Comp. L.	American Journal of Comparative Law
Art.	Article, artigo
B.C. Int'l & Comp. L. Rev.	Boston College International and Comparative Law Review
BGB	Bürgerliches Gesetzbuch
BGH	Bundesgerichtshof
BVerfG	Bundesverfassungsgericht
BVerfGE	Entscheidungen des Bundesverfassungsgerichts
Cardozo J. Int'l & Comp. L.	Cardozo Journal of International and Comparative Law
CF	Constituição da República Federativa do Brasil
Ch.	Chapter
Chi.-Kent L.	Chicago-Kent Law Review
CNMP	Conselho Nacional do Ministério Público
Colum. J. Eur. L.	Columbia Journal of European Law
Colum. L. Rev.	Columbia Law Review
CONAMP	Associação Nacional dos Membros do Ministério Público
CP	Código Penal
CPI	Comissão Parlamentar de Inquérito
CPP	Código de Processo Penal
Crim. Law Forum	Criminal Law Forum
D.	Decreto
DePaul L. Rev.	DePaul Law Review
DF	Distrito Federal
DJ	Diário de Justiça
DL.	Decreto-Lei
DOJ	Department of Justice
DRiG	Deutsches Richtergesetz
EC	Emenda Constitucional
ECHR	European Convention on Human Rights
ECtHR	European Court of Human Rights

ed.	edition, edited by
e.g.	exempli gratia
et al.	et alia
et seq.	et sequentes
FRCP	Federal Rules of Criminal Procedure
FRE	Federal Rules of Evidence
GG	Grundgesetz für die Bundesrepublik Deutschland
GPA	grade-point average
GVG	Gerichtsverfassungsgesetz
Harv. Int'l L. J.	Harvard International Law Journal
Harv. J. L. & Pub. Pol'y	Harvard Journal of Law & Public Policy
Harv. L. Rev.	Harvard Law Review
Hastings L. J.	Hastings Law Journal
HC	habeas corpus
HK-StPO	Heidelberger Kommentar
i.a.	inter alia
IACHR	Inter-American Court of Human Rights
IBCCRIM	Instituto Brasileiro de Ciências Criminais
ICCPR	International Covenant on Civil and Political Rights
i.e.	id est
Ind. L. J.	Indiana Law Journal
J.D.	juris doctor
JECRIM	Juizado Especial Criminal
JGG	Jugendgerichtsgesetz
JVEG	Justizvergütungsgesetz und Justizentschädigungsgesetz
KK-StPO	Karlsruher Kommentar zur Strafprozessordnung
L.	Lei
LC	Lei Complementar
LG	Landgericht
lit.	litera
Loman	Lei Orgânica da Magistratura Nacional
Loy. L.A. Int'l & Comp. L. Rev.	Loyola of Los Angeles International and Comparative Law Review
LSAT	Law-School Admission Test
MG	Minas Gerais
Mich. J. Int'l L.	Michigan Journal of International Law
Mich. L. Rev.	Michigan Law Review
Minn. L. Rev.	Minnesota Law Review
MP	Ministério Público
MP-DF	Ministério Público do Distrito Federal
MPF	Ministério Público Federal
MPU	Ministério Público da União
MüKo-StPO	Münchener Kommentar zur Strafprozessordnung
n.	número
N.C. J. Int'l L. & Com. Reg.	North Carolina Journal of International Law and Commercial Regulation
Nr.	Nummer
N.Y.L. Sch. L. Rev.	New York Law School Review

List of Abbreviations

OAB	Ordem dos Advogados do Brasil
Ohio St. L. J.	Ohio State Law Journal
OLG	Oberlandesgericht
p., pp.	page, pages
para., paras	paragraph, paragraphs
PL.	Projeto de Lei
RBCCrim	Revista Brasileira de Ciências Criminais
Rev.	Review
Rn.	Randnummer
RS	Rio Grande do Sul
sent.	sentence
SK-StPO	Systematischer Kommentar zur Strafprozessordnung
SP	São Paulo
SSW-StPO	Satzger/Schluckebier/Widmaier-Kommentar zur Strafprozessordnung
StA	Staatsanwaltschaft
Stan. J. Int'l L.	Stanford Journal of International Law
STF	Supremo Tribunal Federal
StGB	Strafgesetzbuch
STJ	Superior Tribunal de Justiça
StPO	Strafprozessordung
Súm.	Súmula
SV	Súmula Vinculante
T.	Turma
TJ	Tribunal de Justiça
TRF	Tribunal Regional Federal
U. Chi. L. Rev.	University of Chicago Law Review
U. PA. L. Rev.	University of Pennsylvania Law Review
Urt.	Urteil
U.S.	United States
U.S.C.	United States Code
v.	versus
Va. L. Rev.	Virginia Law Review
Vol.	volume
Wash. L. Rev.	Washington Law Review
Wash. U. Global Stud. L. Rev.	Washington University Global Studies Law Review
W. Va. L. Rev.	West Virginia Law Review
Yale J. Int'l L.	Yale Journal of International Law
Zbornik PFZ	Zbornik Pravnog fakulteta u Zagrebu

Introduction

I. Research Subject

The Brazilian criminal procedure needs reform. The reasons for this are manifold. The current Brazilian Federal Constitution passed in 1988 sets out many procedural rights and guarantees applicable to both Brazilians and foreigners residing in Brazil. In contrast to the very progressive Constitution, the current Code of Criminal Procedure of 1941 was enacted during a dictatorship under a repressive ideology. To adapt the Code of Criminal Procedure to the Constitution, numerous modifications were made to the former, the most important of which took place with the enactment of several laws from 2008 onwards. These laws partly modified both procedural and evidence law and changed the trial setting from an officialized fact-finding to a setting which – although the judge continues to conduct the trial and to be responsible for finding the material truth – allows for a more party-controlled presentation of evidence.

Despite these reforms, the desired changes to the trial setting and, more importantly, in effectively safeguarding the accused's procedural rights were not achieved. Instead, these reforms led to incoherent cross-references and to a mixture of elements of both inquisitorial and adversarial evidentiary arrangements. The latter feature alone is not problematic, as it is rare for a country to have a pure inquisitorial or a pure adversarial procedural model, and it is not uncommon for countries to have features of their legal systems that start converging towards one another. The problem in the current Brazilian criminal procedure lies, however, in the inability in pinpointing its most problematic features and in finding concrete and effective solutions in countering them.

I believe this problem can be largely explained by the lack of tradition of conducting studies in the field of comparative law and namely, in the area of comparative criminal procedure. Furthermore, the basis for comparative law – i.e., conducting systematic and thorough studies on foreign legal systems – is also deficient. For these reasons, many problems arise, such as the misapprehension of fundamental terminology, e.g., *inquisitorial*, *accusatorial*, and *adversarial*, and the resulting arguments made from incorrect premises and inaccurate perceptions. Most importantly, a prevalent unawareness remains concerning the fact that – regardless of a legal system having a predominantly adversarial or a predominantly inquisitorial evidentiary arrangement – specific procedural safeguards must be in place to counter each system's inherent structural deficiencies in an effective manner.

Thus, in view of these blind spots, scholars and practitioners alike have been unable to find helpful solutions to various problems in the Brazilian criminal procedure. Particularly, in finding effective safeguards to protect the defendant's constitutional and procedural rights at trial. I believe the reason for this is not due to a lack of will or effort, but rather, on account of looking for answers in places that are not conducive in finding effective solutions.

II. Research Objectives

This study has five main objectives. The first objective is to examine the development of the normative framework of the Brazilian criminal procedure. This has the purpose of having a better grasp of the mindset behind the enactment of the current Code of Criminal Procedure, the changes in its outline after successive reforms, and to start identifying its most problematic features, particularly regarding the defendant's position at trial.

The second objective is to examine two foreign legal systems in a succinct way, and thus to provide a sample of an adversarial evidentiary arrangement and that of a predominantly inquisitorial one. By way of this examination, I wish to attain the first steps necessary to conduct a study in comparative law, i.e., of having an overview of foreign legal systems.

The third objective is to provide key concepts of comparative law as to fill the gap stemming from the lack of tradition in conducting studies in this area.

The fourth objective is to identify the predominant evidentiary arrangement of the Brazilian criminal procedure and its legal culture as to correctly identify the most problematic features of this legal system.

The last objective is to address the main problematic features of the Brazilian criminal procedure by means of a comparative study in order to make suggestions for its improvement. However, the concrete suggestions themselves are ancillary, as the main focus of this work is to identify the nature of the safeguards needed in countering the main weaknesses of the Brazilian code of criminal procedure.

III. Research Method and Scope of Analysis

I will answer the four last objectives by means of a comparative study using the functional method. The importance of the field of comparative law in fulfilling the objectives set out above and in offering suggestions to the Brazilian criminal procedure cannot be understated. Despite the results of the legal comparison itself being an important aim of this study, its primary contribution is of being a powerful means to better understand and discern the (domestic) legal system under analysis.[1] Thus, conducting comparative studies is an important tool in which to highlight the structural strengths and weaknesses of the Brazilian criminal procedure. To achieve these objectives, I selected the German and US-American legal systems for three main reasons.

First, both countries have influenced and continue to influence many legal systems worldwide.[2] In the Brazilian context, elements of German law have influenced the development of criminal law, while various features of US-American law have influenced the Brazilian criminal procedure.[3]

Second, the United States and Germany have two of the most influential and (possibly) most researched legal systems in the field of comparative criminal procedure and evidence law. This feature coupled with the prolific high-quality research conducted by international scholars on these legal systems result in a substantial amount of literature on these fields of law.

Third, as I wish to furnish two legal systems with different evidentiary arrangements at trial, the United States' adversarial system[4] and Germany's predominantly inquisitorial system are fitting for this task. The examination of these legal systems will provide insights on how each respective trial phase is structured and to give concrete examples on how both these countries counter the inherent structural deficiencies in their respective trial settings. I believe this last feature to be important to this study since it is not uncommon for Brazilian scholars to import elements of foreign legal systems to the Brazilian legal system without having a wider view of how these legal ideas and institutions function in their countries of origin.

For the aforementioned reasons, I believe the analysis of these two legal systems will help address misunderstandings that stem from the lack of systematic research on concrete adversarial and inquisitorial procedural models. And, more specifically, this study will address the misconceptions concerning the German and US-American criminal procedures and evidence law.

---

[1] See infra footnote 1 (Part 3).

[2] *Krey*, Characteristic Features, p. 59; *Grande*, Italian Criminal Justice, pp. 230 et seq.; *Langer*, Legal Transplants to Legal Translations, pp. 1, 2.

[3] The US-American law influenced the Brazilian system in two respects. First, the development of exclusionary rules were based on the US-American case law, see infra Ch. 3 C. IV. 2. b). Second, there has been an increasing development of an institute akin to plea bargaining in the Brazilian criminal procedure (*"acordo"*), in this sense, see *Zilli*, Iniciativa Instrutória do Juiz, p. 24.

[4] Concerning the criminal cases that are disposed of by trial, the US-American trial phase has possibly one of the most adversarial systems in the world. In this sense, see *Pizzi*, Trials Without Truth, pp. 118, 139 et seq. However, this does not apply to the sentencing phase, as this phase greatly differs from the trial phase, in this sense, see infra Ch. 2 B. IV. 2. e).

Due to the vastness of this topic, this work is by no means a comprehensive analysis of the three countries under examination. Rather, my focus lies on the foundations of criminal procedure in each system, coupled with a few selected features of evidence law, which I believe may be very valuable in making suggestions to the Brazilian criminal procedure. To this end, the manner that I circumscribed this work are the following.

As to the *German* criminal procedure, it is important to highlight that in the last few decades, the European Court of Human Rights has become increasingly important in furthering the procedural rights of the accused and those convicted of committing criminal offenses. However, due to time and space constraints, when I examine the German criminal procedure, I will only briefly allude to the rights conferred by the European Convention on Human Rights when applicable.

Regarding the *US-American* law, I had to greatly limit its scope by artificial means. Hence, the analysis of the US-American law is by no means representative of its criminal system. The US-American law – and by extent, criminal procedure and evidence law – has 52 different legal systems, none of which are identical.[5] Owing to the impossibility of addressing both its criminal procedure and evidence law in its entirety, this work will exclusively focus on the federal judicial system for two main reasons.

The first is due to state jurisdictions frequently basing their legal statutes on the federal model. As such, although there are at times considerable differences between the different US-American jurisdictions, the federal system remains to be an important starting point when examining US-American law. The second reason for this choice is due to practical considerations as most of the literature I have found on the subject, particularly in the field of legal comparison, focuses on the federal system.

A caveat is in order regarding this choice. Considering that most criminal cases are disposed of by the state jurisdictions, by focusing on the federal jurisdiction I will only address a small percentage of cases that are adjudicated by American courts. This number is further reduced if I take into consideration that about 90–95 % of federal criminal cases are disposed of by means of plea-bargaining.[6] Hence, at best, less than 10 % of cases that are of the competence of the federal jurisdiction go to trial.

Concerning the legal sources examined, owing to the vastness of both statutory and case law, I will focus on the former. Consequently, I will examine the "law on the books" rather than "law in action". However, I will allude to case law from time to

---

[5] There are a total of 52 legal systems, i.e., the federal jurisdiction, the legal system of the District of Columbia, and the legal systems of each of the fifty states. *LaFave* et al., Criminal Procedure, p. 29.

[6] As early as 1968 *Alschuler* stated that 90 % of criminal cases in both state and federal jurisdictions were disposed of by means of plea bargaining, see *Alschuler*, The Prosecutor's Role, p. 50. For more recent figures, see *Thaman*, World Plea Bargaining, p. 107.

time, as there are several topics – such as that of procedural safeguards – that were established and developed by case law.

Lastly, with regard to the *Brazilian* law, I am fully aware of the limitations in trying to propose suggestions to the Brazilian Code of Criminal Procedure while solely focusing on its legal aspects. I am cognizant that for a foreign legal provision or institute to be taken into consideration, and how or whether it will be implemented in a receiving legal system depends on many factors, such as a country's legal culture, its social, economic, geographical, and political features.[7] Further, to merely suggest that a legal idea or institute be transplanted without taking into account both the features of the legal system of origin and that of the receiving legal system may defeat its purpose.[8] Therefore, in lieu of and owing to the impracticability of finding solutions to the many aspects of the Brazilian criminal procedure that could benefit from improvement, I would like to shed some light as to where the possible answers might come from and to offer some suggestions to its most problematic features.

IV. Structure of the Study

This study is divided into three parts. In the *first part*, I will present the Brazilian criminal procedure by analyzing the development of its normative framework, especially in regard to the changes made to the current Code of Criminal Procedure. This part will be valuable to provide insights regarding the development of the Brazilian legal culture.

The *second part* of this work is divided into three chapters, which correspond to the analysis of each legal system. These chapters have a nearly identical outline and are divided into four parts. In the first part, I will make a brief introduction of the legal system under analysis and further define the scope of analysis of each chapter. In the second part of each country report, I will examine each country's legal sources, court system, key courtroom actors and procedural phases. These initial clarifications are crucial to setting the stage in which to subsequently analyze each country's trial phase and, more specifically, the procedure of evidence taking. The overview of a country's legal structure is a helping tool in identifying and explaining the reasoning behind a country's choice on a set of procedural safeguards over others. Further, the roles and mindset each courtroom actor has throughout the different procedural phases profoundly shape the procedure of evidence taking and vice versa.[9] Therefore, despite many of the terms and key courtroom actors in each of these country reports appearing to overlap, sometimes there are important and marked differences between them, which without a closer inspection may lead to false premises that may com-

---

[7] *Eberle*, The Method and Role of Comparative Law, p. 452.

[8] *Pizzi*, Understanding Prosecutorial Discretion, p. 1373; *Frase/Weigend*, German Criminal Justice, pp. 317, 318; *Damaška*, The Uncertain Fate of Evidentiary Transplants, p. 839.

[9] *Hodgson*, in: Duff et al., The Trial on Trial, vol. 2, pp. 223, 241.

promise the accuracy of the comparative study. In the third part of each country report, I will examine the law of evidence in each system. To this end, I will explore the trial setting, the different types of evidence and how each legal system undertakes evidentiary matters, i.e., the admissibility and exclusion of evidence. Finally, in the last part of each country report, I will identify the main procedural safeguards in countering possible deficiencies within each respective legal system.

In the *third part* of this work, I will present key concepts of comparative law and conduct the comparative study itself. To this end, in Chapter 4, I will offer a theoretical framework in which to provide and clarify fundamental legal definitions in the field of comparative law. For this purpose, I will indicate the main features of the inquisitorial and adversarial evidentiary arrangements, the difference between the truth sought in each procedural model and examine each system's inherent structural strengths and weaknesses. In Chapter 5, I will address the topic of legal transplants and the importance of understanding the receiving country's institutional context – i.e., both its normative framework and legal culture – when conducting comparative studies, and especially, when offering suggestions of improvement to a legal system's shortcomings. Both these chapters will set the stage in which to conduct a comparative study and offer suggestions to improve the Brazilian criminal procedure within the context of its *legal setting* and *legal culture* in Chapter 6.

Part 1

The Development of the Normative Framework of the Brazilian Criminal Procedure

A. Historical Background

The Portuguese first arrived in the (now) Brazilian territory in 1500 and remained there from 1530 – when King João III of Portugal established the colonization of Brazil[1] – until 1822 when the country gained its independence. During most of this period, Portuguese law prevailed in the colonial legal system.

Until the first half of the fifteenth century, the sources of law in Portugal were scattered.[2] To reinforce a centralized monarchy and to facilitate the administration of justice, it was necessary to make a compilation of all the country's legal sources. To this purpose, the Afonsinas Ordinances (*Ordenações Afonsinas*) were enacted in 1446. This was a compilation of laws based on both Roman and Canon law, that were divided into five parts, each of which covered a different area of the administration of justice. Due to its innovative structure, scholars of the time considered it to be a milestone in Portuguese law.[3]

The fifth part of the Afonsinas Ordinances regulated both criminal law and procedure and established the different types of criminal offenses. Due to the strong influence of Canon law, many of these offenses were of a religious nature and those accused of committing them were subject to very harsh punishments. Among them were "flogging, limb amputation, forced labor and exile",[4] while the preferred form of punishment was the death penalty. The main concern when compiling the Afonsinas Ordinances was not whether the punishments were proportional to the crimes committed, but to control the population through fear.[5] For this reason, very few rights were accorded to those accused of having committed crimes and the

---

[1] *Pierangelli*, Processo penal, p. 71.

[2] At that time, Portuguese law was composed of three different sources of law: (i) laws based on Roman and Canon law, (ii) the *forais,* which were royal documents that granted certain royal subjects privileges, and (iii) the local customs and norms. See *Almeida Jr*, O Processo Criminal, p. 109.

[3] *Bittencourt*, Tratado de Direito Penal, p. 89.

[4] *Bittencourt*, Tratado de Direito Penal, p. 90.

[5] *Pierangelli*, Processo penal, p. 56.

practice of committing torture to obtain confessions prevailed well after the compilation of the Afonsinas Ordinances.

During the next 150 years, two further compilations of laws were enacted, the Manuelinas Ordinances (*Ordenações Manuelinas*) in 1521 and the Filipinas Ordinances (*Ordenações Filipinas*) in 1603. Apart from partial changes made in different parts of these ordinances, both these compilations were largely based on the Afonsinas Ordinances.[6]

Although Portugal started colonizing Brazil from 1530 onward, due to the time needed to establish a colonial administration of justice in a territory of continental proportions,[7] the first compilations of Portuguese law to prevail in Brazil were the Filipinas Ordinances.[8] This compilation was in force throughout the colonial period, at first alongside Portuguese statutes (*leis extravagantes*) and from the beginning of the nineteenth century onward,[9] alongside the legislation that were enacted in Brazilian territory. The reason that propelled the enactment of the latter was the arrival of the Portuguese royal family and its court in 1808, who fled to its biggest colony due to Napoleon's threat to invade Portugal. After their arrival, it was necessary to advance the country's administration of justice. To this end, various laws were enacted establishing and developing many new courts and institutions as well as the legal profession.[10]

After Brazil's independence in 1822, the Constituent Assembly (*Assembléia Constituinte*) established that all Portuguese legislation would remain in force in Brazil until new laws were passed to replace them.[11] Soon after, the Brazilian Legislature enacted the Constitution of the Empire in 1824, which established the

---

[6] *Pierangelli*, Processo penal, p. 57.

[7] The gradual colonization of the Brazilian territory started in 1534 when it was divided into 14 lots of lands, called *capitanias hereditárias*. These lots of land were managed by the so-called *donatários*, who were usually a member of the Portuguese nobility and were given the responsibility for the administration of each lot, and had civil and criminal jurisdiction over their appointed territory. In practice, this created a decentralized and somewhat feudal form of administration of justice, due to each *donatário* administering its own form of justice. In 1549, King John III (*Rei João* III) created a Brazilian general government, with the capital in Salvador. Later, in 1573 the country was divided into two General Governments (*governo geral*), the Northern and the Southern governments with the capitals in Salvador and Rio de Janeiro, respectively. In the following centuries, tribunals (*Tribunal de Relação*) were instituted in these capitals in 1609 and 1751, respectively. See *Almeida Jr.*, O Processo Criminal, pp. 142, 143; *Bittencourt*, Tratado de Direito Penal, pp. 89, 90.

[8] *Barros*, Lineamentos, p. 58.

[9] *Pierangelli*, Processo penal, p. 83.

[10] The higher body of judicial administration, the *Tribunal of the Mesa do Desembargo do Paço e da Consciência e Ordens* was transferred from Portugal to Brazil. Further, the court in Rio de Janeiro called *Tribunal de Relação* became the *Casa de Suplicação*, which would later become the higher court of last resort in Brazil (*Superior Tribunal de Justiça*). In this sense, see *Almeida Jr.*, O Processo Criminal, p. 145; *Pierangelli*, Processo penal, p. 83.

[11] *Mirabete*, Processo Penal, p. 38.

country's general provisions and laid out important rights, such as the inviolability of the Brazilian citizens' rights to liberty, individual safety, and property. Among the procedural rights accorded to citizens were (i) not being required to do something or withheld from doing something except by force of law, (ii) the defendant's right not to be prosecuted due to his or her religion, (iii) the need of an arrest warrant to deprive someone of their liberty, (iv) the citizen's equality before the law, and (v) the abolishment of all cruel punishments.[12]

Followed by the enactment of the Constitution, the Criminal Code of the Empire and the Criminal Procedural Code of the Empire were respectively passed in 1830 and 1832. These legislations were influenced by the ideas of liberalism and were a strong reaction to the oppressive Portuguese legislation that had been in force until the respective enactment of these codes.[13] The progressive nature of the Criminal Procedural Code of the Empire[14] led scholars of the time to consider it "a landmark of legal thought and liberal spirit".[15] However, in the following decades after its enactment, the Code of Criminal Procedure of the Empire went through two major reforms. The first took place in 1841 when the conservatives in power believed the newly passed code to be too liberal and unable to curb the changes that were taking place throughout the country.[16] Even though immediately after these reforms were enacted, liberal politicians criticized its reactionary characteristics, it was only more than thirty years later, when the second reform took place, and progressive changes were made to the Code of Criminal Procedure in 1871.[17]

After the second and last Brazilian emperor was deposed in 1889, the Republic of the United States of Brazil (*República dos Estados Unidos do Brasil*) was proclaimed, and in 1891 the National Legislature (*Assembléia Nacional Constituinte*) enacted the first Republican Constitution. Up to that date, the Union had the exclusive power to legislate on criminal procedural law. This changed, however, as article 34, para. 23 of the first Republican Constitution provided that the National Congress (*Congresso Nacional*) had power to legislate on matters of criminal law which were of federal competence. This led scholars and legislators of the time to believe that the Constitution implicitly gave each state the autonomy to organize its criminal procedure on matters of state justice.[18]

As a result, the decentralization of the criminal procedure took place as the state legislatures progressively started enacting their respective codes of criminal pro-

---

[12] Art. 179, paras. 1, 5, 10, 13, 19 of the Constitution of the Empire.

[13] *Marques*, Elementos de Direito, vol. 1, pp. 101, 102.

[14] *Pierangelli*, Processo penal, p. 134; *Marques*, Elementos de Direito, vol. 1, p. 102.

[15] *César Tripoli*, Época Imperial, p. 280.

[16] *Mirabete*, Processo Penal, p. 38.

[17] Among these reforms, there was the implementation of a police force, which to the present date has the responsibility to lead the preliminary investigation (*inquérito policial*). See *Machado*, Investigação Criminal, p. 35.

[18] *Rodrigues*, ABC do Processo Penal, pp. 14, 15.

cedure.[19] The acceptance of the enactment of several state codes of criminal procedure lasted until 1934. In this year, the second Republican Constitution was enacted and it provided that that the Government should appoint a committee to formulate a unified federal Code of Criminal Procedure.[20] To this end, the current Code of Criminal Procedure was enacted and unified the Brazilian criminal procedure in 1941.

B. The Current Code of Criminal Procedure

When the current Code of Criminal Procedure (CPP) was enacted, President Getúlio Vargas governed the country during the period called *Estado Novo,* a dictatorship that lasted almost nine years (1937–1946). His administration was criticized at the time seeing as it was viewed as "totalitarian, dictatorial, conservative and reactionary"[21] and those who objected to his regime in an open manner were perceived as communists, who had to be fought against.

Vargas believed that the Criminal Procedural Code of the Empire of 1832 provided the defendant with excessive procedural rights.[22] For this reason and owing to the need to legitimize Vargas' dictatorship, the government based the new constitution and the new code of criminal procedure on the ideology of Mussolini's fascist regime. As a result, this ideology is reflected in the Constitution of 1937 – which was one of the most backward constitutions in the Brazilian legislative history[23] – and in the original framework of the current CPP. As such, the Italian Code of Criminal Procedure of 1930 greatly inspired the CPP. Mirroring the latter code, the CPP did not have many provisions safeguarding the accused's rights, seeing as they were deemed to be a threat to the state and an enemy to society. The defendant had, therefore, to be fought against and "neutralized".[24]

As a result, the original framework of the CPP had the following characteristics:[25] (i) due to its punitive ideology, the state deemed that those accused of having committed crimes were guilty and, therefore, the presumption of guilt prevailed rather than the presumption of innocence, (ii) there was a vast amount of unchecked

---

[19] *Marques*, Elementos de Direito, vol. 1, p. 108.

[20] Art. 11 of the Transitional Provisions (*Disposições Transitórias*) of the Republican Constitution of 1934. See *Pierangelli*, Processo penal, p. 166; *Melchior*, in: Santoro/Malan/Maduro, Crise no processo penal, p. 45.

[21] See original text in *Giacomolli*, Marcas Inquisitoriais, p. 146, O período foi cunhado como "totalitário, ditatorial, conservador e reacionário".

[22] *Silva Júnior*, Reforma Tópica, p. 28.

[23] *Silva Júnior*, Reforma Tópica, p. 37.

[24] *Giacomolli*, Marcas Inquisitoriais, p. 146.

[25] Despite the CPP having gone through various reforms, many of these features remain in the current CPP. I address the reasons for this in Ch. 5 C. II.

judicial power throughout the criminal procedure, and (iii) those accused of having committed crimes were regarded as an object and a means in which to help the state in finding them guilty. The latter characteristic is exemplified by analyzing the interrogation of the accused at trial, which was considered by both scholars and practitioners alike as a mere means in which to obtain evidence, rather than it being an opportunity for the defendant to defend himself.

I. The Enactment of the Federal Constitution

After the enactment of the CPP, two federal constitutions were promulgated in 1946 and 1964. After each of these enactments, partial reforms were made to the CPP to adapt it to each respective constitution. Interestingly, the changes made to the CPP as to adapt it to the latter Constitution took place in a brutal military dictatorship (from 1964 to 1985).

After this dictatorship ended, the Constituent Power sought to enact a constitution establishing the principles of a democratic society (*Estado Democrático de Direito*), which entailed laying out the essential rights and procedural safeguards of the accused. This was a task of substantial importance due to this new Federal Constitution becoming the primary legal source in Brazil's federalist legal system. As such, when the National Congress sanctioned the Federal Constitution in 1988, it set the minimum threshold that all other statutes should observe. As a result, all statutes should abide by the Constitution and apply their provisions in conformity to the constitutional principles and fundamental guarantees (*garantias fundamentais*).[26]

The overarching importance of the Federal Constitution to the criminal procedure is that it not only sets the fundamental rights and guarantees, which are applicable to all Brazilians and foreigners residing in Brazil, but also that it lays out all the constitutional rights and guarantees that are key to the criminal justice system. Among these latter rights, Art. 5 of the Federal Constitution affords all defendants the right to *audiatur et altera pars,* the right to a full defense, and the presumption of innocence.[27]

Given the new constitutional framework, the need to reform the CPP became crucial seeing as it was not in conformity to the Constitution. This posed a significant problem that the Legislature could only solve by either reforming the current CPP or by enacting a new code of criminal procedure.

---

[26] *Silva Júnior*, Reforma Tópica, p. 51.

[27] These rights are set out in Art. 5 LV, Art. 5 LVII, Art. 5 LVXXIIII CF, respectively. Regarding the latter right, there are Brazilian scholars who state that the principle of non-culpability (*princípio da não-culpabilidade*) prevail in the Brazilian criminal procedure rather than the principle of innocence (*princípio da presunção de inocência*).

II. Modifications to the Code of Criminal Procedure

There were two opposing forces influencing the reform of the criminal procedure.[28] On the one side, there was the need to provide defendants with procedural guarantees, which mirror those set out in the Federal Constitution. On the other side, there was the need to make it more efficient as to better enable the state in combating violent crimes. As such, the main aims sought by the reform committee were to make the CPP more "accusatorial" and efficient.[29]

As to the first aim, an initial clarification must be made regarding the terminology used. In Part 1, I will employ the term *accusatorial* in the manner in which Brazilian scholars employ it, which comprises three different features:

(i) a legal system where different procedural actors are responsible for the accusatory and the adjudicative functions,

(ii) a mixed model, i.e. a legal system that has features of both inquisitorial and adversarial evidentiary arrangements, and

(iii) referring to some features of the adversarial model in its analytical approach, particularly to convey that the presentation of evidence is party-controlled.

For this purpose, I will borrow Langer's description of what Latin American countries mean to convey when they employ the terms accusatorial and inquisitorial. The definition of an accusatorial system is when "criminal procedures (...) are oral and public; distinguish between investigatory and adjudicatory functions (...), includes broad defendant's rights and lay adjudicators and allows the victim to play a larger role in criminal proceedings", whereas an inquisitorial system is a legal system, which "presents the opposite features".[30]

In view of this definition, Brazilian scholars and practitioners deem necessary that for the code of criminal procedure to conform to the Federal Constitution, it should be more "accusatorial". The main criticism to the CPP was the vast amount of judicial discretion, which some critics believe to be incompatible with an accusatorial system. Among the judicial prerogatives are: (i) their right to order a preliminary investigation to be initiated, (ii) to make specific inquiries during trial as to settle any doubts they may have regarding the case before they reach a verdict, and (iii) the right to find the defendant guilty, even though the prosecution believes the defendant to be innocent.[31]

This topic is especially controversial due to the different judicial roles that both scholars and practitioners ascribe to judges. The latter have a variety of responsibilities and in some cases, there seems to be an incompatibility between the

---

[28] *Pellegrini Grinover*, O Processo em Evolução, p. 206.

[29] *Scaranse Fernandes*, in: Prado/Malan, Processo Penal e Democracia, p. 85.

[30] *Langer*, Revolution in Latin American Criminal Procedure, p. 621. I address the legal definitions in the field of comparative law in Ch. 4 B.

[31] Arts. 5 II, 156 II and 385 CPP, respectively.

different roles they may play throughout the procedure. An example of this is that although trial judges are considered to be the main procedural actor at trial and are responsible for finding the material truth, parties are progressively being given more responsibilities and opportunities in co-shaping the procedure of evidence taking.[32] Thus, it remains unclear which of the judicial responsibilities must be allocated or shifted to the parties at trial.

As to the committee's second aim, there were two main reasons in seeking to make the criminal proceedings more *efficient*. On the one hand, it was necessary to effectively fight criminality in a setting, where there were many claims of impunity and violent criminality. On the other hand, efficiency was a means in which to protect criminal defendants seeing as lengthy proceedings affect them financially, socially, professionally, and in the cases of pretrial detention, deprive defendants of their liberty.

A further reason to make the criminal proceedings more efficient was owing to the American Convention on Human Rights (ACHR) setting out that any person detained "shall be entitled to trial within a *reasonable time*"[33] and that "every person has the right to a hearing, with due guarantees and within a *reasonable time* (...) in the substantiation of any accusation of a criminal nature made against him".[34] Despite the fact that the ACHR provides defendants with these rights, there was no equivalent provision in the Brazilian normative framework. This omission was partly solved with the enactment of the Constitutional Amendment EC 45/2004, which added subitem LXXVIII to Art. 5 of the Federal Constitution and set out the (principle of) reasonable length to all judicial and administrative proceedings (*princípio da duração razoável do processo*). Yet, although the Constitution formally sets out this right, the CPP did not provide a proceeding which was conducive to performing trials within a reasonable time.

1. Legislative Reforms

After the enactment of the Federal Constitution, there were several unsuccessful attempts to enact a new code of criminal procedure. In 1992, a group of jurists who were chosen to elaborate a legislative proposal to reform the CPP changed the strategy employed by the previous committees.[35] The new approach was to draft various bills corresponding to different topics of the CPP, which if enacted would have a higher likelihood of making the procedure more efficient and "accusatorial"

---

[32] *Gomes Filho*, in Moura, As Reformas no Processo Penal, pp. 257, 258.
[33] Art. 7 para. 5 ACHR.
[34] Art. 8 para. 1 ACHR.
[35] These Committees were usually named after their respective presidents and were, thus, called Committee (*Comissão*) *Hélio Tornaghi* (1961), Pre-project (*Anteprojeto*) *José Frederico Marques* (1967), and Committee (*Comissão*) *Lauria Tucci* (1983).

(*acusatório*).³⁶ Although, the ensuing project called *Anteprojeto Sálvio de Figueiredo* was not successful, the following reform committee presided by Ada Pellegrini Grinover in 1999,³⁷ which also adopted the policy of partial reforms was successful to a certain extent.³⁸ Each member of the committee drafted a bill to reform a specific area of the criminal procedure, hoping that if all bills were enacted this would lead to a comprehensive reform of the CPP.³⁹

Consequently, the committee presented a total of seven bills covering all areas of the criminal procedure. Of the seven bills presented, five of them were enacted by the National Congress in the following decade. The laws that were enacted reformed provisions regarding the defendant's examination at trial (L. 10.792/03), evidence law (L. 11.690/08), the general outline of the criminal proceedings (L. 11.719/08), jury trial (L. 11.689/08)⁴⁰ and the provisions regulating precautionary measures (L. 12.403/11).⁴¹ I will briefly examine the first three laws as they are the most relevant to this work.

L. 10.792/03 modified several provisions of the CPP concerning the defendant's examination at trial. They set out not only that the examination must occur during the procedure of evidence taking, but also that instead of it being the first proceeding to take place at trial, it must ensue after all the presentation of evidence has been concluded. The aim of this change was to shift the perception of this examination from being a means in which to obtain evidence – thus treating defendants as a means of proof – to treating this examination as an opportunity for defendants to defend

---

³⁶ *Giacomolli*, Marcas Inquisitoriais, p. 152.

³⁷ The Committee presided by Ada Pellegrini Grinover was composed of jurists of the Brazilian Institute of Procedural Law (*Instituto Brasileiro de Direito Processual*). Alongside its president were Petrônio Calmon Filho, Antônio Magalhães Gomes Filho, Antônio Scaranse Fernandes, Luiz Flávio Gomes, Miguel Reale Jr., Nilzardo Carneiro Leão, René Ariel Dotti (latter substituted by) Rui Stoco, Rogério Lauria Tucci and Sidnei Beneti. See *Silva Júnior*, Reforma Tópica, p. 44.

³⁸ *Melchior*, in: Santoro/Malan/Maduro, Crise no processo penal, p. 48.

³⁹ *Giacomolli*, Marcas Inquisitoriais, p. 155; *Silva Júnior*, Reforma Tópica, p. 23.

⁴⁰ L. 11.689/08 modified the legal provisions concerning the *Tribunal do Júri*, the only procedure in the Brazilian criminal justice system in which there is a jury trial. Before this reform took place, the main criticisms to this procedure were due to it being slow and highly formalistic. Hence, this law sought to simplify the jury trial to make it swifter and more efficient. See *Badaró*, in: Assis Moura, As Reformas no Processo Penal, p. 50.

⁴¹ L. 12.403/11 modified and introduced various provisions regarding precautionary measures (*medidas cautelares*) in the criminal procedure. These provisions had the aim to reduce the massive amount of cases of suspects and accused who were ordered to await trial in pretrial detention. To this end, this law established strict legal requirements that must be met for a judge to order a suspect to pretrial detention (*prisão preventiva*). Before the enactment of this law, trial judges only had two options; either to order the accused to pretrial detention, or to let him stand trial in liberty. To remedy this situation, L. 12.403/11 introduced eleven new precautionary measures with differing levels of severity.

themselves and to seek to show their innocence. This change had the further objective of treating defendants as a subject of constitutional and procedural rights.[42]

L. 11.690/08 had the aim of making the procedure more "accusatorial", and as a result, it introduced several changes to the evidentiary arrangement at trial. It modified many aspects of the criminal procedure such as (i) delimitating the admissibility of evidence and which means of proof may substantiate the judge's decision-making;[43] (ii) specifying when evidence is illegal and the provisions regarding its admissibility and exclusion;[44] (iii) granting both victims and witnesses more procedural rights;[45] and (iv) partly changing the control of presentation of evidence, e. g., by shifting the examination of witnesses from it being primarily of the judge's responsibility to it being a party-controlled enterprise.[46]

Lastly, L. 11.719/08 vastly changed the legal provisions regarding the outline of the criminal proceedings, e. g., it separated the criminal proceedings into the common proceeding (*procedimento comum*) and the special proceeding (*procedimento especial*).[47] Additionally, for criminal cases to be adjudicated more swiftly and efficiently, the common proceeding was divided into different "procedural outlines" (*ritos*) according to the abstract number of years of imprisonment of the crime being adjudicated.[48]

2. Outcome of the Previous Reforms

The reforms to the CPP considerably changed the outline of the Brazilian criminal procedure. They were valuable seeing as the legislature introduced them to maximize the effectiveness of the accused's procedural rights and to bring efficiency and an "accusatorial" character to the Brazilian criminal procedure. Despite these reforms partly achieving the committee's anticipated aims, the opinions regarding the aforementioned reforms were far from being uncontested. On the one hand, a considerable number of Brazilian scholars and legal practitioners believed that the aims the reform committee set to achieve were fulfilled. On the other hand, several scholars believed that there were many problematic features resulting from these reforms, particularly concerning the code's lack of consistency. As to the latter argument, I believe the lack of uniformity was due to four main reasons.

The *first* and most important reason is owing to the fact that two of the seven bills proposed by the committee have not yet been enacted. Hence, most provisions

---

[42] See infra Ch. 3 C. III. 1.
[43] See infra Ch. 3 C. II. 1. and Ch. 6 B. II.
[44] Art. 157, chapeau, CPP.
[45] Art. 201 paras. 2 to 5 and Art. 217, chapeau, CPP, respectively.
[46] Art. 212, chapeau, CPP.
[47] Art. 394 CPP.
[48] See infra Ch. 3 A.

concerning the topics of appeals and criminal investigation still follow the systemic of the original wording of the CPP. *Second*, concerning the five bills that were enacted, a considerable amount of time went by between each of their respective enactments, as the first of these bills was enacted in 2003, whereas the last of them was enacted in 2011. As each of these laws came into force, the new provisions were applied within the context of the code's original framework. As a result, the changes in the trial setting and criminal proceedings did not take place in a uniform way. This, in turn, led to a lack of a corresponding (and much-needed) shift in the Brazilian legal culture. *Third*, during the parliamentary discussions that took place before the bills were enacted, the wording of some provisions was changed or suppressed in a way that, at times, greatly reduced the reach of the changes sought.[49] *Lastly*, many original provisions of the CPP that contradicted the wording of the newly enacted ones were not suppressed from the code, which further contributed to the CPP's lack of uniformity.[50]

Although, the main criticisms to the reforms stem from the aforementioned reasons, there are other points of contention surrounding this topic. Many critics believe that the aim of making the procedure more "accusatorial" was not met due to the prevailing amount of judicial power and the lack of division of judicial competency in different phases of the procedure, i.e., there is only one type of judge, who is responsible for deciding on matters of both an investigatory- and adjudicatory nature. As to the aim of making the CPP more efficient, some critics claim that although this objective was partially met, in order to achieve this aim many of the accused's procedural rights were sacrificed.

Regardless of the various arguments adduced, the prevailing opinion is that the CPP is still a long way from providing defendants their constitutionally protected procedural rights. This is owing to the claim that in light of there being no corresponding shift to the legal culture, the repressive mentality that was at the origin of the CPP remains to be pervasive in the legal practice. Hence, there is an overall belief that to change the Brazilian legal culture, a new code of criminal procedure must be enacted.[51] Interestingly, at the same time the laws that changed the provisions regarding evidence law and the jury trial came into force, a new committee was formed to create a proposal to enact a new code of criminal procedure. In the following year, Senator José Sarney presented this committee's legislative proposal to Congress under the number PL 156/09, which is currently under analysis in the Brazilian Chamber of Deputies.[52] As of this writing, it is not yet foreseeable whether or when the National Congress will pass this bill.

---

[49] For an example of this, see infra Ch. 6 B. II.

[50] *Silva Júnior*, Reforma Tópica, p. 25.

[51] *Coutinho*, in: Prado/Malan, Processo Penal e Democracia, p. 261; *Giacomolli*, Marcas Inquisitoriais, p. 162.

[52] This bill became PL. 8.045/10 once it arrived at the Chamber of Deputies.

3. Latest Statutory Modifications

In June 2018, the Ministry of Justice and Public Security presented a legislative proposal (PL. 10.372/18) to the Senate.[53] In contrast to the aforementioned reforms, this bill had as its main aim the repression of violent criminality, and for this reason, it was termed "Package against crime" (*Pacote Anticrime*). To this end, the authoring committee sought to change numerous provisions in the legislation regulating criminal law and criminal procedure as to better equip the state's investigative bodies in streamlining and modernizing the criminal investigation and prosecution.[54] Among the types of criminality this legislation targets are "organized crime, drugs and arms trafficking, private militia, violent crimes and the so-called heinous crimes (*crimes hediondos*)".[55]

On Christmas Eve of 2019, the National Congress enacted L. 13.964/19, which changed various provisions of the Criminal Code, the CPP, and several infra-constitutional laws.[56] Interestingly, despite the seemingly repressive character of the newly enacted law, various provisions were introduced to the CPP which did not have a repressive character. These changes introduced several provisions which were sought by the more liberal scholars, who claimed that the Brazilian criminal procedure did not have an "accusatorial system" nor was it able to guarantee defendants their constitutional right to an impartial trial. Among the many innovations, those of particular interest to this work are:

(i) setting limits to the trial judge's discretionary powers and furthering judicial impartiality by introducing the figure of a pretrial judge. This latter judge is to be solely competent to decide on matters during the investigatory phase and is precluded from adjudicating the case at trial,

---

[53] The original Committee responsible for preparing the preliminary bill were Cesar Mecchi Morales, Érica de Oliveira Hartmann, Gianpaolo Poggio Smanio, José Bonifacio Borges de Andrada, Mônica Barroso Costa, Patrícia Vanzolini, Renato da Costa Figueira, Renato de Mello Jorge Silveira.

[54] Ementa, PL. 10.372/18.

[55] Original wording of Art. 1 PL. 10.372/18: Esta lei modifica a legislação penal e processual penal para aperfeiçoar o combate ao "crime organizado, tráfico de drogas e armas, milícia privada, crimes cometidos com violência ou grave ameaça e hediondos, bem como agiliza a investigação criminal e a persecução penal". The criminal offenses which are considered to be heinous crimes under Brazilian law are set out in L. 8.072/90. Art. 1 provides that among these criminal offenses are i.a., homicide (*homicídio*), intentional bodily injury of a serious nature (*lesão corporal dolosa de natureza gravíssima*), rape (*estupro*), and causing an epidemic which results in death (*epidemia com resultado morte*), as well as some specific cases of theft (*roubo*) and extortion (*extorsão*).

[56] Among the infra-constitutional laws modified by L. 13.964/19 were: L. 7.210/84 (Law on Execution of Prison Sentences), L. 11.343/06 (Law on Combating Narcotics), L. 8.072/90 (Law on Heinous Crimes), L. 9.296/96 (Law on Interception of Telephone Communications), L. 12.037/09 (Law on Criminal Identification of the Civilly Identified) and L. 12.850/13 (Law Against Organized Crime).

(ii) separating the investigative file from the case file, which prior to this reform were both sent to the trial judge after the prosecution filed the bill of indictment,

(iii) the prohibition of a judge in sentencing a case whenever he has had prior contact to inadmissible evidence,

(iv) provisions regulating the chain of custody of evidence,

(v) stricter requirements concerning the judge's duty in the written foundation which leads him to reach a conviction, and

(vi) the creation of a custody hearing.

Most of the provisions introduced to the CPP by L. 13.964/19 came into force on 23.01.2020. However, there were several provisions, which were the object of four motions questioning their constitutionality[57] (ADI) and requests for injunctive relief were made (*liminar*).[58] These motions were filed by various institutions, namely the Association of Brazilian Magistrates (AMB), the Association of Federal Judges of Brazil (AJUFE), and the National Association of the Members of the Public Prosecutor's Office (CONAMP). The object of these motions was to question the constitutionality of some of the newly enacted provisions that instituted the creation of a pretrial judge (*juiz das garantias*), who is solely competent for making decisions in the investigatory phase.[59] This is not surprising considering the country's legal culture,[60] and the normative framework which provide judges with a vast amount of discretionary powers throughout the procedural phases and especially, at trial.

The motions questioning the constitutionality of Arts. 3-A to 3-F CPP were addressed to the Supreme Federal Court; Brazil's constitutional court and the court of last resort regarding matters of constitutional law, which include being competent for trying motions questioning the constitutionality of a federal statute. In January 2020, Justice Luiz Fux examined the motion presented by CONAMP (ADI n. 6.305) and suspended the effectiveness of these legal provisions until the Supreme Federal Court makes a final decision regarding their constitutionality.

The reason adduced by CONAMP in questioning the constitutionality of these provisions was that the creation of a pretrial judge would engender the reorganization of the entire Judiciary (*reorganização de todo poder judiciário*). For this reason, Justice Fux held that these provisions would offend the "federative pact" (*pacto federativo*) due to the Legislative imposing a great change to the Judiciary. He held

---

[57] These motions are called *ações diretas de inconstitucionalidade*, which can be roughly translated as "direct action for the declaration of unconstitutionality". I borrowed the English translation of this term from the official website of the Supreme Federal Court: https://www2.stf.jus.br/portalStfInternacional/cms/verConteudo.php?sigla=portalStfSobreCorte_en_us&idConteudo=120199.

[58] As of this writing, the four motions are ADI n. 6.298, ADI n. 6.299, ADI n. 6.300, and ADI n. 6.305.

[59] Arts. 3-B to 3-F CPP and Art. 157 para. 5 CPP.

[60] In this sense, see Ch. 5 C.

that this violates Art. 125 para. 1 CF, which states that "the jurisdictions of the courts shall be defined in the State Constitutions, and the law of judicial organization shall be of the initiative of the Court of Justice".[61]

---

[61] Further legal provisions adduced by Justice Fux in justifying the suspension of the effectiveness of Arts. 3-A to 3-F CPP were Art. 96, I lit. d and II lit. d CF, Art. 169 CF, Arts. 197 II lit. d ADCT and Art. 109 II and V ADCT.

Part 2

Country Reports

Chapter 1

Germany

A. Introduction

Germany is a Federal Republic composed of 16 territorial units akin to states (*Bundesländer* or *Länder*), which are endowed with wide powers and their own decision-making bodies. It has a federalist structure in which on the one hand, the legislation regulating both criminal and procedural law is federal and applicable nationwide.[1] On the other hand, the public prosecution service, the police, and the court system – with the exception of the Federal Constitutional Court (BVerfG) and the Federal Court of Justice (BGH) – are organized at the state level.[2]

Criminal cases fall under either federal or state competence. Owing to the prosecution being primarily a state affair, (*Sache der Länder*) the individual states investigate and prosecute the large bulk of the criminal offenses. As such, the federal prosecution has the competency to investigate, charge, and prosecute in a very limited number of cases, such as those involving serious offenses that go beyond individual state borders, e.g., in cases of international terrorism.[3]

In German law, regardless of the severity of the criminal offense committed, the cases that are disposed of by trial will follow the same proceeding, which is called *Erkenntnisverfahren*[4] and can be roughly translated as "adjudication proceedings".[5]

---

[1] *Krey/Heinrich*, Deutsches Strafverfahrensrecht, Rn. 34.

[2] *Frase/Weigend*, German Criminal Justice, p. 319; *Krey*, German Criminal Proceedings, pp. 592, 593.

[3] As per Art. 73 (1) Nr. 9a GG. In contrast, Art. 73 (1) Nr. 10 GG sets out the instances in which the federal government and the states work in cooperation, such as lit. c which states that the Federation and the states cooperate concerning the "protection against activities within the federal territory which (...) endanger the external interests of the Federal Republic of Germany".

[4] *Volk/Engländer*, Examens-Repetitorium, Rn. 4.

[5] For reasons of uniformity and accuracy, whenever possible, I will borrow the official translations from the website of the Federal Ministry of Justice and Consumer Protection.

This chapter will solely focus on the felony cases that are disposed of by trial; therefore, I will not address cases that are disposed of by means of diversion (*Einstellung aus Opportunitätsgründen*), summary penal orders, (*Strafbefehlsverfahren*), or by the accelerated proceeding (*Beschleunigtes Verfahren*).[6] For this purpose, this country report is divided into the examination of the criminal procedure (B.) and evidence law (C.), both of which are examined within the field of criminal procedure. Lastly, I will examine the main procedural safeguards in the German criminal procedure (D.).

B. Overview of the Criminal Procedure

I. Legal Sources

The Constitution of the Federal Republic of Germany is the most important source of law followed by the federal statutes.[7] In the area of criminal procedure, there are four main formal sources of law: The Code of Criminal Procedure (StPO), the Courts Constitution Act (GVG), some provisions of the Federal Constitution (GG) and of the European Convention on Human Rights (ECHR).[8]

The StPO is divided into eight parts (termed books), each of which addresses different topics of criminal procedure and evidence law. Books 1 and 2 are of particular importance to this work seeing that they respectively address the general provisions and the proceedings at first instance. As to the GVG, its importance is due to regulating the competence of the public prosecutor's office, the organization of the courts, and the deliberations and voting process that take place immediately before the delivery of judgment in the mixed courts.[9]

The main provisions in the GG that are of most relevance to the criminal procedure are the basic rights (*Grundrechte*), which are set out in Articles 1 to 19.[10] Further

---

Whenever a specific word or translation was not found in the said website, or when for reasons of clarity I employ a term that deviates from the official translation, I will specifically indicate the appropriate source. The translation of the Federal Constitution (GG) is available at: https://www.gesetze-im-internet.de/englisch_gg/index.html. The translation of the Code of Criminal Procedure (StPO) is available at: https://www.gesetze-im-internet.de/englisch_stpo/englisch_stpo.html#p1827. Finally, the translation of the Courts Constitution Act (GVG) is available at: https://www.gesetze-im-internet.de/englisch_gvg/index.html.

[6] These measures are set out in §§ 153 et seq. StPO, §§ 407 et seq. StPO and §§ 417 et seq. stop, respectively.

[7] *Juy-Birmann*, in: Delmas-Marty/Spencer, European Criminal Procedures, p. 292.

[8] Further federal statutes of relevance to this topic are the Youth Courts Law (JGG) and the Criminal Code (StGB).

[9] *Juy-Birmann*, in: Delmas-Marty/Spencer, European Criminal Procedures, p. 294; *Krey/Heinrich*, Deutsches Strafverfahrensrecht, Rn. 35.

[10] *Krey/Heinrich*, Deutsches Strafverfahrensrecht, Rn. 42.

important provisions are Arts. 101 (1), 103 (1), 103 (3), 104 GG.[11] These legal provisions respectively set out the ban of extraordinary courts, the right to a fair trial (*Garantie des gesetzlichen Richters*), the right that "no person shall be punished for the same act more than once under the general criminal laws"[12] and setting out the constitutional guarantees a person has in the event of deprivation of liberty.

The ECHR lays out important procedural rights, such as the defendant's right to (i) a fair trial within a reasonable time (*Recht auf ein faires Verfahren*), (ii) the presumption of innocence (*Unschuldsvermutung*), (iii) the right to have effective legal counsel present (*effective Verteidung*), and (iv) to examine or have examined witnesses against him (*Fragerecht*).[13]

The ECHR came into force in Germany on 3 September 1953,[14] and – formally – it has the rank of a simple law in the German legal framework.[15] As the ECHR is placed below the GG and is in the same level as other federal statutes such as the StPO,[16] *in theory*, German courts are not legally bound by the decisions of the European Court of Human Rights (ECtHR). However, the principle of international law *pacta sunt servanta* has an impact on the German legislature and for this reason, it is "obliged not to enact laws that contradict the ECHR and to repeal existing laws in the event of such contradiction".[17] A further consequence of this principle is that owing to the GG being "friendly towards international law" (*Völkerrechtsfreundlichkeit*), *in practice* German courts interpret German law – and the GG – in conformity with the interpretation of the ECHR by the ECtHR.[18] Thus, although in theory the ECHR has the rank of a simple law, in practice the BVerfG adheres to the jurisprudence of the ECtHR, and thus the Convention has a "soft precedent" (*weicher Vorrang*) in the interpretation of German law.[19]

---

[11] *Krey/Heinrich*, Deutsches Strafverfahrensrecht, Rn. 41.

[12] Art. 103 (3) GG.

[13] Art. 6 para. 1 sent. 1, Arts. 6 para. 2, para. 3 (c), para. 3 (d) ECHR, respectively. See *Ambos*, Internationales Strafrecht, § 10 Rn. 19 et seq.

[14] The law BGB 1.1952 II, 685, 953 of 7.8.1952 implemented the ECHR in the German legal framework in conformity with Art. 59 (2) GG. *Pieroth/Schlink*, Grundrechte, Rn. 56.

[15] *Ambos*, Internationales Strafrecht, § 10 Rn. 2; *Satzger*, Internationales und Europäisches Strafrecht, § 11 Rn. 13.

[16] *Krey/Heinrich*, Deutsches Strafverfahrensrecht, Rn. 63, 64.

[17] See original text in *Krey/Heinrich*, Deutsches Strafverfahrensrecht, Rn. 63, "Allerdings ist die deutsche Legislative (…) verpflichtet, keine Gesetze, die der EMRK widersprechen, zu erlassen und bestehende Gesetze bei einem solchen Widerspruch aufzuheben".

[18] *Krey/Heinrich*, Deutsches Strafverfahrensrecht, Rn. 64; *Satzger*, Internationales und Europäisches Strafrecht, § 11 Rn. 14.

[19] The BVerfG has held that if a decision of the ECtHR significantly changes the factual or legal situation of a decision of the BVerfG, the former can overcome the legal force of the latter. In this sense, see BVerG Urt. from 04.05.2011 – 2 BvR 2333/08; *Ambos*, Internationales Strafrecht, § 10 Rn. 2; *Satzger*, Internationales und Europäisches Strafrecht, § 11 Rn. 14.

II. Court System

In addition to the formal sources of law, there are informal sources; the most important of which is jurisprudence.[20] The Federal Constitutional Court (*Bundesverfassungsgericht*) is the court responsible on having the final word on interpreting the GG[21] and as seen above, it also adheres to the jurisprudence of the ECtHR in interpreting German law. However, in the instances where the GG provides a higher level of protection than the one afforded by the ECHR, the interpretation of the latter cannot lead to a restriction of the rights afforded by the former.[22]

II. Court System

At the first level are the Local Courts (AG), which have the original competence to try cases where a penalty less severe than a four-year sentence of imprisonment is to be expected. These courts fall into three categories which are divided according to the severity of the case. The first category comprises the cases where a penalty more severe than a two-year sentence of imprisonment is not to be expected. In this group, cases are presided by one single professional judge[23] and account for more than 90 % of the criminal cases that are disposed of by the German courts.[24]

The second and third categories comprise the criminal offenses, which have the expectation of being punishable by more than two and less than four years of imprisonment. In this category, cases are tried by a mixed court called the *Schöffengericht*, which is composed of two lay judges and one professional judge.[25] Whenever the public prosecution believes that an additional professional judge is necessary due to the circumstances of a specific case, he may request one to be added to the composition of the court (*erweitertes Schöffengericht*).[26]

At the intermediate level, there are the Regional Courts (LG), which are courts with both original and appellate competence. They are originally competent to try cases that do not fall under the competence of the Local Courts nor of the Higher Regional Courts, and to dispose of criminal offenses, where a sentence of imprisonment exceeding four years is to be expected.[27] These courts are termed the Grand Criminal Divisions (*große Strafkammer*) and are composed of three professional judges and two lay judges.[28] Among the criminal offenses tried by these courts are

---

[20] *Heger/Pohlreich/Kütterer-Lang*, Strafprozessrecht, Rn. 56, 59.

[21] Art. 93 (1) Nr. 1 GG. *Juy-Birmann*, in: Delmas-Marty/Spencer, European Criminal Procedures, p. 293.

[22] *Ambos*, Internationales Strafrecht, § 10 Rn. 2.

[23] § 25 GVG.

[24] *Krey*, German Criminal Proceedings, p. 601.

[25] § 29 (1) sent. 1 GVG; *Krey/Heinrich*, Deutsches Strafverfahrensrecht, Rn. 119.

[26] § 29 (2) sent. 1 GVG; *Volk*, Grundkurs StPO, § 5 Rn. 11.

[27] § 74 (1) GVG.

[28] § 76 (1) sent. 1 GVG; *Krey/Heinrich*, Deutsches Strafverfahrensrecht, Rn. 120.

those which result in the death of the victim (*Schwurgericht*), economic crimes (*Wirtschaftsstrafkammer*) and "serious criminal offenses related to state security"[29] (*Staatsschutzkammer*).[30]

In contrast, the Regional Courts function as an appellate court in cases where there is an appeal (*Berufung*) of a decision which was of the original competence of the Local Courts. In these instances, these courts are called the Small Criminal Divisions (*kleine Strafkammer*) and are composed by one professional judge and two lay judges.[31]

An additional type of court, which has both original and appellate competence is the Higher Regional Court (OLG). The divisions of these courts are called *Senate*, and their composition depend on the circumstances of the case, which can be of either one judge sitting alone, three, or five professional judges.[32] The original competence of these courts is to dispose of criminal offenses that involve national security (*Staatsschutzsachen*)[33] and to dispose of the cases set out in § 120 GVG.[34] In its appellate functions, the Higher Regional Courts are competent to both review certain decisions of the Local Courts (*Sprungrevision*) and of the Regional Courts (*Revision*).[35]

At the top of the pyramid is the Federal Court of Justice (BGH), the country's court of last resort, which only has appellate competence.[36] In matters of criminal law, this court is divided into five Panels for Criminal Matters (*Strafsenate*),[37] each of which is composed of five professional judges.[38] The BGH has jurisdiction to hear and to determine appeals (*Revision*) against first instance rulings of the Higher Regional Courts in cases involving national security. In addition to these instances, the BGH

---

[29] I borrowed the English translation of the term "*Staatschutzkammer*" from *Bohlander*, Principles, p. 41.

[30] These courts are respectively set out in §§ 74 (2), 74c (1) Nr. 1–6 and 74a (1) GVG. *Volk*, Grundkurs StPO, § 5 Rn. 13.

[31] §§ 74 (3), 76 (1) sent. 1 GVG; *Krey/Heinrich*, Deutsches Strafverfahrensrecht, Rn. 128.

[32] § 122 (1) GVG sets out that the court is composed of three professional judges, unless decisions are to be given by a judge sitting alone. In contrast, § 122 (2) GVG sets out the two instances when the court may be composed of five professional judges. In this sense, see *Krey/Heinrich*, Deutsches Strafverfahrensrecht, Rn. 125.

[33] This takes place when the Federal Prosecutor General (*Generalbundesanwalt*) takes over the case due to its particular significance, as per § 74a (2) GVG.

[34] *Volk*, Grundkurs StPO, § 5 Rn. 14; *Krey/Heinrich*, Deutsches Strafverfahrensrecht, Rn. 133.

[35] § 121 (1) Nr. 1 to 3 GVG, and § 335 (2) StPO. In thi sense, see *Krey/Heinrich*, Deutsches Strafverfahrensrecht, Rn. 129.

[36] *Volk*, Grundkurs StPO, § 5 Rn. 6.

[37] As per § 132 (2) GVG, if a Panel for Criminal Matters wishes to reach a decision on a certain matter on questions of law that differs from that of another Panel or that of the Grand Panel for Criminal Matters (*Große Senat für Strafsachen*), the latter is competent to decide on the matter. See *Volk*, Grundkurs StPO, § 5 Rn. 19.

[38] § 139 (1) GVG, *Volk*, Grundkurs StPO, § 5 Rn. 19.

hears appeals against first instance rulings of the Regional Courts that do not fall under the jurisdiction of the Higher Regional Courts.[39]

III. Main Procedural Actors

I will first set the general background of the legal profession in Germany as to subsequently analyze the roles and responsibilities of each procedural actor particularly, in the trial setting.

Regardless of whether a law graduate seeks to work as a judge, a prosecutor, or a lawyer, they must first be a fully qualified lawyer (*Volljurist/Volljuristin*). Law school is completed once a student finishes all necessary course work and successfully passes the first state exam (*Erstes Staatsexamen*). After passing the first state exam, law graduates must go through a two-year apprenticeship called *Refendariat*.[40] This program is tailored in a way to provide graduate students with practical legal experience in different working stations (*Berufsstationen*), i.a., the public prosecutor's office, local courts, in the public administration, and working for private lawyers. At the end of this apprenticeship, law graduates must successfully pass the second state exam (*Zweites Staatsexamen*) to become fully qualified lawyers.

However, for the *Volljuristen* who wish to work as prosecutors or as judges, they must go through a competitive selection process in which their chances of success are based on the candidates' grades on both their state exams. Successful candidates who work for the judicial service, do so in a capacity that usually comprises prosecutorial, judicial[41] and ministerial functions. The judicial service is tailored in this way as to reinforce the idea of prosecutors as judicial officers.[42] Newly hired judicial officers go through a three-year probationary phase after which they receive life tenure employment. As a rule, these professionals rotate between functions, working as either a prosecutor or a judge according to the necessities of the Ministry of Justice. After the probationary phase ends, the capacity in which they will work will depend on the necessities and openings of each department. In some Länder, however, the judicial officer will rotate between the prosecution service, the judiciary, and the Ministry of Justice throughout their whole career.[43]

---

[39] § 135 GVG.

[40] *Boyne*, The German Prosecution Service, pp. 40, 41.

[41] German judges have several rights that civil servants do not have, such as stability and the right not to be removed.

[42] *Perron*, in: Eser/Rabenstein, Criminal Justice, p. 306. This is beneficial as both these procedural actors are the main courtroom actors responsible for seeking the material truth. However, this takes place in different phases of the proceedings, i.e., the prosecution is responsible during the investigatory phase (*Ermittlungsverfahren*) and the presiding judge during the intermediate proceedings and the main hearing (*Hauptverfahren*).

[43] *Boyne*, The German Prosecution Service, p. 41.

1. Judges

There are two types of professional judges, the pretrial judges (*Ermittlungsrichter*)[44] and the trial judges[45] (*erkennender Richter in der Hauptverhandlung* or *Prozessrichter*), who are respectively competent to make decisions in the investigatory and adjudicatory phases.

In the instances where the public prosecutor believes a judicial investigation to be necessary, he submits an application to a pretrial judge to decide on issues which are of a "judge's reservation" (*Richtervorbehalt*).[46] In other words, the pretrial judge is responsible to verify whether the prosecution may employ investigative measures that affect the constitutional and procedural rights of the accused. Among these instances are e.g., the issuing of arrest warrants, whether to conduct physical examinations, and/or telephone surveillances. A further responsibility of the pretrial judge is to secure evidence for trial. A case in point is when a suspect confesses to a prosecutor, the latter may immediately go to a pretrial judge to secure this evidence. Another instance of the pretrial judge securing evidence is the examination of witnesses ahead of trial, which pursuant to the German confrontation clause, may take place in the presence of both the defendant and her defense counsel.[47]

In contrast, trial judges are responsible for deciding whether to bind a case for trial in the intermediate proceedings and if in the affirmative, the presiding judge has the responsibility of conducting and presiding the main proceedings, which include the preparation for the main proceedings and the main proceeding itself (trial).[48] The main tasks of the judges at trial are assessing the evidence and acting as both finder of fact and of law (responsible for the *Tat- und Rechtsfrage*). Additionally, if applicable, trial judges must reach an agreement regarding a negotiated agreement (*Verständigung*) and resume trial, if the initial discussions concerning this agreement fail to occur.[49]

---

[44] Despite the official translation of Ermittlungsrichter being "investigating judge" (as per § 162 StPO), I use the term "pretrial judge" owing to the term "investigating judge" alluding to the figure of the "Untersuchungsrichter". This latter type of judge was the procedural actor responsible for conducting criminal investigations in Germany up to 1975, which was when this figure was abolished and its role was replaced by that of the public prosecutor. See *Bohlander*, Principles, p. 67.

[45] The trial judges are professional judges (*Berufsrichter*), which include the presiding judge (*der Vorsitzende*) and the associate judges (*beisitzende Richter*).

[46] § 162 StPO; *Roxin/Schünemann*, Strafverfahrensrecht, § 9 Rn. 26.

[47] § 58 (2) StPO.

[48] § 238 (1) StPO.

[49] §§ 257c (1) and (4) StPO, respectively.

2. Prosecutors

Prosecutors are participants (*Beteiligte*) rather than parties to the proceedings[50] and while belonging to the executive power, they have a quasi-judicial role.[51] Therefore, regardless of the stage of the procedure, they are bound by the need of being objective as they are deemed to be the guardians of the law.[52] For this reason, German scholars coined the German prosecution "the most objective agency in the world" (*die objektivste Behörde der Welt*).[53] This can be illustrated by the fact that prosecutors may appeal from a conviction and request the trial judge for the defendant to be acquitted if they believe that the law was not correctly applied in a certain case.[54]

The public prosecutor's office (*Staatsanwaltschaft*) has three main roles in the criminal procedure,[55] which are of overseeing the investigatory phase (*Herrin des Ermittlungsverfahrens*), representing the prosecution in both the intermediate and main proceedings (*Vetreterin der Anklage*), and being the authority responsible for the procedure of execution of the sentence (*Vollstreckungsbehörde*).[56] At trial, the prosecutor's role is that of supporting the court in finding the material truth.[57] In fulfilling this role, §§ 160 (1) to (3) StPO lay out the prosecutorial duties in the investigatory phase, which are similar to the court's responsibilities in finding the material truth in the intermediate and in the main proceedings. Along these duties, the prosecution must (i) seek both incriminating and exonerating evidence, (ii) investigate the circumstances of the case which are essential in determining the legal consequences of the criminal offense, and (iii) gather and take evidence when there is concern that it might be lost. Additionally, public prosecutors must verify "the validity of any objection raised by the defense counsel, in order to ensure that the trial can be carried out efficiently".[58]

The fact that prosecutors work for the judicial service, coupled with their responsibility in finding the material truth, further impress on them their concern to do justice. As a result, prosecutors do not view an acquittal or a conviction as losing or

---

[50] *Roxin/Schünemann*, Strafverfahrensrecht, § 9 Rn. 11; *Schäuble*, Strafverfahren und Prozessverantwortung, p. 63.

[51] *Boyne*, The German Prosecution Service, p. 38; *Krey/Heinrich*, Deutsches Strafverfahrensrecht, Rn. 234, 235.

[52] § 160 (1) StPO. See *Krey*, Characteristic Features, p. 598.

[53] *Beulke*, Strafprozessrecht, Rn. 74.

[54] § 296 (2) StPO. Further examples of the objectivity of German prosecutors are set out in §§ 160 (2), 170 (2) sent. 1 StPO. See *Krey/Heinrich*, Deutsches Strafverfahrensrecht, Rn. 244.

[55] *Roxin/Schünemann*, Strafverfahrensrecht, § 9 Rn. 2; *Volk*, Grundkurs StPO, § 6 Rn. 1.

[56] As per § 451 StPO. In this latter capacity, the prosecution demands that the sentenced person pays a fine or is sent to prison.

[57] *Rauxloh*, Plea-Bargaining, p. 86.

[58] *Perron*, in: Eser/Rabenstein, Criminal Justice, p. 310.

winning, or yet, as a criterion for a job well done;[59] rather, this assessment is based on whether the law was correctly applied.[60]

3. Defense Counsel

The right to defense stems from Art. 2 I GG and Art. 6 para. 3 (c) ECHR, which states that if the defendant does not have the financial means to pay for legal assistance, the court must appoint her with legal counsel.[61] The lack of legal counsel present leads to an unbalance between the prosecution on the one side, and the defense on the other side.[62] As per the ECHR, the defendant's right to counsel is essential in guaranteeing a fair trial, and the right of the accused to counsel arises from the very first interrogation of the accused.[63]

The right to defense has a material and a formal aspect.[64] The material aspect pertains to the defendant's right to have assistance of another person in safeguarding his interests, whereas the formal aspect refers to the legal defense itself.[65] In the StPO, the former right is set out by § 137 (1) StPO, which states that the defendant has the right to have assistance of defense counsel "at any stage of the proceedings".[66] As per § 138 (1) StPO, defendants may retain a lawyer for their defense (*Wahlverteidiger*). Whenever a defendant does not have the financial means to retain a lawyer, as there are no public defenders in Germany, a court-appointed counsel will be allocated to him (*Pflichtverteidiger*).[67] Nonetheless, in these instances, the defendant may choose his or her legal counsel and subsequently propose the lawyer in question to the judge, who may only deny the proposed legal counsel if there are strong reasons for him to do so.[68]

As a rule, defendants can waive their right to legal counsel; however, the StPO lays out the instances where such a waiver is not possible due to the presence of legal counsel being mandatory (*Notwendige Verteidigung*).[69] The reasoning for this are various namely, due to the seriousness of the criminal offense, the difficult factual or

---

[59] *Bohlander*, Principles, p. 144.

[60] *Boyne*, The German Prosecution Service, p. 56.

[61] *Krey/Heinrich*, Deutsches Strafverfahrensrecht, Rn. 338.

[62] *Ambos*, Internationales Strafrecht, § 10 Rn. 33.

[63] ECtHR *Salduz v. Turkey*, Nr. 36391/02, *Judgment* 27.11.2008. However, the ECtHR retreated from its latter position, see ECtHR *Beuze v. Belgium*, Nr. 71409/10, *Judgment* 9.11.2018.

[64] *Kindhäuser/Schumann*, Strafprozessrecht, § 7 Rn. 2.

[65] *Kindhäuser/Schumann*, Strafprozessrecht, § 7 Rn. 2.

[66] *Volk*, Grundkurs StPO, § 9 Rn. 31. See infra Ch. 1 C. IV. 2. b).

[67] *Krey/Heinrich*, Deutsches Strafverfahrensrecht, Rn. 339, 426.

[68] *Volk*, Grundkurs StPO, § 11 Rn. 33; *Krey/Heinrich*, Deutsches Strafverfahrensrecht, Rn. 431, 471.

[69] *Krey/Heinrich*, Deutsches Strafverfahrensrecht, Rn. 339, 407.

legal circumstances of the case, or the defendant's inability in defending himself.[70] Thus, in these instances, legal counsel may be appointed to the defendant by either a judge *ex officio* or by request of the public prosecutor.[71]

If the defendant has been requested to reply to the bill of indictment (*Anklageschrift*) and has not yet retained legal counsel, if he expressly requests for legal counsel to be appointed to him, the court must do so immediately.[72] In contrast, § 141 (2) StPO sets out the instances where the defendant must be given court-appointed counsel regardless of him having previously requested the court to do so.

IV. Procedural Phases

1. Investigatory Phase

For reasons of uniformity and clarity, in Part 3, I will refer to the preliminary proceeding (*Ermittlungsverfahren* or *Vorverfahren*) as the "investigatory phase".

a) Evidence Gathering by the State

As seen, in the investigatory phase, the public prosecutor's office is the chief responsible for the investigation and may, in theory, request the police for their assistance in investigating crimes.[73] In practice, however, the manner in which investigations are conducted vary depending on the gravity of the criminal offense in question. In crimes of small and medium gravity, prosecutors usually delegate the investigations to the police, who work autonomously.[74]

Once the investigation is finalized, the police send the prosecution the investigation file and the prosecutors must then determine whether there is enough evidence to charge a suspect. In contrast, in cases involving serious crimes and crimes of higher complexity such as murder, rape, economic and organized crimes, prosecutors tend to be more proactive and investigate alongside the police.[75] Nonetheless, regardless of the level of proactivity of the prosecution during the investigatory phase, an investigative file or dossier (*Ermittlungsakten* or *Akten*) containing all the in-

---

[70] These instances are set out in §§ 140 (1) and (2) StPO. *Volk*, Grundkurs StPO, § 11 Rn. 29 et seq.

[71] *Rogall*, in: SK-StPO, § 136 Rn. 58.

[72] § 141 (1) StPO, *Krey/Heinrich*, Deutsches Strafverfahrensrecht, Rn. 426.

[73] § 161 (1) StPO.

[74] § 163 (1) StPO. *Kühne*, Strafprozessrecht, Rn. 135; *Roxin/Schünemann*, Strafverfahren, § 9 Rn. 21.

[75] *Boyne*, The German Prosecution Service, p. 81.

vestigative steps taken during this phase must be compiled in a very thorough manner.[76]

Once the investigation is concluded, the prosecution must decide whether to bring charges against the suspect or whether to terminate the proceedings (*Einstellung des Verfahrens*).[77] In fulfilling this role, prosecutors are bound to the principle of mandatory prosecution (*Legalitätsprinzip*),[78] which guides the prosecutorial decision-making, both regarding whether to start an investigation and whether to charge a suspect. According to this principle, if there is enough evidence that a criminal offense was committed, the prosecution has the duty to investigate it (*Anfangsverdacht*).[79] Further, once the investigation is concluded, if the standard of "adequate suspicion" (*hinreichender Tatverdacht*)[80] is present – that is, if it is more probable than not that the defendant is guilty of the charges against her – the prosecution must bring charges against the accused.[81] Although this section is located in the chapter reserved to Public Charges (*Öffentliche Klage*), the principle of mandatory prosecution is applicable to all phases of the criminal procedure.[82]

However, despite the principle of mandatory prosecution being vital to the German criminal procedure, in practice, it is usually applied in cases involving serious offenses. In contrast, in crimes of small and medium gravity, the principle of discretionary prosecution (*Opportunitätsprinzip*) applies. The importance of this latter principle is owing to the large number of criminal cases that prosecutors must dispose of daily. Nevertheless, the principle of discretionary prosecution is not synonymous to prosecutorial discretion, nor does it dictate that the prosecution is free from prosecuting a criminal offense. This is because this principle has a normative basis and may only be applied in specific circumstances. The StPO sets out these instances in §§ 153 et seq. and §§ 407 et seq.[83]

---

[76] *Meyer-Goßner/Schmitt*, StPO, § 147 Rn. 14.

[77] *Roxin/Schünemann*, Strafverfahrensrecht, § 40 Rn. 3.

[78] § 152 (2) StPO.

[79] § 152 (2) StPO, *Heger/Pohlreich/Kütterer-Lang*, Strafprozessrecht, Rn. 248.

[80] *Krey/Heinrich*, Deutsches Strafverfahrensrecht, Rn. 262.

[81] As per § 170 (1) StPO. However, if the prosecution verifies that the standard of *hinreichender Verdacht* has not been met, he will terminate the proceedings, as per § 170 (2) sent. 1 StPO. *Heger/Pohlreich/Kütterer-Lang*, Strafprozessrecht, Rn. 264.

[82] This principle mandates that once the charging decision has been made, the prosecution has the duty of leading the charge (*Vertretung der Anklage*). This prosecutorial duty persists, even if the prosecution believes the defendant to be innocent, in which case he must make this position clear to the court at the latest during his closing speeches. For this reason, under no circumstances may the prosecution forego the criminal case.

[83] In practice, a large number os cases are not adjudicated at trial, either because (i) they are terminated due to lack of evidence, e. g., a suspect was not found (20 %), (ii) they are disposed of by §§ 153 et seq. StPO (30–40 %), or (iii) they were disposed of by means of § 153a StPO (10 %). In *Kühne*, Strafprozessrecht, Rn. 308. Slightly differently, *Krey/Heinrich* states that more than 50 % of the criminal cases are disposed of by means of §§ 170 (2), 153 et seq. StPO. *Krey/Heinrich*, Deutsches Strafverfahrensrecht, Rn. 264.

b) Rights of the Defense in the Investigatory Phase

There are two main ways in which the defense may have access to information ahead of trial. First, § 147 (1) StPO affords the defendant's legal counsel the right to request the inspection of the investigation file (*Akteneinsichtsrecht*) that are available to the court and the right to inspect pieces of evidence that are under official custody. The advantage of this right to inspection is that the defendant's defense counsel will have access to both incriminating and exculpatory evidence, which will enable it to have a good basis for judging whether the evidence against her client is enough for a conviction and how to better prepare the defendant's defense. Further, it aids the defense in analyzing the strengths and weaknesses of the evidence gathered by the prosecution.

Despite this right being applicable to all procedural phases, only the defendant's legal counsel has this right, as the defendant herself is barred from having direct access to the investigative file.[84] Owing to the principle of "completeness of the investigative file" (*Grundsatz der Aktenvollständigkeit*), this file must be thorough and contain all the steps partaken throughout the criminal investigation and all information which is relevant to both questions of guilt and to sentencing.[85] For this reason, if there is a chance that the defense's access to parts of the dossier may jeopardize an ongoing criminal investigation, the defense might be refused to have access to either the entirety of the dossier or to parts of it.[86]

The second way in which the defense may have access to information prior to trial is by conducting their own independent investigations. As the StPO does not explicitly provide the defendant with any specific rights or mechanisms to this end, it is up to the defense to choose how to conduct these investigations. Thus, the defense may e. g., hire a detective, or they may conduct the investigation themselves.[87] When conducting investigations, although the defense may search for witnesses to this end, there is no compulsory process in the German law whereby the defense may obtain the said evidence during the investigatory phase.[88]

In addition to the two main options described above, the defense has other means in which to request the prosecution or the pretrial judge to take evidence which may be favorable to the defendant's case. In this sense, it may request the prosecution for exculpatory evidence to be taken.[89] However, in these instances, despite prosecutors usually abiding to this request, owing to their duty of finding the objective facts of the

---

[84] *Meyer-Goßner/Schmitt*, StPO, § 147 Rn. 10.

[85] *Schäuble*, Strafverfahren und Prozessverantwortung, p. 71; *Krey/Heinrich*, Deutsches Strafverfahrensrecht, Rn. 367; *Meyer-Goßner/Schmitt*, StPO, § 147 Rn. 14.

[86] § 147 (2) StPO.

[87] *Schäuble*, Strafverfahren und Prozessverantwortung, pp. 72, 73.

[88] *Frase/Weigend*, German Criminal Justice, p. 341; *Roxin/Schünemann*, Strafverfahrensrecht, § 19 Rn. 63.

[89] § 163a (2) StPO; *Schäuble*, Strafverfahren und Prozessverantwortung, p. 73.

case, it is completely within their discretion whether to comply.[90] A further instance is that if the defendant is examined by a judge during this phase, the defense may rthe examining judge to take individual depositions, which the judge will comply when there is fear that the evidence might otherwise be lost, or when it might prove the defendant's innocence.[91]

2. Intermediate Proceedings: Evidentiary Standard of hinreichender Tatverdacht

After the prosecution has decided to bring charges against a suspect, it sends both the bill of indictment and the investigation file to the court's professional judges,[92] who are competent for the main hearing (*erkennendes Gericht*).[93] It is in this phase called the intermediate proceedings (*Zwischenverfahren*) that based on these written documents, the court's professional judges must decide whether to open the main proceedings. Further, it is also during this phase that the court must decide on matters regarding pretrial detention and provisional placement.[94]

§ 201 (1) StPO sets out that the presiding judge must inform the accused of the bill of indictment and the time limit which she has to apply for individual evidence and to offer objections to the opening of the main proceedings.[95] Further, the court may order individual evidence to be taken to assist it in reaching a decision. The court's decision in both deciding whether to accept the defendant's applications and objections and in requesting individual evidence to be taken, are uncontestable.[96]

If the court decides that there is reason to believe that the standard of "adequate suspicion"[97] (*hinreichender Tatverdacht*) is present, i.e., that it is more probable than not that the defendant is guilty of the charges against her, it will open the main proceedings (*Eröffnungsbeschluss*).[98] The defendant may not appeal from this decision.[99] If, however, the court believes the standard of adequate suspicion was not achieved, or that there are other factual or legal reasons that make it likely that the

---

[90] *Perron*, Beweisantragsrecht, pp. 167 et seq.

[91] § 166 (1) StPO.

[92] § 199 (2) sent. 2 StPO. Lay judges do not participate in the decision whether to open the main proceedings. In this sense, see *Roxin/Schünemann*, Strafverfahrensrecht, § 42 Rn. 7.

[93] § 199 StPO.

[94] § 207 (4) StPO.

[95] *Krey/Heinrich*, Deutsches Strafverfahrensrecht, Rn. 541.

[96] §§ 201 (2), 202 StPO.

[97] I borrowed the English translation of *"hinreichender Tatverdacht"* from *Frase/Weigend*, German Criminal Justice, p. 340.

[98] § 203 StPO; *Kindhäuser/Schumann*, Strafprozessrecht, § 16 Rn. 5.

[99] § 210 StPO; *Trüg/Habetha*, in: MüKo-StPO, § 244 Rn. 10; *Roxin/Schünemann*, Strafverfahrensrecht, § 42 Rn. 17.

accused is innocent,[100] it will not open the main proceedings (*Nichteröffnungsbeschluss*) and will dismiss the case. However, this is only a temporary dismissal (*vorläufige Einstellung*), as the case may be reopened if new facts or evidence are found.[101]

3. Main Proceedings

After the court finds that the evidentiary standard of *hinreichender Tatverdacht* was met, the main proceedings commence (*Hauptverfahren*). This procedure is divided into the preparation for the main hearing and the main hearing itself. It is in the latter phase where both questions of guilt (*Schuldfrage*) and questions of punishment (*Straffrage*) are decided by the court. For reasons of uniformity, in Part 3, I will refer to the main proceedings as the "adjudicatory phase", whereas I will refer to the main hearing itself as "the trial phase" or "trial".

a) Preparation for the Main Hearing

Once the court, who is competent for the trial, opens the main proceedings, the preparation for trial begins (*Vorbereitung der Hauptverhandlung*). It is the presiding judge's responsibility to order the summonses.[102] After the presiding judge sets a date and time for trial,[103] she orders the registry to issue and dispatch the summons to the defendant, its defense counsel, and the witnesses and experts.[104] Following the summoning of the witnesses and experts, the court shall provide both the prosecution and the defense the names of the witnesses and experts in question and the location where they can be found.[105]

When summoning the defendant, the service of summons and of the notification of the date of trial must reach her at least one week prior to trial.[106] An inobservance of this time limit gives the defendant the right to request the hearing to be suspended.[107] The same deadline applies to the summoning of the defendant's court appointed defense counsel and the defendant's chosen defense counsel in cases, where the defendant notified the court of his defense counsel of choice.[108]

---

[100] *Roxin/Schünemann*, Strafverfahrensrecht, § 42 Rn. 14.
[101] § 211 StPO; *Krey/Heinrich*, Deutsches Strafverfahrensrecht, Rn. 540.
[102] § 214 (1) sent. 1 StPO; *Volk*, § 17 Rn. 3.
[103] § 213 (1) StPO; *Heger/Pohlreich/Kütterer-Lang*, Strafprozessrecht, Rn. 346.
[104] §§ 216, 218, 214 (2) StPO, respectively; *Kindhäuser/Schumann*, Strafprozessrecht, § 17 Rn. 4, 5.
[105] § 222 StPO, *Volk*, § 17 Rn. 3.
[106] § 217 (1) StPO.
[107] § 217 (2) StPO.
[108] § 218 StPO.

The public prosecutor's office may summon the witnesses and experts directly,[109] whereas the defendant has two possibilities in which to summon witnesses and experts. She may either request the presiding judge to summon them by a motion to present evidence "indicating the facts on which evidence is to be taken"[110] (*Beweisanträge*), or the defendant may choose to summon them directly.[111]

b) Main Hearing

aa) Determining Attendance of the Procedural Actors and that Evidence is Present

The main hearing (*Hauptverhandlung*) begins when the presiding judge orders the recording clerk or hall attendant to call up the case (*Aufruf der Sache*).[112] The signaling that the case is about to begin is very important seeing that from this point forward, the court may base its conviction on whatever happens in the main hearing, as pursuant to § 261 StPO.[113] Following the calling up of the case, the presiding judge determines whether the defendant, her defense counsel, and the summoned witnesses and experts are in attendance. He must also determine whether documentary and inspection evidence, which the court and prosecution seek to produce at trial, are present.[114] Pursuant to § 243 (2) sent. 1 StPO, after this initial determination, the witnesses must leave the courtroom so that the court may examine the defendant regarding her personal circumstances, as to prevent them from inadvertently being influenced by the testimony of the defendant or that of other witnesses.[115]

bb) Defendant's Examination

The initial examination of the defendant has the purpose of identifying her personal circumstances (*Vernehmung des Angeklagten zur Person*).[116] After this is concluded, the prosecutor reads the charges against the defendant out loud in the main hearing (*Verlesung des Anklagesatzes durch den Staatsanwalt*).[117] This has three main purposes; the first is to make sure that the defendant is aware of the charges against her. Second, to inform the lay judges the exact scope of the charge(s) and the ordinance(s) against the defendant, as they must reach a decision of fact and

---

[109] § 214 (3) StPO, *Volk*, § 17 Rn. 3.

[110] § 219 (1) sent. 1 StPO, *Kindhäuser/Schumann*, Strafprozessrecht, § 17 Rn. 7.

[111] § 220 (1) StPO, *Kindhäuser/Schumann*, Strafprozessrecht, § 17 Rn. 8.

[112] *Arnoldi*, in: MüKo-StPO, § 243 Rn. 8.

[113] *Arnoldi*, in: MüKo-StPO, § 243 Rn. 9.

[114] *Heger/Pohlreich/Kütterer-Lang*, Strafprozessrecht, Rn. 350; *Krey/Heinrich*, Deutsches Strafverfahrensrecht, Rn. 999.

[115] *Arnoldi*, in: MüKo-StPO, § 243 Rn. 16.

[116] *Krey/Heinrich*, Deutsches Strafverfahrensrecht, Rn. 1001.

[117] § 243 (3) sent. 1 StPO. *Arnoldi*, in: MüKo-StPO, § 243 Rn. 23.

law.[118] The reason for this is that contrary to professional judges, lay judges have no access to the investigation file.[119] Third, by reading the charging document, the public in attendance is made aware of the charges against the defendant.

Following the reading of the charges, the presiding judge must instruct the defendant of her right to silence before examining her regarding the charges (*Belehrung des Angeklagten*).[120] Due to this instruction being vital in granting the defendant a fair trial, it must be made in the main hearing, regardless of whether the defendant has previously been made aware of this right.[121] Following this instruction, if the defendant chooses to answer the presiding judge's questions and make a statement, the presiding judge will then proceed to examine the defendant regarding the merits of the case.[122]

cc) Evidence Taking and Closing Arguments

After the examination of the defendant, the presiding judge (presides and) conducts the taking of evidence (*Beweisaufnahme*) to find the material truth.[123] After the presiding judge finishes conducting the evidence taking at trial, both the prosecution and the defense have the right to make their last statements (*Plädoyers/Schlussvorträge*).[124] Pursuant to § 258 (2) StPO, the prosecution has the right to reply at least once to the defense's closing statements (*Recht der Erwiderung*). The presiding judge may, however, grant the prosecution as many replies as she deems pertinent. However, it is vital that the defense's closing statements follows that of the prosecution and that the defendant's right to have the last word is safeguarded.[125]

---

[118] *Frase/Weigend*, German Criminal Justice, p. 355.

[119] In this sense, see infra Ch. 1 C. I. 1.

[120] § 243 (5) sent. 1 StPO.

[121] *Arnoldi*, in: MüKo-StPO, § 243 Rn. 56; however, the previous statements made by the defendant in a judicial interrogation prior to trial can be used against her. As per § 254 StPO, this provision does not exclude calling the police officer as a witness in order to testify on the content of the interrogation. In these instances, the presiding judge may read the recording so that the police officer can confirm or deny its veracity; it is not the content itself that is a means of proof, but rather the police officer's statement regarding its veracity.

[122] The defendant's statements and/or answers to the presiding judge's questions must be made orally. The defendant may also write her statement down and read it out loud at court. Exceptions to an oral statement are only permitted in cases in which the defendant is unable to do so due to physical or psychological reasons. See *Arnoldi*, in: MüKo-StPO, § 243 Rn. 67.

[123] *Heger/Pohlreich/Kütterer-Lang*, Strafprozessrecht, Rn. 361. See infra Ch. 1 C. I. 2. a).

[124] *Krey/Heinrich*, Deutsches Strafverfahrensrecht, Rn. 1016.

[125] § 258 (3) StPO. An interesting feature of the German trial is that owing to prosecutors having an objective role throughout the different procedural phases, if a prosecutor finds that – based on the totality of evidence presented at trial – the defendant is innocent, she will inform the judge of her position during the closing arguments.

dd) Deliberations, Voting and Pronouncement of Judgment

Pursuant to § 260 (1) StPO, the deliberations take place after the defendant's last word and immediately before the delivery of judgment. This is a required proceeding, which occurs in a confidential setting in the deliberations room outside of the main hearing.[126] Although there are no precise stipulations as to how the deliberations should take place or how long they should last,[127] § 194 GVG provides that "the presiding judge shall preside over the deliberations (*Beratung*), ask the questions and collect the votes".

Following the deliberations, the voting process (*Abstimmung*) begins and must ensue in a specific order.[128] In the instances where a rapporteur (*Berichterstatter*) was appointed, he or she must vote first. The following votes are according to seniority, and if two people are of equal seniority, according to age. The order to be followed is that the younger judges vote before the older judges and that the lay judges vote before the professional judges. The presiding judge is the last person to cast his or her vote.

A majority of two-thirds of the total number of votes is required to reach a decision against a defendant regarding both questions of guilt and of the legal consequences of the offense (*Schuldfrage* und *Rechtsfolge*). Considering that the lay judges have the same voting power as the professional judges,[129] depending on the composition of the court, the opinion of the lay judges regarding the defendant's guilt may override that of the professional judges, in which case the latter will have to bend to the former's will.[130] However, in the instances where there is a tie in a mixed court composed of two professional judges and two lay judges, the presiding judge will have the casting vote.[131]

The judgment must be pronounced (*Urteilsverkündung*) within eleven days of the end of the main hearing.[132] Pursuant to § 268 (2) sent. 1 StPO, "the judgment shall be pronounced by reading out the operative provisions of the judgment" (*Urteilsformel*) and by "disclosing the reasons for the judgment" (*Urteilsgründe*). The importance of the presiding judge stating the reasons for reaching her decision in writing is owing to it being the basis of any future appeal.[133]

---

[126] *Maier*, in: MüKo-StPO, § 260 Rn. 8, 30.

[127] *Maier*, in: MüKo-StPO, § 260 Rn. 10.

[128] § 197 GVG.

[129] § 30 (1) GVG.

[130] It should be noted that with the exception of the judges of the BVerfG, trial judges cannot write separate or dissenting opinions. In this sense, see *Bohlander*, Principles, p. 50.

[131] § 196 (4) GVG; however, due to the professional judges' authority and expertise in adjudicating cases, it is not uncommon for the lay judges to follow their reasoning and judgment. In this sense, see *Perron*, in: Eser/Rabenstein, Criminal Justice, p. 305.

[132] § 268 (3) StPO.

[133] The requisites of the reasons of judgment are set out in § 267 StPO.

C. Evidence Law

I. Introduction

1. Finder of Fact: Professional and Lay Judges

As seen, the composition of the courts change depending on the case being tried.[134] On the one side, the bulk of criminal cases are disposed of by the Local Courts, which are presided by a professional judge sitting alone. On the other side, criminal cases that are tried by Local Courts and have a higher degree of complexity and severity and those which are tried in the Regional Courts are mixed courts.[135] The latter courts are comprised of professional judges (*Berufsrichter*) – which include the presiding judge (*der Vorsitzende*) and the associate judges (*beisitzende Richter*) – and of lay judges (*Schöffen*).[136]

The participation of lay judges has its roots in the influence of the ideas brought by the French Revolution, where German jurists were influenced by English jury trials which were deemed to represent the people's interests. Although jury trials were introduced to the German criminal procedure and were eventually abolished in 1924, legislators sought a means of making the criminal justice system accountable to the people.[137] Owing to the belief that "the collaboration of laymen in matters of criminal law lends a great popular support to the administration of justice",[138] the figure of lay judges was introduced to the composition of the Local and Regional Courts.

Lay judges usually serve in this capacity in various cases and for this reason, they acquire a sense of familiarity with the trial setting and with the professional judges.[139] They are – alongside the professional judges – finder of fact and of law, which include questions of guilt and punishment.[140] Further, they "have the right to question both witnesses and expert witnesses, as well as to intervene in the examination of the evidence in any other way".[141] Yet, there are significant differences between the members of the court. Contrary to the professional judges, lay judges do not have access to the investigative nor to the court file (*Gerichtsakten*)

---

[134] See supra Ch. 1 B. II.

[135] *Kindhäuser/Schumann*, Strafprozessrecht, § 12 Rn. 73; *Krey/Heinrich*, Deutsches Strafverfahrensrecht, Rn. 114.

[136] Pursuant to § 45 (1) sent. 2 DRiG, lay judges are bound to secrecy in regards to the court deliberations (*Beratungsgeheimnis*).

[137] *Krey*, German Criminal Proceedings, p. 600.

[138] *Jescheck*, Principles of German Criminal Procedure, p. 244.

[139] *Perron*, in: Eser/Rabenstein, Criminal Justice, p. 305.

[140] § 263 (1) StPO. In this sense, *Perron*, Beweisantragsrecht, p. 119; *Volk*, § 5 Rn. 15; *Krey/Heinrich*, Deutsches Strafverfahrensrecht, Rn. 114.

[141] *Perron*, in: Eser/Rabenstein, Criminal Justice, p. 305.

and thus, they must form their convictions solely based on the evidence that was presented at trial.[142]

2. Trial Setting

a) Officialized Factfinding

The features of the inquisitorial procedural model shape both the roles that the procedural actors play at the trial stage and who has control over the presentation of evidence at trial. In the intermediate phase, the responsibility in the truth-finding enterprise shifts from the prosecution to the court.[143] Due to the *principle of ascertainment of the truth*,[144] it is now the court's task to seek to reconstruct the facts of the case and find out what happened, thereby seeking to find the material or substantive truth. In this setting, evidence is not considered as that of the prosecution or of the defense, but rather of the court.[145] Therefore, it is the court's task to thoroughly examine all evidence that might be relevant in finding what happened, *regardless of and beyond* any motion to take evidence presented by either the prosecution or the defense.[146] To this purpose, in order to streamline the main proceeding, § 238 (1) StPO sets out that it is the responsibility of the presiding judge to conduct the hearing, examine the defendant and the witnesses, and to conduct the procedure of evidence taking at trial. However, although the presiding judge is responsible for conducting the examination of the defendant, the associate judges and lay judges on the one side, and the defense and the prosecution on the other side, may also examine the defendant.[147]

In fulfilling its task to conduct the hearing, the presiding judge will have thoroughly studied the investigative file prior to trial. At trial, he will then decide the order in which he will examine the different means of evidence.[148] A further responsibility of the presiding judge is to verify whether the course and the results of the hearing are being thoroughly registered on record, as per § 273 (3) sent. 1 StPO.[149] Consequently, as a rule, the presiding judge is responsible for making most of the decisions at trial,

---

[142] In this sense, see *Kühne*, Strafprozessrecht, Rn. 116; *Roxin/Schünemann*, Strafverfahrensrecht, § 6 Rn. 16; *Volk*, Grundkurs StPO, § 5 Rn. 15. Contrary to this position, *Kindhäuser* believes that lay judges have the right to access the investigation file, in this sense see *Kindhäuser/Schumann*, Strafprozessrecht, § 12 Rn. 77.

[143] *Schäuble*, Strafverfahren und Prozessverantwortung, p. 64

[144] § 244 (2) StPO; For more details regarding this principle, see Ch. 1 D. I.

[145] *Caianiello/Hodgson*, Discretionary Criminal Justice, p. 8.

[146] *Damaška*, Evidentiary Barriers to Conviction, p. 525; *Frister*, in: SK-StPO, § 244 Rn. 10.

[147] §§ 240 (1) and 240 (2) StPO, respectively.

[148] *Perron*, Beweisantragsrecht, p. 154; *Bohlander*, Principles, p. 113; *Schneider*, in: KK-StPO, § 238 Rn. 2, 3.

[149] *Schneider*, in: KK-StPO, § 238 Rn. 3.

whereas the court itself is only responsible in making decisions in specific instances. One such example is when either the prosecution or the defense objects to "an order by the presiding judge relating to the conduct of the hearing",[150] in which case, the court must decide on the said objection.

b) Rights of the Prosecution and Defense in Participating in the Presentation of Evidence

Although the trial court is responsible for finding the material truth, the prosecution, the defense, the defendant, as well as other procedural actors may co-shape the taking of evidence at trial. I will now briefly examine the main avenues the StPO provides the prosecution and defense to do so, namely through the right to cross-examine witnesses and experts (*Kreuzverhör*), to ask questions (*Fragerecht*), to make statements during evidence taking (*Erklärungsrecht*), and to present the court a motion to take evidence (*Beweisantragsrecht*).

First, based on the Anglo-American evidence law, § 239 StPO sets out that the prosecution and the defense may jointly request the presiding judge for them to examine witnesses and experts by means of cross-examination. In these instances, after both the defense and the prosecution conclude their respective examinations, the presiding judge may pose questions to the said witnesses and experts. There are, however, two limitations to the applicability of this right. First, both the prosecution and the defense may only cross-examine the experts and witnesses who were named by them; thus, experts and witnesses that were named by the court cannot be subjected to cross-examination.[151] Second, this right only applies to requests by the defense counsel and prosecution. Hence, the private accessory prosecutor (*Nebenkläger*) and private plaintiffs (*Privatkläger*) are not permitted to cross-examine experts and witnesses. Interestingly, although this provision was initially created as a means to compliment the court's truth finding activities, it is currently in disuse.[152]

Second, § 240 StPO affords the prosecution and the defense the right to ask questions. This provision also sets out that the presiding judge shall permit the associate judges and the lay judges to ask questions to the defendant, witnesses, and experts.[153] It is up to the presiding judge alone when to grant this right and to decide whether the person who made the request to ask questions may do so before or after he has examined the defendant, witness, or expert in question. The prosecution and the defense may ask direct questions to either the defendant, the witnesses, and the

---

[150] § 238 (2) StPO.

[151] *Schneider*, in: KK-StPO, § 240 Rn. 5.

[152] I will examine the reasons for the disuse of cross-examination in German trials in Ch. 5 B. III. 1.

[153] For court-appointed experts to prepare for their opinion (*Gutachten*), they also have the right to ask the defendant and witnesses questions, to be present while the defendant and witnesses are examined, and to ask them questions in this occasion, as per §§ 80 (1) and 80 (2) StPO, respectively.

experts they wish to inquire until the person in question is not dismissed by the presiding judge.[154] However, this right only encompasses the right to ask questions, and does not entail the right to make declarations or statements, nor to prepone the closing statements.[155]

In addition to the aforementioned procedural actors, defendants may also ask questions to the witnesses and experts. This is in accordance with Art. 6 para. 3 (d) ECHR, which states that the defendant has the right to examine the witnesses against her and those on her behalf.[156] The importance of this right is that contrary to the court who, as a rule, examines witnesses in a detached and objective manner, the defense may try to heavily attack and impeach witnesses against the defense, as a means in which to unearth inconsistencies and even potential untruthfulness.[157] However, § 240 (2) sent. 2 StPO expressly states that the defendant is not permitted to ask the co-defendant any questions, owing to the concern that this could disrupt the procedure of evidence taking. For this reason, if the defendant has any questions to the co-defendant, he must ask his questions through his defense counsel or through the presiding judge.[158]

Third, § 257 StPO affords the defendant (para. 1), and upon request the prosecution and the defense counsel (para. 2), the possibility to make statements after each single piece of evidence is taken. This is an important means for the defense to co-shape evidence taking by seeking to show the court their respective standpoint.

The last and most important means to allow for the defense to co-shape evidence taking is by means of it requesting the court to take evidence. This motion permits the prosecution, the defense, and the defendant to file an application to the court responsible for hearing the case to take additional evidence. Due to the importance of the motion to take evidence and its potential in effectively co-shaping the trial setting, I will examine it in more detail when I address the procedural safeguards of the German criminal procedure.[159]

II. Methods of Proving Facts

1. Exceptions to the Need of Proof

Although, as a rule, facts need to be proven at trial, there are exceptions to the need of proof (*negative Beweisbedürftigkeit*). There are facts that while relevant do not need to be proven due to them either being obvious facts (*offenkundige Tatsachen*), or

---

[154] § 248 StPO.
[155] *Schneider*, in: KK-StPO, § 240 Rn. 5.
[156] *Kindhäuser/Schumann*, Strafprozessrecht, § 6 Rn. 22.
[157] *Schäuble*, Strafverfahren und Prozessverantwortung, p. 95.
[158] *Schneider*, in: KK-StPO, § 240 Rn. 7.
[159] See infra Ch. 1 D. II.

due to them being the opposite of these evident facts.[160] These facts comprise both facts of general knowledge (*allgemeinkundigen Tatsachen*) and facts known to the court (*gerichtskundigen Tatsachen*). On the one hand, acts of general knowledge are those that are widely well-known and that are available from readily reliable sources and can range from a variety of areas of expertise such as geography, history, medicine, politics, physics among many others. Nonetheless, geographical and temporal limitations may apply to such facts,[161] owing to the possibility that a fact may only be evident within a specific geographical area and time. On the other hand, facts known to the court are those in which a judge either obtained them by virtue of her experience of working as a judge, or facts that are usually well-known or are readily available to all judges.[162] For this reason, facts obtained by a judge due to private reasons, or facts that are only known to a judge due to a case she is presently adjudicating, are not facts known to the court.[163]

2. Strict and Discretionary Forms of Proof

As to the facts that need to be proven at trial, this may be done by either strict or discretionary forms of proof. It is important to be aware of the difference between them as they have differing degrees of formality, they serve different purposes, and must abide by different principles. Concerning their purpose, facts that concern questions of guilt (*Schuldfrage*) and questions of punishment (*Straffrage*) may only be proven by means of the strict forms of proof[164] (*Strengbeweis*). This type of proof comprises four different types of evidence that are expressly provided by the StPO. In contrast, the discretionary forms of proof (*Freibeweis*) are not regulated by the StPO and may be used for all other purposes, such as matters of a purely procedural nature.[165] Among these matters are e. g., whether the procedural requirements to reject a motion to take evidence are fulfilled and regarding all evidence taking that takes place outside of the main hearing. However, in cases where the evidence is pertinent to *both* questions of guilt and punishment and procedural concerns (*doppelrelevante Tatsachen*), these matters require to be proven by strict forms of proof.[166]

The second distinction between these forms of proof is regarding the principles each of them must abide by. On the one hand, when examining discretionary forms of proof, the court must only abide by the *principle of ascertainment of the truth* and by the right to a fair hearing (*Grundsatz des rechtlichen Gehörs*).[167] Conversely, the strict

---

[160] *Eisenberg*, Beweisrecht, Rn. 16.
[161] *Eisenberg*, Beweisrecht, Rn. 19.
[162] *Eisenberg*, Beweisrecht, Rn. 24, 26, 27, 32.
[163] *Eisenberg*, Beweisrecht, Rn. 24, 28.
[164] *Roxin/Schünemann*, Strafverfahrensrecht, § 24 Rn. 2.
[165] *Roxin/Schünemann*, Strafverfahrensrecht, § 24 Rn. 3.
[166] *Heger/Pohlreich/Kütterer-Lang*, Strafprozessrecht, Rn. 365.
[167] *Eisenberg*, Beweisrecht, Rn. 36; *Frister*, in: SK-StPO, § 244 Rn. 12a.

forms of proof provided by the StPO are governed not only by the *principle of ascertainment of the truth*, but by all evidentiary principles, e. g., the principles of orality, immediacy, and publicity.[168]

In the following sections, I will examine the defendant's examination at trial (*Vernehmung der Angeklagte*) and the four types of strict forms of proof, i. e., witnesses (*Zeugenbeweis*), experts (*Sachverständige*), documentary evidence (*Urkundenbeweis*), and inspection (*Augenscheinsbeweis*).

III. Means of Evidence

1. Defendant

Pursuant to § 244 (1) StPO, after the presiding judge examines the defendant regarding the merits of the case, the taking of evidence commences. Although the examination of the defendant does not take place at the procedure of evidence taking per se and is not one of the four strict forms of proof, the defendant's declarations at trial may be helpful to the court in finding the material truth and in preserving evidence.[169] This is owing to the legal nature of the examination of the defendant being both a means of evidence and a means of defense (*Doppelcharakter der Vernehmung*).[170] It is a means of evidence sensu lato, since it is possible for a judge to find the defendant guilty based on her confession, or on statements she gave under examination.[171] In contrast, it is a means of defense due to it safeguarding the defendant's right to a fair hearing[172] and the right to defend herself.

§ 243 StPO sets the sequence of steps that take place at trial, and that (as a rule) must be followed, such as that the examination of the defendant must take place before the procedure of evidence taking. However, although the structure of the hearing as a whole must be maintained, it is possible for the procedural steps to slightly deviate from the order set out in this provision.[173] This is the case when the defendant wishes to make statements at a later moment, i.e., after the procedure of

---

[168] *Eisenberg*, Beweisrecht, Rn. 35.

[169] *Kühne*, Strafprozessrecht, Rn. 792; *Roxin/Schünemann*, Strafverfahrensrecht, § 25 Rn. 1.

[170] However, it should be noted that most German scholars see this proceeding as a means of defense. In this sense, see *Rogall*, in: SK-StPO, § 136 Rn. 18.

[171] *Roxin/Schünemann*, Strafverfahrensrecht, § 25 Rn. 1. However, *Kühne* contends that the defendant's confession can only serve as evidence in which to base a verdict if there are no other evidence that contradicts the said confession. Otherwise, the verdict may be appealed due to the incompleteness of the assessment of evidence. In this sense, *Kühne*, Strafprozessrecht, Rn. 792.

[172] *Roxin/Schünemann*, Strafverfahrensrecht, § 25 Rn. 4.

[173] *Arnoldi*, in: MüKo-StPO, § 243 Rn. 7.

C. Evidence Law

evidence taking has already started,[174] in which case the court must allow the defendant to do so.

§ 136 (2) StPO is a provision applicable to all phases of the procedure[175] and reinforces the examination of the accused as a means of defense due to it providing her an opportunity to dispel the evidence against her and to present facts that are beneficial to her case.[176] As to the examination itself, it may take place both during the pretrial phase and at trial. Regardless of the procedural phase in which it takes place, the examination of the accused or of the defendant will follow the same structure.[177] §§ 136 and 243 StPO respectively set out the examination conducted by a judge in the pretrial phase and in the trial phase.[178]

At trial, after the presiding judge ascertains that the formal forms of proof are present and asks the witnesses to leave the courtroom, she will then examine the defendant as to her personal circumstances (*Vernehmung des Angeklagten zur Person*),[179] which the defendant has the duty to answer.[180] The duty to answer to these questions is owing to them having the sole purpose of identifying the defendant's identity (*Feststellung der Identität*). Among these questions, the defendant is asked to state her full name, the date and place of birth, her marital status, address, and nationality.[181] However, there are questions that are both pertinent to identify the defendant and that are conducive in answering questions of guilt and punishment. In these instances, these questions are to be conducted at a later moment when the court examines the defendant regarding the circumstances of the case.[182]

Ensuing this first examination, the prosecutor reads the charges against the defendant, which allows the lay judges, the public in attendance, and the defendant

---

[174] *Frister*, in: SK-StPO, § 243 Rn. 5, 62, 63.

[175] *Rogall*, in: SK-StPO, § 136 Rn. 4.

[176] *Pizzi/Perron*, Crime Victims in German Courtrooms, p. 46; *Frister*, in: SK-StPO, § 243 Rn. 62–63.

[177] As to the examination of the accused by the prosecutor or by the police during the investigatory phase, both will follow the procedure set out in § 136 as laid out in § 163a (3) sent. 2 StPO concerning the prosecution and § 163a (4) sent. 1 StPO as to the police.

[178] The two exceptions to this are laid out in §§ 136 (1) sent. 2 and 136 (2) StPO, which apply to all phases of the procedure. These provisions respectively set out the instructions to be given to the accused concerning her procedural rights and the right to produce evidence in her favor.

[179] §§ 243 (1), 243 (2) sent. 1, 243 (2) sent. 2 StPO, respectively.

[180] However, there are scholars who despite acknowledging that the defendant's statutory right to silence only encompasses questions regarding the merits of the case, criticize the fact that defendants must answer questions with the purpose of identifying their identity. This is because they believe that forcing the defendant to an "active participation in the identification process" (*Verpflichtung bei einer aktiven Mitwirkung bei der Identifizierung*) violates the defendant's right not to incriminate itself, and thus violates the *nemo tenetur* principle. In this sense, see *Frister*, in: SK-StPO, § 243 Rn. 27.

[181] *Frister*, in: SK-StPO, § 243 Rn. 26; *Arnoldi*, in: MüKo-StPO, § 243 Rn. 21.

[182] *Roxin/Schünemann*, Strafverfahrensrecht, § 25 Rn. 5.

herself to be informed of the charges against her.[183] The presiding judge then instructs the defendant on her rights (*Belehrung des Angeklagten*), namely:[184] (i) the right not to answer questions addressed to her concerning the merits of the case (*Schweigerecht*),[185] (ii) the right to consult with her defense counsel before being examined, and if she is not yet represented by counsel, the right to retain one, and (iii) the right to request evidence to be presented in her favor. As previously seen, owing to the importance of these instructions in granting the defendant a fair trial, they must be made in the main hearing, regardless of whether the defendant has previously been made aware of them.[186]

Following these instructions, the presiding judge will examine the defendant regarding the merits of the case (*Vernehmung des Angeklagten zur Sache*). This examination includes questions which help the court assess the defendant's guilt and which are relevant to sentencing.[187] For these reasons, the presiding judge may ask the defendant whether she has a criminal record, her education and profession, information about her family and social environment, questions that aim to discover the historical events of the criminal offense, and the "internal and external circumstances of the offense".[188] Additionally, the presiding judge may ask the defendant about her relationship to the witnesses and, if applicable, to the co-defendants.[189]

Usually, the preferable way to examine the defendant is to allow her to narrate the facts of the case giving the defendant the opportunity to deny the facts against her and to introduce facts that support her claim.[190] However, in cases where the defendant is having difficulties in narrating the facts or simply has nothing else to add, the presiding judge may ask her specific questions.[191] Due to the principle of orality (*Mündlichkeitsprinzip*), the defendant's statements and/or answers to the presiding judge's questions must be made orally.[192] However, this requirement does not mean that the defendant's statements must be made spontaneously. A case in point is that the defendant may bring to trial written notes to be read out loud, or she may write

---

[183] § 243 (3) sent. 1 StPO.

[184] §§ 136 (1) and 136 (2) StPO.

[185] § 243 (5) sent. 1 StPO.

[186] As to the consequences of the failure to instruct the defendant of these rights, see infra Ch. 1 C. IV. 2. b).

[187] *Frister*, in: SK-StPO, § 243 Rn. 25; *Kühne*, Strafprozessrecht, Rn. 794.

[188] *Frister*, in: SK-StPO, § 243 Rn. 68, "die äußere und innere Seite der Tat".

[189] *Roxin/Schünemann*, Strafverfahrensrecht, § 25 Rn. 8.

[190] *Arnoldi*, in: MüKo-StPO, § 243 Rn. 62; *Roxin/Schünemann*, Strafverfahrensrecht, § 25 Rn. 8.

[191] *Arnoldi*, in: MüKo-StPO, § 243 Rn. 62.

[192] However, this is not applicable to the pretrial phase, as the accused may answer the prosecution's questions in writing, as per § 163a (1) sent. 2 StPO.

down her entire statement to read it out loud at court.[193] Furthermore, the defendant's defense counsel may also read these statements out loud.

2. Witnesses

Seeing as witnesses are people who witnessed facts that are relevant to the case, the object of their testimony cannot include legal assessments, their opinions, and conclusions.[194] There are three requisites that need to be present for a person to be competent to be a witness (*Zeugnisfähigkeit*),[195] namely having original perception of the facts of the case (*Wahrnehmung*), remembering what happened (*Speicherung und Erinnerung*), and the ability to reproduce/communicate what took place (*Wiedergabe*). In principle, any person who fulfills these three main requisites may be a witness. There are no legal restrictions to certain groups of people, such as people with mental and physical incapacity, children,[196] the defendant's spouse or family, or people convicted of crimes.[197] Nevertheless, there are certain situations where a person is precluded from being a witness due to having a procedural role at trial that is incompatible with that of a witness,[198] e. g., being a trial judge, prosecutor, or a private plaintiff (*Privatkläger*).

If a trial judge, lay judges,[199] or registry clerk take the stand as a witness, give statements in writing, or "disclose private personal knowledge of the case in the trial",[200] they are precluded from participating in further proceedings. Further, as is the case regarding prosecutors, if they wish to testify, they must previously receive permission to do so.[201] However, differently than judges, once a prosecutor receives permission to testify, another prosecutor must be present at trial while the representative for the prosecution is taking the stand.[202]

---

[193] Exceptions to oral statements are only permitted in cases in which the defendant is unable to do so due to physical or psychological reasons. In this sense, see *Arnoldi*, in: MüKo-StPO, § 243 Rn. 67.

[194] *Eisenberg*, Beweisrecht, Rn. 1003; *Kühne*, Strafprozessrecht, Rn. 795.

[195] *Eisenberg*, Beweisrecht, Rn. 1363.

[196] There is no legal statute that prescribes the minimum age in which children may testify as witnesses; for this reason, a child's competency as a witness will be decided on a case-by-case basis. However, there are provisions, such as §§ 241a, 247a, 255a (2) StPO that aim to protect vulnerable and underage witnesses. See *Eisenberg*, Beweisrecht, Rn. 1002.

[197] *Bohlander*, Principles, p. 148; *Eisenberg*, Beweisrecht, Rn. 1000.

[198] *Roxin/Schünemann*, Strafverfahrensrecht, § 26 Rn. 1.

[199] §§ 22 Nr. 5 and 31 StPO, respectively. See also *Eisenberg*, Beweisrecht, Rn. 1007.

[200] *Bohlander*, Principles, p. 148.

[201] § 54 (1) StPO.

[202] *Eisenberg*, Beweisrecht, Rn. 1017 et seq. If a representative for the prosecution is not present, this gives cause to an absolute grounds for appeal, as per § 338 Nr. 5 StPO.

In regard to the defendant's defense counsel, she may take the stand as a witness and subsequently continue her duties and responsibilities after her testimony.[203] However, in cases where the defendant has appointed counsel (*notwendige Verteidigung*),[204] due to the "judicial duty of care" (*Fürsorgepflicht des Gerichts*), the court must assign the defendant legal counsel while the defendant's appointed legal counsel is testifying.[205]

a) Rights and Duties

Witnesses have several right and duties. Among their rights are the right to legal counsel (*Zeugenbeistand*) and to compensation (*Zeugenentschädigung*). The former right is set out in § 68b (2) StPO, which lays out that "a witness who does not have the assistance of legal counsel at his examination and whose interests meriting protection cannot be taken into account in another way shall be assigned counsel". With respect to legal compensation, § 71 StPO provides that witnesses shall be remunerated pursuant to the Judicial Remuneration and Compensation Act (JVEG). However, the remuneration will only take place if the witness makes a request to this end either orally or in writing.[206] The remuneration may cover the witness's loss of earnings, traveling costs, and additional costs and expenditures.[207]

In contrast, witnesses have three main duties, namely, to attend trial (*Erscheinenspflicht*), to testify truthfully (*Wahrheitspflicht*), and to take an oath (*Eidespflicht*).[208] Regardless of the procedural phase in question, all witnesses under the German jurisdiction who were summoned by a judge, or a prosecutor must attend trial.[209] By "judge", this not only encompasses trial judges, but also pretrial judges, requested judges (*ersuchter Richter*), and assigned judges (*beauftragter Richter*). Additionally, the duty to attend trial applies regardless of whether a witness has the right to refuse testimony.[210]

---

[203] *Eisenberg*, Beweisrecht, Rn. 1014. This is because §§ 138a, 138b StPO provide an exhaustive list of the cases in which a defendant's defense counsel must be excluded. Therefore, since these provisions do not prohibit the defense counsel from giving evidence as a witness, they are permitted to testify.

[204] § 140 StPO.

[205] Despite §§ 58 (1), 243 (2) sent. 1 StPO setting out that the witnesses must leave the courtroom while the other witnesses and the defendant are taking the stand, the same does not occur when the defendant's defense counsel takes the stand as a witness due to the defendant's right to have counsel present. See *Eisenberg*, Beweisrecht, Rn. 1014.

[206] *Eisenberg*, Beweisrecht, Rn. 1206.

[207] §§ 5, 6, 22 JVEG.

[208] *Heger/Pohlreich/Kütterer-Lang*, Strafprozessrecht, Rn. 366a.

[209] §§ 48 (1) sent. 1, 161a (1) sent. 1 StPO. *Roxin/Schünemann*, Strafverfahrensrecht, § 26 Rn. 11.

[210] *Eisenberg*, Beweisrecht, Rn. 1055.

C. Evidence Law

A witness who fails to obey a summons without a "sufficient and timely excuse for his non-appearance"[211] or absents himself at trial without permission of the presiding judge[212] is considered absent and will incur in one of the penalties of § 51 (1) StPO.[213] Among these penalties are the costs caused by the failure to attend trial (*Auferlegung der Kosten*) and a coercive fine (*Ordnungsgeldverhängung*), both of which must be imposed when the witness first absents himself. If the coercive fine cannot be collected, a coercive detention (*Ordnungshaft*) may be imposed, and in cases of repeated non-appearance, the court may order the witness to be brought to court by force (*zwangsweise Vorführung*).[214]

This duty also entails that all witnesses must answer to questions both regarding their identity (*Angaben zur Person*)[215] and regarding the facts of the case (*Angaben zur Sachen*).[216] As to the witnesses that have the right to refuse testimony, while as a rule, they must answer to the questions related to their identity, they are excused from answering questions concerning the facts of the case.[217] Witnesses that fail to answer to the facts of the case or choose not to answer to specific questions while answering to others are liable to the penalties of § 70 StPO, which include the same penalties as those applicable to the witness who fails to attend court.

Witnesses must testify truthfully; nonetheless, contrary to the duty to attend trial, if a witness answers untruthfully at court, they are not liable to the penalties under § 70 StPO. However, the court must instruct witnesses of the criminal consequences of incorrect or criminal statements,[218] i.e., false testimony and perjury.[219]

Lastly, *in theory* witnesses must take an oath, which may be of either a religious or a non-religious nature[220] and are usually taken after the witness's testimony.[221] However, *in practice*, witnesses rarely take oaths as the court only asks a witness to do so when it believes that taking an oath will make it more likely that the person in question will testify truthfully.[222]

---

[211] § 51 (2) StPO.

[212] § 248 StPO.

[213] §§ 51, 161a (2) StPO; *Kühne*, Strafprozessrecht, Rn. 811.

[214] *Kühne*, Strafprozessrecht, Rn. 811.

[215] § 68 (1) sent. 1 StPO.

[216] §§ 69, 70 StPO. *Eisenberg*, Beweisrecht, Rn. 1084.

[217] *Eisenberg*, Beweisrecht, Rn. 1085.

[218] § 57 sent. 1 StPO; *Kühne*, Strafprozessrecht, Rn. 811.1.

[219] Depending on the nature of the untruthful statements, the witness might be liable to §§ 153 et seq., 257, 258, 164, 185 et seq., 263 StGB.

[220] §§ 57, 64 StPO.

[221] § 59 (2) StPO.

[222] *Roxin/Schünemann*, Strafverfahrensrecht, § 26 Rn. 39, 42.

b) Particularities of the Examination of Witnesses

The judges,[223] the prosecution,[224] the defendant,[225] and the private plaintiff (*Privatkläger*)[226] may summon witnesses. It is up to the presiding judge to decide the order in which to examine witnesses.[227] However, in practice, the court usually first examines the witnesses that present inculpatory evidence followed by those that present evidence favorable to the defendant.[228] As to witness examination itself, many judges conduct this examination by asking open-ended questions and usually let the witnesses narrate in their own words all "he knows about the subject of his examination".[229] After the witness finishes narrating the events, the presiding judge begins to ask questions.

There are instances where the court must either order a witness or the defendant to leave the courtroom. This takes place when the court believes that the presence of the defendant may hinder the witness or a co-defendant from answering truthfully to its questions. In these instances, the court will order the defendant to leave the hearing room during the examination so that the witness does not have to face the defendant while testifying.[230] If, however, the court believes that a witness's well-being may be at imminent risk should he be examined in the presence "of those attending the main hearing, the court may order the witness to remain in another place during the examination".[231] In these instances, a simultaneous audio-visual transmission of the testimony shall be provided in the courtroom. Additionally, § 247a (1) sent. 4 StPO lays out that a witness's testimony shall be recorded if there is concern that the witness in question will not be available for examination in a future main hearing and the recording is necessary for establishing the truth.

As to minors, it is the presiding judge's responsibility to conduct the examination of witnesses who are under 18 years of age. The associate judges, prosecutor, the defendant, the defense, and the lay judges may request the presiding judge to ask these witnesses questions. In turn, the presiding judge will only allow them to do so, if she deems that asking the minor direct questions will not be harmful to his well-being.[232]

---

[223] §§ 214 (1) sent. 1, 223 StPO.

[224] §§ 161a (1), 214 (3) StPO set out that the public prosecutor may summon witnesses in the investigatory phase and in the adjudicatory phase, respectively.

[225] § 220 (1) StPO.

[226] § 386 (2) StPO.

[227] § 238 (1) StPO, see also *Pizzi/Perron*, Crime Victims in German Courtrooms, p. 44.

[228] *Julius*, in: HK-StPO, § 244 Rn. 4.

[229] § 69 StPO; *Pizzi/Perron*, Crime Victims in German Courtrooms, pp. 42, 43.

[230] § 247 StPO.

[231] § 247a (1) StPO. As per § 58a (1) Nr. 1 StPO, this provision is also applicable to witnesses who are under 18 years of age.

[232] § 241a (2) StPO.

3. Experts

Experts may be appointed at all phases of the procedure. In the pretrial phase, they may be appointed by either the police or by the public prosecutor's office.[233] In contrast, at trial, the court may appoint an expert whenever it deems necessary to appoint a professional to help it with areas outside of its expertise. In these instances, the said experts are considered "aides to the judge" (*Gehilfe des Gerichts*). Regardless of the procedural moment in which an expert is retained, their expertise is limited to the facts, rules of experience, and to the conclusions they reach.[234]

Experts can either be court-appointed or privately retained. As per § 73 (1) StPO, it is the court's prerogative as to whether to appoint an expert and if it decides to do so, it also has discretion in choosing which expert or experts it wishes to appoint. Thus, apart from the specific instances set out in the StPO in which the court must consult with an expert,[235] as a rule, there is no legal provision compelling the court to do so. For this reason, the court may refrain from retaining an expert in cases, where it believes it has enough expertise in the matter.[236] However, if the court needs an expert and publicly registered experts are available, these experts must be appointed over nonregistered experts.[237] Once a court appoints an expert, the prosecutor, the defendant and, if applicable, the private plaintiff may challenge the said expert for the same reasons a judge may be challenged.[238]

Conversely, the defense may appoint a privately retained expert.[239] However, due to it being up to the court whether to appoint an expert, it is not bound to the suggestions of experts made by other procedural actors.[240] In regard to the prosecution, although both the defense and the prosecution may appoint experts, it is very uncommon for the latter to do so in the trial phase. This is due to the prosecution's role as the chief responsible for the investigatory phase, and for this reason, if it deemed necessary to the case to appoint an expert, it would have done so prior to trial.

---

[233] §161a (1) StPO.

[234] *Roxin/Schünemann*, Strafverfahrensrecht, § 27 Rn. 2.

[235] Such instances are: (i) to bring a defendant to a psychiatric hospital to be held under observation so that the preparation of an opinion concerning her mental condition may take place (§ 81 StPO), (ii) in cases where there is a possibility that the defendant might have to be placed in a psychiatric hospital, a detention center (*Entziehungsanstalt*) or a preventive detention facility, termed *Sicherungsverwahrung* (§ 80a StPO), (iii) when a postmortem or autopsy takes place (§§ 87 et seq. StPO), (iv) when there is suspicion of poisoning (§ 91 StPO), (v) when there is suspicion of counterfeiting money or official stamps (§ 92 StPO), (vi) in molecular genetic investigations (§ 81g (3), § 81g (4), § 81h (3) sent. 1 StPO).

[236] § 244 (4) StPO. See *Bohlander*, Principles, p. 155.

[237] § 73 (2) StPO.

[238] § 22 Nr. 1–4 StPO.

[239] §§ 220, 245 StPO.

[240] However, pursuant to § 245 (2) StPO, if the court dismissed the defense's appointment of an expert, it may compel the court to accept it by means of a motion to present evidence (*Beweisantrag*).

At times, experts may seem like witnesses due to having similar duties, e. g., the right to being compensated[241] and the right of refusing to render an opinion in the same instances a witness may refuse to give testimony.[242] However, privately retained experts are not akin to witnesses as may be the case in other legal systems.[243] Thus, although they do have similar features to those of witnesses, there are important differences between them. First, although both experts and witnesses have the task to relay facts to the court,[244] the expert is called upon at trial mainly to give an opinion and draw conclusions from facts. This contrasts with the testimony of witnesses, who are called upon to relay past facts that they have personally witnessed.[245] Second, due to witnesses having an original perception of the facts that took place they are not replaceable, whereas experts are.[246] Third, pursuant to § 80 StPO, to prepare their expert opinion (*Gutachten*), experts have additional rights in comparison to witnesses. These are, namely, the right to ask questions to both the witnesses and the defendant (para. 1), the right to inspect the written dossier, and of being present while both the witnesses and the defendant are being examined by the court (para. 2).

4. Documentary Evidence

Documents are writings that contain information, which may be used for evidential purposes and can be presented at court in the main proceedings. As a rule, if the court believes that contents of a document are necessary to establish the truth of a matter, as per § 244 (2) StPO, it will read parts of the documents out loud at trial. However, § 249 (2) StPO sets out an exception to this, in which case the "self-reading procedure" (*Selbstleseverfahren*) will take place. Simply put, the judges, the prosecution, the defendant, and her defense counsel will then read the whole content of the document outside of trial.[247]

However, there are three instances, where the "self-reading procedure" cannot take place and the document must be read out loud at trial. The first is set out in § 253

---

[241] § 84 StPO.

[242] § 76 sent. 1 StPO.

[243] In the US-American legal system, expert witnesses are considered to be witnesses. However, the concept of expert witnesses in an adversarial setting – i.e., where each expert witness seeks to further its respective party's case – is a foreign concept in German criminal trials. Thus, owing to the roles of the privately retained experts not being comparable to those of an expert witness, these terms should not be used interchangeably. See infra Ch. 2 C. III. 1.; *Bohlander*, Principles, p. 147.

[244] *Bohlander*, Principles, pp. 147, 152.

[245] This also applies to cases where a witness was only able to notice the facts due to her knowledge in a specific area of expertise. These witnesses are the so-called *Sachverständige Zeugen*, and despite them being called "expert" witnesses, they are merely witnesses who happen to have expert knowledge. For this reason, the rules of evidence applicable to them are those applicable to witnesses (§ 85 StPO).

[246] *Roxin/Schünemann*, Strafverfahrensrecht, § 27 Rn. 4.

[247] § 249 (2) StPO.

(1) StPO, which states that in cases where a witness or an expert cannot remember a fact, their previous examination may be read out loud to refresh their memory. The second instance is that a defendant's previous confession, which was "in a judicial record or in an audio-visual recording of an examination may be read out loud or played back"[248] at trial. The last instance is when the defendant makes a contradiction between her statement at trial, and a previous statement, and such contradiction cannot be clarified without interrupting the trial.[249]

A further matter that affects the reading of documents out loud is the "principle of examination in person" (*Grundsatz der persönlichen Vernehmung*). This principle is set out in § 250 StPO, which mandates that whenever the proof of a fact is based on the observation of a person, this "person shall be examined at the main hearing" and cannot be replaced by reading out loud the record of the witness's previous examination or her written statement.

There are three clarifications that need to be made regarding the principle of examination in person. First, whenever the reading of documents does not have the purpose of proving a fact of relevance to either question of guilt or punishment,[250] discretionary forms of proof are permitted. Thus, records of examinations, written statements, and certificates may be read out loud.[251] Second, as per § 255a (1) StPO, concerning the previous examinations of witnesses, whenever the cited exceptions to § 250 StPO state that a record of a witness's previous examination may be read out loud, this also entails the prospect of "the showing of an audio-visual recording of a witness examination". Third, the principle of examining a person in court has exceptions, which are set out in §§ 251, 253, 254, 255a, 256 StPO.[252]

The first set of exceptions is set out in § 251 StPO, which states the precise instances when the record or the written statement of a previous examination of a witness, an expert, or the co-defendant, may be read out loud (*Urkundenbeweis durch Verlesung von Protokollen*). This provision is divided into two groups. First, when the documentary evidence stems from a non-judicial examination (*nicht richterlichen Vernehmung*), i.e., examinations conducted by the police or the prosecution.[253] Second, when it stems from a judicial examination (*richterlichen Vernehmung*).[254] If the court decides to order for a document to be read out loud at trial, it must indicate

---

[248] § 254 (1) StPO.

[249] § 254 (2) StPO.

[250] *Eisenberg*, Beweisrecht, Rn. 2099.

[251] § 251 (3) StPO.

[252] As there is no prohibition to hearsay evidence, these provisions do not prohibit a police officer from testifying at court but only prohibit them from reading the defendant's examination out loud.

[253] As per § 251 (1) StPO. This takes place whenever the prosecution, the defendant, and his defense counsel consent to the court reading the document out loud, and when either the witness, the expert or the co-defendant in question have died or can no longer be examined at court within a foreseeable period. §§ 251 (1) Nr. 1 and 251 (1) Nr. 3 StPO, respectively.

[254] § 251 (2) StPO.

the reasons for doing so regardless of the document stemming from a judicial or a non-judicial examination.[255] Additionally, the documentary evidence in question must be read in its entirety, unless the procedural actors (*Prozessbeteiligte*) agree in only reading parts of it.[256]

The second set of exceptions to the principle of examining a person at court is set out in § 253 StPO, which provides the instances where a witness or an expert either forget a fact or contradict a previous statement at trial. Thus, the previous statements may be read out loud to respectively refresh their memory, or to establish or correct a contradiction (*Protokollverlesung zur Gedächtnisunterstützung*).[257] In the instances where a witness cannot recall the events/facts of the case, the court may read the former examination as a means in which to refresh her memory. However, it is the witness's reaction to the reading out loud of the document, which is the evidence and not the document itself.[258] Finally, regardless of the reason that justified the reading out loud of the documentary evidence, it must be circumscribed to the subject matter in which the forgetfulness or contradiction occurred.[259]

The third set of exceptions to the principle of examining a person at court is set out in § 254 StPO, which provides the reading out loud of judicial examinations regarding the defendant's confessions and contradictions (*Verlesung eines richterlichen Protokolls bei Geständnis oder Widersprüchen*). § 254 (2) StPO has the same wording as § 253 (2); thus, as is the case regarding witnesses, if the defendant states something at trial, which contradicts a previous statement he has made, this latter statement may be read out loud at trial.

Finally, the last set of exceptions to the principle of examining a person at court is set out in § 256 StPO, which provides the reading out loud of statements made by official authorities and experts (*Verlesung der Erklärungen von Behörden und Sachverständigen*).

5. Inspection

Inspection is evidence, which can be perceived with the five senses, i.e., through the sense of taste, sight, touch, smell, and sound,[260] and may occur in any phase of the proceedings.[261] This type of evidence may be replaced by any other means of strict forms of proof. This is so because contrary to § 250 StPO – which states that

---

[255] § 251 (3) sent. 2 StPO.

[256] *Eisenberg*, Beweisrecht, Rn. 2143.

[257] However, for the court to avail itself of this option, it must have previously exhausted all other means of evidence that could substitute the evidence which was forgotten or that could lead to clarifying the contradiction. In this sense, see *Eisenberg*, Beweisrecht, Rn. 2161.

[258] *Eisenberg*, Beweisrecht, Rn. 2163.

[259] *Eisenberg*, Beweisrecht, Rn. 2165.

[260] *Bohlander*, Principles, p. 161.

[261] *Eisenberg*, Beweisrecht, Rn. 2220.

whenever proof of a fact is based on the observation of a person, oral evidence cannot be replaced by documentary evidence – there is no such provision in the StPO concerning the prohibition to substitute inspection evidence for another type of evidence.[262] On the contrary, "it is generally indispensable to supplement inspection evidence with other means of proof, since inspection cannot provide evidence for certain facts in isolation, but rather must establish an additional relationship to the concrete facts of the case".[263]

There are two types of inspections. The first type is the judicial inspection (*Richterlicher Augenschein*), which takes place whenever "the trial court, a requested judge or an assigned judge personally perceives the object of the inspection".[264] When this type of inspection takes place, the court shall give the public prosecutor, the defendant, and his defense counsel prior notice, as to allow them to be present at the inspection.[265] Further, whenever a judicial inspection takes place with the aid of experts, the defendant may request the court for his own experts to be summoned to the hearing.[266] If the court rejects this request, the defendant may summon the expert herself, and the defendant's privately appointed experts are permitted to join in the inspection as long as they do not hinder it.[267]

In the instances where a judicial inspection takes place outside of the main hearing (*außerhalb der Hauptverhandlung*) due to efficiency reasons or due to a concern of loss of evidence,[268] this inspection must be recorded stating the date and time, the procedural actors involved, what took place, and whether the essential formalities have been observed.[269] This record may later be read out loud at trial as documentary evidence.[270] In contrast, the judicial inspections that take place at trial (*innerhalb der Hauptverhandlung*) are not to be on record as per §§ 168 and 168a StPO, due to them being part of the evidence taking itself. This is the case regardless of whether the object of inspection finds itself in the courtroom. Therefore, as per § 273 (1) StPO, "the record must indicate the course and the results of the main hearing in essence and shall indicate that all essential formalities have been observed". As such, for the

---

[262] *Eisenberg*, Beweisrecht, Rn. 2223.

[263] *Eisenberg*, Beweisrecht, Rn. 2223a, "[Dagegen ist im All] eine Ergänzung des Augenscheinbeweises durch andere Beweismittel unverzichtbar, da Augenscheinsobjekte nicht isoliert Beweis für bestimmte Tatsachen erbringen können, sondern vielmehr zusätzlich eine Beziehung zum konkreten Tatgeschehen hergestellt werden muss".

[264] *Eisenberg*, Beweisrecht, Rn. 2226, "Um eine richterliche Augenscheinseinnahme handelt es sich, wenn entweder das erkennende Gericht selbst oder ein beauftragter bzw ersuchter Richter das Augenscheinsobjekt sinnlich wahrnimmt".

[265] §§ 168c (5) sent. 1, 168d (1) StPO.

[266] § 168d (2) sent. 1 StPO.

[267] § 168d (2) StPO.

[268] *Eisenberg*, Beweisrecht, Rn. 2239.

[269] §§ 168 sent. 1, 168a (1) StPO.

[270] § 249 (1) StPO.

inspection to be considered by the court at the assessment of evidence (as per § 261 StPO), it must be recorded.

The second type of inspection are the non-judicial inspections (*Nichtrichterlicher Augenschein*), which take place when a person has sensory perceptions of the object of inspection and presents them at trial on behalf of the court. When the person in question has expertise regarding the object of inspection, they will be considered as court-appointed experts and the object of inspection will be regarded as expert evidence and the rules of expert evidence shall apply.[271] If, however, the person who has sensory perceptions of the object of inspection in question has no expertise regarding the object of inspection, they are called "assistants to inspection" (*Augenscheinsgehilfe*).[272]

IV. Admissibility of Evidence

1. Admissibility of Evidence and Rationale Behind Limiting or Excluding Evidence

Although one of the main aims of the German criminal procedure is to ascertain the material truth, at times it must give way to other aims or public interests that are of equal importance, and that may in fact further the finding of truth.[273] An illustration of this is § 55 (1) StPO, which provides witnesses that are related to the defendant the right to refuse to testify. Apart from the instances set out in this legal provision, these witnesses may only refuse to answer to questions that will incriminate them should they answer. Thus, absent this legal provision, these witnesses would either be forced to lie to protect their relative, or their testimony would be impaired. Should this happen, in the best case, this would fail to help the court in finding the truth and in the worst case, it would actively thwart the court in its truth finding duties.

Therefore, the rationale behind limiting or excluding otherwise admissible evidence is to circumscribe the state's power in the pursuit of establishing the truth, which cannot be sought at all costs. To this end, limits must be set to the prosecuting authorities[274] and to the judge's prerogatives in finding the truth.[275] This is a consequence of the principle of the rule of law (*Rechtsstaatsprinzip*)[276] and the prohibition of treating the defendant as a mere object of the proceedings. Additionally,

---

[271] *Eisenberg*, Beweisrecht, Rn. 2261.

[272] *Eisenberg*, Beweisrecht, Rn. 2262.

[273] *Eisenberg*, Beweisrecht, Rn. 329; *Kindhäuser/Schumann*, Strafprozessrecht, § 1 Rn. 15, 18; *Krey/Heinrich*, Deutsches Strafverfahrensrecht, Rn. 20 et seq.

[274] The police and prosecution's responsibilities in seeking the truth are set out in § 163 StPO and in §§ 160 (1) and 160 (2) StPO, respectively. The judges' responsibilities to this end are set out in § 244 (2) StPO.

[275] *Kühne*, Strafprozessrecht, Rn. 880.1.

[276] Art. 20 (3) GG.

this stems from the state's duty of not only protecting its citizens by prosecuting a crime once it has been committed, but of also protecting citizens from the state's authority (*Staatliche Gewalt*).[277]

For this purpose, there are instances where there is a prohibition of evidence (*Beweisverbote*) that may be applicable to all phases of the procedure and is addressed to actions by the state rather than those of private citizens. This term comprises the prohibition in both obtaining evidence[278] (*Beweiserhebungsverbot*) and in exploiting a determined piece of evidence once it has already been gathered (*Beweisverwertungsverbot*). In regard to the latter, this occurs once there has been a violation in obtaining the evidence in question.[279] This is the case when the evidence is gathered in violation of either statutory or constitutional rights or provisions. The prohibition of exploitation of evidence may stem from either a legal provision or from a construction by the jurisprudence of the German Constitutional Court; as for example, the defendant's right to personality.[280] The consequence of this prohibition is that depending on the circumstances, a piece of evidence obtained in violation to a legal provision will be barred from being considered by the court in assessing the evidence or in taking it into consideration in its decision-making.[281]

2. Statutory and Constitutional Rules Excluding or Limiting Evidence

a) Protection of the Defendant's Right of Personality

The Federal Constitutional Court construed the general right of personality (*das allgemeine Persönlichkeitsrecht*) from two other constitutional rights namely, the right to free development of one's personality (*Recht auf die freie Entfaltung seiner Persönlichkeit*) and the right to human dignity (*Schutz der Menschenwürde*).[282] This right seeks to protect individuals from state interference in their personal sphere. However, there are varying degrees of interference permitted that are dependent on which of the defendant's personal sphere is affected. Thus, depending on the three personal domains (*Sphäre*) in question, the evidence gathered by the state may vary

---

[277] *Kühne*, Strafprozessrecht, Rn. 880.

[278] The prohibition in obtaining evidence is further divided into three different categories. The first is called the prohibition on the topic (*Beweisthemaverbot*), which refers to certain topics that cannot be the object of evidence gathering, such is the case of evidence that entail public secrets (e. g. § 54 StPO). The second category is the prohibition due to the method used to gather evidence being illegal (*Beweismethodeverbot*), as for example, in the instances set out in § 136a StPO. The last category is the *Beweismittelverbote*, which are means of evidence that cannot be used to prove a fact (e. g. §§ 52 et seq., §§ 81c, 250, 252).

[279] *Kühne*, Strafprozessrecht, Rn. 881.

[280] BVerfGE 34, 238.

[281] *Eisenberg*, Beweisrecht, Rn. 356.

[282] Art. 2 (1) GG and Art. 1 (1) GG, respectively; *Pieroth/Schlink*, Grundrechte, p. 91, Rn. 391.

from it being exploited at trial to it being fully prohibited from being presented at trial.

The first domain is the social sphere (*Sozialsphäre*), which is an area that is not protected from the state, and consequently, all evidence that solely affects this sphere may be exploited at trial. The second area is the private sphere (*Schlichte Privatsphäre*) and it is given a higher amount of protection from the state due to it affecting rights that should be protected from state interference (*relativ geschützter Bereich*). For evidence stemming from this sphere to be exploited at trial, the state's interest in prosecuting the case must be weighed against the defendant's right to privacy.[283] Usually the higher the level of reprehensibility of a crime, the higher the chances of the evidence in question to be admitted at trial. The last and the most protected sphere is the *Intimsphäre*, i. e., the "core areas of the defendant's private life" (*Kernbereich privater Lebensgestaltung*). Evidence that stems from this sphere is absolutely prohibited from being explored at trial.[284]

b) Nemo Tenetur Se Ipsum Accusare

The nemo tenetur principle (*nemo-tenetur-Grundsatz*) may be considered a constitutional principle due to it stemming from three constitutional rights: the principle of human dignity, the general right of personality, and the principle of the rule of law.[285] The first dimension of this right is that regardless of the procedural phase in which the defendant choses to testify regarding the merits of the case, she is not compelled to tell the truth ("*der Beschuldigte ist nicht wahrheitspflichtig*").[286] Further, as long as the defendant does not incur in one of the criminal provisions set out in the StGB, the defendant is not prohibited from telling a lie.[287]

Additional dimensions of this principle are the right of the accused to silence, to consult an attorney, and the duty to instruct the accused of both these rights, which are set out in § 136 (1) StPO and are applicable to all phases of the criminal procedure.[288]

The *right to silence* is one of the defendant's most important procedural rights. § 136 (1) sent. 2 StPO sets out *a contrario* that the defendant's right to silence at trial only regards the merits of the case, owing to the first part of the defendant's examination merely seeking to identify the person taking the stand. In other words, it

---

[283] *Volk/Engländer*, Examens-Repetitorium, Rn. 258.

[284] *Volk/Engländer*, Examens-Repetitorium, Rn. 258.

[285] Art. 2 (1) GG, Art. 1 (1) GG, and Art. 20 (3) GG, respectively. See *Roxin/Schünemann*, Strafverfahrensrecht, § 25 Rn. 2.

[286] *Bohlander*, Principles, p. 146; *Kühne*, Strafprozessrecht, Rn. 793.

[287] The criminal provisions (*Tatbestände*) set out in the StGB are §§ 145d, 164, 185 et seq. In this sense, see *Kindhäuser/Schumann*, Strafprozessrecht, § 6 Rn. 14.

[288] *Rogall*, in: SK-StPO, § 136 Rn. 4.

seeks to ascertain whether the person being examined is the person that is being accused of having committed the criminal offense.[289]

Regarding as to whether judges may interpret the defendant's right to silence to his detriment, there are some factors that need to be taken into consideration. Whenever the defendant refuses to answer all the questions posed to her, the trial judges may not interpret this in any way that is prejudicial to the defendant, and, therefore, her silence cannot be considered in the assessment of evidence, as per § 261 StPO.[290] However, if the defendant only answers to selected questions while refusing to answer to others, her "partial silence" (*partielles Schweigen*) can be used against her. Nevertheless, this is not applicable when the defendant answers to questions regarding a specific criminal offense while remaining silent as to the commission of other offenses, for which she is also standing trial.[291]

Depending on the specific circumstances, the failure to instruct the defendant of her rights may have different legal consequences.[292] § 136 (1) StPO sets out which procedural rights the *examining authorities* must inform the accused prior to her examination. By stating "examining authorities", this provision refers to a state investigative body (*staatliches Ermittlungsorgan*), which usually entail the police, the prosecution, and the judge.[293] However, if an expert wishes to ask the defendant questions, he must necessarily instruct the defendant of her right to silence prior to doing so. If the expert fails to instruct the defendant of this right, the defense will ask the court for the testimony to not be allowed as evidence.

As to the people subject to the examination, this provision only addresses the accused and the defendant. This is because during the examination of a suspect, she will initially be regarded as a witness and, therefore, the provisions applicable to the examination of witnesses apply.[294] If however, there is a slight amount of evidence indicating that she in fact committed the criminal offense, she will then be regarded as an accused and from that moment forwards, the procedural rights set out in § 136 StPO will apply.

As § 136 (1) sent. 2 StPO lays out both the right to silence and the right to legal counsel, the failure to instruct the accused or defendant of the said rights may result in the prohibition to exploit the evidence which result from the examination.[295] However, there are limitations to the prohibition of exploiting evidence that stem from the court's failure in instructing the defendant. This is because the prohibition and its limits will vary depending on the instruction which did not take place.

---

[289] See *Rogall*, in: SK-StPO, § 136 Rn. 43; *Roxin/Schünemann*, Strafverfahrensrecht, § 25 Rn. 5.
[290] *Roxin/Schünemann*, Strafverfahrensrecht, § 25 Rn. 32.
[291] *Roxin/Schünemann*, Strafverfahrensrecht, § 25 Rn. 33.
[292] § 136 (1) sent. 2 StPO.
[293] *Roxin/Schünemann*, Strafverfahrensrecht, § 24 Rn. 31.
[294] *Rogall*, in: SK-StPO, § 136 Rn. 13.
[295] *Eisenberg*, Beweisrecht, Rn. 373, 374.

Two considerations must be taken into account regarding the failure to instruct the accused of her *right to silence*. First, whenever inquiries are made to a person in the investigatory phase (*Befragung*) and the state investigative body does not have an initial suspicion (*Anfangsverdacht*) against the person in question, there is no need to inform this person of her right to silence. The same applies if the suspect makes spontaneous statements without being prodded to this end (*Spontanäußerungen*).[296]

Second, when analyzing the examination of the accused, there are three different scenarios to examine as each of them have different outcomes.

(i) In the instances where the accused has previous knowledge of her right to silence and nevertheless, decides to make statements, the judge's instructions to the accused to this end would have been unnecessary. Thus, failure to do so would not result in the prohibition to explore evidence.

(ii) In the instances, where the defendant was oblivious of her right to silence, there must be a further analysis regarding the circumstances of this unawareness. In this scenario, evidence may be admissible if the defendant was made aware of this right at trial and his defense counsel expressly agrees to the use of the said evidence.[297]

(iii) Evidence may be exploited by the court upon a "dissent/objection solution" (*Widerspruchlösung*). According to this solution, the defendant's defense counsel may express her objection to the defendant being examined without prior instruction regarding her right to silence until the moment set out in § 257 StPO.[298] Thus, pursuant to this provision, after evidence has been taken in each individual case, the defendant shall be asked whether he has anything to add and upon request, the defense counsel shall be given the opportunity to make statements after his examination and after evidence has been taken in each individual case. However, there is a limitation to the dissent/objection solution. Due to the prohibition of evidence usually targeting evidence, which is prejudicial to the accused's case, this solution is only applicable in these instances.[299] Therefore, if the accused's statements were beneficial to her case, the objection solution cannot be invoked.

As to the failure to instruct the accused of her *right to consult with her defense counsel*, due to this right being as important as the accused's right to silence, it must be made known to the accused since her very first examination.[300] For this reason, failure to instruct the defendant about this right incurs in a prohibition of exploring evidence obtained from the examination. However, differently than the right to si-

---

[296] *Volk/Engländer*, Examens-Repetitorium, Rn. 251.
[297] *Rogall*, in: SK-StPO, § 136 Rn. 79.
[298] *Volk/Engländer*, Examens-Repetitorium, Rn. 249.
[299] *Rogall*, in: SK-StPO, § 136 Rn. 81.
[300] *Rogall*, in: SK-StPO, § 136 Rn. 47.

C. Evidence Law

lence, the right to consult an attorney and to effectively contact one stems from the right to a fair trial and the right to a defense.[301]

c) Prohibited Methods of Examining the Accused

§ 136a StPO lays out both the prohibited methods of examining the accused (*verbotene Vernehmungmethode*) and the consequential prohibition of exploitation of evidence stemming from these methods. This provision is applicable to all procedural phases and is the main provision protecting the accused's right to decide whether to make statements.[302] Its aim is to safeguard the freedom of the accused to make statements without being coerced, induced, or tricked to incriminate herself. This prohibition is applicable not only to the accused's examination, but also to the examination of witnesses and experts, as set out in §§ 69 (3) and 72 StPO.

As per § 136a (2) sent. 1 StPO, the addressees of these prohibitions are the state investigative bodies (*staatliche Ermittlungsorgane*), i.e., the police, public prosecutors, and judges.[303] Consequently, the use of prohibited methods in obtaining evidence by third parties without the state's participation is not a reason for the evidence in question to be prohibited from being exploited at trial. Paras. 1 and 2 set out examples of prohibited methods of examining the accused.[304] As per para. 1, the methods that affect the accused's freedom to make up her mind and decide for herself whether to make statements are namely, "ill-treatment, induced fatigue, physical intervention on the body, the administration of drugs, torture, by means of deception or hypnosis." As per para. 2, the methods that impair the accused's memory (*Erinnerungsvermögen*) and their cognitive faculties, and her ability to understand the options she has in which "to defend herself and to assess the consequences of her statements accurately" (*Einsichtsfähigkeit*)[305] are also prohibited.

§ 136a (3) sent. 1 StPO states that the prohibitions set out in paras. 1 and 2 apply regardless of the accused's consent. This is the only instance in the German criminal procedure of a legal provision explicitly setting out an absolute prohibition of exploration of evidence (*absolutes Verwertungsverbot*).[306] Additionally, by way of § 136a (3) sent. 2 StPO, this prohibition also applies to the court reading the transcript of the testimony at trial, which resulted from this examination.[307]

---

[301] *Rogall*, in: SK-StPO, § 136 Rn. 91.

[302] *Diemer*, in: KK-StPO, § 136a Rn. 1.

[303] This provision is also applicable to court-appointed experts in the instances where they examine witnesses or the defendant. *Diemer*, in: KK-StPO, § 136a Rn. 5.

[304] The methods set out in this provision are not enumerative. See *Kühne*, Strafprozessrecht, Rn. 891.

[305] *Diemer*, in: KK-StPO, § 136a Rn. 35, Die Einsichtsfähigkeit ist hier das Vermögen der Auskunftsperson, die Verdachtslage, ihre "Verteidigungsmöglichkeit und die Folgen ihrer Aussagen zutreffend einzuschätzen".

[306] *Eisenberg*, Beweisrecht, Rn. 357.

[307] *Diemer*, in: KK-StPO, § 136a Rn. 39.

d) Witnesses' Rights and Duties to Refuse to Testify

Depending on the circumstances of a specific case, a witness may have the right to refuse to testify (aa)) or a duty to refuse to give testimony (bb)).

aa) Right to Refuse to Testify

The reasoning behind witnesses having the right to refuse to testify (*Zeugnis-* und *Auskunftsverweigerungsrecht*) is that although the finding of truth is one of the main aims of the procedure, there should be a balance between this aim and other important interests and relationships. The StPO sets out three instances in which a witness has the right to refuse to testify.

The first instance is that, as per § 55 (1) StPO, any witness may refuse to give information (*Auskunftsverweigerungsrecht*) to which the reply would subject her, or her relatives to the risk of being prosecuted for a criminal or a regulatory offense (*Ordnungswidrigkeit*).[308] Due to the nature of this right, apart from the instances where a witness has the right to refuse to give testimony due to other reasons set out in §§ 52 et seq. StPO, the witness must testify, only refusing to give an answer regarding questions that may incriminate her or a family member. The court must instruct the witness of her right not to answer to incriminating questions whenever there are relevant pointers that her statement may incriminate her.[309] If a witness is a relative of the defendant, the court must inform her of both these rights. Further, every time the witness wants to exercise her right not to reply to an answer, she must declare her refusal to give information (*Weigerungserklärung*).

The second instance is set out in § 52 (1) StPO, whereby people who are a relative of the defendant have an unrestricted right to refuse to give testimony (*Zeugnisverweigerungsrecht der Angehörigen des Beschuldigten*).[310] The term "relative" comprises the defendant's fiancé, spouse, life partner, descendant, ascendant, or sibling. Further relatives are those collaterally related to the third degree, i.e., their parents' siblings or their siblings' children, and those related by marriage to the second degree.[311] The right to refuse to give testimony on personal grounds is a personal right and for this reason, the only person entitled to waive it is the witness herself.[312] As this right has an objective criterium, i.e., if a person is one of the people enumerated in § 52 (1) StPO, there is no further need to prove that there is a conflict of interest in testifying.[313]

---

[308] A set out in § 52 (1) StPO.
[309] § 55 (2) StPO. *Eisenberg*, Beweisrecht, Rn. 1121.
[310] *Kühne*, Strafprozessrecht, Rn. 812.1.
[311] *Kühne*, Strafprozessrecht, Rn. 812.1.
[312] *Eisenberg*, Beweisrecht, Rn. 1223.
[313] *Eisenberg*, Beweisrecht, Rn. 1212.

Pursuant to § 52 (3) sent. 1 StPO, the presiding judge must inform the relative of the defendant of his right to refuse to give evidence before each examination. After the presiding judge's instruction – as is the case regarding the witness's right not to incriminate oneself – the witness must expressly state that it does not want to give testimony on personal grounds. There are two main consequences to this; the first is that if the person in question makes any statements, it cannot be used as a means of evidence. The second effect is that if the person who is related to the defendant exercises her right to refuse to testify, this cannot be prejudicial to the defendant's case in any way.[314]

The third and last instance a witness may refuse to testify is on professional grounds. The objectives of this right are to both enable the protection of professional secrecy and to safeguard the relationship between the members of certain professions on the one side, and the people who seek their advice or assistance on the other side.[315] § 53 (1) StPO exhaustively specifies the group of people who may refuse to testify due to their profession (*Zeugnisverweigerungsrecht der Berufsgeheimnisträger*). Among them are clergymen, the accused's defense counsel, attorneys, notaries, doctors, dentists, psychotherapists, pharmacists, midwives, and drug dependency counselors.

The people who benefit from the duty to secrecy are the ones that can release a professional from his right to refuse to give testimony. According to § 53 (2) StPO once the people named in para. 1, Nr. 2 to 3b are released from their duty to secrecy, they cannot refuse to testify. However, if the other professionals cited in para. 1, are released from their duty to secrecy, this will merely influence their opinion, as the final decision as to whether to testify is up to the professional in question. Also, when exercising the right to refuse testimony, the affected professionals may choose to either reveal the secret, refuse to do so in its entirety, or reveal parts of it.[316]

bb) Duty to Refuse to Testify

Contrary to the circumstances analyzed above, there are instances where a witness has a duty to refuse to testify. As per § 54 StPO, this takes place when due to a person's profession as a public official, they have a corresponding duty of secrecy. Thus, for the person in question to testify at court, they need a prior authorization to do so (*Aussagegenehmigung für Angehörige des öffentlichen Dienstes*).[317] Absent this authorization, the witness must refuse to testify.[318] Among the public officials that are

---

[314] *Eisenberg*, Beweisrecht, Rn. 1228.
[315] *Eisenberg*, Beweisrecht, Rn. 1234.
[316] *Eisenberg*, Beweisrecht, Rn. 1255.
[317] § 54 (1) StPO.
[318] Failure to do so may incur in the criminal offense set out in § 353b StGB. *Roxin/ Schünemann*, Strafverfahrensrecht, § 26 Rn. 32.

bound to this authorization are judges,[319] civil servants, soldiers, undercover agents, parliamentarians, and members of the federal and state governments. The purpose of this provision is "to protect public interests of secrecy as they are necessary to effectively fulfill tasks of public interest".[320]

For the people listed in para. 1, they may only testify present an authorization from their hierarchical superiors, whereas the people listed in para. 2 are subject to the specific provisions set out for each category. As per para. 3, the president (*Bundespräsident*) may choose whether he wishes to testify and may refuse to do so if his testimony is detrimental to either the federation (*Bund*) or a state.

D. Evidentiary Principles and Procedual Safeguards

The StPO has provisions which both address the main evidentiary principles (*Beweisgrundsätze*)[321] and a procedural safeguard that aims to remedy a structural weakness in the German inquisitorial trial setting. On the one hand, §§ 244 (2) and 261 StPO address the court's responsibility of taking and assessing evidence at trial (*Beweissamlung* and *Beweiswürdigung*)[322], which are embodied in the principle of ascertainment of the truth[323] and the principle of free evaluation of evidence. On the other hand, §§ 244 (3) to (6) and 245 (2) StPO provide for the right of both the prosecution and the defense to present to the court a motion to take evidence, thus enabling them to co-shape the procedure of evidence-taking at trial.

I will presently examine these evidentiary principles as they are key in governing the court's evaluation of proof and guiding and setting limits to the court's decision-making. Following this analysis, I will examine the motion to take evidence from the defense's standpoint, as I seek to primarily examine the defendant's procedural safeguards in the German criminal procedure.

---

[319] Professional judges are subject to the regulations applicable to public officials, as laid out in §§ 46, 71 DRiG.

[320] *Eisenberg*, Beweisrecht, Rn. 1259, "Sinn und Zweck des § 54 ist es, öffentliche Geheimhaltungsinteressen zu wahren, soweit dies erforderlich ist, um Aufgaben im Gemeinwohlinteresse wirksam erfüllen zu können".

[321] *Ott*, in: KK-StPO, § 261 Rn. 1.

[322] *Julius*, in: HK-StPO, § 244 Rn. 1.

[323] The English translation of this principle in the website of the Federal Ministry of Justice is "the inquisitorial system". However, I do not think that this is an adequate term to explain this principle; thus, for reasons of clarity I borrowed the English translation of "*Aufklärungspflicht des Richters*" from Volker Krey, Characteristics Features of German Criminal Proceedings, p. 603.

I. Principle of Ascertainment of the Truth

§ 244 (2) StPO sets out the main provision establishing the German evidentiary arrangement at the trial setting[324] by mandating that the court shall establish the (material) truth ex officio (*Aufklärungspflicht des Richters*).[325] To this end, it must "extend the taking of evidence to all facts and means of proof relevant to the decision".[326] Therefore, it is the court's task to thoroughly examine all evidence that might be of relevance in finding the historical events of the case and in doing so, it must "ensure that the evidentiary material is as complete as possible".[327] The court must fulfill this task regardless of and beyond any motion to take evidence presented by the parties.[328]

In fulfilling her tasks, apart from a few exceptions set out in the StPO – e.g., the defendant's right to have the last word – the presiding judge has the prerogative to define the order in which she wishes to take evidence at trial. As seen, this is due to the presiding judge having to thoroughly examine the investigative file prior to trial in order to have the most amount of information possible. Based on this examination, she will decide on how to best conduct the taking of evidence in a way that is the most conducive to verify at trial whether the information contained in the investigative file can be confirmed.

II. The Defendant's Right to Request the Court to Take Evidence

Although the presiding judge is responsible for taking evidence at trial, the prosecution and the defense[329] may co-shape this procedure by requesting the court to take additional evidence by means of the *Beweisantragsrecht*. However, owing to the structure of the German criminal procedure, the defense is the main key courtroom actor which exercises this right.[330] This is because the prosecutor is the chief responsible for the criminal investigation (*Herrin des Ermittlungsverfahrens*) and the procedural actor responsible for supporting the court in finding the material truth. Hence, the prosecutor has already thoroughly investigated all inculpatory and ex-

---

[324] *Bohlander*, Principles, p. 163; *Eisenberg*, Beweisrecht, Rn. 1; *Krehl* in: KK-StPO, § 244 Rn. 32, 40.

[325] In Germany, this principle is also referred to as *Ermittlungsprinzip*, *Instruktionsmaxime*, *Amtsermittlungsgrundsatz*, *Amtsaufklärungspflicht* and *Untersuchungsgrundsatz*. As to the court's duty in finding the truth, see *Krehl* in: KK-StPO, § 244 Rn. 28; *Frister*, in: SK-StPO, § 244 Rn. 10.

[326] § 244 (2) StPO; *Meyer-Goßner/Schmitt*, § 244 Rn. 11.

[327] *Grande*, in: Jackson et al., Crime, procedure and evidence, p. 156.

[328] *Frister*, in: SK-StPO, § 244 Rn. 10; *Krehl* in: KK-StPO, § 244 Rn. 32, 34.

[329] The private accessory prosecutor (*Nebenkläger*) and the private prosecutor (*Privatkläger*) are also eligible to request a motion to take evidence; see *Eisenberg*, Beweisrecht, Rn. 168; *Krehl*, in: KK-StPO, § 244 Rn. 97.

[330] *Schäuble*, Strafverfahren und Prozessverantwortung, p. 101.

culpatory evidence prior to having indicted the accused. It is for this reason that although in theory the prosecution may request the court to take additional evidence by means of the *Beweisantragsrecht*, in practice, it has very little reason to do so.

The motion to take evidence is an important means in which to remedy structural weaknesses of the trial setting, which could stem from both the investigatory phase and the intermediate proceedings.[331] As previously seen, in the investigatory phase, the defense counsel has the right to access the investigative file and the right to request the prosecution for evidence to be taken in his defense.[332] Therefore, apart from these instances, there are not many possibilities in which the defendant can "co-shape" the prosecutorial investigation.

As seen, in the intermediate proceedings, the professional judges of the court, who are competent in hearing the main hearing, decide whether the evidentiary standard of *hinreichender Tatverdacht* was met. Seeing that these judges base their decision on the investigation file and have prior knowledge of the case ahead of trial, there is a risk that they might be biased against the defendant prior to trial.[333] For this reason, the *principle of ascertainment of the truth* is an unsuitable means in which to remedy this deficiency, due to it being a subjective rather than an objective criterion in which to base the suitability of a determined means of evidence.[334] Hence, the motion to take evidence is an efficient way in which to force the court to examine additional evidence in favor of the defendant that is relevant to the question of guilt and to the legal consequences (*Schuldfrage* and *Rechtsfrage*).[335] This is because absent a ground to refuse the motion, the court is obliged to take the evidence in question, even if it deems the requested evidence to be unnecessary.[336]

There are three formal requisites that a motion to take evidence must meet. First, the applicant must present it to the court at trial, i.e., from the moment the court determines the presence of the procedural actors until the beginning of the pronouncement of the judgment.[337] Although this motion may be presented orally to the court, applicants usually present an abbreviated reference to a written pre-formulated and substantiated motion.[338] The second and third requisites are that the applicant must state the factual allegation she wishes to prove and to specify the type of evidence "that is meant to furnish that proof".[339]

---

[331] *Trüg/Habetha*, in: MüKo-StPO, § 244 Rn. 11.

[332] See supra Ch. 1 B. IV. 1. b).

[333] For a brief examination on the risk of judicial bias in the inquisitorial evidentiary arrangement, see infra Ch. 4 B. IV. 1.

[334] *Trüg/Habetha*, in: MüKo-StPO, § 244 Rn. 11.

[335] *Eisenberg*, Beweisrecht, Rn. 139; *Schmitt*, in: Meyer Goßner, § 244 Rn. 18.

[336] *Schäuble*, Strafverfahren und Prozessverantwortung, p. 98.

[337] § 246 (1) StPO; *Eisenberg*, Beweisrecht, Rn. 178, 178a.

[338] *Perron*, Beweisantragsrecht, p. 182.

[339] *Bohlander*, Principles, p. 164. See also *Eisenberg*, Beweisrecht, Rn. 138.

The enforceability of the motion to take evidence is guaranteed, owing to the court only being permitted to reject it when one of the strict instances set out in the §§ 244 (3) sent. 2, 244 (4), 244 (5), and 245 StPO are present.[340] Due to these criteria being exhaustive, the court may not reject a motion outside of the scope of these provisions, by stating e. g., that the motion was belatedly submitted or that the court has already made up its mind regarding the defendant's guilt.[341] This is owing to the prohibition of anticipation of evidence (*Verbot der Beweisantizipation*), whereby the court cannot reject a motion to take evidence on the basis that it is futile because the opposite has already been proven or because a confirmation of the evidence is not to be expected.[342]

The set of objective criteria vary in its strictness depending on the type of evidence in question and on whether the evidence to be taken is already present at trial. In the main proceedings, the strictest grounds for refusal of this motion are regarding evidence that is already present at trial, as per § 245 (2) StPO. The second strictest grounds for refusal of the motion to take evidence is concerning evidence that is yet to be produced at trial, as per §§ 244 (3) to (5) StPO.

The justifications for rejecting a motion to take evidence that is yet to be introduced at trial has varying degrees of strictness depending on the type of evidence the applicant wishes the court to present. The strictest criteria are applied to the motion to take evidence regarding (i) witnesses or documents, whereas the grounds for refusal of a motion to take evidence concerning (ii) experts and (iii) inspection or concerning witnesses who are abroad are less strict.[343]

The grounds for refusing the taking of evidence regarding the presentation of a witness or a document are the following. As per § 244 (3) sent. 2 StPO, whenever an applicant requests the court to take these types of evidence, if the evidence in question is inadmissible, the court *must* reject the said motion. In contrast, sent. 3 of this legal provision provides that, there are instances in which the trial court may reject the motion if it so chooses. The following instances are when (i) the evidence is of common knowledge (*Offenkundigkeit*), (ii) the evidence is irrelevant to the decision (*Bedeutungslosigkeit*), (iii) the fact has already been proven (*Erwiesensein*) (iv) the evidence is completely unsuitable (*völlige Ungeeignetheit*), (v) the evidence is unobtainable (*Unerreichbarkeit*), (vi) the defense seeks the presentation of a determined piece of evidence with the intent to protract the proceedings (*Verschleppungsabsicht*), and (vii) an allegation to be proven to exonerate the defendant can be treated as if the alleged fact were true (*Wahrunterstellung*).

---

[340] *Perron*, in: Alexander Bruns (ed.), Festschrift für Rolf Stürner, p. 876.

[341] *Eisenberg*, Beweisrecht, Rn. 139a; *Roxin/Schünemann*, Strafverfahrensrecht, § 45 Rn. 31.

[342] *Schäuble*, Strafverfahren und Prozessverantwortung, p. 97.

[343] §§ 244 (3), 244 (4) and 244 (5) StPO, respectively.

The presiding judge is responsible for making a ruling regarding the concession of the motion to take evidence.[344] However, it is the court's decision to reject this motion and it is "obliged to provide extensive written reasoning in justifying its finding".[345] The reason for this thorough reasoning is that should there be an appeal, the grounds for refusal will be carefully examined and scrutinized by the appellate court.[346]

III. Principle of Free Evaluation of Evidence

§ 261 StPO consecrates the principle of free evaluation of evidence[347] (*der Grundsatz der freien richterlichen Beweiswürdigung*) whereby the court shall decide according to its free conviction from the evidence that was presented at trial. For this reason, there are no rules of formal evidence (*strikte Beweisregeln*) that govern the court's assessment of evidence in forming her conviction.[348]

There are three main limitations to this standard of proof. First, the free evaluation of evidence limits itself only to the evidence and statements that were orally discussed at trial; thus, also safeguarding the principles of orality, immediacy, and publicity.[349] As a result, the court is absolutely prohibited from exploiting evidence that was not presented at trial, i.e., the moment the presiding judge orders the recording clerk to call the case up until the moment the defendant has the right to have his last word.[350] The reasoning behind this is to avoid the court basing its decision on the contents of the investigative file without verifying whether the contents in the said file can be confirmed at trial in the full scope of the aforementioned principles.

Second, the reasoning behind a decision is personal (*höchstpersönlich*) and although it is a decision based on a subjective certainty (*subjektive Gewissheit*), the court must state the rational-objective factual basis (*objektive Tatsachengrundlage*) that led it to its decision.[351] In concretizing the former element, the reasons behind the court's decision must be laid out in the judgment,[352] as a means in which to control the subjectivity that is inherent in a decision. To this end, there are "guidelines" regarding the principle of free evaluation of evidence: (i) the written foundation must be very thorough, (ii) the subjective certainty must stem from a high objective probability that the defendant is guilty,[353] (iii) the reasoning must be free from logical errors and

---

[344] § 244 (6) StPO. See *Perron*, Beweisantragsrecht, p. 206.
[345] *Perron*, in: Eser/Rabenstein, Criminal Justice, p. 312
[346] *Perron*, in: Eser/Rabenstein, Criminal Justice, p. 312.
[347] *Damaška*, Evidence Law Adrift, pp. 21, 45.
[348] *Velten*, in: SK-StPO, Vor § 261 StPO Rn. 30; *Ott*, in: *KK-StPO*, § 261 Rn. 3.
[349] *Velten*, in: SK-StPO, § 261 StPO Rn. 46; *Ott*, in: KK-StPO, § 261 StPO Rn. 1.
[350] §§ 243 (1) and 258 StPO, respectively; *Velten*, in: SK-StPO, § 261 StPO Rn. 46, 47.
[351] *Frase/Weigend*, German Criminal Justice, p. 344; *Eisenberg*, Beweisrecht, Rn. 89, 91.
[352] *Eisenberg*, Beweisrecht, Rn. 100a.
[353] *Krehl* in: KK-StPO, § 244 Rn. 29.

contradictions, and (iv) scientific knowledge must be respected, e. g., expert evidence.

The vital importance of this written foundation, which states the reasons for reaching a decision is that in the case of an appeal, the appellate court's criteria for examining the decision's validity will be based on whether the elements set above were fulfilled.[354] Hence, the objective factual basis is met by the court having to "give an exhaustive assessment of each piece of evidence and each sign of evidence (*Beweisanzeichen*) and take into account all factors essential to the reaching of a judgment[355]."

Third, when there is a prohibition of evidence (*Beweisverbote*), the court cannot take such evidence into account when assessing the evidence that was presented at trial. This applies regardless of whether this prohibition stems from constitutional or statutory provisions, or due to it colliding with other procedural rights and principles.[356]

Chapter 2

The United States of America

A. Introduction

The United States of America has a federal government, which is divided into 50 states. Each state has its own criminal justice system, and its own executive and legislative systems.[357] Additionally, there is the jurisdiction of the District of Columbia and the federal jurisdiction, which is responsible for disposing of all federal crimes nationwide. Thus, the US-American legal system has 52 different judicial systems and although at times, they may be similar to one another, none of them are identical.[358]

Owing to the impossibility of addressing the American criminal procedure and evidence law in its entirety, this work will exclusively focus on the federal judicial system.[359] Considering that most criminal cases are disposed of by the state jurisdictions, by focusing on the federal jurisdiction, I will only address a small per-

---

[354] *Eisenberg*, Beweisrecht, Rn. 96.

[355] *Eisenberg*, Beweisrecht, Rn. 100, "[Das Gericht] hat auch jede Beweistatsache und jedes Beweisanzeichen erschöpfend und unter Berücksichtigung aller für die Urteilsfindung wesentlichen Gesichtspunkte zu würdigen."

[356] *Eisenberg*, Beweisrecht, Rn. 112.

[357] *Gilliéron*, Public Prosecutors, p. 15.

[358] *LaFave* et al., Criminal Procedure, p. 4.

[359] Part 1 of Title 18 of the United States Code specifies all the criminal offenses that fall under the federal jurisdiction (18 U.S.C. §§ 1–2725).

centage of cases that are adjudicated by American courts.[360] This number is further reduced if I take into consideration that about 90–95 % of criminal cases are disposed of by means of plea-bargaining.[361] Hence, at best, less than 10 % of cases in the federal jurisdiction go to trial. Nonetheless, the fact that the majority of criminal cases are disposed of by means of plea bargaining does not reduce the importance of the criminal cases that are disposed of by trial, as they play a crucial role in directly influencing the plea negotiations.[362] This is because the full panoply of rights of the adversarial system is afforded to defendants at trial, i.a., the right to a jury trial and the strict rules on admissibility of evidence. Thus, the structure of the trial is a driving force behind plea negotiations, and according to Perron, "even the possibility of a potential trial along the lines of the adversarial model is enough to significantly influence the basis of the plea-arrangements".[363]

In addition to focusing on the criminal cases that are adjudicated by the federal courts, this study will solely address felony cases that go to trial.[364] In examining this legal system, the present country report entails two different areas of law: criminal procedure (B.) and evidence law (C.). While the former studies the rules applicable to the investigation and prosecution of criminal cases and the outline of the procedural phases, the latter examines the admissibility of evidence at trial.[365] Following an overview of both these areas of law, I will examine the procedural safeguards in the federal jurisdiction (D.), which are analyzed either within the domain of criminal procedure or of evidence law.

Regarding the legal sources examined, as this is a common law system, it has as its primary legal sources both statutory and case law.[366] Due to the vastness of case law, I will focus on the former, i.e., I will examine "law on the books" rather than "law in action". For this purpose, my guiding points are the Federal Constitution and its Amendments, the Federal Rules of Criminal Procedure, and the Federal Rules of Evidence. Nevertheless, I will sometimes refer to case law as there are specific features of federal law – particularly in regard to the development of several constitutional and procedural safeguards – that are inextricable from the examination of precedent.

---

[360] *Burnham*, Introduction, p. 174.

[361] As to the percentage of cases that are disposed of by means of plea bargaining, see footnote 6 (Part 1).

[362] *Thaman*, in: Perron (ed.), Die Beweisaufnahme im Strafverfahrensrecht, p. 503.

[363] *Perron*, in: Eser/Rabenstein, Criminal Justice, p. 307.

[364] As per 18 U.S.C. § 3156(a)(3), felonies are criminal offenses punishable by a maximum term of imprisonment of more than a year.

[365] *Graham*, Evidence, p. 1.

[366] *Thompson* et al., An Introduction, p. 7.

B. Overview of the Criminal Procedure

I. Legal Sources

The main sources of statutory law in criminal procedure are primarily the US-Constitution, followed by the federal statutes.[367] The most important provisions of the US-Constitution are set in the Bill of Rights,[368] which provides the procedural rights of the accused throughout the different procedural phases. Of particular importance to this study are the 4th, 5th, 6th, 8th and 14th Amendments to the Constitution.

The most important federal statute regulating criminal procedure is the Federal Rules of Criminal Procedure (FRCP), which was drafted and promulgated by the Supreme Court,[369] and later approved by Congress, and is binding to all federal courts.[370] The United States Code (U.S.C.) is also an important legal source in the federal jurisdiction; titles 18 and 28 are of most relevance to this work, as they respectively set out provisions of both criminal law and criminal procedure and establish the organization of the federal courts.

Although not being the main focus of this work, case law plays a crucial role in the US-American legal system. Its importance is due to the principle of *stare decisis* ("to stand by that which is decided"[371]), which asserts that the final decisions of higher courts' are both binding to the originating court and to all lower federal courts.

---

[367] The importance of the former is owing to Article VI of the Constitution and to *Marbury v. Madison*, where the Supreme Court ruled that the Constitution of the United States is the Law of the Land. In this sense, see *Marbury v. Madison*, 5 U.S. 137 (1803); *Scheb/Sharma*, An Introduction to the American Legal System, p. 20.

[368] When the US Constitution came into force in 1789, it did not include any civil rights. To remedy this, the founding fathers outlined the main civil liberties in the so-called Bill of Rights, i.e., in the first ten amendments to the United States Constitution. The main concern in outlining these civil liberties was to protect the citizens from the national government owing to the fear that stemmed from the abuses that took place in the country during English rule. It is for this reason that initially the Bill of Rights was not applicable to the states, as at the time, the individual states were not viewed as a threat to the American citizens. As further amendments were added to the U.S. Constitution – which now totals 27 – several of the civil liberties that once applied exclusively to the federal government are now also applied to the states. The constitutional basis for this was the 14th Amendment to the Constitution which introduced the "due process" and "equal protection" clauses. This took place in large part during the so-called "Warren-court revolution", between 1961 and 1967, when not only several of the provisions of the Bill of Rights were transposed to the states, but also the rights of the accused were significantly expanded. See *Belknap*, The Supreme Court, p. 1; *Scheb/Sharma*, An Introduction to the American Legal System, pp. 18, 19; *LaFave* et al., Criminal Procedure, pp. 58 et seq.

[369] The Supreme Court presented its final draft to Congress, which due to recognizing the importance of these rules, decided to approve them instead of letting it "become automatically effective". See *Thompson* et al., An Introduction, p. 283; *Saltzburg/Martin/Capra*, FRE Manual, §PT 1.03, PT 1–4.

[370] *Dressler/Michaels*, Understanding Criminal Procedure, pp. 2, 3.

[371] *Britz*, Criminal Evidence, p. 7.

II. Court System

The federal jurisdiction has a three-tiered court system. In the first level are the district courts, which are divided into 94 districts and each judicial district has a district court.[372] Pursuant to Art. 3 of the Federal Constitution, Congress authorizes the specific cases where the district courts have jurisdiction in civil and criminal matters.[373]

In the second level are the circuit courts, which are intermediate appellate courts that have jurisdiction in reviewing the district courts' final decisions.[374] There are thirteen circuit courts in total. The two first circuit courts cover the District of Columbia, i. e., the United States Court of Appeals for the District of Columbia Circuit and one circuit court which covers all federal judicial districts, i. e., the United States Court of Appeals for the Federal Circuit.. The remaining eleven circuit courts cover the states; thus, depending on where the final judgment of the district court took place, the parties will have the right to appeal to the appropriate circuit court competent to review this district court's final decision.[375]

At the top of the pyramid is the Supreme Court of the United States, which has a "hybrid function", i. e., it has both original jurisdiction and has the ultimate appellate jurisdiction on federal issues. TheSupreme Court's original jurisdiction is set out in Art. 3 Section 2 of the Federal Constitution of the United States and in 28 U.S.C. § 1251. In its jurisdiction as court of last resort, all federal courts must abide by its rulings,[376] as it has the final word in interpreting the Constitution.[377] Thus, it "exercises appellate jurisdiction over cases appealed from the United States Courts of Appeals".[378] The Supreme Court of the United States may also review a final judgment by the highest court of a state by writ of certiorari, when it involves a point of federal law that is contrary to "the Constitution, treaties, or laws of the United States".[379]

---

[372] 28 U.S.C. § 132(a); *Burnham*, Introduction, p. 174.

[373] The jurisdiction of the district courts is set out in 28 U.S.C. § 85.

[374] 28 U.S.C. § 1291.

[375] As per 28 U.S.C. § 41.

[376] However, only the State Supreme Courts have the final say regarding the interpretation of their respective state Constitutions, see *Dressler/Michaels*, Understanding Criminal Procedure, pp. 2, 3.

[377] The Supreme Court of the United States not only has the final word in judicial matters but owing to judicial review, it also has the power to examine the constitutionality of acts of both other branches of government. In this sense, see *Thompson* et al., An Introduction, p. 27; *Roberson/Winters*, Evidence for Criminal Justice, p. 15.

[378] *Burnham*, Introduction, p. 176.

[379] 28 U.S.C. §§ 1254, 1257.

III. Main Procedural Actors

Judges, prosecutors, defense attorneys, and public defenders are all lawyers. Before starting law school, students must complete four years of undergraduate studies, and in some universities, they must additionally present their undergraduate GPA and take the LSAT to apply to graduate school.[380] Successful students must then study three years of law school to earn their J.D. To become a lawyer, law graduates must pass the Exam of the American Bar Association (Bar Exam) from the respective state in which they wish to practice law. As there is no separate Federal Bar Examination, a lawyer who has passed a State Bar Exam "must go to a local federal district court and obtain a certificate entitling them to practice in that district".[381]

Below, I will briefly analyze and distinguish each main procedural actor, particularly concerning their roles in the procedure of evidence taking at trial.

1. Judges

In the first instance of the federal jurisdiction, there are two types of judges: magistrate judges and district court judges. The Federal Magistrates Act authorizes each district court to decide and specify the responsibilities of the magistrate judges depending on the court's specific needs and caseload.[382] Magistrate judges are, therefore, "subordinate judicial officers",[383] who may have different responsibilities depending on what each district court judge chooses to delegate them.[384] As a rule, the main responsibilities of the magistrate judge are[385] (i) to dispose of misdemeanor cases, (ii) to conduct the initial proceedings, such as the preliminary hearing in felony cases,[386] and (iii) to make decisions in pretrial matters in both misdemeanor and felony cases, e. g., issuing search and arrest warrants, and setting bail.[387]

In contrast, district court judges are responsible for adjudicating felony cases once the grand jury issued an indictment in the federal jurisdiction. Pursuant to Art. 2, Section II of the US-Constitution, the President appoints district court judges with the advice and the consent of the Senate. As to grant them autonomy in

---

[380] *Friedman/Hayden*, American Law, p. 250.
[381] *Burnham*, Introduction, p. 137.
[382] *Mc Gabe*, A Guide to the Magistrate Judges System, p. 20.
[383] *Thompson* et al., An Introduction, p. 38.
[384] *Burnham*, p. 186.
[385] *Mc Gabe*, A Guide to the Magistrate Judges System, pp. 19, 20.
[386] An exception to this can be observed in felony cases where the prosecution files an information rather than an indictment, as per FRCP 5.1(a)(3).
[387] 28 U.S.C. § 636.

their rulings, federal judges are appointed for life and their salaries cannot be reduced.[388]

From now on, to facilitate both the analysis of the US-American legal system in this chapter and in Part 3, I will use the term magistrate judge in the sense of subitems (ii) and (iii) set above. That is, to refer to judges who have judicial competence to make decisions in the investigatory phase and in the adjudicatory phase up to the moment, where the charges against the accused must be screened by verifying whether the evidentiary standard of probable cause has been met. In contrast, I will employ the term trial judge to refer to the judicial competence in the hearing of arraignment onwards and specially, in the trial phase.[389]

2. Prosecutors

Federal prosecutors belong to the Department of Justice (DOJ) and have the responsibility of charging and prosecuting federal crimes. There are currently 93 U.S. Attorneys, who work in 94 districts, one for each federal judicial district,[390] and an Attorney General, who is the head of the DOJ.[391] Both the Attorney General and the U.S. Attorneys are nominated by the President and subsequently confirmed by the Senate and can be removed by the President at any time.[392]

The Federal Guidelines which guide federal prosecutors are the United States Attorney's Manual, and the Criminal Resource Manual, coupled with memoranda from their respective Attorney Generals.[393] However, due to these guidelines having an internal nature, if prosecutors do not follow these rules, they are solely accountable to the DOJ seeing that there are no exterior mechanisms to enforce, intervene or limit the prosecutorial discretionary powers.[394]

Prosecutors are parties to the proceedings, who have various roles and responsibilities. In the pretrial phase, they have the duty to decide whether there is probable cause to charge a suspect and, if in the affirmative, which charges to file

---

[388] *Thompson* et al., An Introduction, p. 39. I will analyze the district court judges' roles and responsibilities in more detail when I examine the adversarial trial setting in Ch. 2 C. I. 2. b).

[389] A caveat is in order, the manner in which I employ the terms *magistrate judge* and *trial judge* may not completely overlap with the responsibilities of magistrate judges and district court judges in all criminal proceedings.

[390] Only 93 U.S. Attorneys work in 94 judicial districts, as one single U.S. Attorney is competent for the districts of Guam and Northern Mariana Islands. In this sense, see Executive Office for the United States Attorneys (2011), p. 1; *Thompson* et al., An Introduction, p. 45.

[391] 28 U.S.C. § 503. Among the several roles of the Attorney General, he represents the United States in legal matters and gives advice and opinions to the President when so requested. In cases, which are exceptionally severe or important, the Attorney General appears in person before the Supreme Court, as set out in 28 U.S.C. § 511.

[392] 28 U.S.C. § 503, 28 U.S.C. § 541(a) and 28 U.S.C. § 541(c), respectively.

[393] *Podgor* in: Wade/Luna, Transnational Perspective, p. 10.

[394] *Davis*, Arbitrary Justice, p. 15.

against him. In fulfilling these tasks, prosecutors have a far-reaching amount of discretionary power. Once the charging decision is made, the prosecution has the responsibility of leading the criminal case to its conclusion. Namely, by seeking to assure a conviction, which can occur either by taking the case to trial or by negotiating a plea agreement, where the accused will then plead guilty to the charges as negotiated with the defense.

In deciding whether to file a bill of indictment against a suspect, prosecutors must consider whether they have enough evidence to prove to a grand jury that there is probable cause for a case to go to trial. If the grand jury believes that probable cause exists, it will issue an indictment. The prosecutor will then have the responsibility of introducing evidence that furthers their case at trial and of seeking to prove to the jury every element of the criminal offense beyond a reasonable doubt.

Owing to the adversarial trial setting, some scholars believe that the prosecution is more interested in winning the case than finding the truth and serving justice.[395] However, many scholars contest this view arguing that prosecutors are interested in seeking justice and seeing that defendants receive a fair trial.[396] The reason for these contradictory views is likely due to the prosecution's distinct standpoints in the different phases of the procedure. In the pretrial stage, prosecutors have no interest in prosecuting innocent citizens and seek to find the objective facts of the case, and consequently, they seek to find the truth and to serve justice.[397] However, once they believe probable cause is present for a case to go to trial, i.e., that there is a reason to believe that the accused committed the crime in question, the prosecution's stance shifts. That is, owing to its conviction of the defendant's culpability, the prosecution seeks to win the case by proving to the factfinder all elements of the criminal offense.[398]

3. Defense Counsel

There are different types of defense counsel. The first type are the privately retained attorneys, who are usually lawyers that work at a private practice and are chosen by defendants who have the financial means to retain them. The second type are the public defenders, who work for the government and are appointed to defendants who do not have the financial means to retain counsel and have the task to

---

[395] *Frankel*, The Search for Truth, p. 1038; *Pizzi*, Soccer, Football and Trial Systems, p. 369; *Langer*, From Legal Transplants to Legal Translations, p. 21; *Findley*, Adversarial Inquisitions, p. 912; *Boyne*, The German Prosecution Service, pp. 4, 5.

[396] In this sense, see *Thompson* et al., An Introduction, p. 46; *Britz*, Criminal Evidence, p. 64; *Ingram*, Criminal Evidence, p. 101. See also ABA Model Rules, Rule 3.8.

[397] See infra Ch. 4 B. III.

[398] *Thaman*, in: Perron (ed.), Die Beweisaufnahme im Strafverfahrensrecht, p. 503; *Perron*, in: Eser/Rabenstein, Criminal Justice, p. 308.

represent the defendant at all stages of the proceeding.[399] The third type of counsel are the court-appointed counsel, who are usually lawyers who work on a pro bono basis or are "private attorneys who are paid by the state on a case-by-case basis to represent indigent defendants".[400]

The Sixth Amendment to the Constitution lays out that criminal defendants have the right to counsel at trial. This right extends to all "critical stages" of the prosecution, which also comprise lineups, pretrial hearings, and pretrial discovery.[401] The right to counsel entails not only counsel being present, but also its effective assistance. The defense counsel's main role is to protect the defendants' legal and constitutional rights both before and during trial and to further their interests.[402] Since the prosecution must prove that the defendant committed all elements of the crime, if one element rests unproven, the jury must consider the defendant not guilty. Therefore, the defense counsel has the duty to investigate and gather evidence prior to trial, so that it can present evidence at trial which sheds doubt on the prosecution's case and instill in the jury reasonable doubt concerning at least one of the elements of the crime.

In fulfilling this task, the defense may have different tactics, such as trying to exclude evidence that is prejudicial to their client, introducing evidence contrary to the prosecution's case, trying to impeach the witnesses for the prosecution, and if applicable, presenting an alibi or an affirmative defense, e.g., presenting a claim of self-defense, or an insanity defense. A further role of the defense counsel is to "establish a proper record for appellate review";[403] i.e., if the judge excludes evidence favorable to the defense or admits evidence that is favorable to the prosecution's case, pursuant to FRE 103, the defense must make a claim of error at trial for the judge's ruling to be preserved for appeal.

IV. Procedural Phases

1. Investigatory Phase

a) Evidence Gathering by the State

After a crime is committed, the police are responsible for finding the perpetrator of the criminal offense. To this end, they have many options in which to gather evidence, such as, questioning the victim, the eyewitnesses and the people who were near the crime scene, as well as analyzing the crime scene and looking into possible suspects. When the police believe there is enough evidence against a suspect that amounts to

---

[399] FRCP 44(a); *Ingram*, Criminal Evidence, p. 778.
[400] *Thompson* et al., An Introduction, p. 46.
[401] See infra Ch. 2 D. I. 1.
[402] *Ingram*, Criminal Evidence, p. 104.
[403] *Roberson/Winters*, Evidence for Criminal Justice, p. 18

probable cause, they may make an arrest.[404] Following an arrest,[405] the suspect is taken to the police station, where her name, the time of arrest and the offense she allegedly committed are recorded.[406] The police may further identify the suspect by taking her pictures and fingerprints.

b) Rights of the Defense Prior to Trial

In the US-American trial setting, the parties are responsible for presenting their respective cases. Thus, it is the defense's responsibility to gather evidence, which is favorable to the accused during the investigatory phase. In achieving this aim, the defense may conduct the investigation themselves, or – depending on their financial resources – they may hire a private detective to this end. The pretrial investigation entails searching for evidence favorable to the defense's case; for this purpose, the defense may seek and question witnesses, search for documents, and hire expert witnesses. The FRCP sets out three main ways in which the defense may acquire evidence prior to trial, namely by means of (i) discovery, (ii), subpoenas and (iii) depositions. I will briefly describe each one of these mechanisms, particularly the latter, as I will address (i) and (ii) in more detail when I examine the main procedural safeguards in the US-American criminal procedure and evidence law.[407]

The right to discovery is the right that both parties have to present a motion to the court, to request the opposing party to hand in certain types of information that is in its possession or control.[408] As per FRCP 17, the right to subpoena is a means by which the defendant may request the court to compel people to testify or to produce a document or object at trial.

The right to a deposition is a means in which the parties may preserve evidence prior to trial, by presenting a motion requesting the court to take a deposition of a witness ahead of trial. To this end, the party must state the reasoning for believing that there is a risk that the said witness may not be available for examination at trial.[409] As per FRCP 15(a)(1), the court may grant the party this motion "because of exceptional circumstances and in the interest of justice". Additionally, the court may request the deponent to produce documents or objects that do not fall under the rules of privilege.

The party that wishes to take the deposition must give the other party written notice of the deposition's date and location and inform it of "the name and address of

---

[404] Pursuant to FRCP 5(b), if the police arrest a suspect without an arrest warrant, a complaint "must be promptly filed in the district where the offense was allegedly committed.".

[405] In most felony cases, defendants remain detained during trial. See *Thaman*, in: Perron (ed.), Die Beweisaufnahme im Strafverfahrensrecht, p. 494.

[406] *LaFave* et al., Criminal Procedure, p. 15.

[407] See infra Ch. 2 D. I. 1. and Ch. 2 D. I. 2., respectively.

[408] *LaFave* et al., Criminal Procedure, p. 18; and FRCP 12(b)(4)(B).

[409] *Thaman*, in: Perron (ed.), Die Beweisaufnahme im Strafverfahrensrecht, p. 514; *Schäuble*, Strafverfahren und Prozessverantwortung, p. 313.

each deponent".[410] Should the defendant be in custody, the party must also give written notice to the officer who has custody of the defendant.[411]

The main difference between the right to subpoena and the right to deposition regarding the statements of oral witnesses, is that in the former, a party requests the court for the witness to appear at trial, whereas the latter is a means in which to preserve evidence prior to trial, owing to the risk that the deponent may not be able to testify at trial.

2. Adjudicatory Phase

a) Issuance of a Complaint and Initial Appearance

Once there is probable cause against a suspect, either a police officer or the prosecutor files a formal charging document termed complaint.[412] From this moment forward, the prosecutor oversees the proceedings and has full discretionary powers concerning the charging decision.[413] Once the complaint is filed before a magistrate judge, the suspect becomes a defendant, and will have her first appearance before the former.[414] The initial appearance before the magistrate is an important procedural moment for two reasons.

First, the magistrate judge is competent to decide on matters of detention and release. Therefore, in cases where the police arrested a suspect without an arrest warrant, the magistrate must determine whether probable cause was present to arrest the suspect.[415] In contrast, in cases in which a complaint is filed and the suspect is at liberty; if the magistrate verifies that the complaint establishes probable cause to believe that an offense has been committed and that the defendant committed it, she must issue an arrest warrant against the defendant.[416] Further, it is during the initial appearance that the magistrate will deliberate whether to grant the defendant bail.

Second, it is in the initial appearance that the magistrate informs the defendant of the charges against her and of her procedural rights, such as the right to counsel and to request that counsel be appointed to the defendant if she cannot afford one.[417] In

---

[410] FRCP 15(b)(1).

[411] FRCP 15(b)(2).

[412] FRCP 3.

[413] Thus, in cases where the police filed a complaint, the prosecutor may decide to change the charges filed against the defendant, make additional charges, or drop the charges altogether. See *LaFave* et al., Criminal Procedure, p. 14.

[414] *LaFave* et al., Criminal Procedure, p. 15.

[415] As per FRCP 5(a)(1)(A), the police may make an arrest with or without a warrant. In the latter cases, the suspect must be taken to a magistrate judge after the arrest took place. See also *Dressler/Michaels*, Understanding Criminal Procedure, p. 7.

[416] FRCP 4(a).

[417] FRCP 5(d)(1)(A) and FRCP 5(d)(1)(B), respectively.

addition to these rights, the magistrate will also instruct the defendant about her right to silence and to a preliminary hearing.[418]

b) Grand Jury or Preliminary Hearing: Evidentiary Standard of Probable Cause

Before arraignment, there needs to be a further screening of the charges against the defendant with the aim of checking the prosecution's discretionary powers.[419] There are two different ways to do this: through the grand jury by means of an indictment and through the preliminary hearing by means of an information. Indictment is "a formal written statement made by the grand jury accusing a person of a crime",[420] whereas information is "a criminal charge brought by the prosecutor without a grand jury indictment".[421]

Pursuant to the Fifth Amendment to the Constitution, an accused will only answer "for a capital, or otherwise infamous crime" after the grand jury issues an indictment. In this respect, FRCP 7(a)(1) provides that an "offense must be prosecuted by an indictment if it is punishable: by death; or by imprisonment for more than one year", i.e., in felony cases.[422] However, in cases involving felonies that are not punishable by death, the defendant may waive her right to prosecution by indictment in an open court. In these instances, the screening of the prosecution's case will take place by information rather than by indictment.[423]

In prosecutions by indictment, the grand jury is responsible for deciding whether there is enough evidence to take a case to trial.[424] The grand jury is a group of jurors composed of 16 to 23 members, that stem from the same group of potential jurors as the jury trial.[425] The purpose of this procedure is to protect defendants against weak cases that are devoid of "proof of guilt".[426] Interestingly, although defendants have a constitutional right to a grand jury, they have fewer rights in this proceeding than in the preliminary hearing. This is due to the former proceeding being conducted behind closed doors, where neither the magistrate, the defense counsel nor the defendant are present.[427] Therefore, due to only the prosecutor and the witnesses for the prosecution

---

[418] Respectively, FRCP 5(d)(1)(D) and (E).
[419] *Saltzburg/Capra*, American Criminal Procedure, p. 999.
[420] *Marcus* et al., The Rights of the Accused, p. 117.
[421] *Marcus* et al., The Rights of the Accused, p. 117.
[422] For the definition of felony, see supra footnote 364 (Part 2).
[423] FRCP 7(b); see also *Smith v. United States*, 360 U.S. 1, 9 (1959).
[424] FRCP 6(a)(1), 18 U.S.C. § 3321.
[425] *LaFave* et al., Criminal Procedure, p. 17.
[426] *Thompson* et al., An Introduction, p. 14.
[427] *Thaman*, in: Perron (ed.), Die Beweisaufnahme im Strafverfahrensrecht, p. 500.

being present,[428] the jurors only hear the prosecution's case to the extent that the prosecution wishes to present it to them. Consequently, with exception to privileged communications, the prosecution may present to the grand jury evidence that would not have been held admissible at trial.[429]

After the evidence is presented, the grand jurors deliberate and vote. Rarely failing to issue an indictment and to the secretive nature of this proceeding,[430] there are many scholars who criticize the grand jury as a means in which to verify whether probable cause is present and as a mechanism to control the prosecution's discretionary powers.[431] Nonetheless, the grand jury is considered to be an effective way to protect the rights of the accused, as it prompts prosecutors to screen their case more thoroughly and abstain from prosecuting cases they believe to be weak.

In contrast to the grand jury, a criminal case will be prosecuted by information in misdemeanor cases or in felony cases where the accused waived his right to prosecution by indictment. The preliminary hearing follows an adversarial setting and resembles a trial, where the accused has the right to counsel and each party presents its case to a magistrate judge in open court.[432] With the exception of testimonial privilege, the parties may present all the evidence they possess, including those which would not be held admissible at trial.[433] However, in this setting, opposing counsel usually do not present all evidence they have at their disposal, but rather, only the amount necessary either to show that the standard of probable cause has been met or to show its absence.

It is the prosecution's responsibility to show that the standard of proof of probable cause is present,[434] and at the end of this hearing, the magistrate judge must verify whether there is probable cause to bind the case to trial.[435] As per FRCP 5.1(f), "if the magistrate judge finds no probable cause to believe an offense has been committed or the defendant committed it", she must "dismiss the complaint and discharge the defendant".

Once the grand jury or the preliminary hearing ends and the grand jurors or magistrate find(s) that there is probable cause for the case to go to trial, different

---

[428] FRCP 6(d)(1); *Thompson* et al., An Introduction, p. 51; *Saltzburg/Capra*, American Criminal Procedure, p. 1004.

[429] FRE 1101(d)(3). See *Thompson* et al., An Introduction, p. 282; *Ingram*, Criminal Evidence, pp. 37, 38.

[430] *Marcus* et al., The Rights of the Accused, pp. 124, 125; *Saltzburg/Capra*, American Criminal Procedure, p. 1002.

[431] *Perron*, in: Eser/Rabenstein, Criminal Justice, p. 305.

[432] *Thaman*, in: Perron (ed.), Die Beweisaufnahme im Strafverfahrensrecht, p. 500; *Whitebread/Slobogin*, Criminal Procedure, p. 623.

[433] FRE 1101(d)(3); FRCP 5.1(e); *Saltzburg/Capra*, American Criminal Procedure, p. 1030.

[434] *Whitebread/Slobogin*, Criminal Procedure, p. 625.

[435] *Saltzburg/Capra*, American Criminal Procedure, p. 1030.

documents will be issued. In the case of a grand jury, jurors will issue an indictment in the trial court, which will then replace the complaint as the charging document. In contrast, once the magistrate believes there is probable cause for a case to go to trial, the prosecutor must file an information in the trial court, which will replace the complaint as the charging document. Regardless of the type of the document in question, both indictment and information must contain the essential facts of the offense charged and must have been signed by a prosecutor.[436]

c) Arraignment and Pretrial Motions

Arraignment is a proceeding that is held in open court before the judge competent for adjudicating the criminal case at trial. As per FRCP 10(a), the defendant will be given a copy of the charging document and will be informed of the charges against her. The defendant will then be asked to plead to the indictment or information, i. e., she will then either plead not guilty, guilty or *nolo contendere*.[437]

By pleading guilty, the defendant admits to having committed the charges against her, whereas by pleading *nolo contendere* the defendant conveys that it does not wish to contest the allegations. The latter plea cannot be used against the defendant in a civil case.[438] For the court to accept the plea of guilty or *nolo contendere*, it must address the defendant in open court and inform her of her procedural rights. Among these rights are: to plead not guilty, to be represented by counsel, the right "to confront and cross-examine adverse witnesses, to be protected from self-incrimination, to testify and present evidence and to compel the attendance of witnesses".[439] After informing the defendant of her rights, the court will then inform her that these rights are waived if the courts accept the guilty plea or *nolo contendere* plea. Thus, by accepting either of these pleas, the trial does not take place and the judge sets a date for sentencing.[440]

However, if the defendant chooses to plead not guilty, she maintains her innocence and denies having committed the charges against her. In this case, the court will then set a date for trial.[441] The court may also specify a deadline for the parties to present the pretrial motions, and if it fails to do so, if the parties wish to present written motions, they must do so before the trials begins.[442] The pretrial motions have various purposes namely, to produce evidence (discovery)[443] and to suppress evidence that

---

[436] FRCP 7(c)(1).
[437] FRCP 11(a)(1).
[438] *Whitebread/Slobogin*, Criminal Procedure, p. 724.
[439] FRCP 11(b)(1). See *Thaman*, in: Perron (ed.), Die Beweisaufnahme im Strafverfahrensrecht, p. 500.
[440] *LaFave* et al., Criminal Procedure, p. 19.
[441] *LaFave* et al., Criminal Procedure, p. 18.
[442] FRCP 12(c)(1).
[443] See infra Ch. 2 D. I. 1.

was obtained in violation to the constitution or to a federal statute.[444] Both the right to discovery and the motion to suppress evidence are important means to enable the parties in knowing the strength or weaknesses of the opposing party's case. A case in point is that if the trial court makes a ruling to exclude a piece of evidence the prosecution wishes to present at trial, the prosecution may decide to drop the case. Conversely, if the trial judge admits the said evidence or chooses to suppress crucial evidence the defense wishes to present, the defendant may choose to plead guilty to the charges in exchange for a plea agreement.[445]

d) Trial

The questions of guilt and those of punishment are addressed in different procedural phases. At the trial phase, the factfinder will solely decide regarding the defendant's guilt, whereas the determination of the sentence the defendant will receive if found guilty is addressed in the sentencing phase. Pursuant to the Sixth Amendment to the Constitution, the defendant has a right to a trial by jury; nonetheless, he may waiver this right in writing.[446] If the prosecution consents to this waiver and the court approves it, a bench trial will take place, i.e., a single judge will decide regarding both matters of fact and of law. However, defendants usually choose to have a trial by jury, due to preferring to take their chances with twelve lay people who must (as a rule) decide unanimously as to whether they are guilty.[447]

I will now examine the general steps that take place at trial. All these steps are applicable to jury trials, whereas the opening statements, the procedure of evidence taking, and the closing arguments are applicable to both jury and bench trials.

aa) Jury Selection

The process of selecting potential jurors from a jury pool is called *voir dire*. It is through the *voir dire* that the judge and the parties attempt to uncover possible biases in favor of or against the defendant and, therefore, attempt to panel an impartial jury.[448] The preferred way in which to question potential jurors for possible biases is by the trial judge asking them direct questions.[449] Following the judge's questions, the

---

[444] *Thompson* et al., An Introduction, pp. 51, 52. If a party fails to present a motion to exclude evidence prior to trial, the party in question is waiving her right to challenge the exclusion of the evidence in question. In this sense, see *Roberson/Winters*, Evidence for Criminal Justice, p. 187; FRCP 12(b)(3)(C).

[445] *Roberson/Winters*, Evidence for Criminal Justice, pp. 187, 192 et seq.

[446] FRCP 23(a)(1).

[447] FRCP 23(b)(1), *Newton/Welch*, Understanding Criminal Evidence, p. 51.

[448] *Cooper*, Voir Dire, p. 270; *Dressler/Michaels*, Understanding Criminal Procedure, p. 12.

[449] *Bradley* believes that FRCP 24(a) should state that the court *must* conduct voir dire, i.e., making it mandatory for judges to examine potential jurorsmodifying this rule, he believes that the voir dire, and consequently, the jury trial would be swifter and more efficient. As a result,

parties are allowed to ask the jurors questions if the courts finds them to be proper.[450] When a party believes a potential juror to be biased, they may challenge them in two different ways. The first means is by challenging a juror for cause, which takes place when either the prosecution or the defense believes that based on a juror's answer, he could be prejudicial to the respective party's case. Each party has an unlimited number of challenges for cause.[451] The second means of challenging a potential juror is by peremptory challenges, which is used when a party believes a juror to be biased but cannot prove or explain to the trial judge the reasoning behind this.[452] Contrary to the challenges for cause, each party has a limited number of peremptory challenges.[453]

Once the jury is paneled, jurors may not speak to one another or to any other person concerning the facts of the case. Thus, due to them being prohibited to make any private inquiries, jurors must make decisions regarding the facts of the case based solely on the evidence presented to them at trial.[454]

bb) Opening Statements, Evidence Taking, and Closing Arguments

The opening statements is the parties' opportunity to present to the factfinder that which they believe the evidence will show.[455] However, while doing so, the parties cannot anticipate the presentation of evidence that are under the rules of evidence. The prosecution begins the opening statements followed by the defense. The defense may, however, choose to postpone its opening statements and present them after the prosecution has finished presenting its case-in-chief. The importance of these statements is due to them being the first contact the finder of fact has with the case and the moment where they start forming their first impressions as to whether the defendant is guilty or innocent.[456]

After the parties present their opening statements, the procedure of evidence taking begins. Each opposing counsel presents their respective case and decide the

---

more defendants would have the right to a jury trial, and this, in turn, would contribute to reduce the number of criminal cases that are disposed of by means of plea bargaining. See *Bradley*, Reforming the Criminal Trial, pp. 661, 664.

[450] *Graham*, Evidence, p. 3.

[451] *Cooper*, Voir Dire, p. 269.

[452] However, parties may not challenge a juror by means of a peremptory challenge owing to the juror being of a certain gender or race.

[453] According to FRCP 24(b)(2), the prosecution has the right to six peremptory challenges in felony cases, whereas the defense has the right to ten peremptory challenges. However, as per FRCP 24(b)(1), whenever the prosecution seeks the death penalty in capital cases, each side has the right to twenty peremptory challenges.

[454] *Newton/Welch*, Understanding Criminal Evidence, p. 53.

[455] *LaFave* et al., Criminal Procedure, p. 400.

[456] *Newton/Welch*, Understanding Criminal Evidence, p. 54.

order in which they wish to present evidence.[457] They present their respective cases in front of the trial judge, who will act as an impartial umpire and who will decide on matters of admissibility and exclusion of evidence upon an objection of one of the parties.[458] The prosecution starts presenting its case-in-chief, owing to it having the burden of proving to the trier of fact that the defendant is guilty beyond any reasonable doubt. After the prosecution rests its case, the defense may make its opening statements if it has not previously done so. As per FRCP 29(a), the defense may also motion the trial judge for a judgment of acquittal, which is a request for the court to dismiss the case when the defense believes the prosecution did not prove every element of the offense.[459]

If the court finds that the prosecution's case-in-chief was deficient, it may either permit the prosecution to present additional evidence, or it will "order the jury to return a verdict of acquittal".[460] However, if the court denies the motion – as is usually the case – the defense has the task to instill on the jury a reasonable doubt that the defendant is not guilty. The defense may accomplish this task in a variety of ways: (i) by presenting an affirmative defense, (ii) by presenting evidence to prove the defendant's innocence, and (iii) by attacking the evidence presented by the prosecution, by finding faults and shortcomings to its case-in-chief, e. g., impeaching the witnesses for the prosecution.

After the defense rests, the prosecution's rebuttal may ensue, i.e., when the prosecution contests the defense's case-in-chief. The prosecution must restrict itself to the evidence presented by the defense, such as proving that an affirmative defense presented by the opposing party is untruthful. Depending on the circumstances, after the prosecution's rebuttal evidence, the defense may present its rejoinder evidence. In so doing, the defense must attain to the facts and evidence presented by the prosecution in its case in rebuttal.[461]

Once the procedure of evidence taking is concluded, each party presents their closing arguments. This is an opportunity the parties have to summarize their respective cases and to convince the factfinder of the truthfulness of their side. Contrary to the opening statements, the parties may refer to all evidence, which was presented at trial.[462] This is because the closing statements are not based on new evidence, and thus, it is an additional opportunity for the parties to clarify the evidence and to further imprint on the jury the strength and veracity of their respective case.[463] As a

---

[457] *Langer*, Legal Transplants to Legal Translations, p. 21.

[458] *Damaška*, Evidence Law Adrift, p. 87.

[459] Despite the motion for acquittal usually taking place after the prosecution rests its case, it may also take place once both parties rested their cases, as well as after the jury reached its verdict.

[460] *LaFave* et al., Criminal Procedure, p. 1398.

[461] *Newton/Welch*, Understanding Criminal Evidence, p. 55.

[462] *Newton/Welch*, Understanding Criminal Evidence, p. 55.

[463] *Newton/Welch*, Understanding Criminal Evidence, p. 56.

rule, the prosecution presents their closing arguments followed by the defense. However, due to the prosecution having the burden of proof of proving every element of the criminal offense beyond a reasonable doubt, after the defense presents their closing arguments, the prosecution has the right to the last word.[464] During these last closing arguments, the prosecution must restrict its arguments to those presented by the defense in its closing arguments.[465]

cc) Jury Instructions, Jury Deliberation, and Announcement of the Verdict

Either prior to or following the closing arguments, the trial judge must make the final instructions to the jury as to enable them to decide the facts of the case.[466] Subsequently, the deliberation of the jury takes place in a setting of complete secrecy, which is owing to the panel of jurors being required to reach their decision without any external influence. If a juror has any doubts regarding a certain fact that transpired in court, they may ask the trial judge to clear such matters. Once the jurors reach their decision, it is final and they need not explain their thought processes as to how they reached the verdict.[467] After the jurors reach a unanimous decision, the announcement of the verdict must be made in open court.[468]

e) Sentencing Phase

In both jury and bench trials, once the factfinder reaches a decision regarding the defendant's guilt and announces the verdict, the trial is concluded. Should the factfinder find the defendant guilty, the determination of the sentence the defendant will receive is addressed in a separate proceeding called the sentencing phase. As a rule, trial judges base their verdict on the presentence investigation, which is prepared by a probation officer and submitted to the court.[469] The setting of the sentencing phase considerably differs from the trial setting;[470] furthermore, both the courtroom actors and the aims of each phase vary considerably.[471] The trial judge's stance shifts

---

[464] As per FRCP 29.1.
[465] *Graham*, Evidence, p. 5.
[466] See infra Ch. 2 D II 2.
[467] *Newton/Welch*, Understanding Criminal Evidence, p. 57.
[468] FRCP 31(a).
[469] FRCP 32(c)(1)(A). See also *Thompson* et al., An Introduction, p. 56.
[470] *Ingram*, Criminal Evidence, p. 39.
[471] The first substantial difference between the sentencing phase and the trial phase is that when the probation officer prepares the presentence investigation, he may base it on evidence that was gathered during the investigatory phase which has not been presented at trial. For more information on the sentencing phase, see *Thaman*, in: Perron (ed.), Die Beweisaufnahme im Strafverfahrensrecht, p. 505; *Pizzi/Perron*, Crime Victims in German Courtrooms, pp. 45, 46; *Pizzi*, the American "Adversary System"?, pp. 850, 851; *Pizzi*, in: Jackson et al., Crime, procedure and evidence; *Thompson* et al., An Introduction, p. 56.

from that of a passive referee to an active role, which "is responsible for determining both the relevant facts, and more particularly, the sentence".[472]

C. Evidence Law

I. Introduction

The main source of statutory law is the Federal Rules of Evidence (FRE), which was drafted and promulgated by the Supreme Court,[473] and later approved by Congress. In addition to the FRE, case law is vital in the creation and development of the regulation of evidentiary matters in the federal courts. As mentioned, evidence law is a subject in itself and is not studied as being part of the subject of criminal procedure[474] as is the case in other legal systems.[475] This is because the FRE govern evidentiary issues applicable to both criminal[476] and civil trials. The following analysis will focus almost exclusively on statutory law, i.e., on the provisions of the FRE that are applicable to criminal trials.

Before addressing the specifics of evidence law, I will now examine two features of the procedure of evidence taking at trial, which some scholars believe are responsible for shaping evidence law:[477] the trier of fact (1) and the control of pro-

---

[472] *Perron*, in: Eser/Rabenstein, Criminal Justice, p. 307.

[473] *Saltzburg/Martin/Capra*, FRE Manual, §PT 1.03, PT 1–4.

[474] *Nijboer*, Common Law Tradition, p. 301.

[475] This is the case in the German and Brazilian criminal procedures; in this sense, see Ch. 1 A. and Ch. 3 A., respectively.

[476] Even though I am limiting this research to evidence law as applied in a trial setting, it is interesting to state that evidence law directly affects plea-bargaining. As seen, for the past century, the vast majority of cases in both state and federal jurisdictions are disposed of by plea-bargaining. For this reason, scholars such as *Roberts* (see *Roberts*, in: Jackson et al., "Crime, procedure and evidence") believe that the judge's rulings on the admission or exclusion of evidence directly affect plea bargaining negotiations. This is because depending on the judge's ruling, it may strengthen or weaken a party's case, and therefore, evidence law directly influences both the leverage the prosecution has in proposing a deal and the defendant's decision on whether to accept the deal or to plead not guilty. See also *Kaye* et al., McCormick, p. 13.

[477] However, this is not an uncontroversial topic, as critics of this view contend that the shaping of modern evidence law cannot be explained due to these two factors alone. Many scholars believe that evidence law "serves additional purposes than regulating jury trials" (see *Allen/Alexakis*, in: Jackson et al., Crime, procedure and evidence, p. 338). *Langbein* (see *Langbein*, Historical Foundations of the Law of Evidence) contends that the modern Anglo-American Law of Evidence cannot be explained due to Jury trials alone, since according to his estimates the latter was developed in the 12th century, whereas the former was only developed in the late 18th century. In explaining the development of evidentiary rules, *Langbein* states that these rules were influenced by the fact that "informal jury control declined" from the mid-18th to the mid-19th century, due to the "rise of the adversary criminal procedure" That is, due to the presence of opposing counsel (p. 1197), which "pressured the judge toward passivity". In a system of trial that was commonly conducted by lawyers (…), the judge came to play a much

1. Finder of Fact: Jury and Bench Trials

The overwhelming majority of federal felony cases that are disposed of by trial are jury trials.[478] The importance of the defendant's right to a jury trial is such that it is set out in both Art. 3 Section 2 of the US-Constitution and the Sixth Amendment to the Constitution. Jury trials are bifurcated trials. On the one hand, a group of lay people decide regarding the facts of the case and are, at times, also responsible for deciding on "specific questions regarding the assessment of punishment".[479] On the other hand, the trial judge is responsible for deciding the law to be applied to the case should the jury find the defendant to be guilty.[480]

It is important to underline that jurors need not explain how they reached the verdict.[481] Thus, there is no way in which to control the thought processes that went through the individual jurors' minds while deciding whether the defendant is guilty or not guilty. It is possible that not even jurors are exactly aware of all the thought processes that led them to reach their decision.[482] Further, since the decision should be reached collectively, there is no process in which to verify what were the previous opinions of each juror before deliberations started, and whether and to what extent these initial opinions changed due to interactions and/or pressures from the majority of the jurors. As a rule, due to the impossibility of knowing what the juror's thought processes are during evidence taking and during jury deliberations, it is necessary to control the evidence that is presented to them at trial. For this reason, the evidence that is presented to the jurors is previously sifted as to avoid that they hear inadmissible, confusing, untrustworthy, or biased evidence.[483] Consequently, owing to

---

less active role in producing the evidence" (p. 1198). However, due to the impossibility of addressing all factors that influence modern US-American evidence law, I would like to concentrate on factors that I believe are pertinent to this study. Jury trials and party-controlled presentation of evidence may not explain all nuances of evidence law, but they can certainly partially explain how evidence law is shaped, even if these factors are merely correlated to the shaping of evidence law and no irrefutable causal link is found between them.

[478] *LaFave* et al., Criminal Procedure, p. 1396.

[479] *Perron*, in: Eser/Rabenstein, Criminal Justice, p. 307. One such example is in capital cases, where if the jurors find the defendant to be guilt it is up to them to decide whether the judge should impose a death penalty or a life sentence. In this sense, see also *Thaman*, in: Perron (ed.), Die Beweisaufnahme im Strafverfahrensrecht, p. 504.

[480] As seen in footnote 479 (Part 2), the exception to this rule is in capital cases where the trial judge cannot pass a death sentence without a jury.

[481] *Pizzi/Perron*, Crime Victims in German Courtrooms, p. 49; *Lempert*, in: Jackson et al., Crime, procedure and evidence, pp. 404, 405; *Newton/Welch*, Understanding Criminal Evidence, p. 57.

[482] *Damaška*, Evidence Law Adrift, pp. 44, 45.

[483] FRE 403.

the lack of specifics as to how the factfinder reached its decision, strict evidentiary rules are necessary for the parties to have some degree of control over the factfinder's decision-making.[484]

Differently than in jury trials, in bench trials, the trial judge may state the grounds in reaching a verdict.[485] This is because FRCP 23(c) sets out that before the court announces the defendant's guilt, one of the parties may request the court to state its reasoning in open court or in a written decision. In the instances where neither party requests the judge for his reasoning in reaching the decision, the appeal will not be based on a written decision. Thus, in the latter instance and in jury trials, the FRE bring a certain amount of formalism to the procedure.

The defendant may waive her right to a jury trial,[486] in which case a bench trial will take place. In bench trials, the trial judge is both finder of fact and of law.[487] Thereby the trial judge must decide on matters of credibility, decide on the probative value of the evidence presented by the parties, and make rulings on law.[488] Seeing that in bench trials, the trial judge has the responsibility of "deciding which facts have been properly proven"[489] and applying the laws to the case, the rules of evidence tend to be more relaxed, owing to the belief that a professional judge is better equipped than lay jurors in dealing with evidentiary matters.

2. Trial Setting

a) Party-Controlled Presentation of Evidence

The adversarial nature of the US-American trial setting considerably shapes evidence law. Each party has the duty to collect, evaluate and present evidence as best they can to secure the best possible outcome for each respective side. This is because this system believes that through the clash of both parties, the formal truth will come out.[490] For this reason, there are times when each party sifts the evidence they wish to present at trial, not necessarily by its probative strength, but according to the impact it will have on the ultimate factfinder.[491] Accordingly, the prosecution and the defense

---

[484] *Damaška*, Evidence Law Adrift, pp. 44, 46; *Perron*, in: Eser/Rabenstein, Criminal Justice, p. 307.

[485] *Lempert*, in: Jackson et al., Crime, procedure and evidence, p. 402.

[486] The waiver of the right to a jury trial was set out in *Patton v. United States*, which established that the defendant has the right to waive his constitutional right to a jury trial in non-capital cases. See *Patton v. United States*, 159 U.S. 500 (1895). For a defendant's waiver to be valid, it must be made intelligently and voluntarily, as provided in *United States v. Jackson*, 390 U.S. 570 (1968)

[487] *Roberson/Winters*, Evidence for Criminal Justice, p. 16.

[488] *LaFave* et al., Criminal Procedure, p. 1397.

[489] *Ingram*, Criminal Evidence, pp. 36, 96.

[490] *Boyne*, The German Prosecution Service, p. 4.

[491] *Damaška*, Evidence Law Adrift, p. 84.

must prepare their cases thoroughly before going to trial. This includes coaching witnesses on how to phrase their answers and better convey information in a manner that is most beneficial to each respective case. The parties' control over the presentation of evidence comprises not only evidence sensu stricto, but also other forms of proof, as they may make stipulations regarding facts, and unilaterally waiver rights.[492]

Due to the partisan control of evidence, it is necessary to regulate the admission and exclusion of evidence, as a means of controlling the quality of the evidence presented to the factfinder,[493] i.e., so that each counsel presents the best evidence possible.[494] To this end, "the prohibition against use of undisclosed evidentiary material is an effective sanction to maintain the integrity of the competitive fact-finding enterprise".[495] Owing to the very nature of the adversarial setting, it is the opposing counsel who invokes the exclusionary rules that apply in the case, and, therefore, evidence law "comes to life"[496] when one of the parties of the case invokes them.

b) The Role of the Trial Judge

aa) Role as an Umpire

The main role of trial judges is that of an umpire, who "preside over the proceedings and see that order is maintained".[497] In fulfilling this task, judges have various responsibilities during the procedure of evidence taking, such as ensuring that the constitutional and procedural rights of the defendant are respected. Although truth finding is one of the objectives of the criminal procedure, it is not its only aim. Hence, depending on the circumstances, the finding of the truth must be weighed against other aims, such as procedural fairness. In safeguarding due process, trial judges usually have vast discretionary powers to preside over trial and to make decisions regarding evidentiary matters.

First, the court is responsible for making decisions regarding the admissibility of evidence,[498] whereas the decision regarding the probative value of a proffered item of evidence is left to the jury to decide. The reason for this is that the court is better equipped than the jury to assess certain *preliminary questions* of fact; such is the case regarding the determination of whether a witness is qualified, a privilege exists, or

---

[492] See infra Ch. 2 C. II. 2.
[493] *Nance*, Understanding Responses to Hearsay, p. 468.
[494] *Roberts*, in: Jackson et al, Crime, procedure and evidence, p. 314.
[495] *Damaška*, Evidence Law Adrift, p. 84.
[496] *Damaška*, Evidence Law Adrift, p. 87.
[497] *Perron*, Beweisantragsrecht, p. 395; *Roberson/Winters*, Evidence for Criminal Justice, p. 16.
[498] *Graham*, Evidence, p. 1.

evidence is admissible.[499] Pursuant to FRE 104(a), when weighing these considerations, the court is not bound by evidence rules, except privilege. Therefore, for a court to analyze whether an item of evidence is admissible, it may, for example, take into consideration hearsay statements.[500] In assessing these matters, trial judges decide on a case-by-case basis and have a great amount of discretion in doing so, as appellate courts usually uphold the trial judge's decision, due to the belief that judges have a clearer perception of the events that transpired. This is because it is difficult for the appellate court to evaluate the conditions surrounding the events that transpired by merely reading the trial record.[501]

As a rule, the court has discretion whether to make decisions in the presence of the jury. There are instances, however, in which this discretion is curtailed, as FRE 104(c) sets out when the trial court must conduct a hearing outside of the jury's earshot. These are namely, when (i) it concerns the admissibility of a defendant's confession, (ii) the defendant choses to take the stand, or (iii) "justice so requires".[502]

As to preliminary questions, FRE 104(b) provides that "when the relevance of evidence depends on whether a fact exists, proof must be introduced sufficient to support a finding that the fact does exist". In such cases, the trial judge must decide if there is a reasonable probability that a jury would find that the fact in question exists.[503] If the court believes the evidence to be relevant, it will admit it, so that the jury may decide as to its weight and credibility, since the probative value of a determined evidence, that is, the weight and credibility of a witness's testimony, is up to the jury to decide.[504]

Second, the court should "exercise reasonable control over the mode and order of examining witnesses and presenting evidence",[505] so that the procedure is conducive to finding the truth and being efficient. Generally, parties have great latitude in presenting evidence, as the court does not have access to information of either party's case. For this reason, judges are wary of intervening in the presentation of evidence, as in so doing they may inadvertently hinder the finding of the truth rather than advance it.[506] Nonetheless, there are instances when the trial judges may intervene, particularly whenever: "(i) the parties ask for a ruling, (ii) when the judge wishes to

---

[499] FRE 104(a).

[500] *Graham*, Evidence, p. 9.

[501] *Weinstein/Berger*, Student Edition, § 6.01[5] [b] (6–9).

[502] FRE 104(c)(3). Among these instances are those which affect the defendant's constitutional rights, such as the failure to give a Miranda warning and issues regarding search and seizure. In this sense, see *Graham*, Evidence, p. 9.

[503] *Graham*, Evidence, p. 8.

[504] There are cases, however, in which the trial judge must weigh the probative value of a determined evidence against its prejudicial effects. See infra Ch. 2 C. IV. 2. a).

[505] FRE 611(a).

[506] *Thaman*, in: Perron (ed.), Die Beweisaufnahme im Strafverfahrensrecht, p. 507; *Weinstein/Berger*, Student Edition, § 2.02[2] (2–5).

clarify matters, or (iii) when something out of the ordinary takes place that warrants intervention".[507]

Usually, the trial judge has discretion in these matters and will not have his decision overturned unless the "appellate court finds a clear abuse of discretion that seriously damaged a party's right to a fair trial".[508] Thus, as long as "each party is afforded the opportunity to present his own evidence and to meet that of his opponent, he is scarcely in a position to complaint of a deviation or lack thereof from the normal witness examination".[509]

Third, FRE 611(a)(3) states that the trial judge must protect witnesses from being harassed by the parties during their testimony.[510] In fulfilling this task, the court may control the questions posed by the prosecution and the defense, although it will only exclude a question if one of the parties' raise an objection to the said question.[511] In conducting this role, appellate courts also usually uphold both the trial judge's decision to intervene at trial or to abstain from doing so. As seen, this is owing to the appellate court not having access to the nuances of witness examination as it is not possible for them to be properly conveyed on record.[512] An illustration of this is the manner in which the parties address the witness, such as the tone of their voice and the witness's responses to the questioning.

bb) Judicial Discretion in Presenting Evidence

In addition to the trial judges' role as an umpire, FRE 614 provides them the prerogative to present evidence, as it sets out that the court may call and examine witnesses regardless of which party called them. Nonetheless, apart from expert witnesses, if the trial judge calls a witness, this is usually seen as an "unwarranted intrusion into the adversary system favoring one party or another and thus should be undertaken only when clearly required in the interests of justice".[513]

This is because in the adversarial trial setting judicial neutrality is linked to the concept of passivity.[514] Thus, as a rule, trial judges will usually not intervene in the presentation of evidence unless one of the parties makes an objection to the opposing

---

[507] *Weinstein/Berger*, Student Edition, § 2.02[2] (2–4).
[508] *Graham*, Evidence, p. 717.
[509] *Graham*, Evidence, p. 715.
[510] See *Alford v. Unites States* (1931); *Thompson* et al., An Introduction, pp. 198 et seq.
[511] *Thompson* et al., An Introduction, p. 195.
[512] *Weinstein/Berger*, Student Edition, § 2.02[2] (2–8).
[513] *Graham*, Evidence, p. 717.
[514] See *Frankel*, The Search for Truth: An Umpireal View. If judges act in a way that shows bias to one side, it might give cause to reversible error. Involuntarily presenting evidence that supports one party may lead to the trial judge being deemed biased and/or having its decision reversed on appeal. See also *Damaška*, Evidence Law Adrift, pp. 75, 82, 90, 123.

party's proffered evidence.[515] For this reason, if the court decides to examine a witness, it must "maintain an appearance of impartiality and neither become an advocate for a particular party nor display hostility to anyone".[516] As the presentation of evidence is a "party-controlled contest", it is deemed that if the trial judge were to call and examine a witness, he would both lose his neutrality and interfere in the presentation of evidence, as the information would stem from a third party rather than from the dialectic process itself. For these reasons, trial judges are usually wary of calling and examining witnesses, as this may lead to their decision being overruled by an appellate court.

II. Methods of Proving Facts

1. Evidence: Direct and Circumstantial Evidence

The parties may present either direct or circumstantial evidence. Direct evidence is that which is "based on personal knowledge"[517] and it is "evidence that proves a fact without the need for a juror to infer or presume anything from it".[518] In contrast, circumstantial evidence is that in which a fact is established and the juror must make inferences or presumptions as to a second fact.[519] Therefore, once real or testimonial circumstantial evidence is presented to the jury, it is up to the jurors to draw inferences or presumptions as to whether that fact is true.[520] Usually due to the surreptitious nature of crimes, most evidence tends to be circumstantial; however, the degree of "indirectness" of this type of evidence varies from case to case.

There is neither a legal differentiation concerning direct and circumstantial evidence nor is there a difference concerning the weight to be given to each of them.[521] Thus, whereas a specific jury may find a defendant guilty solely based on circumstantial evidence, another set of jurors may find the defendant not guilty despite the prosecution basing its case on direct evidence.

2. Alternatives to Formal Proof

There are cases where it would be unreasonable to expect the parties to prove every piece of information or fact that is presented to the jury.[522] If this were required,

---

[515] *Saltzburg/Martin/Capra*, FRE Manual, p. xiv.
[516] *Graham*, Evidence, p. 719.
[517] *Ingram*, Criminal Evidence, p. 107.
[518] *Thompson* et al., An Introduction, p. 82.
[519] *Ingram*, Criminal Evidence, p. 108.
[520] *Thompson* et al., An Introduction, p. 83.
[521] *Ingram*, Criminal Evidence, pp. 108, 119.
[522] *Ingram*, Criminal Evidence, p. 119.

it would lead to confusing the jury and making their fact-finding role more complicated and make trials even more costly and lengthy. To avoid this, case and statutory law developed four alternatives to formal proof, i.e., exceptions to the need of proving all facts in contention.

The first alternative to formal proof is *judicial notice* which is a means that courts have at their disposal to determine whether a matter is true without having to go through "ordinary evidentiary means".[523] FRE 201(b) sets out that there are facts which are "generally known within the trial court's territorial jurisdiction" or "can be accurately and readily determined from sources whose accuracy cannot reasonably be questioned". These facts can range from a variety of different areas of expertise, such as geography, medicine, or physics. The court may take judicial notice on its own initiative or at the request of one of the parties.[524] Regardless of who takes the initiative, both parties have the right to be heard concerning the taking of judicial notice.[525] Further, as per FRE 201(f), the court must instruct the jury that it is up to them to accept a judicial notice "as conclusive".

The second exception to the need of proof are *presumptions*, which is "a legal practice whereby a court accepts the existence of one fact from the existence of another fact that has already been proven".[526] There are two classifications of presumptions; the first of which are divided into rebuttable and conclusive presumptions. Rebuttable presumptions are those, where the party affected by it may produce evidence to contradict the presumption in question. This is the case when a person who has gone missing for various years is considered to be deceased, and the opposing party introduces evidence of the said person's whereabouts. Conversely, conclusive presumptions are those in which the parties may not introduce evidence to contradict it. A case in point is the presumption of knowledge of the law; if this presumption were rebuttable, it would be nearly impossible to convict criminal defendants who claim that they were not aware that the conduct for which they are facing trial was illegal.

The second classification of presumptions is divided into presumptions of law and presumptions of facts. On the one hand, presumptions of law are those that the law mandates the jurors to regard a fact as true from the beginning of the trial, as for example, the presumption of innocence. Since this presumption is rebuttable, if the prosecution has a strong case and can prove to the jury beyond a reasonable doubt that the defendant is in fact guilty, the jury may rebut this presumption. On the other hand, presumptions of facts are those that appear in the course of the trial as each party presents their respective case.[527]

---

[523] *Thompson* et al., An Introduction, p. 88.
[524] FRE 201(c).
[525] FRE 201(e).
[526] *Thompson* et al., An Introduction, p. 98.
[527] *Thompson* et al., An Introduction, p. 100.

The third alternative to formal proof are *inferences*, which occur when a jury deduces a fact to be true due to the deduction of a previous fact that has already been proven to be true. Although inferences are similar to presumptions, there are marked differences between them; the most important of which is that presumptions are mandatory, whereas inferences are not. The second difference is that while the court may control presumptions, inferences are virtually incontrollable due to them being the result of the thought processes of each individual juror.[528]

The last exception to the need of proof are the *accepted stipulations*, which are agreements where both parties concur that a fact or facts are true. Stipulations save the jurors a large amount of time, owing to them not having to decide on matters that are not essential to factfinding.[529]

III. Types of Evidence

1. Testimonial Evidence: Defendant, Witnesses and Expert Witnesses

Testimonial evidence is the oral testimony by witnesses at open court,[530] which are either direct or circumstantial. There are three types of witnesses: (i) *lay witnesses*, which are people who have personal knowledge of the facts of the case, (ii) the *defendant* whenever he chooses to testify at court,[531] and (iii) *expert witnesses*, which are people who may testify owing to their "knowledge, skill, experience, training or education".[532] Among the many rights conferred to witnesses, the most important of them is the right against self-incrimination, set out by the Fifth Amendment to the Constitution.[533] However, one particularity of this right in regard to the defendant is that if she chooses to take the stand, she is automatically waiving her right to silence. For this reason, during the defendant's examination, when she is subject to cross-examination by the opposing party, the defendant may not raise her right to silence, due to having waived it by choosing to testify.

a) Witness Competency

Pursuant to FRE 601, "every person is competent to be a witness unless the FRE provide otherwise". Therefore, unlike the restrictions common law historically imposed on certain groups of people, the FRE impose no such limitations. Hence, certain groups of people, i.e., those with possible mental incapacity, children, the

---

[528] *Thompson* et al., An Introduction, p. 99.
[529] *Thompson* et al., An Introduction, p. 108.
[530] FRCP 26.
[531] *LaFave* et al., Criminal Procedure, p. 1395; *Graham*, FRE in a Nutshell, p. 249.
[532] FRE 702.
[533] *Thompson* et al., An Introduction, p. 184.

defendant's spouse, people convicted of committing crimes, and personal and/or religious beliefs cannot be an impediment for a person to be a witness at trial.[534]

The decision whether a person is competent to be a witness is up to the trial judge, who usually has great discretion to decide this matter on a case-by-case basis. If a party wishes to present a witness, it is their responsibility to prove to the court that the person in question is competent.[535] If the court deems necessary, it may question the potential witness and order a psychological or psychiatric examination.[536] However, as a rule, courts tend to allow witnesses to testify.[537] Once the trial judge deems a witness competent to testify, it is up to the jurors to decide the amount of weight and credibility they will give to the witness's testimony.

For a judge to deem a witness competent, there are four requirements that must be met, which are applicable to all witnesses. First, the witness must have *personal knowledge* of the event.[538] This does not mean that the witness must have perceived the facts of the case in its entirety; however, she must have personal knowledge of facts that are relevant to the case. Further, it is not necessary for the witness to have known at the time she perceived the facts that a criminal offense was taking place and that these facts could later be helpful in shedding light on the matter.

The second and third requisites are that the witness must have the ability to both *recollect* what happened and to *communicate* these facts to the trier of fact. Thus, if there are any mental or physical reasons that hinder a person from recalling or communicating to the trier of fact what took place, this person cannot be deemed competent to testify.

Fourth, witnesses must *take an oath or make an affirmation* before they take the stand, by which they declare that they will tell the truth.[539] The slight difference between them is that an oath is a declaration based on religious beliefs ascertaining that the witness will testify truthfully and declares the legal consequences of not doing so. In contrast, an affirmation has no religious implications and is a consequence of the First Amendment to the Constitution, which lays out the freedom of religion, or a lack thereof. For this reason, an affirmation must merely convey the witness's commitment in telling the truth and that the person in question is aware of the legal consequences of failing to do so. There are instances when a simplified version of an oath or an affirmation will suffice, as is the case when people with mental disabilities or children take the stand. In these instances, the trial judge must

---

[534] *Thompson* et al., An Introduction, p. 118.

[535] *Thompson* et al., An Introduction, p. 118.

[536] *Graham*, FRE in a Nutshell, pp. 229, 230.

[537] As a rule, the higher courts usually uphold the court's decision unless there is proof that the trial judge abused her discretionary powers or that there was plain error. In this sense, see *Gardner/Anderson*, Criminal Evidence, p. 128.

[538] FRE 602.

[539] FRE 603.

make sure that the person in question understands the importance of telling the truth and that there will be consequences if she fails to do so.

b) Examination of Witnesses

The parties may examine witnesses by means of direct and cross-examination. As a rule, each party examines their own witnesses by means of direct examination, i.e., by asking them either general or specific questions. The former questions are usually open-ended questions, to which the witness will answer by narrating the facts to the best of their knowledge, whereas the latter questions are those concerning particular facts.[540] The decision on whether to ask a general or a specific question is left to the party examining the witness, as the law makes no distinction between them.[541] In practice, however, general questions are not the preferred way to examine a witness, as they are too open and unpredictable and consequently any information can come up. As the aim of the parties during examination is to control the witness as to control the evidence that is presented to the jury, usually the parties ask the witnesses specific questions.[542]

After the party that called the witness directly examines her, the opposing party may cross-examine the witness in question. The importance of cross-examination is that a party may then examine the testimony and credibility of a witness with the intent of unearthing inconsistencies, untruthfulness, and omissions in their statements. To this end, a party may cross-examine the opposing party's witness by means of leading questions. As the name implies, these are questions that lead the witness to answer in a way that the examining party wishes to hear.[543]

As a rule, a party may not ask their own witnesses leading questions, unless the witness in question is deemed hostile or unresponsive,[544] or when they need help in developing their testimony. The latter may take place when the witness is either having difficulty to remember the facts, is nervous or afraid, has physical or mental problems, or is a child.[545]

Regarding the subject matter of cross-examination by means of leading questions, FRE 611(b) sets out that these questions "should not go beyond the subject matter of the direct examination and matters affecting the witness's credibility". Thus, if the prosecution wishes to examine the defense's witness on additional matters, it may do so by means of direct examination.

---

[540] *Graham*, Evidence, p. 58.
[541] *Kaye* et al., McCormick, p. 23.
[542] *Pizzi*, Trials without Truth, p. 127.
[543] *Graham*, Evidence, p. 59.
[544] FRE 611(c)(2).
[545] *Graham*, Evidence, p. 61.

aa) Credibility and Rehabilitation of Witnesses

As seen above, the weight and credibility to be given to a witness's testimony is up to the jurors to decide. For this reason, the witness's credibility is crucial to a party's case, as it conveys to the jurors the likelihood that the witness will testify in a truthful manner. Conversely, an important piece of evidence or fact of the case may not be conveyed to the jury if the jurors do not believe that the witness is truthful.

Graham defines credibility as "dependent upon the willingness of the witness to tell the truth and upon her ability to do so".[546] For this reason, it is a good tactic for a party to discredit the opposing party's witness with the aim of hampering their case. A means of doing so is by a technique of cross-examination called impeachment, by which a party tests the opposing witness's credibility.[547] This technique has the intent to show to the factfinder that the witness has, i.a., eventual biases, given prior inconsistent statements, defects of competence (in perceiving, recollecting, and communicating the facts of the case), and by showing evidence of a witness's previous criminal conviction.

Once a witness has been impeached by the opposing party, the party calling the witness may seek to rehabilitate him by bolstering his credibility. For this reason, as a rule, a party may only attest to a "witness's character for truthfulness after it has been attacked".[548]

Due to the importance of this topic in shaping the US-American trial setting and in being one of the mechanisms of safeguarding the defendant's Sixth Amendment Confrontation Clause,[549] I will now examine the circumstances in which a party may impeach a witness. First, it is important to distinguish whether the matter being impeached is collateral or not collateral to the case. If the matter is collateral to the case, the party may not introduce extrinsic evidence to rebut the witness's testimony and must accept the answer given by the witness. In contrast, if the matter is not collateral to the case, the party impeaching the witness may introduce extrinsic evidence to contradict her testimony.[550]

bb) Impeachment of Witnesses

A party may either impeach their own witness or impeach the opposing party's witness. The latter type of impeachment may take place in a variety of instances, such as impeaching the opposing party's witness for (i) bias or prejudice, (ii) previous criminal convictions, (iii) character, (iv) inconsistent statements, (v) the inability to

---

[546] *Graham*, FRE in a Nutshell, p. 247.

[547] *Gardner/Anderson*, Criminal Evidence, p. 127; *Graham*, FRE in a Nutshell, p. 249.

[548] FRE 608(a). In this sense, see *Ingram*, Criminal Evidence, pp. 363, 364; *Graham*, FRE in a Nutshell, p. 267.

[549] See infra Ch. 2 D. I. 3.

[550] *Graham*, FRE in a Nutshell, p. 249.

perceive or recall events, and (vi) using the defendant's prior confession for impeachment purposes.

As a rule, a party may impeach its own witness in two circumstances.[551] The first is when a witness testifies to something the party calling him could not foresee, as for example, the witness contradicts its prior testimony or says something that might be prejudicial to the case. In these instances, the party calling the witness is justified in impeaching him, as a means of trying to minimize the damage made by the witness's testimony. The second reason is in cases when it is preferable for a party to impeach its own witness than to wait for the opposing party to do so by means of cross-examination.[552] This can be illustrated either when a witness receives a "favorable treatment" by the prosecution for testifying, or when the witness has a criminal conviction, or yet, when he might have a bias in favor of or against the defendant.[553] In such cases, it is preferable for the jury to hear this information from the party who called the witness rather than by the opposing counsel.[554]

(i) As to impeaching the opposing party's witness, either the defense or the prosecution may do so when there is reason to believe that the witness has a *bias in favor of or against* the defendant. This is because the witness's stance toward the defendant or its relationship with him will have a bearing on its testimony, and thus, the jury must be aware of these factors when determining whether to believe the witness under examination.

(ii) A party may also impeach a witness by evidence of a criminal conviction.[555] As this regards non-collateral matters, if the witness in question denies having a prior conviction, the party impeaching her may introduce extrinsic evidence to contradict this statement.[556] However, there are three limitations to impeaching a witness for a criminal conviction; the first is regarding the severity of the said conviction. For the trial judge to admit the witness's conviction, the crime should be punishable by death or by imprisonment, which exceeds one year. When the witness in question is the defendant, as a rule, her conviction may only be admitted if the trial judge rules that its probative value outweighs its prejudicial effect.[557] Nevertheless, a criminal conviction is to be admitted regardless of the amount of the years of imprisonment regarding crimes, which involve dishonest or false statements. The reasoning for this

---

[551] FRE 607.

[552] *Thompson* et al., An Introduction, p. 159.

[553] According to *Graham* (*Graham*, FRE in a Nutshell, p. 301) "this process was never treated as impeachment of a party's own witness, but rather as anticipatory disclosure designed to reduce the prejudicial effect of the evidence if revealed for the first time on cross-examination".

[554] *Graham*, FRE in a Nutshell, p. 301.

[555] FRE 609.

[556] *Graham*, FRE in a Nutshell, p. 281.

[557] FRE 609(a)(1)(B). I examine the instances where the court must conduct a balancing test between the probative value and the prejudicial effects of a proffered piece of evidence in Ch. 2 C. IV. 2. a).

is that these crimes are relevant in showing to the jury the witness's lack of credibility.[558]

The second limitation to presenting evidence of a witness's criminal conviction is if the conviction dates back to more than ten years. In such cases, for this evidence to be admissible, the party impeaching the witness must show that the probative value of the evidence outweighs its prejudicial effects. Further, the party that wants to introduce this evidence must present the opposing party written notice of its intention to present the witness's criminal conviction at trial. The last limitation to this rule is that the opposing party may not present evidence of a witness's criminal conviction, if he has been subjected to pardon, annulment, or certificate of rehabilitation.

(iii) A party may attack a previous witness's character by presenting the testimony of the "witness's reputation for having a character for truthfulness of untruthfulness, or by testimony in the form of an opinion about that character".[559] The term given to a person presenting the testimony in question is called a character witness. When a character witness testifies regarding the reputation of the witness being impeached, he must have previously discussed with other people regarding the witness's reputation, or he must have been present at these discussions. Therefore, it is not necessary for the character witness to have had direct contact with the witness being impeached. However, a character witness that testifies in the form of an opinion to discredit a witness must have had direct contact with the said witness.[560] Regardless of whether a party presents testimony of a witness's reputation for having a character for truthfulness or untruthfulness or in the form of an opinion about his character, impeaching a witness for character is usually a collateral matter.[561] In this sense, FRE 608(b) sets out that extrinsic evidence "to prove specific instances of the witness's conduct" is not admissible.[562]

(iv) When a witness makes inconsistent statements, i.e., saying something and later contradicting it, the jurors might not know whether the first or the second statement is true, or yet, if either of them is true.[563] In such cases, the party may impeach the witness, as this has a bearing on demonstrating to the jury that the witness in question is not truthful.

(v) An important tactic in questioning a witness's truthfulness is to impeach a witness's ability to perceive or recall events. A case in point is when a witness attests to having seen the defendant on the night of the crime and the party conducting the examination is able to prove that the witness has a severely impaired vision. As a result, the party may then prove to the factfinder that the witness could not have

---

[558] FRE 609(a)(2).
[559] FRE 608(a).
[560] *Graham*, FRE in a Nutshell, pp. 280, 281.
[561] *Graham*, FRE in a Nutshell, p. 272.
[562] FRE 608(b). However, this does not apply to criminal convictions under FRE 609.
[563] *Roberson/Winters*, Evidence for Criminal Justice, p. 192; *Ingram*, Criminal Evidence, p. 357.

properly recognized the person who, for example, committed a crime that took place on a rainy and cloudy night. This fact would have a bearing regarding the witness's competence to testify, seeing that she was not able to clearly perceive the events in question.

(vi) If the defendant chooses to take the stand and denies having committed the criminal offense for which she is standing trial, the prosecution may use her prior confession to impeach her testimony. This is because denying the commission of a crime is not a collateral matter, and thus, the prosecution may introduce extrinsic evidence to contradict the defendant's testimony.[564] However, for the defendant's prior confession to be admissible at trial, it must have been made freely and voluntarily.[565]

2. Real Evidence: Documentary and Demonstrative Evidence

Real evidence refers to any physical evidence and comprises both documentary and demonstrative evidence. Documentary evidence usually encompasses a vast array of evidence, i.e., conventional written documents, such as contracts, certificates, and letters, text messages, emails, documents saved on cloud, and messages on social media. In contrast, demonstrative evidence, is that which helps the jury to understand the circumstances of the crime, such as photos of the crime scene, diagrams, charts, and taking the jury to visit the crime scene.

Real evidence is considered to be the most "persuasive type of evidence",[566] as it lacks subjectivity, as opposed to oral evidence, which is totally dependent on the subjectivity of the person giving testimony. As to their admissibility, real evidence usually follows the same rules applicable to testimonial evidence. Nonetheless, there are two features which are peculiar to real evidence, namely authentication and the best evidence rule.

Authentication is the verification of whether a purported piece of evidence is what its proponent claims it to be. It is of particular importance for the admissibility of written documents in the broad sense of the term,[567] Pursuant to FRE 901(a), to verify the authenticity of a document, "the proponent must produce evidence sufficient to support a finding that the item is what the proponent claims it is". This is the case, when, for example, a party claims a document is authentic, while the opposing party claims it to be a forgery. When making a decision regarding the admissibility of the evidence in question, the trial judge must solely verify whether the evidence presented shows that the item is what the proponent claims it to be and that the jury

---

[564] This is not the only instance where the prosecution may introduce the defendant's prior confession at trial; see infra Ch. 2 C. IV. 2. e); *Schäuble*, Strafverfahren und Prozessverantwortung, p. 374.

[565] *Ingram*, Criminal Evidence, p. 361.

[566] *Thompson* et al., An Introduction, p. 234.

[567] *Thompson* et al., An Introduction, pp. 213, 243.

would also find the evidence to be authentic.⁵⁶⁸ This is because the authenticity of a piece of evidence does not have to be exhaustively proven as the decision of whether it is defective and the weight to be given to the evidence is up to the jury to decide.⁵⁶⁹

The *best evidence rule* is a "rule of preference" in which an original piece of evidence is preferable to the presentation of secondary evidence. This rule is also termed "Documentary Originals Rule".⁵⁷⁰ As the name suggests, it only applies to contents of written documents in the broad sense of the word. As a result, this rule is not applicable to demonstrative evidence. Usually, the best evidence rule applies in two situations; either when a party introduces a piece of evidence and the opposing party disputes its content, or when a witness must remember the contents of a document.⁵⁷¹ In these cases, owing to non-original documents being deemed less trustworthy due to the risk of them being falsified or altered,⁵⁷² there is a preference for the parties to present original evidence at trial. However, this rule is not applicable when the content of a piece of evidence is not under dispute, or when the parties make a stipulation regarding the contents of the item in question.⁵⁷³

There are two main differences between authentication and the best evidence rule. First, while the former has the aim of verifying whether a proffered item is genuine, the latter only applies when the content of an item is under dispute, and thus, it is necessary for the party presenting the item to furnish the original copy of the documentary evidence.⁵⁷⁴ Second, the responsibility in deciding the weight to be given to a piece of evidence differs between them. On the one hand, the decision of authentication is up to the jurors to decide, i.e., it is up to the jurors to decide whether they believe a document to be authentic, as the trial judge must only verify if the piece of evidence is what the proponent claims it to be. On the other hand, the best evidence rule is a matter of judicial competence, i.e., the trial judge must verify whether the proffered piece of evidence is in fact an original.⁵⁷⁵

---

[568] *Thompson* et al., An Introduction, p. 214.
[569] *Ingram*, Criminal Evidence, p. 564.
[570] *Thompson* et al., An Introduction, pp. 223, 224.
[571] *Thompson* et al., An Introduction, p. 223.
[572] *Ingram*, Criminal Evidence, p. 587.
[573] *Thompson* et al., An Introduction, p. 232.
[574] *Thompson* et al., An Introduction, p. 224.
[575] *Thompson* et al., An Introduction, p. 233.

IV. Admissibility of Evidence

1. Admissibility of Evidence and Rationale Behind Limiting or Excluding Evidence

As per FRE 402, relevant evidence is admissible unless the Federal Constitution, a federal statute, the FRE or other rules prescribed by the Supreme Court provide otherwise. Therefore, all relevant evidence is admissible except when a "rule or interpretation" expressly states differently.[576] For evidence to be relevant, FRE 401 lays out that it must both have "any tendency to make a fact more or less probable than it would be without the evidence" and that "the fact is of consequence in determining the action". As previously seen, the decision concerning the admissibility and exclusion of evidence at trial of the trial judge's responsibility, whereas the decision regarding the probative value to be given to a proffered item of evidence is left to the jury to decide.

When the court makes a ruling admitting or excluding evidence, either the prosecution or the defense may claim error in this ruling.[577] To preserve a claim of error for appeal, this error must affect a substantial right of the party. Moreover, there are some requirements that must be met depending on whether a claim of error concerns the admission or the exclusion of evidence. If a party believes that the court admitted improper evidence, it must timely object to its admission and specifically state the grounds for objecting to the evidence in question.[578] Conversely, if the court makes a ruling excluding a party's proffered evidence, the affected party must make an offer of proof indicating the exact content the evidence seeks to prove.[579] However, regardless of the court having admitted or excluded evidence, if the court makes a definite ruling on the record, the affected party "need not renew an objection or offer of proof to preserve a claim of error for appeal".[580]

There are two main reasons for limiting or excluding otherwise admissible evidence. First, because of the adversarial trial setting, there are instances when admitting a proffered piece of evidence may hinder the search for the truth rather than advance it.[581] As the factfinders are, as a rule, a group of lay people, the presentation of evidence must be previously sifted, so that only evidence that is relevant and material may reach the jury. Accordingly, "many of the provisions in the FRE are

---

[576] *Ingram*, Criminal Evidence, p. 215.

[577] There are three types of error: harmless error, prejudicial/reversible error, and plain error. The former does not affect a party's substantial right, whereas prejudicial error and plain error do. The difference between the latter is that prejudicial error is only taken into consideration by the appellate court if a claim of error was preserved for appeal, whereas plain error may be taken into consideration by an appellate court even if the party affected did not preserve a claim owing to the error in question affecting the fundamental integrity and fairness of the trial.

[578] FRE 103(a)(1).

[579] FRE 103(a)(2); *Weinstein/Berger*, Student Edition, § 2.03[4] (2–28).

[580] FRE 103(b).

[581] *Weinstein/Berger*, Student Edition, § 1.01[2][b] (1–4)(1–5).

C. Evidence Law

designed to increase the likelihood of accurate determinations".[582] However, there are instances, where it does not suffice for the evidence to be relevant and material. In addition, the evidence must not risk "confusing and bringing confusion"[583] to the factfinder and, therefore, it is necessary to verify whether the evidence is really that which its proponent claims it to be. Such is the case regarding many aspects of witness testimony, such as witness competency and credibility, the admissibility of hearsay, and issues concerning the admissibility of real evidence, such as the best evidence rule and – to a certain extent – authentication.

Second, although ascertaining the truth is an important aim of evidence law,[584] depending on the circumstances of a specific case other aims must prevail due to various extrinsic policies.[585] These extrinsic policies may have either a constitutional or a statutory basis. An illustration of a statutory limitation is privilege, as it seeks to preserve interests and relationships, such as marital harmony, and the trust between a patient and her psychotherapist. In contrast, an example of a constitutional reason is set out in the Fourth Amendment to the Constitution, which aims to protect the accused from unreasonable searches and seizures, and thus seeks to discourage and deter the police from obtaining evidence in an illegal manner.

2. Statutory and Constitutional Rules Excluding or Limiting Evidence

a) Probative Value v. Prejudicial Effects

FRE 403 sets out that "the court may exclude relevant evidence if its probative value is substantially outweighed by a danger of one or more of the following" prejudicial effects. The importance of this rule is that, as in principle, all relevant evidence is admissible, FRE 403 is a means in which to counter the flow of evidence and give the trial judge a "generalized option"[586] to exclude otherwise relevant evidence.[587] By relevant evidence, this rule is applicable to all types of evidence, i.e., both direct and circumstantial evidence on the one side, and testimonial and real evidence on the other side.[588]

Therefore, the court must conduct a balancing test where the probative value of the proffered evidence is weighed against its prejudicial effects.[589] Due to the preference of the FRE towards the admissibility of evidence over its exclusion, the court should

---

[582] *Weinstein/Berger*, Student Edition, § 1.01[2][b] (1–4)(1–5).
[583] *Weinstein/Berger*, Student Edition, § 1.01[2][b] (1–4)(1–5).
[584] FRE 102.
[585] *Weinstein/Berger*, Student Edition, § 1.01[2][b] (1–4)(1–5).
[586] *Graham*, Evidence, p. 26.
[587] *Gold*, Federal Rules of Evidence 403, p. 497.
[588] *Weinstein/Berger*, Student Edition, § 6.02[1] (6–18).
[589] As per FRE 609(a)(2), the only exception to this rule is concerning impeachment by evidence of a criminal conviction proving a dishonest act or false statement.

make this balancing test by conferring the maximum amount of probative value to a proffered item of evidence, while evaluating the minimum amount of prejudicial effects to its admission.[590] When balancing these two weights, the evaluation may entail one or various prejudicial effects.[591] The court does not necessarily need to state on record its reasoning behind the balance, but rather, it must be inferred that such a balancing test occurred.[592] As is usually the case regarding the court's ruling on evidentiary matters, – particularly concerning the admission and exclusion of evidence – this decision is usually upheld by the appellate courts due to the great level of subjectivity and the contextual nature of these decisions.

The balancing test of FRE 403 is distinct from the analysis of whether proffered evidence is admissible under FRE 401.[593] In the latter, the court must simply analyze whether it considers the evidence to be relevant and material, whereas in the former, the court's assessment involves other considerations. Among these considerations are (i) whether there are alternatives to the proffered evidence, (ii) the importance of this item of evidence to the proponent's case, and (iii) eventually whether a limiting instruction would suffice in lessening its prejudicial effects.[594]

FRE 403 sets out the "prejudicial effects", stating that these are "unfair prejudice, confusing the issues, misleading the jury, undue delay, wasting time, and needlessly presenting cumulative evidence".[595] Regarding the first prejudicial effect of *unfair prejudice*, it is to be expected, that evidence presented by a party is prejudicial to the opposing side. For this reason, for the exclusion of a piece of evidence to be warranted, it must be unfairly prejudicial, i.e., evidence which "has a tendency to suggest decision on an improper basis, (...) such as bias, sympathy, hatred, contempt, retribution or horror".[596] In these instances, the jurors may find the defendant guilty or not guilty solely based on the effect this evidence had on them,[597] which would lead the jury to base their decision on emotional rather than rational reasons.

As seen on conducting this balancing test, the court must assess whether a party has evidentiary alternatives to the proffered evidence that are less prejudicial. If that is not the case, the evidence in question will rarely be excluded.[598] This is better exemplified regarding demonstrative evidence when it comes to photos or recordings of a victim of a violent crime. In these cases, federal courts usually allow the presentation of this type of evidence.[599] However, the court must consider the number of

---

[590] *Weinstein/Berger*, Student Edition, § 6.02[2] (6–23).
[591] *Graham*, Evidence, p. 26.
[592] *Weinstein/Berger*, Student Edition, § 6.02[2] (6–21).
[593] *Weinstein/Berger*, Student Edition, § 6.02[1] (6–22).
[594] *Graham*, Evidence, p. 27.
[595] FRE 403.
[596] *Graham*, Evidence, p. 27.
[597] *Ingram*, Criminal Evidence, p. 218.
[598] *Weinstein/Berger*, Student Edition, § 6.02 (6–24).
[599] *Weinstein/Berger*, Student Edition, § 6.02 (6–24).

photos the party wishes to present, whether they are black and white or in color, and the reasoning behind wishing to present them to the factfinder.

The second and third prejudicial effects, which can be arranged into the same group due to its similarity are *confusing the issues* and *misleading the jury*. Both these effects could distract the jury from the matter at hand and could either lead the jurors to a wrongful conclusion or cause them to overvalue the probative value of proffered evidence.[600] Hence, the admissibility of such evidence would confuse and mislead the jury rather than help it reach an informed decision.[601]

The last prejudicial effects are *undue delay, waste of time, and needless presentation of cumulative evidence*. These three prejudicial effects have a similar reasoning, i.e., time considerations; if such evidence were admissible, it would result in the trial being unduly delayed. The needless presentation of cumulative evidence may in a sense, be considered as a waste of time, as it occurs when a party persists in introducing evidence to support the veracity of a fact, despite it having been previously proven. Such is the case of presenting numerous witnesses who testify to the same events and all of them are corroborating each other's perceptions and repeatedly narrating the same events.

b) Privilege Against Compulsory Self-Incrimination

The Fifth Amendment to the Constitution provides that no one "shall be compelled in any criminal case to be a witness against himself", thus establishing the defendant's constitutional right against self-incrimination and coerced confessions.

The Miranda warnings are an extension to the right against self-incrimination in the pretrial phase. In *Miranda v. Arizona*,[602] the Supreme Court held that the police must instruct the defendant of her Miranda rights prior to interrogating her. This warning must inform the suspect of her right to remain silent, to have legal counsel present, and if she cannot afford to retain one, that she may have counsel appointed to her. The Supreme Court established that there are two instances when the police must instruct the defendant of these rights, namely (i) whenever a suspect is in custody or has her freedom circumscribed by the police and (ii) whenever the police wish to interrogate the suspect "with a view to obtaining incriminating statements".[603] If these two conditions are present and the police fails to instruct the defendant of these

---

[600] *Graham*, Evidence, p. 28; *Ingram*, Criminal Evidence, p. 222.

[601] *Ingram*, Criminal Evidence, p. 220. Additionally, if the trial judge were to remedy these effects by having to give lengthy judicial instructions about the admissibility of this evidence, the probative value of the proffered evidence would be outweighed by these prejudicial effects. In this sense, see *Weinstein/Berger*, Student Edition, § 6.02 (6–30) (6–32).

[602] *Miranda v. Arizona*, 384 U.S. 436 (1966).

[603] *Ingram*, Criminal Evidence, p. 774.

rights, anything the defendant says in these circumstances will not be admissible as evidence at trial.[604]

At trial, as per the privilege against compulsory self-incrimination, the defendant is not obliged to take the stand and the prosecution may not infer to the jury that the defendant is guilty due to not wanting to testify.[605] Whenever the defendant chooses to testify, he may only do so after the prosecution established a prima facie case, i.e., after the defendant has heard all the evidence and witnesses against her. This feature furthers the standpoint of the defendant's examination as a means of defense, as it increases the defendant's chances to defend herself of the specific charges and of the evidence presented against her.[606]

There are two limitations to the right against self-incrimination. First, if the defendant chooses to waive this right and takes the stand, she may not choose to answer some questions while invoking her right against self-incrimination regarding the specific questions she does not wish to answer. Further, when the defendant takes the stand, she must take an oath to swear to tell the truth, and as a result, if she lies while testifying, the defendant might be liable for perjury. Second, the defendant's right against self-incrimination is only applicable to testimonial evidence.[607] Consequently, the defendant does not have a corresponding right regarding physical evidence, such as writing samples, showing a part of her body, being photographed or fingerprinted, participating in line-ups, and providing a DNA sample.[608]

c) Search and Seizure

Pursuant to the Fourth Amendment to the Constitution people should be secure "in their persons, houses, papers and effects against unreasonable searches and seizures" and that a warrant can only be issued upon probable cause "particularly describing the place to be searched and the persons or things to be seized". Although the wording of this Amendment does not specify who a person is protected from, it has been interpreted to mean that people are to be protected against the actions of the government.[609] In the context of a criminal investigation, this Amendment's main rationale is to discourage the police from obtaining evidence in an illegal way. This is achieved by sanctioning illegal actions by means of this exclusionary rule. In other words, evidence obtained in violation of the Fourth Amendment to the Constitution

---

[604] *Graham*, Evidence, p. 9. An exception to this prohibition is if the defendant chooses to take the stand at trial and ends up contradicting himself. In this sense see supra Ch. 2 C. III. 1. b) bb).

[605] *Whitebread/Slobogin*, Criminal Procedure, p. 874; *Saltzburg/Capra*, American Criminal Procedure, p. 1081.

[606] *Damaška*, Evidentiary Barriers to Conviction, p. 528.

[607] *Ingram*, Criminal Evidence, p. 770.

[608] *Thompson* et al., An Introduction, p. 234.

[609] *Saltzburg/Capra*, American Criminal Procedure, p. 38.

will not be admissible at trial. By excluding the said evidence, this may have very serious consequences to a criminal case, which may even lead to the charges being dismissed.[610] The gravity of the consequence of evidence gathered in violation to this Amendment is to further the aim of deterring the police from acting in an unconstitutional manner.

d) Privilege

Privileges are specific instances when a witness has the right to refuse to testify and the specific instances when a person can keep a witness from testifying.[611] Contrary to the majority of the rules of evidence, privilege is not limited to the trial phase, and applies to all stages of the criminal procedure.[612] The reasoning behind this is that although the finding of truth is one of the main aims of the procedure, there are other aims that are just as important and that, at times, must prevail. Thus, there are interests and relationships that are more important than the admissibility of relevant evidence, e.g., protecting certain types of relationships, such as those between husband and wife. For this reason, privilege may bar a witness from being compelled to testify not for reasons such as lack of authenticity or bias, but rather due to the aim of protecting certain interests and relationships.

Initially the Supreme Court promulgated thirteen rules addressing privileges.[613] However, Congress discarded this catalogue due to not wishing that these rules massively prevented the admissibility of otherwise admissible evidence and hindered the finding of truth.[614] As a result, precedent will govern the claims of privilege except for the instances set out in FRE 501, i.e., when prescribed in the "the United States Constitution; a federal statute; or rules prescribed by the Supreme Court". As to the proposed rules to the FRE, which were not adopted, Congress has adopted them as "standards", i.e., as a means to help the courts in deciding whether privilege is applicable in criminal cases.[615] These standards are flexible enough to permit federal courts to develop new privileges, to change existing ones, and – apart from three existing privileges[616] – to determine on a case-by-case basis whether privilege rules are applicable. Thus, courts make this determination by balancing the interests of the

---

[610] *Whitebread/Slobogin*, Criminal Procedure, p. 19.

[611] *Thompson* et al., An Introduction, p. 281.

[612] FRE 1001(c).

[613] *Weinstein/Berger*, Student Edition, § 18.02[1] (18–3).

[614] *Broun*, Giving Codification a Second Chance, pp. 769, 770; *Weinstein/Berger*, Student Edition, § 18.02[1] (18–3).

[615] *Broun*, Giving Codification a Second Chance, p. 770; *Weinstein/Berger*, Student Edition, § 18.02[3] (18–9). These "standards" are also called Supreme Court standards.

[616] Apart from three established privileges, i.e., attorney-client-, psychotherapist patient- and marital privileges.

admissibility of the evidence and its probative value, on the one side, and the interest of keeping such evidence confidential, on the other side.[617]

To illustrate this topic, I will briefly analyze the three privileges that are not determined on a case-by-case basis. To this end, I will examine both the FRE 502 and the standards Congress adopted as a foundation for federal courts to analyze the matter.

The first privilege is the *attorney-client privilege*, which is set out both in FRE 502 and in Standard 503.[618] This privilege protects the communications held between a client and her attorney,[619] as the reasoning behind it is to encourage clients to communicate freely with their attorneys, without fear of being compelled to disclose the content of their conversations at trial.[620] If it were not for this type of privilege, clients would not receive proper counsel, and the defendant's right to counsel in criminal proceedings would be void.

Pursuant to Standard 503(a)(4), communication is confidential whenever the client believes she is only communicating with her attorney or those that "are in rendition of legal services". Therefore, if the client choses to reveal the content of the said communications to a third party, confidentially between the client and her attorney is void and the privilege is deemed to be waived. Standard 503(c) provides that both the client and the attorney have the claim of the privilege, although the latter only has this claim "on behalf of the client".

The second case is the *psychotherapist-patient privilege*, which is laid out in Standard 504 and has "considerable force",[621] due to being cited by the Supreme Court.[622] The reasoning behind this privilege is to enable people to feel at ease to seek psychiatric or psychological treatment. The rationale applied to this privilege is the same as that of the attorney-client privilege, i.e., if a person were compelled to disclose the content of confidential communications between her and her physician, the social costs would be higher than that of finding the truth. The meaning conferred to confidential communications applies when the patient believes that the conversation being held is restricted to her and her physician. As per standard 504(c), the privilege may be claimed by the patient, or by the psychotherapist who may do so on behalf of their patients.[623]

---

[617] *Weinstein/Berger*, Student Edition, § 18.02[3] (18–10), (18–11).

[618] *Weinstein/Berger*, Student Edition, § 18.03 (18–22).

[619] The criteria for being a lawyer are subjective rather than objective, what is decisive is that the client is either speaking to a lawyer or she believes the person she is talking to is a member of the bar.

[620] *Weinstein/Berger*, Student Edition, § 18.03[1] (18–22).

[621] *Weinstein/Berger*, Student Edition, § 18.04[1] (18–47).

[622] *Klein*, Psychotherapist-Patient Privilege, p. 701.

[623] By psychotherapist, according to Standard 504 (a)(2) this is "a person authorized to practice medicine" or "a person licensed or certified as a psychologist". *Weinstein/Berger*, Student Edition, § 18.04[1] (18–50).

The third type of privilege is the *marital privilege*, which has two different facets, i.e., it applies to both testimonial privilege and to confidential marital communications. These two privileges differ regarding both their rationale and who has claim to it. The testimonial privilege regards to "all testimony against a spouse on any subject, including non-confidential matters"[624] and applies during the union of a valid marriage. Once the marriage has ended, it is no longer applicable.[625] In this type of spousal privilege, the Supreme Court vested the privilege in the spouse who is called as a witness; hence, it is up to the witness to decide whether to testify. Conversely, the confidential marital communications privilege persists after the dissolution of marriage. This is because the rationale behind this privilege is that communications between husband and wife should be fostered and encouraged, and for this reason, either spouse may claim the privilege.[626]

e) Hearsay

FRE 801(c) sets out the definition of hearsay, which is when (i) a declarant makes an out-of-court statement that is witnessed by a person, who testifies to its contents at trial, or (ii) a "written or recorded statement of an out-of-court declarant",[627] which is introduced at trial.[628] Pursuant to FRE 801(a), a statement is "a person's oral assertion, written assertion, or nonverbal conduct, if the person intended it as an assertion", whereas FRE 801(b) provides that declarant is "the person who made the statement".

Contrary to FRE 401, which lays out that all relevant evidence is admissible unless stated otherwise; FRE 802 states that hearsay is not admissible unless a federal statute, the FRE, or rules prescribed by the Supreme Court provides otherwise.[629] The reasoning for this rule is because hearsay evidence is considered to be untrustworthy.

As previously examined,[630] there are four requirements to witness competency. Three of these requisites must be taken into consideration in assessing whether the witness is apt to testify, i.e., original perception of the events, and recollection and ability to communicate the said events to the trier of fact.[631] Even if all these requirements are fulfilled, there are still risks to testimonial evidence. In seeking to mitigate the risks that are inherent to this evidence, three conditions must be met to increase the odds that a witness's testimony will be truthful, and to enable the parties

---

[624] *Weinstein/Berger*, Student Edition, § 18.05 (18–67) (18–68).

[625] *Thompson* et al., An Introduction, p. 119.

[626] *Weinstein/Berger*, Student Edition, § 18.05 (18–67) (18–68).

[627] Written or recorded out-of-court statements are subject to FRE 1002. See *Graham*, Evidence, p. 78.

[628] *Graham*, Evidence, p. 86.

[629] *Weinstein/Berger*, Student Edition, § 14.02[1] (14–4).

[630] See supra Ch. 2 C. III. 1. a).

[631] *Graham*, Evidence, pp. 83, 84.

in finding eventual inconsistencies or mistakes in their testimony. These conditions are that the witness:[632] (i) must make an in-court statement, i.e., that she must testify at trial, (ii) must take an oath or make an affirmation, and (iii) that the witness's testimony is subject to cross-examination. Remarkably, the three conditions set out to minimize testimonial risks are usually not fulfilled in hearsay statements.[633] However, the FRE sets out exceptions to the inadmissibility of hearsay when the declarant's out-of-court statement is believed to be trustworthy and thus may be admissible due to the circumstances which further its trustworthiness. I will now examine some of these exceptions below.

FRE 803 sets out the exceptions to the rule against hearsay irrespective of whether the declarant is available as a witness. Some examples of these exceptions are "present sense impression", "excited utterance", and public and family records. Conversely, FRE 804 provides the exceptions to the rule against hearsay in cases in which the declarant is not available as a witness, i.e., the witness cannot testify at trial due to an illness, death, refusal to testify, or for other reasons.[634] Illustrations of this are statements made under the belief of imminent death and statements against interest.

FRE 805 addresses the possibility of "Hearsay within Hearsay", which states that "a hearsay within hearsay is not excluded by the rule against hearsay if each part of the combined statements conforms with an exception to the rule". Theoretically, there is no limitation regarding the number of layers of hearsay that may be admissible under this rule. However, the bigger the level of hearsay exceptions within each other, the higher the probability than the evidence in question is untrustworthy.[635] In these instances, the trial judge should make a balancing test pursuant to FRE 403.

FRE 807 lays out a "residual exception" to the hearsay rule stating that a hearsay statement does not need to necessarily be excluded if it is not covered by a hearsay rule exception. This is so because an out-of-court statement may be trustworthy, material, highly probative, and yet, there might be no hearsay exception that covers the statement in question. This residual exception should be used sparingly and out-of-court statements without a hearsay exception should be admissible only in cases where the proffered evidence has a high amount of probative value and there is a great need for the evidence in question.[636] Therefore, even if the proffered evidence has a great probative value, if there are alternatives to the hearsay evidence, the out-of-court statement will likely be excluded.[637]

---

[632] *Weinstein/Berger*, Student Edition, § 14.01 (14–2).
[633] *Graham*, Evidence, pp. 77, 78.
[634] FRE 804(a).
[635] *Weinstein/Berger*, Student Edition, § 14.05 (14–32).
[636] *Weinstein/Berger*, Student Edition, § 14.04 (14–25).
[637] *Weinstein/Berger*, Student Edition, § 14.04 (14–29).

Pursuant to FRE 806, regardless of whether an out-of-court statement is covered by a hearsay exception (in the instances which fall under FRE 801(d)(2)(C), (D), or (E)), a party may use the statement to impeach the opposing party's witness.[638] Therefore, there is no need in which to lay a foundation before impeaching a witness in cases of prior inconsistent statements, which allows the opposing party "to examine the declarant as under cross-examination if the party calls her as a witness".[639]

Finally, regardless of whether an out-of-court statement is covered by a hearsay exception and whether it may theoretically be admitted as evidence, the trial judge may still exclude the said statement pursuant to FRE 403. That is, if the trial judge believes that the probative value of the out-of-court statement is substantially outweighed by its prejudicial effects.[640]

D. Procedural Safeguards

I. Safeguards to the Adversarial Trial Setting

As seen in this chapter, in the adversarial trial setting, each party has the duty to collect, evaluate, and present evidence to secure the best possible outcome for each respective side.[641] In view of the state's favorable position in gathering evidence prior to trial, and the resulting advantage in evaluating and presenting evidence at trial, certain constitutional and procedural safeguards must be in place to further the equality of arms. For this reason, there is the need for safeguards both from the standpoint of gathering evidence prior to trial and from the standpoint of presenting evidence and testing the strength and truthfulness of the opposing party's case at trial. I will now examine the three main safeguards furthering these rights, namely the discovery rights from the defense's standpoint (1.), the Compulsory Process Clause (2.) and the Confrontation Clause (3.).

1. Discovery Rights of the Defense

The right to discovery has a statutory basis and enables both the prosecution and the defense to have access to information that is in possession or control of the opposing party.[642] Its importance is due to a variety of reasons, namely: (i) equipping both parties with information to make a more informed decision regarding plea negotiations, and in these not taking place, (ii) in equipping the parties in being better

---

[638] *Weinstein/Berger*, Student Edition, § 14.03 (14–10).
[639] *Weinstein/Berger*, Student Edition, § 14.06 (14–33).
[640] *Thompson* et al., An Introduction, p. 369, *Weinstein/Berger*, Student Edition, § 6.05 (16–19).
[641] See supra Ch. 2 C. I. 2. a).
[642] *LaFave* et al., Criminal Procedure, p. 18.

prepared (prior to) at trial, (iii) reasons of efficiency, such as avoiding the need for continuances, and lastly (iv) saving resources in gathering information prior to trial, thus using these resources in other pursuits.

The importance of this safeguard from the defense's standpoint is that it equips the defense with access to evidence in possession or control of the prosecution prior to trial. Hence, in the absence of the discovery rights, it would be likely that the defense would at best, spend a considerable amount of time and resources to have access to the said information, and at worse, it would have little to no means of having access to evidence in possession or control of the prosecution.[643] For this reason, the right to discovery "helps equalize the contest between the state and the defendant".[644]

Due to the types of criminal offenses that fall under the competence of the federal jurisdiction, the FRCP do not grant the defense broad discovery rights as do statutes in some individual states.[645] Nonetheless, FRCP 16(a) sets out seven instances, where the prosecution must disclose evidence upon a request by the defense. These instances can be divided into four broad groups:

(i) oral or written statements made by the defendant, which are in possession of the prosecution,[646]

(ii) the defendant's prior criminal record,[647]

(iii) inspection of documents and objects,[648] as well as reports of any physical or mental examinations and of any scientific test or experiment, which are under the possession and control of the government,[649] and

(iv) summary of any testimony of an expert witness, which the prosecution intends to use in its case-in-chief.[650]

In addition to the aforementioned instances, the defense may have access to information in control or possession of the prosecution in two further circumstances. The first is regarding the testimony of lay witnesses, where the Supreme Court decided in *Jencks v. United States*[651] that the defense may have access to the written and recorded statements of the witnesses for the prosecution. However, the prose-

---

[643] *Whitebread/Slobogin*, Criminal Procedure, p. 672.

[644] *Whitebread/Slobogin*, Criminal Procedure, p. 681.

[645] *Saltzburg/Capra*, American Criminal Procedure, p. 1084.

[646] As to FRCP 16(a)(1)(A), this applies when the prosecution intends to use the defendant's written and recorded statements at trial. As per FRCP 16(a)(1)(B), written or recorded statements must either be in the prosecution's possession or control or made in response to an interrogation by someone the defendant knew to be part of the government, or they were given by the defendant in a grand jury and were recorded.

[647] FRCP 16(a)(1)(C).

[648] FRCP 16(a)(1)(E).

[649] FRCP 16(a)(1)(F).

[650] FRCP 16(a)(1)(G).

[651] *Jencks v. United States*, 353 U.S. 657 (1957).

cution must only grant the defense this information after it has directly examined these witnesses at trial.

Second, although there is no "general constitutional right to discovery in criminal cases",[652] the Supreme Court has established in *Brady v. Maryland*[653] that the defendant has a constitutional right to have access to evidence within the possession or control of the prosecution that is "exculpatory and material to guilt or punishment".[654] Hence, if the prosecution fails to hand in exculpatory evidence, there is a violation of due process regardless of whether the prosecution was acting in good or bad faith.[655] This constitutional right also applies even in the instances, where the defense has not made a request for evidence, if the evidence in question is of a substantial value, i.e., when the omission of the evidence "creates a reasonable doubt that did not otherwise exist".[656]

In contrast, as per FRCP 16(b)(1), there are instances in which the prosecution has a corresponding right to request information in possession of the defense, due to "reciprocal discovery". Thus, when the prosecution complied with the defense's request to inspect documents, objects, or reports of examinations and tests, the defense must grant a request by the prosecution for discovery of the corresponding information. This applies as long as the evidence is in possession of the defense, and it intends to use the item in question in its case-in-chief at trial.[657] The same applies concerning the summary of any expert witness's testimony that the defense intends to use in its case-in-chief.[658]

Nevertheless, there are instances where access to information is precluded to either one or both of the parties. The first instance concerns evidence that is precluded from the prosecution due to the defendant's privilege against self-incrimination, i.e., the prosecution cannot request for information that violates this right.[659] The second instance is that, as a rule, the defense is precluded from having access to grand jury transcripts.[660] There are, however, three exceptions to this; the defendant has the right (i) to his recorded grand jury testimony, (ii) to the grand jury testimony of the lay witnesses after they have been examined under direct examination at trial, and (iii) to exculpatory information that is material to the case. The third and last instance is that both parties are precluded from having access to work-product information, i.e.,

---

[652] *Saltzburg/Capra*, American Criminal Procedure, p. 1080.
[653] *Brady v. Maryland*, 373 U.S. 83 (1963).
[654] *LaFave* et al., Criminal Procedure, p. 1365.
[655] *LaFave* et al., Criminal Procedure, p. 1368.
[656] *Saltzburg/Capra*, American Criminal Procedure, p. 1005.
[657] FRCP 16(b)(1)(A) and (B).
[658] FRCP 16(b)(1)(C).
[659] *Whitebread/Slobogin*, Criminal Procedure, p. 672.
[660] FRCP 16(a)(3).

neither party may have access to reports or memoranda made by each respective party, which were "prepared in anticipation of litigation".[661]

2. Compulsory Process Clause

The Sixth Amendment to the Constitution provides the accused "to have compulsory process for obtaining witnesses in his favor", thus setting out the Compulsory Process Clause, which together with the Confrontation Clause "constitutionalize the law of witnesses in criminal cases".[662] The *Compulsory Process Clause* seeks to enable the defense to prepare its case and encompasses three rights.

The first right contained is the right to examine witnesses. In *United States v. Nixon*, the Supreme Court found that the Compulsory Process does not only entail the defendant's right to secure "the attendance of witness at trial",[663] but rather that it "undergirds the entire presentation of a defendant's case, from the right to discover witnesses in his favor to the right to compel them to testify over the claims of privilege".[664]

The second right encompassed by the Compulsory Process Clause is the defendant's right to testify. Until very recently, despite witnesses having a privilege against self-incrimination, the defendant had no corresponding right to take the stand if he so wished. It was only in *Rock v. Arkansas*[665] that the Supreme Court explicitly established that the right to testify was a defendant's constitutional right which derived from the Compulsory Process Clause, the Due Process Clause, and the Fifth Amendment's privilege against self-incrimination.[666]

The third and main right is the defendant's right to subpoena witnesses. In the US-American legal system it is up to the defendant to summon his own witnesses. Hence, the subpoena is a means in which to enforce the summoning of witness.[667] This right is implemented in the federal jurisdiction by FRCP 17, which provides that the defendant may use the "court's subpoena power to compel persons to appear as witnesses or to produce designated documents and objects *at trial*".[668] This right is also applicable to indigent defendants when the defendant "shows an inability to pay the witness's fees and the necessity of the witness's presence for an adequate de-

---

[661] *Whitebread/Slobogin*, Criminal Procedure, p. 671.
[662] *Westen*, Compulsory Process, p. 192.
[663] *Westen*, Compulsory Process, p. 192.
[664] *Westen*, Compulsory Process, p. 193.
[665] *Rock v. Arkansas*, 483 U.S. 44 (1987).
[666] *LaFave* et al., Criminal Procedure, p. 1395.
[667] *Schäuble*, Strafverfahren und Prozessverantwortung, p. 338.
[668] *LaFave* et al., Criminal Procedure, p. 1382.

fense".[669] If the defense is able to fulfill both these requisites, the government will pay for the "process costs and witness's fees".[670]

When issuing a subpoena, courts usually have a certain amount of discretion in deciding whether to subpoena witnesses and the number of subpoenas it will issue.[671] As such, for a defendant to exercise his right to subpoena, the evidence sought must be admissible at trial,[672] i.e., he must show that the witness or object sought is "relevant, material, and useful"[673] to his defense.

The right to subpoena and to discovery have some overlapping features, such as enabling the defendant to have access to information. Nonetheless, there is a significant difference between these safeguards. On the one hand, a subpoena is a command directed to all persons, and contains a command for a witness to attend trial at a determined time or place, or yet, for a person to attend trial to produce documents or objects either before trial or "before they are to be offered as evidence".[674] On the other hand, discovery is a request by a party to have access to information which is either in possession or in control of the opposing party.[675] Thus, whereas a subpoena may be directed to all people, discovery is a request for information between the parties. A further difference between them, is that discovery is a pretrial motion which has the aim to gather information prior to trial, whereas the subpoena is a request for a person to attend a specific proceeding, which usually takes place at trial.

3. Confrontation Clause

The Sixth Amendment to the Constitution affords the accused the "right to be confronted with the witnesses against him", thus setting out the Confrontation Clause. Due to the adversary nature of the American trial, whenever applicable, the rights accorded to the defendant are also extended to the prosecution, who also has the right to present its own witnesses, and to confront the defendant's witnesses.[676] Since *Mattox v. United States*,[677] the Confrontation Clause has been deemed to be synonymous to the right of cross-examination, which is a party's right to examine the testimony and credibility of the witnesses of the opposing party.

---

[669] FRCP 17(b).

[670] FRCP 17(b).

[671] *Marcus* et al., The Rights of the Accused, pp. 208, 209.

[672] *LaFave* et al., p. 1382.

[673] *Marcus* et al., The Rights of the Accused, p. 209.

[674] FRCP 17(c)(1).

[675] *LaFave* et al., Criminal Procedure, p. 1383.

[676] *Kaye* et al., McCormick, p. 6.

[677] *Mattox v. United States*, 156 U.S. 237 (1895). *Marcus* et al., The Rights of the Accused, p. 141.

The Confrontation Clause is considered to be a stronghold of the truth finding process in the American criminal procedure.[678] Throughout its history, the Supreme Court has defined the scope of the Confrontation Clause and set exceptions to this right. It was more recently in *Crawford v. Washington*[679] that the Supreme Court held that this Clause "is meant to prevent the admission of *testimonial* statements by declarants who are not subject to cross-examination either at the time statements are made or at trial".[680] Hence, the Supreme Court deemed that only out-of-court statements that are testimonial were to be subjected to the Confrontation Clause.[681] The court then proceeded to stipulate features in which to identify and differentiate "testimonial" statements from "non-testimonial" statements. These features differ depending on (i) to whom the statement is addressed to, (ii) the level of formality surrounding the witness's interrogation, and (iii) the primary concern of the person to whom the statements are being addressed.

As a rule, testimonial statements are those in which the law enforcement's primary concern is to gather relevant evidence against the defendant for a future criminal prosecution, and usually involves a certain level of formalism.[682] In contrast, out-of-court statements have a higher probability of being nontestimonial when they are made in an informal setting, and, as a rule, are not addressed to someone in law enforcement.[683] If a statement is in fact made to a law enforcement agency, the interrogation's primary concern is "to enable police assistance to meet an ongoing emergency".[684]

Although, as a rule, statements are presumed to be inadmissible whenever the defense does not have the opportunity to subject the declarant of an out-of-court testimony to cross-examination, there are four circumstances in which testimonial statements are admissible.[685] First, whenever the defense had a prior opportunity to cross-examine the declarant (e. g. in the preliminary hearing), his testimony will be admissible, even if the said declarant is later found to be unavailable, despite the prosecution's efforts in procuring them.

Second, whenever there is a forfeiture to the right to confrontation, i. e., the declarant is unavailable, due to the defendant willingly hindering or coercing him not to testify. In these instances, prosecution must prove the forfeiture by a preponderance of the evidence.[686] Some lower courts deem there is a forfeiture of the right to cross-

---

[678] *Weinstein/Berger*, Student Edition, § 14.01[1] (14–2).

[679] *Crawford v. Washington*, 541 U.S. 36 (2004).

[680] *Whitebread/Slobogin*, Criminal Procedure, p. 843.

[681] *Marcus* et al., The Rights of the Accused, p. 154.

[682] *Whitebread/Slobogin*, Criminal Procedure, p. 844.

[683] *Whitebread/Slobogin*, Criminal Procedure, p. 845; *Marcus* et al., The Rights of the Accused, p. 165.

[684] Such is the case when a person calls the police to ask for assistance.

[685] *Whitebread/Slobogin*, Criminal Procedure, p. 847.

[686] *Whitebread/Slobogin*, Criminal Procedure, p. 851.

examination in murder cases, regardless of the prosecution having to prove that the defendant killed the declarant due to the specific objective of thwarting him from testifying at trial.

Third, when the declarant is available and the defense was given the chance to confront him at trial, all prior testimonial statements are admissible. This is also applicable when the defendant had the prior opportunity to cross-examine the declarant during a preliminary hearing. Lastly, the testimonial statement will be considered admissible when it is not used for the purpose of proving the truth of a fact, but to impeach a statement made by the defendant which contradicts the testimonial statement in question.

At the statutory level, the FRCP provide for the implementation of the confrontation clause at trial, which is safeguarded by means of the cross-examination.[687] As seen, the parties may conduct cross-examination by means of leading questions and by impeaching the opposing party's witnesses. Owing to the US-American evidence taking occurring in a trial setting where the parties are the sole responsible for gathering, preparing, and presenting evidence at trial, the latter technique of cross-examination can be a powerful way for the defense to unearth inconsistencies, untruthfulness, and omissions in the statements of the witnesses for the prosecution. If done in a skillful manner, cross-examination may instill in the jury a reasonable doubt as to the defendant's guilt.

II. Safeguards to Lay Factfinding

The jury trial is a distinctive feature of the American criminal justice system, and a defendant's constitutional right in all felony cases. The importance of the right to a jury trial is such that prior to the independence of the United States, it was viewed by the colonists as a "valuable safeguard of liberty and the palladium of free government".[688] In *Duncan v. Louisiana*, the Supreme Court established that jury trials are "an inestimable safeguard against the compliant, biased, or eccentric judge".[689] By allowing for lay participation in the factfinding process, it is deemed that the accused is protected against the government. Nonetheless, due to its very premise of lay factfinding, safeguards must be in place to both sift the evidence that is presented to the jurors and to guide them in their decision-making. I will presently examine both safeguards to this end, namely the rules regarding the admissibility and exclusion of evidence (1.) and the court's instructions to the jurors (2.).

---

[687] *Schäuble*, Strafverfahren und Prozessverantwortung, p. 330. For the implementation of the Confrontation Clause at trial, see supra Ch. 2 C. III. 1. b).

[688] *Whitebread/Slobogin*, Criminal Procedure, p. 764.

[689] *Duncan v. Louisiana*, 391 U.S. 145 (1968).

1. (Strict) Rules as to the Admissibility and Exclusion of Evidence

As previously seen, jurors need not explain how they reached their verdict.[690] For this reason, there is no way in which to control the thought processes that went through the *individual* jurors' minds while deciding whether the defendant is guilty or not guilty. Additionally, owing to the decision being reached *collectively*, there is no process in which to verify what were the previous opinions of each juror before deliberations started, and whether and to what extent these initial opinions changed due to interactions and/or pressures from the majority of the jurors.

As a rule, due to the impossibility of checking what goes through the jurors' minds during evidence taking and during jury deliberations, it is necessary to control the evidence that is presented to them. Therefore, the evidence brought to the jurors is previously sifted to avoid that they hear inadmissible, confusing, untrustworthy, or biased evidence.[691] To this end, strict evidentiary rules are necessary for the parties to have some degree of control over the factfinder's decision-making.[692]

The need for evidentiary rules is heightened by the fact that in jury trials and – if not otherwise stipulated – in bench trials, the trier of fact does not need to state the reasons for its decision.[693] Therefore, in such cases, an appeal is not based on a written decision stating the reasoning behind the finding of guilt.[694] In this scenario, the FRE brings a certain amount of formalism to the procedure.

2. Jury Instructions

The importance of the jury instructions cannot be overstated, considering that it may be used as a basis for an appeal. Due to jurors being completely unaware of matters of evidence law, criminal law and criminal procedure, trial judges must make instructions to the jury "at various points throughout the trial".[695] The instructions commence during voir dire, where the trial judge instructs prospective jurors of their obligations and what awaits them should they be selected as jurors.[696] After the voir dire is finalized and the jurors are selected, the trial judge proceeds to give the jury the preliminary instructions. This includes, explaining to the jurors basic legal concepts, such as "reasonable doubt, the presumption of innocence, the nature of evidence (direct and circumstantial), and the judge's authority to judge credibility".[697]

---

[690] *Newton/Welch*, Understanding Criminal Evidence, p. 57.

[691] FRE 403.

[692] *Damaška*, Evidence Law Adrift, pp. 44, 46.

[693] However, as per FRCP 23(c), if a party requests the court to state its reasoning in open court prior to it announcing the verdict, the court must comply.

[694] *Damaška*, Evidence Law Adrift, p. 46.

[695] *LaFave* et al., Criminal Procedure, p. 1408.

[696] *LaFave* et al., Criminal Procedure, p. 1409.

[697] *LaFave* et al., Criminal Procedure, p. 1409.

The court will also give the jurors the final instructions before they deliberate, which usually takes place either prior to or following the closing arguments.[698] The trial judge proceeds to instruct the jury in matters of law to enable them to decide as to the facts of the case. This entails the "elements of the crime, the elements of any lesser included offenses, any defenses raised by the evidence, and on the burden of proof".[699] As per FRCP 30(a), if a party so wishes, it may request the judge in writing to instruct the jury "on the law as specified in the request".[700] In these instances, the court must inform the parties of its ruling regarding this request before the closing arguments take place.[701] After the jury begins the deliberations, the jurors may have additional questions regarding the case and may need instructions on how to deal with them. In such cases, the trial judge will have a considerable amount of discretion in deciding whether and how to answer to these questions.[702]

Chapter 3

Brazil

A. Introduction

Brazil is a Federal Republic composed of 26 states and the federal district. Although it has a federal structure in which each federal unit has its own Legislative, Judiciary and Executive bodies, the legislation regarding criminal law and criminal procedure is federal and applicable nationwide.[703] Accordingly, there is only one jurisdiction in criminal matters (*justiça comum penal*), where criminal offenses are disposed of by either federal courts (*justiça federal*) or by state courts (*justiça estadual*).[704] As there is but one jurisdiction, regardless of whether a criminal offense is tried in a federal or in a state court, it will follow the same procedural outline.[705] This is because the differences between the outline of criminal proceedings is not de-

---

[698] FRCP 30(c).

[699] *Roberson/Winters*, Evidence for Criminal Justice, p. 12, *Graham*, Evidence, p. 5.

[700] See also *Thaman*, in: Perron (ed.), Die Beweisaufnahme im Strafverfahrensrecht, p. 508.

[701] FRCP 30(b).

[702] *LaFave* et al., Criminal Procedure, p. 1409.

[703] Art. 22 I CF, Art. 1, chapeau, CPP.

[704] Art. 109 I to IX CF sets out the specific instances that fall under the federal competence. As the state competence has a residual nature, it is competent to disposes of all cases that do not fall under the federal competence.

[705] Despite the outline of the proceedings being the same, there are some small differences between the federal and the state competence, such as some of the procedural deadlines (*prazos processuais*). One such example is the total amount of days in which the chief of police has to conclude a criminal investigation, i. e., ten days in cases involving non-federal criminal offenses (art. 10, chapeau, CPP) and 30 days in cases involving federal criminal offenses (art. 66, L. 5.010/66).

termined whether a crime is of federal or state competence, but rather whether a criminal offense must be disposed of by the so-called "common proceeding" (*procedimento comum*), or by the "special proceeding" (*procedimento especial*).[706]

Most criminal cases tried by the Brazilian courts are disposed of by means of the *common proceeding*, which comprises three different "procedural outlines" (*ritos*).[707] The allocation of a criminal case to a specific procedural outline is determined by the number of years of imprisonment by which a criminal offense is punishable.[708] The ordinary procedural outline (*rito ordinário*) disposes of criminal offenses punishable by a minimum of four years of imprisonment, whereas the summary procedural outline (*rito sumário*) disposes of criminal offenses punishable by a period superior to two years and inferior to four years of imprisonment. Finally, the highly summarized procedural outline (*rito sumaríssimo*) disposes of criminal offenses punishable by a maximum of two years of imprisonment.[709]

The CPP mostly focuses on the ordinary procedural outline since it affords the accused the most procedural rights due to the higher complexity and gravity of the cases adjudicated.[710] As the procedural phases of this procedural outline are applied in a subsidiary manner to the other two types of common proceedings and to the special proceedings, the CPP only sets out the features of the summary procedural outline which differ from the general framework.[711] As to the highly summarized procedural outline, its normative framework is set out in L. 9.099/95, which sets out the adjudication of misdemeanors and petty infractions.[712]

---

[706] Art. 394, chapeau, CPP.

[707] The words *rito* and *procedimento* can be translated into English as "proceeding". However, I translated the word "*rito*" as "procedural outline" as to differentiate it from the word "procedimento", and also to highlight the fact that depending on the "*rito*" in question, the procedural phases of a criminal case – especially during the adjudicatory phase – may be considerably different.

[708] Art. 394 para. 1, I to III CPP.

[709] Art. 98 I CF provides that the Union (União) and the states should create special courts (*Juizados Especiais Criminais*) to dispose of both civil suits of lesser complexity and criminal offenses of lesser offensive potential (see footnote 712 (Part 2)). To this end, the Union enacted L. 9.099/1995 to establish these courts and provide the outline of the highly summarized procedural outline. Because one of the main aims of this type of procedural outline is to quickly dispose of criminal cases, the trial setting of the highly summarized procedural outline greatly differs from those of the ordinary- and summary procedural outline. One such example is that in the former the judge has the possibility of disposing a case by means of the decriminalizing measures (*institutos descriminizadores*), which include a measure akin to diversion (*transação penal*).

[710] An illustration of this is that whereas in the summary procedural outline the defense may call up to five witnesses at trial, in the ordinary procedural outline, this number is raised to eight witnesses, as per Arts. 532 and 401, chapeau, CPP, respectively.

[711] Art. 394 para. 5 CPP.

[712] Art. 61 L. 9.099/95 defines these criminal offenses as "crimes of lesser offensive potential" (*crimes de menor potencial ofensivo*) and comprise both (i) petty infractions (*con-

The "*special proceedings*" comprise various types of proceedings that were created to adjudicate cases, which have specific circumstances either regarding (i) the persons involved, i. e., either the perpetrator or the victim of a criminal offense, or (ii) regarding specific features of the criminal offense, such as its complexity and/or gravity. Thus, there are various instances, where a criminal case must be tried in accordance with specific provisions set out by either the Federal Constitution or by an infra-constitutional law. An example of the former,[713] is the creation of the "Jury Institution"[714] (*Instituição do Júri*), which is competent to dispose of cases involving criminal offenses that were willfully committed against a person's life.[715]

Due to the impracticability of addressing all three modalities of the common proceedings and the various types of special proceedings, I will focus on the ordinary and summary procedural outlines, which apart from a few exceptions, have an almost identical structure and are applicable to dispose of felonies, which are punishable by more than two years of imprisonment.[716] In addition to these two procedural outlines, I will occasionally allude to the Jury Institution for two main reasons. First, owing to it disposing of serious criminal offenses which involve complex factual and legal questions, it provides defendants with the highest number of procedural rights in the Brazilian criminal justice system. Second, it is the only instance of lay factfinding in adjudicating felony cases in this legal system.

For these purposes, this country report is divided into the examination of the criminal procedure (B.) and evidence law (C.), both of which are examined within the Brazilian criminal procedure. Thus, when I examine this legal system's procedural safeguards (D.), they are also comprised within this field of law.

B. Overview of the Criminal Procedure

I. Legal Sources

The main source of law is the Federal Constitution, where Art. 5 sets out the majority of the defendant's constitutional rights and guarantees (*direitos funda-*

---

travenções penais), which are laid out in L. 3.688/41, and (ii) misdemeanors (*crimes*) which are provided in the Criminal Code (CP).

[713] Art. 5, XXXVIII CF.

[714] For reasons of uniformity and accuracy, whenever possible, I will borrow the official translations from the website of the Brazilian Federal Supreme Court. However, due to the absence of translations of legal terms and institutions from Portuguese into English, I had to create new translations for various words in Portuguese. The translation of the Federal Brazilian Constitution of 1988 into English is available at: https://www2.stf.jus.br/portalStfInternacional/cms/verConteudo.php?sigla=portalStfSobreCorte_en_us&idConteudo=120010.

[715] See infra Ch. 3 C. I. 1.

[716] Art. 394 para. 1, I and II CPP.

mentais). As seen, all statutes should abide by it and apply their provisions in conformity to the constitutional provisions.

Ranking below the Federal Constitution and above all other infra-constitutional legislation, is the American Convention on Human Rights (ACHR).[717] Its hierarchy in the Brazilian normative framework is a relatively new development. The ACHR was introduced into the Brazilian legal framework on 06.11.1992 by means of D. 678/92,[718] and until 2008, it had the same rank as that of an ordinary legislation (*lei ordinária*). This changed in 2008 due to a ruling by the Supreme Federal Court – the country's constitutional court and the court of last resort regarding matters of constitutional law.

Due to the ACHR being a treaty with the aim of furthering human rights, the STF modified its earlier legal understanding regarding the hierarchy of international human rights treaties in the Brazilian legal framework. In this ruling,[719] the STF adopted the Supra-Legality Theory (*Teoria da Supralegalidade*), by which international human rights treaties rank below the Federal Constitution but outranks all other Brazilian legislation (the latter comprises all statutory legislation which I will address below). This is especially important as the ACHR provides every person with various procedural rights, such as the right to liberty and – in having been accused of committing a criminal offense – the right to a fair trial.[720]

As to the infra-constitutional legislation, the main statute regulating both criminal procedure and evidence law is the CPP, which, i.a., sets out the roles and responsibilities of the main procedural actors, lists examples of the types of evidence that may be presented at trial, and sets out the ordinary and summary procedural outlines, as well as the outline of the jury trial. Further important statutes are the Penal Code (CP) and various infra-constitutional laws (*leis especiais or leis extravagantes*), that provide and regulate several criminal and procedural matters, which are not included in the CPP.[721] Among these topics are (i) the regulation of petty infractions,[722] (ii) the creation of special courts competent for disposing of both petty infractions and misdemeanors, and establishing the framework of the highly summarized procedural outline,[723] and (iii) the regulation of various types of special

---

[717] The ACHR is usually referred to by Brazilian scholars as San José Pact (*Pacto de São José da Costa Rica*).

[718] The introduction of the ACHR to the Brazilian normative framework is owing to Art. 5 para. 2 CF setting out that the "The rights and guarantees expressed in this Constitution do not exclude other deriving from (…) international treaties in which the Federal Republic of Brazil is a party."

[719] RE 466343 (03.12.2008).

[720] As set out in Arts. 7 and 8 ACHR, respectively.

[721] *Mossin, Compêndio* de Processo Penal, p. 69.

[722] DL. 3.688/41 (*Lei das Contravenções Penais*).

[723] See supra footnotes 709 and 712 (Part 2).

proceedings, such as those which aim to curb domestic and familial violence against women.[724]

In addition to the aforementioned laws, there are infra-constitutional laws which regulate the roles, responsibilities, and prerogatives of the main procedural actors, namely those of (i) public defenders,[725] public prosecutors,[726] (iii) judges,[727] and (iv) private attorneys.[728]

Lastly, an important legal source peculiar to the Brazilian legal system are the *súmulas vinculantes* (SV), roughly translated as "binding summary". These are summaries of precedents issued by the Supreme Federal Court either *ex officio* or upon request. These binding precedents have the purpose of fostering a certain amount of efficiency and legal certainty (*segurança jurídica*) to future lawsuits involving similar issues.[729] The subject matter of the SV are rulings of the Supreme Federal Court on topics of a constitutional nature which are controversial, and which this court has previously dealt with on repeated occasions.[730] They are binding to all judicial bodies including the Supreme Federal Court itself[731] and the Public Administration; thus, a judicial decision, which is contrary to the wording of a SV must be annulled.[732]

---

[724] L. 11.340/96 (*Lei Maria da Penha*).

[725] The Public Defender's Office is divided into that of the Union (*Defensoria Pública da União*), which i.a., comprise the federal Public Defender's Office and that of the Federal District (*Defensoria Pública Federal*), on the one side, and Public Defender's Office of the states (*Defensoria Pública dos Estados*), on the other side. The organization and attribution of the members of the former are regulated by LC 80/1994, whereas the legislation regulating the latter is of each individual state's competence.

[726] Just like the Public Defender's Office, The Public Prosecutor's Office is also divided into that of the Union (*MPU*), which comprise, i.a., the Federal Public Prosecutor's Office (MPF), and that of the Federal District (*MP-DF*) on the one side, and the Public Prosecutor's Office of the States *(Ministério Público dos Estados)* on the other side. LC 75/93 provides the organization, the roles, and prerogatives of federal prosecutors and those of the DF. In contrast, L. 8.625/1993 sets out the general rules for the organization of the Public Prosecutor's Office in the state level. For the division of the Public Prosecutor's Office, see *Tourinho Filho*, Manual, pp. 415 et seq.

[727] The organization of the federal courts, and the prerogatives, duties, and responsibilities of federal judges is set out in LC 35/79 (*Loman*).

[728] L. 8.906/94 is the Statute of the Brazilian Bar Association (*Estatuto da OAB*) which regulates the practice of law by private attorneys.

[729] Binding summaries were introduced to the Brazilian legal system by Art. 103-A CF by means of the EC n. 45/2004 and are regulated by 11.417/96. Those of interest to the criminal procedure are the súmulas vinculantes 11 and 14.

[730] The decisions of the STF are applicable to those made by either one of the two Panels (1 T. and 2 T.) or by full bench judgments. *Mendes/Branco*, Curso de Direito Constitucional, pp. 992 et seq.

[731] According to Art. 103-A CF, the STF may only diverge from a binding summary if it expressly revokes it, in which case the procedure to revoke it will follow the same procedure as its enactment.

[732] *Mendes/Branco*, Curso de Direito Constitucional, pp. 992 et seq.

II. Court System

Both the state and federal courts have a three-tiered system. In the first level, criminal cases are respectively tried in the Criminal Courts (*varas criminais*) and in the Federal Courts (*varas federais*). Apart from a few exceptions, e. g., felonies that are of the competence of the jury trial,[733] criminal cases in the first instance are adjudicated by one professional judge.

In the second level are the intermediate appellate courts; the courts of state competence are called Courts of Justice (TJ), whereas those of federal competence are called the Federal Regional Courts (TRF). The latter courts are divided into five regions, each of which comprise several states. In contrast to the courts in the first instance, as a rule, all appellate courts are collegial courts.

At the top of the pyramid are the two higher courts – the Supreme Federal Court (STF) and the Superior Court of Justice (STJ) – that have both original and appellate competencies.[734] As seen, the STF is both the country's constitutional court and the court of last resort regarding matters of constitutional law. Differently, the STJ is a new court established by the current Federal Constitution and is the highest appellate court concerning non-constitutional points of law (*legislação infraconstitucional*) that do not fall under either the labor, military, or electoral jurisdictions.[735]

III. Main Procedural Actors

As a rule, judges, prosecutors, and public defenders are lawyers. To become a lawyer, students must complete five years of law school in a recognized university and have a minimum of two years of work experience as a legal intern.[736] Once these requirements have been met, law graduates must pass both phases of the Brazilian Bar Examination (*Prova da OAB*). For law graduates who wish to work at a law firm, they may do so as soon as they successfully pass the bar exam. However, for those who wish to work as a judge, a prosecutor, or a public defendant[737] after passing the

---

[733] A professional judge adjudicating a criminal offense involving organized crimes may, for reasons of security, request for additional judges to participate in adjudicating the case in question, as per Art. 1 para. 1 L. 12.694/2012.

[734] Arts. 102 and 105 CF set out both the appellate and original jurisdiction of each respective higher court.

[735] Art. 105 III CF.

[736] These internships may be held at a law firm or a governmental institution, such as the public prosecutor's office, public defender's office, or working for a judge, or as is the case in some universities, at the law school's internship center (*escritório modelo*).

[737] Judges, prosecutors, and public defenders have a high level of stability due to having the right not to be removed (except for Art. 93 VIII CF) and irreducibility of compensation. Further, after two years in office, judges and prosecutors have life tenure and may only loose office after a final and unappealable judicial decision. As to public defenders, after two years in office they acquire stability, i.e., loss of office is dependent on an administrative proceeding. In this sense,

Bar Exam, they must additionally pass a civil servant's entrance examination (*concurso público*).[738] There are different exams for each profession with differing levels of difficulty and requisites,[739] e. g., law graduates, who wish to become judges must have a minimum of three years of experience as a lawyer before applying to this entrance examination.[740]

I will presently examine the roles the main procedural actors play, particularly at the procedure of evidence taking at trial.

1. Judges

As of this writing, there is only one type of judge, who combines both the roles of a pretrial judge and that of a trial judge. This is problematic seeing that depending on the city where a criminal offense is being adjudicated, this feature may lead to the disregard of the defendant's procedural right to an impartial trial. This is because a single judge may be competent to decide – in the same criminal case – on matters of both an investigatory and of an adjudicatory nature. Despite the probability of this taking place in big cities being minor due to the large number of courts competent in adjudicating criminal cases, this risk is highly increased in smaller cities owing to the limited number of criminal courts (*varas criminais*) in a specific district (*comarca*). Thus, in smaller districts, it is not uncommon for the same judge to be responsible to make decisions throughout all phases of the same criminal case.

However, the current scenario of there being only one type of judge will change if certain provisions of L. 13.964/19 which currently have their efficacy suspended, come into force. If this is the case, the aforementioned judge, would then become the trial judge, termed *juiz da instrução ou julgamento*,[741] and would be solely responsible for adjudicating criminal cases. This is because Art. 3-B of L. 13.964/19 sets out a pretrial judge, termed "*juiz das garantias*", who would be responsible for overseeing the legality of the criminal investigation and to both safeguard the suspect's (*indiciado*) individual rights as that of the people directly affected by the

---

see Art. 95 I to III CF (judges), Art. 17 I and II LC 75/93 (prosecutors) and Art. 43, 88, 127 LC 80/94 (public defenders).

[738] Owing to these professionals being well paid and having a high level of stability, these exams are highly competitive. Consequently, successful candidates usually have a considerable amount of knowledge in law.

[739] The entrance examination for those who wish to become judges are set out in Art. 93 I CF c/c Art. 78 LC 35/79. The entrance examination for those who wish to become public defender's is set out in Art. 134 para. 1 CF c/c Art. 24, LC 80/94. Art. 129 para. 3 CF sets out the entrance examination for those who wish to become public prosecutors in general; and Art. 45 LC 40/81 set out the entrance examination for those who wish to work for the Public Prosecutor's Office of the States (MP) whereas Arts. 183 and 187, LC 75/93 set out the entrance examination for those who wish to become prosecutors at the Public Prosecutor's Office of the Union (MPU).

[740] Art. 93 I CF.

[741] As before the enactment of L. 13.964/19, there was only one type of judge, the terms for pretrial judges and trial judges were only created with the enactment of this law.

criminal investigation. As per Art. 3-C CPP, the pretrial judges would only be competent to make rulings on matters that involve the investigation of felonies and would thus be precluded from adjudicating criminal cases. These changes to the CPP are vital in furthering the defendant's position at trial, as it would significantly lower the risk of judicial bias.[742]

2. Prosecutors

The main roles and responsibilities of public prosecutors are set out in Arts. 127 to 129 CF, and for this reason, no federal statute may change these prerogatives.[743] As a rule,[744] public prosecutors[745] are parties to the proceedings, who are responsible for filing a bill of indictment and once they decide to charge someone, they must seek to obtain the defendant's conviction.[746] If a prosecutor deems that there is enough evidence to believe that an offense has been committed and that the police were able to identify its author, due to the principle of mandatory prosecution (*princípio da obrigatoriedade*)[747] she must file a bill of indictment against the suspect. Once the prosecution makes its charging decision, it has the responsibility of leading the criminal case to its conclusion.

---

[742] See Ch. 6 A. II. 2. b).

[743] *Pacelli/Fischer*, Comentários ao CPP, p. 534.

[744] There are two instances where a private prosecution (*ação penal privada*) may take place in criminal cases. The first instance takes place in cases of "exclusive private prosecution" (*ação penal privada exclusiva*), which take place when a criminal offense called "crimes against honor" (*crimes contra a honra*) is committed. In these cases, the victim is the sole person who may file a complaint (*queixa*) against the accused. These criminal offenses are set out in Arts. 138, 139, 140, chapeau, CP. The second instance where a private prosecution takes place is when the prosecution fails to file a complaint within the legal deadline. In such instances, the victim may file a complaint against the accused, as per Art. 5 LIX CF.

[745] Public prosecutors are part of the Public Prosecutor's Office MP, and they are referred to by different terms depending on whether they work for the state or federal jurisdiction. In the first instance, public prosecutors prosecuting non-federal and federal criminal offenses are respectively called *Promotores de Justiça* and *Procuradores da República*.

[746] As per Art. 129 I CF. Contrary to their role in civil procedures – where prosecutors are considered to be the guardians of the law (*custos legis*) – in criminal matters, most young scholars consider the prosecution to be a party to the proceedings. In this sense, see *Marques*, Elementos de Direito, vol. 2, pp. 39 et seq.; *Lopes Jr.*, Direito Processual Penal, 11th ed., p. 104; *Pacelli/Fischer*, Comentários ao CPP, pp. 534, 539; *Capez*, Curso de Processo Penal, p. 228; *Badaró*, Processo Penal, pp. 295, 296; *Karam*, in: Prado/Malan, Processo Penal e Democracia, pp. 402 et seq.; *Nicolitt*, Manual de Processo Penal, p. 488; *Silva Júnior*, Reforma Tópica, p. 76. Contrariwise, there are some scholars who deem the prosecution to be an "impartial party" ("*parte imparcial*") in the criminal proceedings, e.g., *Pacelli/Fischer*, Comentários ao CPP, pp. 534, 539; *Tourinho Filho*, Manual, pp. 406, 407; *Lopes Jr.*, Direito Processual Penal, 11th ed., p. 104; *Nucci*, CPP Comentado, p. 704.

[747] The terms might cause some confusion to German readers due to the principle of mandatory prosecution being called *princípio da obrigatoriedade* (*Legalitätsprinzip*), whereas the principle of discretionary prosecution is termed *princípio da legalidade* (*Opportunitätsprinzip*).

3. Defense Counsel

The right to defense counsel is explicitly set out in the Constitution,[748] and in the ACHR.[749] In the Brazilian legal framework, this right stems from the constitutional principle of (the right to a) full defense (*princípio da ampla defesa*), which comprise both the defendant's right to defend herself (*autodefesa*) and the right to have assistance of legal counsel present in all parts of the proceedings (*defesa técnica*).[750] Owing to both the latter principle and the principle of audiatur et altera pars (*princípio do contraditório*), the trial judge must adhere to both aspects of the full defense.[751] As a result, if a judge tries a defendant without any defense counsel by her side, this will constitute an absolute nullity for violation of both constitutional and statutory law.[752]

There are three types of legal counsel. Seeing that the vast majority of defendants do not have the financial means of retaining an attorney in criminal cases, the first and by far the most common type of legal assistance is provided by public defenders (*defensores públicos*).[753] In contrast, defendants that do have the financial means to pay for legal counsel may retain the services of an attorney of their choice[754] or choose to be represented by a public defender.[755] In both the aforementioned instances, legal counsel is respectively termed *defensor constituído* and *advogado constituído*, as the defendant chose the person representing him.

The third type of legal representation is the court-appointed counsel (*defensor dativo*). Legal counsel is appointed to the defendant in two different circumstances. First, whenever a public defender's office is understaffed and does not have enough public defenders available to represent all citizens that seek their assistance. Second, whenever the defendant goes to trial without having previously retained legal counsel, the trial judge will appoint him one irrespectively of the defendant's financial means.[756] In the latter instance, Art. 263 sole paragraph CPP *a contrario*

---

[748] Art. 5 LV CF. The CPP implicitly sets out the right to counsel in Arts. 261 and 366.

[749] Art. 8 para. 2 lit. d and lit. e ACHR.

[750] *Scaranse Fernandes*, Processo Penal Constitucional, pp. 255 et seq.; *Grilo*, Defesa Técnica, p. 39; *Pacelli*, Curso de Processo Penal, pp. 51, 339.

[751] Therefore, the judge must inform the defendant of his right to silence and – in its absence – appoint him legal counsel. Although the defendant may only waiver his right to defend himself, he cannot waive his right to legal counsel. In this sense, see *Lopes Jr./Gloeckner*, Investigação Preliminar, pp., 471, 479; *Malan*, in: Prado/Malan, Processo Penal e Democracia, p. 154.

[752] *Nicolitt*, Manual de Processo Penal, p. 496; *Malan*, in: Prado/Malan, Processo Penal e Democracia, p. 158; *Choukr*, CPP Comentado, vol. 1, p. 492.

[753] Art. 5, LXXIV and Art. 134, chapeau, and paras. 1 to 4 CF.

[754] *Capez*, Curso de Processo Penal, p. 239.

[755] *Nicolitt*, Manual de Processo Penal, p. 500.

[756] *Pacelli/Fischer*, Comentários ao CPP, p. 547; *Capez*, Curso de Processo Penal, p. 240.

provides that if the defendant does not have the financial means to pay for the legal services of the court-appointed counsel, the state will cover all costs.

IV. Procedural Phases

1. Investigatory Phase

For reasons of uniformity and clarity, I will refer to the investigation phase (*investigação criminal*) as the investigatory phase.

a) Evidence Gathering by the State

In the investigatory phase, there are two main actors, who have the legitimacy to conduct criminal investigations; these are the chief of police and the public prosecutor's office. In most cases, once a crime is committed, there is a police investigation (*inquérito policial*) presided by the chief of police, termed *delegado de polícia*. These are law graduates[757] who passed a civil servant's entrance examination to work either for the Civilian Police (*Polícia Civil*), in criminal cases that fall under state competence or for the Federal Police (*Polícia Federal*), in cases that fall under federal competence.[758]

When investigating crimes, the chief of police must document all steps taken in the criminal investigation and has a vast array of prerogatives at her disposal.[759] This investigation is conducted in a partisan manner, where the police mostly focuses on searching for inculpatory evidence.[760] This is owing to the chief of police having the task to gather enough evidence to prove that a crime was in fact committed (*prova da materialidade*) and to identify the person who committed it (*autoria do crime*).[761] Once the chief of police has gathered both these elements,[762] the criminal investigation is concluded. After he has finished compiling the investigation file (*relatório*), he must then send this file to the judge, who in turn, will send it to the public prosecutor's office.[763]

---

[757] Art. 3 L. 12.830/13.

[758] Art. 144 paras. 1 and 4 CF, respectively. In this sense, see *Badaró*, in: Ambos (ed.), Polícia e Investigação, p. 257.

[759] Art. 6 I to X CPP.

[760] *Vieira*, in: Ambos (ed.), Polícia e Investigação, p. 355.

[761] Art. 4, chapeau, CPP.

[762] These elements are termed the "minimum evidentiary standard" (*lastro mínimo probatório*).

[763] As per Art. 10 para. 1 CPP. In this phase of the proceedings, the judge merely conducts an examination of an administrative nature to verify whether the time frame stipulated by law to conclude the investigatory phase was respected. See *Tourinho Filho*, Manual, p. 156.

Once the public prosecutor receives the investigation file, she has three options.[764] First, if she finds that there is not enough evidence to charge a suspect or to prove the materiality of a crime, she may return the investigative file to the chief of police for further inquiries.[765] Second, if she believes that either no crime was committed, or that further inquiries would not suffice to file a complaint, she will request the criminal investigation to be archived (*arquivamento*).[766] Third, if, however, the prosecutor finds that there is enough evidence to believe that an offense has been committed and that the police were able to identify its author, the evidentiary standard of justified cause (*justa causa*) has been met and the prosecutor must file a complaint.[767]

The STF has ruled that the public prosecutor's office may conduct criminal investigations in a subsidiary and exceptional manner.[768] The former applies either when the chief of police is unwilling to investigate, or when the facts of the case reveal that the police force is intentionally trying to thwart criminal investigations. In contrast, the exceptional character of the prosecutorial investigative role is that they may only investigate the commission of specific criminal offenses. Only when either of these conditions are met may the public prosecutor's office investigate. In such instances, they will have all the prerogatives that are usually conferred to the chief of police at their disposal.

b) Rights of the Defense in the Investigatory Phase

The investigatory phase is an administrative and written procedure, which is secretive in nature as to guarantee the effectiveness of the investigative measures employed by the investigative bodies (*sigilo do inquérito policial*). Due to its very nature, the procedural rights that are usually accorded to the defendant at trial are not

---

[764] Lopes Jr./Gloeckner, Investigação Preliminar, p. 321.

[765] Art. 16 CPP.

[766] As of this writing, Art. 28 CPP states that once the public prosecutor's office requests the criminal investigation to be archived (*arquivamento*), if the judge considers that the reasons adduced by the prosecutor are unfounded, it may send the investigative file to the attorney general", who will either file a bill of indictment herself or designate a prosecutor to do so. It is only when the attorney general also believes that the criminal investigation should be archived, that the judge must comply with this decision. This may change, as the wording of Art. 28 CPP was modified by L. 13.964/19. However, as of this writing, this legal provision has its effectiveness suspended by the STF.

[767] Interestingly, although it is unequivocal that public prosecutors are bound by the principle of mandatory prosecution (*princípio da obrigatoriedade*), this principle is not *expressly* set out in neither the Federal Constitution, nor in any infra-constitutional legislation. However, this principle is implicitly set out in Art. 24, chapeau, CPP, which states that the bill of indictment *must* be filed by the public prosecutor's office. However, the termed employed ("*será*") is open to interpretation as it may both signify the possibility of the public prosecutor's office filing a bill of indictment and requiring the public prosecutor's office to do so.

[768] RE 593.727/MG. In the Brazilian legislative framework, resolutions 181 and 183 CNMP set out that the public prosecutor's office may conduct criminal investigations.

granted to the accused in this phase.[769] Thus, the principles to a contradictory hearing, to full defense in its full scope and to the so-called *princípio do juiz natural*,[770] i. e. the defendant's right to a "competent, independent, and impartial court previously established by law"[771] are not mandatory in this procedural phase, and thus cannot be enforced. Nonetheless, the accused and her defense counsel have certain rights during this phase, namely:

First, as per Art. 5 LXII and LXIII CF, arrestees must be instructed of their right to remain silent and to have the assistance of legal counsel. Further, the arrestee's identity and the place in which he is being held must be informed to a judge, and, additionally, to either a family member or to a person specified by him. The latter provision is essential in furthering the defendant's right to a defense. This is because if a judge does not immediately release the defendant in cases of an illegal arrest, a family member of the defendant or a person appointed by him may contact the public defender's office to prepare his defense, thus safeguarding the defendant's right to counsel in the pretrial phase.[772]

Second, pursuant to the Statute of the Brazilian Bar Association[773] and to SV 14, the defense may have access to the investigation file and to all the steps of the investigation that have already been concluded.[774] Therefore, the defense counsel can only be denied access to information contained in the investigation file regarding ongoing investigative measures. However, this right is limited to the defendant's legal counsel, as the accused herself is completely barred from having direct access to the investigation file.

Third, Art. 14, chapeau, CPP provides the defense the possibility of requesting the police to carry out "tasks" or investigations (*diligências*). However, it is fully within the police's discretion whether to carry out these investigations.[775]

Fourth, in 2018, the Federal Council of the Brazilian Law Association enacted Provision 188, which provides the so-called *investigação defensiva*, i. e., it affords the defense the right to conduct investigative measures. For this purpose, the defense may gather evidence in any procedural moment it wishes.[776] For this reason, the defense cannot be hindered from (legally) investigating and gathering evidence and may hire detectives and legal experts for this purpose.[777] According to this provision, the evidence the accused or her legal counsel unearths are not subject to discovery;

---

[769] *Badaró*, in: Ambos (ed.), Polícia e Investigação, pp. 260, 261.
[770] Art. 5 XXXVII and LIII CF.
[771] Art. 8 para. 1 ACHR.
[772] *Grilo*, Defesa Técnica, p. 48.
[773] Art. 7 XIII to XV and Art. 7 para. 1 L. 8.906/94.
[774] *Saad*, in: Santoro/Malan/Maduro, Crise no Processo Penal, p. 311.
[775] See infra Ch. 3 D. II. 2. and Ch. 6 B. I. 2. a).
[776] Arts. 1 and 2 Provision 188/2018.
[777] Arts. 4 and 7 Provision 188/2018.

thus, there is no legal obligation in which to force the defense to disclose evidence to the prosecution or to the police.[778] Although theoretically Provision 188 was an important step in advancing the defendant's right in co-shaping trial, by allowing him to gather evidence, it did not set out any means in which to enforce this right. Thus, the extent and effectiveness of this right is hampered, and in practice this provision is of little practical importance.

Lastly, the newly enacted L. 13.964/19, introduced the custody hearing in the Brazilian criminal justice system (*audiencia de custódia*), whereby whenever a person is arrested for a crime that cannot be subject to bail (*crime inafiancável*), the police's failure to show an arrest warrant will not prevent her arrest. Nonetheless, in these instances, the defendant must immediately be taken to the judge who issued the arrest warrant for a custody hearing.[779]

2. Adjudicatory Phase

As mentioned in the beginning of this chapter, I will now focus on the ordinary and the summary procedural outlines, which are applicable to dispose of criminal offenses that are punishable by more than two years of imprisonment. For the sake of uniformity, from now on I will refer to these procedural steps as the adjudicatory phase. Moreover, although there is only one type of judge who is responsible for both deciding on investigatory and adjudicatory matters, from now on, I will refer to this judge as the trial judge. This is for reasons of clarity and uniformity for when I examine the key concepts of comparative law and conduct the comparative study in Ch. 6.

a) Filing a Bill of Indictment and the Evidentiary Standard of Justa Causa

Whenever the prosecution verifies that the standard of proof of "justified cause" has been met, she must file a bill of indictment (*oferecimento da denúncia*). As per Art. 41 CPP, this document must contain the description and circumstances of the criminal offense and the identification of the accused (*qualificação do acusado*) – or in its absence, the information by which she may be identified – and the exact charges against her.[780] In this charging document, the prosecution must name the oral testimony it seeks to present at trial, under penalty of preclusion.

---

[778] Art. 6 Provision 188/2018.

[779] Art. 287 CPP.

[780] The term used to describe the precise charges against the defendant is *classificação do crime*.

In the instances the prosecution bases the bill of indictment on the criminal investigation (*inquérito*),[781] she must also send the investigation file to the trial judge to be attached to the case file (*autos do processo*).[782] Once the judge competent to adjudicate the case[783] receives the charging document, she must verify whether the minimum evidentiary standard of justified cause has been met. If she believes that the evidentiary standard has not been met or that the conditions for filing a bill of indictment were not fulfilled,[784] she must dismiss it (*rejeição da denúncia*). In contrast, if these conditions have been met, the judge competent to adjudicate the case will accept the bill of indictment (*recebimento da denúncia*) and will subsequently order the accused to be summoned (*citação*) to file the initial written reply to the bill of indictment within ten days.[785]

b) Filling a Written Reply to the Bill of Indictment and Setting a Date for Trial

In the written reply to the charging document (*resposta à acusação*), the defendant may include all that is relevant to her defense, which entails all exculpatory evidence she wishes to present at trial. To this end, the defense may present documents, highlight any weaknesses in the bill of indictment, and to offer evidence to rebut the prosecution's claims.[786] Additionally, as per Art. 396-A, chapeau, CPP, it is in the written reply to the bill of indictment that the defendant may list the witnesses he wishes to summon himself. However, whenever the defense wishes the judge to summon these witnesses (*notificar as testemunhas*), it must expressly request the court to do so, and state the need for the court to summon the witnesses rather than the defense summoning them itself.[787]

The consequence of the court summoning the witnesses rather than the defense is that if the witness fails to attend trial, the court may impose them the legal sanctions set out in the CPP, which include coercively bringing the witness in question to court.[788] In contrast, if the defense fails to expressly request the court to summon the listed witnesses, if a witness fails to attend trial, there is no means in which the

---

[781] There are cases where there is no need for a formal criminal investigation (*inquérito policial*), as is the case when a suspect is arrested while committing a criminal offense (*preso em flagrante*).

[782] Art. 12 CPP.

[783] If the STF finds Art. 3-B, chapeau, XIV CPP to be constitutional, the pretrial judge will be competent to decide whether the minimum evidentiary standard of justa causa has been met.

[784] As per Art. 395 I to III CPP.

[785] Art. 396, chapeau, CPP.

[786] Art. 396-A, chapeau, CPP; *Nucci*, CPP Comentado, pp. 999, 1000.

[787] *Brasileiro de Lima*, Manual de Processo Penal, p. 1315; *Nucci*, CPP Comentado, p. 1000.

[788] Arts. 218 and 219 CPP.

defense may enforce their attendance.[789] A further consequence regarding witness testimony is that the written reply to the bill of indictment is the only procedural moment where the defendant may indicate the name of the oral witnesses[790] he wishes to present at trial.[791]

Once the trial judge receives the written reply to the charging document, she has two options. The first option is to summarily acquit the defendant (*absolvição sumária*) when the trial judge finds that one of the instances set out in the exhaustive list of Art. 397 CPP are present.[792] In such cases, the defendant's summary acquittal creates *res judicata* in the substantive sense (*coisa julgada material*).[793] However, if the trial judge does not summarily acquit the defendant, she will then set a date and time for the procedure of evidence taking to commence, which implicitly means that the receipt of the bill of indictment was confirmed (*ratificação do recebimento da denúncia*). The trial judge will then summon the defense and the prosecution, and if applicable, the private accessory prosecutor (*assistente de acusação*) informing them the time and place of the trial.[794]

c) Procedure of Evidence Taking

Due to the constitutional principle, which mandates that all judicial proceedings must have a reasonable length (*princípio da duração razoável do processo*), the trial judge must conclude the procedure of evidence taking (AIIJ) within 60 days of its commencement.[795] Although it is the judge's responsibility to preside this hearing, Art. 400, chapeau, CPP sets out the order of the evidence to be presented at trial.

---

[789] *Rangel*, Direito Processual Penal, p. 541; *Nucci*, CPP Comentado, pp. 1000, 1001.

[790] On the one hand, as the bill of indictment must be presented prior to trial, some scholars believe there is a mitigation to this rule as they believe it would be unfair to completely prohibit the defense from presenting witnesses in their favor at a later procedural moment. According to these scholars, the defense is allowed to indicate fictitious names as witnesses, to allow the defense more time in which to search for additional witnesses. In these instances, the defense may substitute the name of the fictitious witness for the real ones prior to the procedure of evidence taking at trial. This practice is not set out in the CPP as it was created as a means in which to counter this code's formalism. On the other hand, other scholars contend that the trial judge should not permit this practice, and states that the defense may only furnish the incorrect names of the witnesses, if the witness in question has not yet been located, in this sense, see *Nucci*, CPP Comentado, p. 1000.

[791] *Pacelli/Fischer*, Comentários ao CPP, p. 872. See infra Ch. 3 C. III. 2. a).

[792] The exhaustive list comprises: (i) the existence of a cause that either excludes the illegality of the fact (*excludente de ilicitude*, Art. 23, chapeau, CP) or the defendant's guilt (*excludente da culpa*, Art. 26, chapeau, CP), (ii) the fact narrated is not a crime or (iii) the defendant's criminal liability ceases to exist (*extinção da punibilidade*, Art. 107 CP).

[793] *Brasileiro de Lima*, Manual de Processo Penal, p. 1323; *Badaró*, Processo Penal, p. 622.

[794] Art. 399, chapeau, CPP.

[795] Art. 400, chapeau, CPP.

Whenever applicable, the hearing should start with the victim's statements (*declarações do ofendido*) concerning her identity, the circumstances of the crime and who the author of the crime is or who she presumes this person to be and allowing the victim to indicate relevant evidence for this purpose.[796] After the victim's statements, the examination of the prosecution's witnesses take place, followed by those of the defense (*oitivas das testemunhas de acusação e de defesa*).[797] During witness examination, the parties directly ask the witnesses questions, and after both the prosecution and defense have finished inquiring them, the trial judge may supplement the inquiry.[798]

Following the witnesses' examination, the hearing and examination of the court expert(s) ensues followed by that of the party-appointed experts. When applicable, following these examinations, the confrontation between the parties and the witnesses and the recognition of people or things take place.[799] The last act of the hearing is the examination of the defendant. This has the purpose of enabling defendants to previously hear both the prosecution's and the defense's case in their totality before either testifying or invoking their right to remain silent.

Once all evidence has been produced, the parties and, when applicable, the accessory private prosecution may request further "supplementary inquiries" whenever they consider it to be necessary in view of the circumstances or facts ascertained in the instruction (*diligências complementares*).[800]

d) Closing Arguments and Sentencing

After the conclusion of the procedure of evidence taking, the prosecution followed by the defense will have twenty minutes to orally present their closing arguments, which may be extended for a further ten minutes.[801] In cases where there are multiple defendants, each defendant will have a total of thirty minutes to present their closing arguments.[802] Following the closing speeches, the trial judge renders a decision. However, in certain cases, due to the complexity of the case or due to the number of co-defendants, the judge may grant the parties five days to present their written closing arguments (*apresentação de memoriais*) instead of presenting them orally.[803]

---

[796] Art. 201, chapeau, CPP.

[797] *Nicolitt*, Manual de Processo Penal, p. 550.

[798] Art. 212, chapeau, and Art. 212, sole paragraph, CPP.

[799] These procedures are respectively termed *acareações* and *reconhecimento de pessoas ou coisas*.

[800] Art. 402 CPP.

[801] Art. 403, chapeau, CPP. In cases where there is a private accessory prosecutor (*assistente de acusação*), she has ten minutes to make her closing speeches, in which case the defense will have ten further minutes to address them.

[802] Art. 403 para. 1 CPP.

[803] Art. 403 para. 3 CPP. The presentation of the closing speeches – either written or orally – is an essential procedural step. Thus, if the defense is not given the opportunity to present its

In such cases, after the trial judge receives the written closing arguments, she will then have ten days to render her decision.[804]

C. Evidence Law

I. Introduction

1. Finder of Fact: Professional Judges

Professional judges preside over criminal cases sitting alone and are thus both finders of fact and of law.[805] The only exception to this rule is whenever a criminal offense was committed with the intent to take another person's life, in which case defendants have a constitutional guarantee to a jury trial.[806] Owing to the factfinders being lay people, the Jury Institution is a bifurcated procedure. In the first phase named the Preliminary Instruction (*Instrução Preliminar*), the trial is presided over by a trial judge, who must verify whether there is probable cause to bind the case to a jury trial. If the trial judge believes this to be the case, the second phase of the procedure named *Plenário do Júri* ensues. In this phase, a trial judge oversees the jury trial (*o juiz presidente do Plenário do Júri*) and is responsible for the finding of punishment and sentencing, whereas the jury are the finders of fact and of certain points of law.[807] Due to lay factfinding, there are features of the jury trial which are distinctive to this setting and are not featured in any other type of criminal proceeding.[808]

---

closing speeches, this will constitute an absolute nullity (*nulidade absoluta*) as the defendant will be considered as having been formally represented (*formalmente defendido*), but "materially defenseless" (*materialmente indefeso*). However, as per S. 523 STF, if the closing speeches have been deficient, it will only be annulled if the defense demonstrates to the trial judge its deficiency.

[804] *Brasileiro de Lima*, Manual de Processo Penal, p. 1334.

[805] This applies not only to the ordinary and summary procedural outlines, but also to the highly summarized procedural outline (JECRIM).

[806] As per Art. 74 para. 1 CPP, the jury trial is competent to adjudicate four criminal offenses: homicide, instigation or aiding in committing suicide infanticide and abortion.

[807] Arts. 482 chapeau, 483 I-V, 483 paras. 3 and 4 CPP; *Silva Júnior*, Reforma Tópica, pp. 244 et seq.

[808] The most important of these features is that defendants have the right to the so-called *plenitude de defesa*, which defers from the principle to a full defense, as the defense can present non-legal arguments to the jury, which would not be permissible in any other type of proceeding. This included the use of hypnosis and the presentation of psychographic letters (*cartas psicografadas*) from the victim. Another example concerns witness examination; in the second phase of the Jury Trial, the trial judge is responsible for examining witness and the defendant, and it is only after he has concluded the said examinations, that the parties may directly question them, as per Art. 473 chapeau CPP. If the jury wishes to formulate questions to the witnesses and to the defendant, they may only do so through the judge who will formulate the questions and relay them to the person in question, as per Art. 473 para. 2 CPP.

2. Trial Setting

The current trial setting has gone through various changes, which led to a partial shift in regard to the procedural actor(s) who are responsible for presenting evidence at trial.[809] Until 2008, the trial judge alone was the sole responsible for conducting the procedure of evidence taking. However, as seen, after the enactment of L. 11.690/2008, various features of the trial setting were modified as to allow for a more party-controlled presentation of evidence. As a result, the trial judge no longer has absolute control over the presentation of evidence. And, as of this writing, although the trial judge remains to be the main procedural actor responsible for evidence taking, the current trial setting has elements of both party-controlled and officialized fact-finding.

Initially, it is important to state that all evidence presented at trial is considered to be that of the criminal proceeding (*processo*). This is due to the evidentiary principle of evidence sharing (*princípio da comunhão da prova*), which states that although the prosecution and defense seek to present evidence to further their respective cases, once the evidence is presented at trial, it "can be used by any of the key courtroom actors",[810] i.e., namely by both parties and by the court.[811] For this reason, Art. 401 para. 2 CPP provides that if a party decides to withdraw from calling a witness it has previously appointed, the trial judge may call and examine the witness in question. Further, although not expressly stated in the CPP, due to the principle of evidence sharing, many scholars believe that a party may only withdraw from calling a witness that has been indicated in the bill of indictment or in its written response with the opposing party's consent. Thus, absent this consent, if the opposing party wishes to examine the witness in question, it must be given the opportunity to state its reasons for wishing to call the said witness.[812]

a) Elements of Officialized Fact-Finding

The trial judge retains a significant amount of responsibilities at trial (*poderes instrutórios do juiz*), the most important of which are presiding over trial, and of conducting the procedure of evidence taking and the defendant's examination.[813] The judges' duties at trial stem from the principle of ascertainment of the truth (*princípio da verdade material ou real*), which mandates their responsibility in searching for the material truth.[814] In addition to this principle, the principle of "official impulse"

---

[809] See supra Part 1 B. II. 1.

[810] *Silva Júnior*, Reforma Tópica, p. 139, A prova (...) pertence ao processo "de modo que pode ser utilizada por qualquer um dos sujeitos do processo".

[811] *Capez*, Curso de Processo Penal, p. 411; *Nucci*, CPP Comentado, p. 411.

[812] In this sense, see *Távora/Alencar*, Curso de Direito Processual Penal, p. 657; *Silva Júnior*, Reforma Tópica, pp. 139, 140.

[813] Art. 251 CPP. See *Tourinho Filho*, Manual, p. 421.

[814] See infra Ch. 3 D. I.

(*princípio do impulso oficial*) states that once the trial judge receives the bill of indictment, she is responsible for propelling the case forward until its conclusion.[815] To perform these tasks, the trial judge normally has the investigative file at its disposal. This is because whenever a bill of indictment is based on a police investigation, the investigative file is sent to the trial judge and is attached to the case file.[816] At the procedure of evidence taking, the judge has three main responsibilities.

First, during the interrogation of the defendant, the trial judge plays a central role as the *sistema presidencialista* applies, i.e., she fully controls the examination. Only after she has finished examining the defendant, may the parties direct their questions to the judge, who will then relay them to the defendant, if she considers the said questions to be pertinent and relevant to the case.[817]

Second, once the parties conclude their respective examinations of oral evidence, i.e. after the examination of the victim(s), witnesses, and informants, the trial judge may do so, when she believes that certain aspects of an oral statement need further clarification.[818]

Third, the trial judge and the parties may address their questions to the court-appointed experts in writing. If the trial judge believes that there is a need to clarify the questions asked by the parties, or in cases where further questions arise from the previous answers, the expert in question will have to testify at court so that the judge and the parties may question her orally.[819]

Lastly, pursuant to Arts. 209, chapeau, and 234 CPP, trial judges may call and examine additional witnesses to those appointed by the parties and they may arrange for the presentation of documents, which they consider relevant to the case to be attached to the case file (*juntada aos autos*). Additionally, as per Art. 156 II CPP, trial judges may ask for inquiries to be carried out to clarify questions or dispel any doubts on a relevant issue during evidence taking (*realização de diligências*).[820]

---

[815] *Capez*, Curso de Processo Penal, p. 65; *Távora/Alencar*, Curso de Direito Processual Penal, p. 82; *Nucci*, CPP Comentado, pp. 584, 585.

[816] If the STF find Art. 3-C para. 3 CPP to be constitutional, the trial judge will no longer have access to the investigative file, as it will be kept at the registry of the court, where only the parties may have access to it.

[817] Art. 188 CPP. There are some authors that believe that the parties should be allowed to ask the defendant direct questions. In this sense, see *Nucci*, CPP Comentado, p. 524.

[818] Art. 212, sole paragraph, CPP. See HC 111.815/SP.

[819] I will address this topic in more detail infra Ch. 3 C. III. 4.

[820] In this sense, see *Mirabete*, Processo Penal, p. 314; *Marques*, Elementos de Direito, vol. 2, pp. 5 et seq.; *Zilli*, Iniciativa Instrutória do Juiz, pp. 180 et seq.; *Jardim/Amorim*, Direito Processual Penal, pp. 80, 310. There are many scholars who believe that the judicial prerogatives set out in Art. 156 II, Art. 209, chapeau, and Art. 234 CPP must be interpreted restrictively, as they believe that the parties are the sole procedural actors who should be allowed to present evidence at trial. According to these scholars, the judge should only carry out inquiries in cases in which he deems them to be to necessary in order to clarify certain matters or doubts that the parties were unable to dispel. In this sense, see *Capez*, Curso de Processo Penal,

At times, the judicial responsibility in finding the material truth is also present prior to trial. A case in point is that the judge competent to adjudicate the case may also order the anticipated production of evidence, which are considered to be urgent and relevant.[821] This may take place when the judge believes that there is an unsurmountable reason that prevents a witness or the victim to attend trial for a long or uncertain period. The reasons for the latter are namely, due to an infirmity, to old age or due to a witness or the victim moving to a country which has no extradition laws with Brazil. In such cases, the court notifies the parties to ensure that the production of the evidence in question is conducted while safeguarding the defendant's procedural rights to audiatur altera pars and to a full defense.[822]

b) Elements of Party-Controlled Presentation of Evidence

As of this writing, although the trial judge is the main responsible for conducting the trial and examining the evidence, the prosecutor and the defense are considered to be parties to the proceedings and may present evidence that further advances their respective cases in three instances.

First, when filing either the bill of indictment or the written reply to this charging document, the prosecution and the defense must respectively appoint the names of the witnesses they wish to examine at trial. Further, during the examination of the victim, witnesses and informants, the parties have the responsibility of directly questioning these people (*inquirição direta*), whereas the trial judge only has an ancillary role during these examinations.

Second, upon a previous request to the trial judge, the parties may examine court-appointed experts by asking them to clarify the evidence presented by them and directly asking them additional questions.[823] Further, the parties may request the trial judge to allow them to appoint their own privately retained experts, who will then be heard during evidence taking at trial.

Third, due to the principle of "the parties' own responsibility" (*princípio da autorresponsabilidade das partes*), whenever one of the parties commits an error or is inactive in its role, they must assume the consequences of their mistakes.[824] This furthers the parties' roles and responsibilities in co-shaping the procedure of evidence taking.

---

pp. 370, 407; *Tourinho Filho*, Manual, p. 582; *Nicolitt*, Manual de Processo Penal, p. 701. However, there are scholars that believe that judicial discretion should be limited owing to it going against the "accusatory principle". In this sense, see *Choukr*, CPP Comentado, vol. 1, p. 447; *Pacelli*, Curso de Processo Penal, pp. 343, 444.

[821] Art 156 I CPP.
[822] See Ch. 6 B. II.
[823] Art. 159 para. 5 I CPP.
[824] *Capez*, Curso de Processo Penal, p. 411.

II. Methods of Proving Facts

1. Information Gathered in the Investigatory Stage and Evidence Sensu Stricto

Depending on the procedural phase in which a piece of information is gathered, the said information will have a specific terminology and probative value. During the investigatory phase, the police collect informative elements (*indícios ou peças de informação*) that although at times are referred to as evidence,[825] are not evidence in its strict legal sense (*provas em senso stricto*).[826] This is due to the informative elements being gathered in a procedural phase, which has an administrative, written, and secretive nature. For this reason, Art. 155, chapeau, CPP lays out that the trial judge may not base his decision *solely* on informative elements.[827] In this sense, most Brazilian scholars hold that the trial judge may only consider informative elements in her decision-making as *obiter dicta*, but never as *ratio decidendi*. Hence, for the trial judge to consider these informative elements as evidence, they must be produced at trial, where the defendant has the constitutional right to a full defense and audiatur et altera pars,[828] and where the trial judge competent to dispose of the case is present during the whole instruction (*princípio do juiz natural*).[829]

An important topic that Brazilian scholars also address in the context of Art. 155, chapeau, CPP is the probative value of the evidence stemming from the anticipated production of evidence (*produção antecipadas de provas*). The judge competent to adjudicate the case may order the anticipated production of evidence in two instances. The first instance is regarding precautionary measures (*provas cautelares*), which take place when the trial judge orders the anticipated production of evidence, e. g., due to the belief that there is an unsurmountable reason that prevents a witness or the victim to attend the trial for a long or uncertain period. In these instances, the court must notify the parties of the date in which the taking of evidence will take place to ensure that the production of the evidence in question is conducted while safeguarding the defendant's procedural rights.[830] For this reason, although the evidence is taken by the trial judge prior to trial, it is considered to be evidence in the strict sense as the three aforementioned procedural rights afforded to the defendant at trial are safeguarded.

---

[825] As per Art. 6 III CPP which states that "as soon as the police becomes aware of the commission of a criminal offense it must (...) gather all *evidence* which serves to clarify the facts".

[826] *Zilli*, O Pomar e as Pragas, p. 2; *Lopes Jr./Gloeckner*, Investigação Preliminar, p. 323.

[827] See infra Ch. 6 B. II.

[828] *Lopes Jr./Gloeckner*, Investigação Preliminar, p. 468.

[829] This right comprises both the principle to the jurisdiction of a lawful judge (*princípio do juiz natural*) and the principle of immediacy (*princípio da imediaticidade/imediação*). In this sense, see *Lopes Jr./Gloeckner*, Investigação Preliminar, p. 317.

[830] Arts. 155, chapeau, and 156 I CPP.

The second type of evidence which may be taken prior to trial is the evidence which is considered to be "unrepeatable" due to its perishable nature (*provas irrepetíveis*). This type of evidence usually refers to expert evidence, such as the corpus delicti exam (*exame de corpo de delito*).[831] This type of evidence is examined by court-appointed experts who are deemed to be impartial owing to them being subject to some of the provisions applicable to judges to ensure judicial impartiality.[832] For this reason, there is the presumption that this type of evidence is produced by trustworthy and impartial procedural actors.[833] Further, as the expert evidence must be later presented at trial – where all of the defendant's procedural rights are safeguarded – it is also considered to be evidence sensu stricto.

2. Direct and Circumstantial Evidence

Although both direct and circumstantial evidence are admissible at trial, there is a certain amount of confusion on the judicial nature (*natureza jurídica*) of the latter type of evidence, owing to the CPP[834] and various scholars referring to circumstantial evidence by the term "*indícios*". The reason for this is that the same term is frequently used not only to refer to circumstantial evidence, but also to refer to informative elements. In truth, the appropriate term for circumstantial evidence are *provas indiciárias*, as it is evidence in the strict legal sense and is a valid means of proof that has a similar probative value as that of direct evidence (*provas diretas*), seeing as they are both produced at trial.

Despite circumstantial evidence being evidence sensu stricto, there is an ongoing debate among scholars on whether the trial judge may base a conviction on circumstantial evidence, as some scholars believe that a judge may not convict a defendant based on this type of evidence alone.[835] However, the majority of Brazilian scholars believe that circumstantial evidence may base a conviction as long as there are several pieces of circumstantial evidence that combined with the totality of the evidence presented at trial, may lead the trial judge to find the defendant guilty.[836]

---

[831] Brazilian scholars have some interesting considerations regarding this particular type of expert evidence. Owing to the principle of the free evaluation of evidence (*livre convencimento motivado*), the formal rules of evidence (*prova tarifada*) were abolished in the Brazilian criminal procedure. However, various Brazilian scholars contend that this is not the case owing to the CPP mandating that the corpus delicti exam must be made by an official expert to prove the fact that a crime has been committed (*materialidade do crime*). Normally, the corpus delicti exam cannot be replaced by any other means of evidence individually, not even by the defendant's confession. Nonetheless, there is an exception to this rule, which is when it is not possible to perform this examination, due to the disappearance of the remains or traces of the object in question. In such cases, as per Art. 167 CPP, oral testimony may supplant it.

[832] Art. 275 CPP.

[833] See Ch. 3 C. III. 4.

[834] Art. 239 CPP.

[835] *Tourinho Filho*, Manual, p. 639.

[836] *Badaró*, Processo Penal, p. 506.

III. Means of Evidence

The means of evidence provided by the CPP are not exhaustive, as the provisions set out in Arts. 158 to 250 CPP are merely exemplificative (*provas nominadas*).[837] Among the different types of evidence, there is no aprioristic hierarchy between them[838] and none of them have absolute probative power.[839] Consequently, a single piece of evidence that goes against all other means of evidence is not enough to support a criminal conviction.[840]

I will presently examine the most common types of evidence presented at trial (*meios de prova*), namely the defendant (*o réu*), witnesses (*prova testemunhal*), the victim (*ofendido*), experts (*peritos e prova pericial*) and documentary evidence (*prova documental*).

1. Defendant

The legal nature of the examination of the defendant is that of both a means of evidence and a means of defense.[841] The latter aspect was furthered by L. 11.719/2008, which shifted the defendant's examination from being the first act of the procedure of evidence taking to it being the very last. As such, by the time the defendant is examined by the trial judge, both inculpatory and exculpatory evidence have been previously examined by the judge, and when applicable, by the parties. Hence, based on all the evidence that was offered at trial, the defendant may make an informed decision on whether to answer to the judge's and the parties' questions in whichever way she believes to be most favorable to her case.[842]

---

[837] *Capez*, Curso de Processo Penal, p. 405; *Tourinho Filho*, Manual, pp. 572, 573. Contrariwise, the means of evidence that are not set out in the CPP are the so-called "unnamed means of evidence" (*provas inominadas*).

[838] *Choukr*, CPP Comentado, vol. 1, pp. 441, 442.

[839] *Lopes Jr./Gloeckner*, Investigação Preliminar, p. 502. For this reason, the trial judge may decide contrary to that which is proven by means of expert evidence, as per Art. 182 CPP.

[840] However, this is not to say that a single piece of evidence is not enough for a criminal conviction. There are instances in which this might suffice for a conviction, such as the case of the testimony of a police officer, or the victim's statements in a case involving a criminal offense of a sexual nature.

[841] Regarding the defendant's examination, there are scholars that believe it to be both a means of evidence and a means of defense. In this sense, see *Tornaghi*, Curso de Processo, pp. 362, 363; *Greco Filho*, Manual de Processo, p. 200; *Mirabete*, Processo Penal, p. 266; *Marques*, Elementos de Direito, vol. 2, p. 386; *Zilli*, Iniciativa Instrutória do Juiz, p. 186; *Nicolitt*, Manual de Processo Penal, p. 730. In contrast, there are several scholars that believe the defendant's examination to be predominantly or exclusively a means of defense. In this sense, see *Lopes Jr.*, Direito Processual Penal, 11ᵗʰ ed., p. 231; *Tourinho Filho*, Manual, p. 592; *Badaró*, Processo Penal, p. 451; *Nucci*, CPP Comentado, p. 497; *Pacelli*, Curso de Processo Penal, p. 49.

[842] *Pacelli*, Curso de Processo Penal, p. 388.

In the instances where the evidence presented at trial is mostly detrimental to the defendant, it might be beneficial for her to confess or to present mitigating circumstances as to receive a lesser punishment. Conversely, if the evidence against the defendant is weak, it might benefit her to deny having committed the criminal offense. The defendant has yet another option, which is to exercise her constitutional right to remain silent. For these reasons, the principle of full defense is implemented in both aspects during the defendant's examination, i. e., it is the main occasion the defendant has in which to express her right to defend herself at trial,[843] while having the mandatory assistance of legal counsel, as mandated by Art. 185, chapeau, CPP.

In contrast, the examination of the defendant is a means of evidence because if she wishes to answer to the judge's questions, these answers will be taken as evidence and may be used by the trial judge in convicting her. One such example is when the defendant choses to confess. However, for a confession (*confissão*) to be taken as a means of evidence, it must be made voluntarily and explicitly at trial.[844] As to its probative value, the confession is to be considered as only one piece of evidence among many. Thus, for the trial judge to convict a defendant, the confession must be corroborated by other pieces of evidence presented within the totality of all evidence produced at trial (*conjunto probatório*).[845]

Therefore, if a defendant makes a confession without any other pieces of evidence corroborating the said confession, its probative value is not absolute.[846] The reason for this is that believing a confession to be true without corroborating evidence may lead to a faulty conclusion. This is owing to the risk that a defendant may confess to a crime which he did not commit due to reasons of financial gain, altruism, mental illness or due to wanting to give the real perpetrator of the criminal offense a chance to escape.[847] For this reason, the CPP provides the defendant the opportunity to retract her confession or yet, to confess to certain facts of the crime while denying other facts.[848]

a) Examining the Defendant

The examination of a person suspected or accused of committing a crime may occur both during the pretrial phase and at the procedure of evidence taking, which are respectively conducted by the police and the trial judge.[849] Although both pro-

---

[843] *Nucci*, CPP Comentado, p. 523.

[844] The defendant's confession at the pretrial phase of the proceedings is solely an informative element (*indícios ou pecas de informação*). See *Nucci*, CPP Comentado, p. 532.

[845] Art. 197 CPP. See *Capez*, Curso de Processo Penal, p. 120.

[846] *Tourinho Filho*, Manual, p. 607; *Nicolitt*, Manual de Processo Penal, p. 741.

[847] *Tourinho Filho*, Manual, p. 607.

[848] Art. 200 CPP. See *Nucci*, CPP Comentado, pp. 543, 544.

[849] Art. 6 V and Art. 187, chapeau, CPP, respectively.

cedures are termed *interrogatório*, it is only in the latter procedure that the defendant has the mandatory right to i.a., counsel being present and audiatur altera pars.[850]

Prior to the defendant's examination at trial, regardless of whether the defendant is free or detained in jail pending trial, she has the right to a private meeting with her defense counsel.[851] During the trial phase, whenever the trial judge examines the defendant by means of videoconference, the defense counsel will remain at court, whereas the defendant will have an *ad hoc* public defender present with her in the correctional facility where she is being held. Also, pursuant to Art. 185 para. 5 CPP, during this examination, both the defendant and the *ad hoc* public defender must have access to telephone channels for the private communication between them and the defendant's legal counsel at court.

Regardless of where the defendant's examination takes place, this examination is divided into two phases with a preliminary phase taking place before the examination itself.[852] In the preliminary phase, the identification of the defendant takes place before the trial judge examines him and has the purpose of ascertaining whether the person taking the stand is the same person as that who was accused of committing the crime (*qualificação do réu* or *obtenção de dados qualificativos do réu*).[853] To this purpose, the trial judge will ask the defendant about her personal circumstances, such as her name, age, address, place of work and whether she can read and write.[854] After this initial identification is concluded, the trial judge must instruct the defendant of her right to silence in both parts of the examination, i.e., during the examination of the defendant regarding the facts of her life (*interrogatório sobre a pessoa do acusado*) and the facts of the case (*interrogatório sobre o mérito*).[855]

The trial judge then proceeds to question the defendant regarding her address, profession, place of work and general questions about her life, which in turn, include whether the defendant has been previously arrested or prosecuted. If the defendant

---

[850] If the defendant's legal counsel is not present during the defendant's examination, this will constitute an absolute nullity for violation of both constitutional and statutory law, i.e., Art. 5 LV CF and Arts. 185, chapeau, Art. 564, III, "c" and Art. 572 (*a contrario*) CPP.

[851] In cases where the defendant is being questioned from the prison in which he is being held, he must have direct and private access to her defense counsel, who is present in the main hearing, as per Art. 185 para. 5 CPP.

[852] The defendant's examination is set out by Arts. 185 to 187 CPP. However, there is no uniform position in regards as to whether the defendant's examination is divided into two or three phases. For the scholars that support the former, see *Choukr*, CPP Comentado, vol. 1, p. 512. For those who support the latter, the defendant is initially identified, and after this first step, the two phases of the examination take place, i.e., the qualification of the defendant and examination as to the facts of her life and the examination as to the merits of the case. In this sense, see *Nucci*, CPP Comentado, pp. 515, 517, 518.

[853] Art. 186, chapeau, CPP.

[854] *Nucci*, CPP Comentado, p. 515.

[855] Art. 187, chapeau, CPP.

answers in the affirmative to the latter question, the trial judge will ask her whether any sentence has been imposed and the circumstances surrounding it.[856]

After the first part of the interrogation is concluded, the trial judge proceeds to examine the defendant as to the facts of the case,[857] where the defendant can respond whether the accusation made against her is true. If the defendant claims the accusation to be untrue, the judge will proceed by questioning her whether she knows who committed the criminal offense and whether she was with the said perpetrators either before or after the commission of the criminal offense in question. During this examination, the defendant may offer further clarifications, indicate evidence in her favor, present an alibi, and whether she wishes to express herself concerning the evidence presented against her.[858] Additionally, the defendant may make statements concerning whether she knows any of the victims and witnesses that are to be examined, or have previously been examined, and if so, whether she has anything to claim against them. Further clarifications may be made as to whether she has previously seen the instrument of crime and if she knows of other facts and details that may be helpful in clarifying the case. Lastly, prior to concluding the examination, the trial judge must ask the defendant whether there are any final statements she wishes to make.

Once the trial judge finishes examining the defendant, the parties have the opportunity to direct their questions to the judge, who will then orally transmit them to the defendant if she considers them to be pertinent and relevant to the case.[859] Some scholars see this measure as both a means in which to protect the defendant from (a possible) aggressive questioning by the prosecution and in protecting the defendant from misguided questions made by the defense.[860]

After the examination of the defendant is concluded, pursuant to Art. 196 CPP, the trial judge may at any time – either *ex officio* or by requirement of one of the parties – renew this examination. If this takes place, the trial judge must state the reasons that led her to do so. The re-examination of the defendant usually happens when[861] (i) a judge is replaced in the middle of the trial due to retirement or to being promoted, (ii) procedural mistakes were committed in the original examination (*erros processuais*), (iii) new oral testimony was admitted and the defendant wishes to comment on them, or (iv) the defendant has previously confessed and wishes to retract the said confession.

---

[856] Art. 187 para. 1 CPP.

[857] Art. 187 para. 2 I to VIII CPP.

[858] Art. 189 CPP.

[859] Art. 188 CPP. The sequence of the procedural actors who may direct their questions to the trial judge are the public prosecutor followed by the private accessory prosecutor (*assistente de acusação*), the co-defendants' legal counsel and the defendant's legal counsel. See *Nicolitt*, Manual de Processo Penal, p. 734.

[860] *Nucci*, CPP Comentado, pp. 523, 524.

[861] *Nucci*, CPP Comentado, p. 531.

b) Duty to Attend Trial and Exception to the Defendant's Examination at Court

As a rule, defendants are examined by the trial judge in the courtroom. However, there are exceptional instances, where judges may examine defendants who are detained pending trial by means of videoconference. This may occur, either by the judge's decision *ex officio* or by requirement of the parties.[862] Regardless, once the judge decides to examine the defendant per videoconference, she must notify the parties of her decision within ten days of the interrogation.[863] Due to its exceptional nature, for the judge to examine the defendant by means of videoconference, one of the situations set out in Art. 185 para. 2 I-IV CPP[864] must be present and the trial judge must substantiate her reasons for doing so in writing.[865] Further, according to Art. 185 para. 7 CPP, whenever the alternatives for examining the defendant at court are not viable, the defendant must then be brought to court for the trial judge to examine her.

2. Witnesses

As per Art. 202 CPP, in theory any person may be a witness as there are no priori restrictions to witness competency. However, when testifying, they must limit themselves to the facts they have witnessed and (as a rule) should not express their personal opinions regarding them. An exception to this is when the witness's opinion

---

[862] Art. 185 para. 2 CPP. The examination of the defendant by videoconference is applicable to all three "common proceedings" (*procedimento comum*). As to jury trials, the defendant may only be examined by videoconference in the first part of the trial (*Instrução Preliminar*), i.e., the part of the trial where a professional judge examines whether there is probable cause to bend the case to trial. As to the second part of trial, i.e., when the jury trial takes place (*Plenário do Júri*), the defendant's examination by videoconference is prohibited due to the factfinders being lay people who need to have direct contact to both the defendants and the witnesses in the broad sense.

[863] Art. 185 para. 3 CPP.

[864] Pursuant to Art. 185 para. 2 I to IV CPP, the circumstances in which a judge may examine a defendant by videoconference are: "I. when there is risk to public security, when there is reasonable suspicion that the defendant is either part of a criminal organization or that he may try to escape while being brought to trial. II. To enable the participation of the defendant in court, due to illness or other personal circumstances. III. To prevent the defendant from influencing the witness's testimony, in cases, where it is not possible to examine the witnesses by videoconference and IV. Due to reasons of public order." This last item is heavily criticized, due to the use of terminology, which is vague and lack a concrete definition.

[865] Due to the defendant's examination by videoconference being of an exceptional nature if the trial judge requests it without one of the requisites of Art. 185 para. 2 I-IV CPP being present, this proceeding will be subject to absolute nullity. In this sense, see *Nicolitt*, Manual de Processo Penal, p. 737.
Nucci, CPP Comentado, pp. 508 et seq.

is inseparable from the narrative of the facts,[866] as the assessment of the evidence is of the trial judge's responsibility.

Differently than in other countries,[867] the term witness is closely related to the probative value to be given to an oral testimony. Thus, in the Brazilian criminal procedure there are two types of witnesses sensu lato; these are witnesses in the strict sense (*testemunhas*) and the so-called informants (*informantes*). There are two main differences between them. First, for a person's testimony to be considered that of a witness sensu stricto, it must be made at trial in front of the trial judge. For this reason, all statements that were made outside of court, e. g., during the investigatory phase, are to be considered as statements made by informants rather than witnesses. Second, for a person's statements to be considered as that of a witness sensu stricto, the person being examined must have the duty to tell the truth. In contrast, informants do not have this corresponding duty.

Witnesses in sensu stricto have three main duties at trial, which are to tell the truth, to testify and to attend trial. As per the first duty, witnesses must make a solemn promise to tell the truth before testifying (*dever de prestar o compromisso com a verdade*).[868] This solemn promise has the aim of morally nudging a witness to this end. However, the CPP provides that some people are either exempt from their duty to tell the truth or that of testifying at trial. In such cases, the person who witnessed facts that are relevant to the case may be heard by the court as an informant rather than as a witness sensu stricto. The reasoning behind this is due to the belief that the probative value stemming from a statement given under specific circumstances or stemming from a specific group of people, are not to be considered of equal probative value to the statements of a witness sensu stricto. One such example is the testimony of a person who is mentally ill or under the age of fourteen. At times, this may also be applicable to the statements of people who are related to the defendant. Although, as a rule, the defendant's relatives may refuse to testify, at times, they must give statements when due to the peculiarities of the case, there are no other ways in which to obtain relevant evidence regarding the facts and circumstances of the criminal offense.[869] Therefore, in these instances, the defendant's relatives do not have the duty to tell the truth and are to be examined by the trial judge as informants rather than witnesses sensu stricto.

Regarding the witness's duty to testify, it applies to both the testimony itself and the duty to inform the court of her personal circumstances (*qualificação*), such as her name, age, address, profession, place of work, and whether she is related to any of the parties.[870] Regardless of whether a witness fails to tell the truth or remains silent when questioned, if she does not have a corresponding legal right to refuse to do so, she is

---

[866] Art. 213 CPP.
[867] See supra Ch. 1 C. III. 2. and Ch. 2 C. III. 1.
[868] Art. 203 CPP.
[869] Art. 206 CPP.
[870] Art. 203 CPP. See *Nucci*, CPP Comentado, pp. 566, 567.

liable for false testimony (*falso testemunho*), as per Art. 342 CP.[871] This is because, as a rule,[872] the criminal offense of false testimony is applicable to witnesses who lie on the stand and to those that remain silent absent a legal excuse to do so.[873]

Lastly, as per Art. 206 CPP, witnesses must attend trial when regularly summoned. If they fail to attend trial without giving the court a justifiable reason, the trial judge may order the bailiff to coercively bring the witness in question to court, with the aid of police force if necessary.[874] Additionally, depending on the extent of the witness's resistance in being brought to court, he may face an indictment of contempt of court (*crime de desobediência*).[875] In these instances, the trial judge may additionally order the witness to pay a fine and to pay for the costs resulting of the trial judge having to order a bailiff to coercively bring him to court by force.[876]

a) Summoning Witnesses

As to the number of witnesses that testify at trial, the prosecution may summon in total and the defense may summon per indictment a total of eight witnesses sensu stricto[877] in the ordinary procedural outline and five witnesses in the summary procedural outline.[878] Further, if co-defendants are standing trial together, each of them will have the right to summon eight witnesses. The numbers set above only apply to the people that are considered as witnesses in the strict sense, and for this reason, they are referred to as "numbered witnesses" (*testemunhas numerárias*). Hence, informants and witnesses who were named by other witnesses, the so-called "referred witnesses" (*testemunhas referidas*), are not included in the above-mentioned numbers.[879] Additionally, victims of a criminal offense are not considered to be witnesses because they do not have to make a solemn promise to tell the truth and due to having an interest in the case's outcome.[880]

---

[871] This topic is controversial, as some scholars believe that witness's liability does not stem from the legal oath per se, but rather pursuant to Art. 342 CPP. In this sense see, *Tourinho Filho*, Manual, p. 624. In contrast, there are scholars that contend that witnesses are only liable for false testimony if they make a solemn promise to tell the truth. In this sense, see *Nucci*, CPP Comentado, pp. 562, 563.

[872] For exceptions, see infra Ch. 3 C. IV. 2. c).

[873] *Choukr*, CPP Comentado, vol. 1, p. 547; *Nucci*, CPP Comentado, p. 573.

[874] Art. 218 CPP.

[875] As per Art. 330 CP.

[876] Art. 219 CPP. The fine is proportional to the witness's economic conditions and may vary between one to ten minimum wages.

[877] This illustrates the high amount of formalism of the Brazilian criminal procedure. I address the reasons for the existence of this feature in the Brazilian legal culture in Ch. 5 C. I.

[878] Arts. 401, chapeau, and Art. 532 CPP, respectively.

[879] Art. 209, para. 1 CPP. See *Nicolitt*, Manual de Processo Penal, p. 550.

[880] Both informants and victims are termed *testemunhas não numerárias*, which roughly translates as "uncounted witnesses".

As to the procedural moment in which the parties must indicate the witnesses they wish to present at trial, both the prosecution and defense must name them in the bill of indictment and in the written response to the indictment, respectively. If they fail to do so, their right to present witnesses precludes, and the only way they may question them is if they request the judge to produce the witness as that of the court's (*testemunhas do juízo*).[881] The problem with this practice lies that in such cases, it is within the trial judge's discretion whether to admit the witness in question, as there are no mechanisms in which to compel the court to summon and examine them at trial.[882]

Pursuant to Art. 209, chapeau, CPP, the trial judge may summon and hear additional witnesses whenever she considers it to be necessary. However, unlike oral testimony indicated by the parties, there are no restrictions to the number of additional witnesses the judge may summon and examine. Although the CPP does not state the procedural moment the trial judge may hear these additional witnesses, in practice this usually occurs either after the "numbered witnesses" indicated by the parties were examined or after the procedure of evidence taking is concluded.[883] If the trial judge examines the witnesses in the latter procedural moment, the witnesses of the court will be heard as "supplementary inquiries" (*diligências complementares*).[884]

b) Examining Witnesses

I will now describe the examination of oral testimony, which comprise the examination of witnesses sensu stricto, informants, and the victim. It is only for reasons of expediency that I will use the term witness to analyze the examination of all oral testimony in this subitem. The reason for doing so is owing to the outline of the examination of oral testimony being located in Chapter VI of the CPP, which addresses the examination of witnesses.

There are two main characteristics to witness examination, the first of which is set out by Art. 204, chapeau, CPP which states that their testimony must be given orally.[885] However, there are some practices that are permitted, e. g., witnesses are permitted to briefly consult their notes concerning the facts of the case, and either one

---

[881] Art. 401, para. 1 CPP. See *Brasileiro de Lima*, Manual de Processo Penal, p. 1316; *Nucci*, CPP Comentado, p. 589.

[882] I will address this topic in more detail in Ch. 6 B. I. 2. b) aa).

[883] *Nucci*, CPP Comentado, pp. 589, 590.

[884] Art. 402 CPP.

[885] An exception to the duty to testify orally are afforded to witnesses that are exempt from this duty owing to their office, as per Art. 221 para. 1 CPP. If they choose to, the president, his vice-president, the presidents of the Federal Senate and the House of representatives, and the chief justice of the Supreme Federal Court may give a written testimony instead of an oral one. In such cases, the parties will submit their questions to the judge who will then relate them to the aforementioned officials, as per Art. 220 CPP.

of the parties or the trial judge may read parts of the indictment out loud as a means in which to activate the witness's memory.[886]

The second characteristic is that, as a rule, witness examination must take place in the courtroom. However, there are two exceptions to this rule, namely when either a witness is unable to attend trial due to a serious illness or old age[887] and whenever there is concern that the defendant's presence may cause the witness to feel fear, intimidation, or embarrassment. In the latter case, either the defendant will be asked to leave the courtroom, in which case, his defense counsel will remain inside, or the witness will have to leave the courtroom and will be examined by the parties and the trial judge by means of videoconference.[888]

The examination of the oral evidence will greatly differ depending on whether the person giving statements is an adult or a minor.[889] Adult witnesses must be examined separately, so that they cannot hear each other's testimony[890] and as a rule, the prosecution's witnesses are heard first followed by those of the defense (*oitivas das testemunhas de acusação e de defesa*).[891]

Up to the reform of the CPP in 2008, the *sistema presidencialista* with regard to the examination of witnesses persisted, i.e., the trial judge was responsible for examining witnesses. Thus, it was only after the trial judge concluded his examination, that the parties could then direct their questions to the trial judge who would then relay them to the witness, if he found the question to be pertinent and relevant to the case. The reasoning behind this system was that by sifting the questions directed to the witnesses, this would protect them from offensive or inducive questions.[892] As previously examined, it is for this very reason that the *sistema presidencialista* persists concerning the examination of the defendant.[893]

---

[886] Art. 204, sole paragraph, CPP.

[887] Art. 220 CPP.

[888] Art. 217, chapeau, CPP.

[889] The specificities as to the examination of minors are provided by L. 13.431/2017. This law sets out that the examination of minors in cases where they are either a victim or a witness to a criminal offense which involved violence (Art. 4 I-IV). This special procedure is called *depoimento sem dano* and aims to protect minors from further trauma and victimization (Arts. 1 and 8). However, depending on the circumstances of the case, it may also be applicable to victims and witnesses between 18 and 21 years of age and (Art. 3, sole paragraph). The specific steps the judge must take are set out in art. 12, L. 13.431/2017.

[890] Art. 210, chapeau, CPP.

[891] Art. 400 sets out the order of presentation of witnesses, which must be followed under penalty of relative nullity (*nulidade relativa*). That is, if it can be proven that the defendant was found guilty because of the inversion in in the examination of the witnesses, said examination will be annulled and must start from the beginning. See *Nicolitt*, Manual de Processo Penal, p. 550.

[892] *Nucci*, CPP Comentado, p. 595.

[893] Scholars such as *Barcelos de Souza* believe that the sistema presidencialista should have persisted concerning the examination of witnesses as to protect them from offensive or inducive questions. See *Souza*, Novas Leis de Processo, p. 15.

After the enactment of L. 11.690/08, which changed the wording of Art. 212, chapeau, CPP, each party may directly question the witnesses (*inquirição direta*). As seen, first the witnesses summoned by the prosecution are heard, followed by those summoned by the defense. Therefore, whenever the former witnesses are heard, the prosecution,[894] followed by the defense may ask them questions, whereas when the latter are heard, the order is reversed, i.e., the defense questions the witnesses, followed by the prosecution. After both the parties finish questioning the witnesses, the judge may supplement the examination whenever she wishes to clarify certain points.[895] However, although the parties are responsible for conducting the examination of witnesses, the trial judge may still deny either party from asking certain questions, whenever she believes that they have no relation to the case or are repetitive.[896]

When addressing the topic of witness examination, it is important to clarify a widespread misconception. Although some Brazilian scholars refer to the practice of questioning witnesses in the Brazilian trial setting as akin to the cross-examination as practiced in the US-American system,[897] this is an erroneous comparison. The reason for this is that Art. 212, chapeau, CPP sets out that each party must examine both their own witnesses and the opposing party's witnesses by means of direct examination. Thus, contrary to the main feature of the US-American cross-examination, the examination of the opposing party's witnesses is not conducted by means of leading questions. Furthermore, the parties are discouraged to ask these types of questions, as Art. 212, chapeau, CPP *expressly* states that the trial judge should not allow the parties to ask witnesses questions that may induce a specific answer, i.e., leading questions.

A second important distinction between the examination of oral witnesses in the Brazilian setting which greatly differs from the US-American cross-examination is that in the latter legal system although the trial judge may ask witnesses questions, in practice it is very uncommon for a US-trial judge to do so. This is owing to the US-American adversarial trial setting and, consequently, to the belief that if trial judges act in a more active manner, they may be losing their more passive stance, and thus their impartiality.[898] Conversely, as the Brazilian trial judge is responsible for con-

---

[894] When applicable, whenever the witnesses summoned by the prosecution are heard, the private accessory prosecutor (*assistente de acusação*) asks the questions directly after the prosecution and before the defense. In contrast, when the witnesses summoned by the defense are heard, the order is reversed, i.e., the private accessory prosecutor asks the questions directly after the defense and before the prosecution.

[895] *Badaró*, Processo Penal, p. 627. I address this topic in more detail in Ch. 5 B. III. 2.

[896] Art. 212, chapeau, CPP.

[897] *Silva Júnior*, Reforma Tópica, pp. 138, 139, 173 et seq.

[898] See infra Ch. 4 B. III.

ducting evidence taking, it is not uncommon for him to ask witnesses questions, as it is the judge's responsibility to find the objective facts of the case.[899]

3. Victim

Whenever applicable, the victim will start her statements by clarify her identity, which include stating her name, address, and profession. Subsequently, she will inform the court the circumstances of the crime committed and who she thinks the author of the crime is or who she presumes it to be. She may also indicate evidence that she believes to be important to the case.[900]

There are many similarities between victims and witnesses, such as being examined in a similar manner and having the duty to attend trial and to make statements. For this reason, if a victim fails to attend trial without giving any valid reasons for her absence, the trial judge may order her to be brought to trial.[901] Yet, despite having many similarities, there are key differences between victims and witnesses, namely that the former (i) do not have to make a solemn promise to tell the truth,[902] (ii) they make "declarations" (*declarações do ofendido*)[903] rather than being "examined" by the parties and the trial judge, (iii) they have an interest in the case's outcome, particularly because the criminal conviction also serves as a civil enforcement order should a civil case ensue (*título executivo cível*) and (iv) they may present evidence at trial, which they believe might be helpful in clarifying the case.[904]

As is the case regarding the defendant's statements, due to the victim not being a witness, she has no obligation to tell the truth and, therefore, is not liable to being prosecuted for perjury (*falso testemunho*).[905] However, she is prohibited from incriminating an innocent person for a crime when she knows the person in question has not committed under penalty of being liable for slander (*denunciação caluniosa*).[906]

---

[899] Even if the concept of the search for the material truth is going through changes, as the trial setting is slowly allowing for more party-controlled presentation of evidence, the fact remains that the judge's role in finding the truth remain to be ingrained in the Brazilian legal culture. See infra Ch. 4 C. II. and Ch. 5 C. II.

[900] Art. 201, chapeau, CPP.

[901] Art. 201 para. 1 CPP.

[902] *Choukr*, CPP Comentado, vol. 1, p. 550.

[903] Art. 201, chapeau, CPP.

[904] Art. 201, chapeau, CPP.

[905] *Nicolitt*, Manual de Processo Penal, p. 249.

[906] Art. 339 CP.

4. Experts

There are three types of professionals who aid the trial judge in her decision-making in areas outside of her expertise.[907] These professionals fall into two groups: court-appointed experts (sensu lato) and privately retained experts. The former grouping comprises both official experts (*peritos oficiais*) and the so-called "appointed experts" (*peritos nomeados*). Official experts are professionals who hold a diploma of higher education and who usually must pass a civil servant's entrance examination (*concurso público*) to work in a specific area of expertise. They "belong to a special organ of the State, which has the responsibility to exclusively produce said expertise".[908] In the absence of an official expert, the trial judge may order the production of expert evidence to be carried out by two "appointed experts", who have technical qualifications related to the nature of the examination.[909]

The CPP sets out that the trial judge and the parties may address their questions to the official experts and to the appointed experts in writing, by means of the so-called *quesitos*.[910] This right is also extended to the private accessory prosecutor (*assistente de acusação*) and to the victim. The parties' written questions must be presented ten days in advance of the proceeding in which the court-appointed expert will present her findings.[911] This is due to court-appointed experts (in the broad sense) having to be informed of the date set for trial and the questions directed to her within at least ten days prior to trial.[912] If the judge grants the parties' request, the expert will usually hand in the expert report (*laudo pericial*) and the answers to the parties' questions in writing.[913] However, in the instances where the trial judge believes that there is a need to further clarify the questions asked by the parties, or in cases where further questions arise from the previous answers, the expert in question will have to attend trial and testify so that the trial judge and the parties may question her orally.[914]

The enactment of L.11.690/2008 introduced another feature in the trial setting with the aim of allowing the parties to present evidence at trial. As per the new wording of Art. 159 para. 3, the parties may request the trial judge for permission to

---

[907] The CPP sets out the instances, where experts are necessary to assist the trial judge's decision-making, such as Art. 158, chapeau, CPP.

[908] *Nucci*, CPP Comentado, p. 455, "(...) pertence a órgão especial do Estado, destinado exclusivamente a produzir perícias".

[909] Art. 159 para. 1 CPP.

[910] Arts. 159 para. 3, 176, chapeau, CPP. See also *Nucci*, CPP Comentado, pp. 488, 489.

[911] Arts. 159 para. 3 and 159 para. 5 I CPP. Failure to comply to these deadlines only leads to irregularity and not nullity.

[912] Art. 159, para. 3 CPP. According to Art. 160, sole paragraph and Art. 278 CPP, if the deadline of ten days is met and the official expert fails to appear at trial, the trial judge may order her to be coercively conducted to trial (*condução coercitiva*).

[913] *Nucci*, CPP Comentado, pp. 459.

[914] *Nucci*, CPP Comentado, pp. 459.

appoint privately retained experts of their choice (*assistentes técnicos*).[915] This request may take place either before or after the presentation of the expert evidence by the official expert. If the trial judge permits the parties to retain their own expert, she will notify them of her decision.[916] In such cases, the privately retained expert may participate in the proceedings after the official expert concluded the examination of the evidence and finished writing the expert report, and if applicable, after having answered the party's questions orally. It is only then that privately retained experts may have access to the object to be examined by her and may write her report (*parecer do assistente técnico*).[917]

Although this modification to the CPP gave the parties a higher degree of participation over the presentation of evidence, the probative value of evidence presented by court-appointed expert differs from that presented by privately retained experts. This is because court-appointed experts are subject to some of the same provisions applicable to judges,[918] e.g., they may be challenged by the same reasons judges may be challenged (*casos de suspeição*).[919] For this reason, there is the presumption that evidence produced by a court-appointed expert is produced by an impartial procedural actor.

5. Documentary Evidence

The CPP has a broad definition of documents. Art. 232, chapeau, defines them as any writing of a public or private nature that may also comprise both digital and audiovisual records. More specifically, documents are any "materialized manifestation, by means of spelling, symbols, drawings, that are a form of expression of language or communication in which it is possible to understand its content".[920] Contrary to witness testimony, where the parties must name the witnesses they wish to present in a specific procedural moment under penalty of preclusion, both parties may introduce documentary evidence at any stage of the proceedings.[921] Further, Art. 234 CPP sets out that if the trial judge is made aware of a documentary evidence that is relevant to either the prosecution or the defense's case, she may order the

---

[915] The privately retained experts are akin to expert witnesses in the US-American evidence law, as they are experts whose services are retained by the parties.

[916] Art. 159 para. 4 CPP.

[917] Art. 159 para. 5 II CPP.

[918] Art. 275 CPP.

[919] Art. 280 CPP.

[920] *Pacelli*, Curso de Processo Penal, p. 448, "Documento [é] qualquer manifestação materializada, por meio de grafia, de símbolos, de desenhos e, em enfim, que seja uma forma ou expressão de linguagem ou de comunicação, em que seja possível a compreensão de seu conteúdo".

[921] Art. 231 CPP. See *Scaranse Fernandes*, Processo Penal Constitucional, p. 78; *Badaró*, in: Ambos (ed.), Polícia e Investigação, p. 263.

evidence in question to be attached to the case file and to be taken as evidence at trial regardless of the absence of a request by the parties to this end.

As to the authenticity of documentary evidence, there are a few particularities regarding this topic which is dependent on the piece of evidence in question. First, the authentication of copies of photographs have the same probative value as the original photographs.[922] Second, for copies of public documents to have the same probative value as the original document, the former must first be compared to the latter in the presence of the authority by which it is being presented.[923] Lastly, whenever the authenticity of a private document is contested by either one of the parties or by the trial judge, the handwriting and the document's signature must be submitted to a court-appointed expert to settle the matter.[924]

IV. Admissibility of Evidence

1. Admissibility of Evidence and Rationale for Limiting or Excluding Evidence

As previously seen, the trial judge is responsible for finding out the historical events and the circumstances surrounding the commission of a criminal offense. To this end, all means of evidence are accepted provided that they do not violate constitutional or statutory provisions, legal principles,[925] or the "best practices" (*bons costumes*).[926]

The acceptability of all means of evidence is furthered by Art. 155, chapeau, CPP, which sets out the principle of probative freedom (*princípio da liberdade probatória*). Further, the sole paragraph of Art. 155 CPP states that the civil law's restriction to evidence is not applicable to criminal procedures, with exception of those that relate to a person's status, such as that which aims to prove a person's marital status, date of birth, citizenship, and parentage. Nonetheless, there are limitations to the admissibility of evidence on account of statutory and constitutional provisions, which set out restrictions in the methods of obtaining evidence (*obtenção da prova*). The reasoning behind these provisions are due to the need of safeguarding other procedural aims that are of equal or higher importance than truth-finding. For this reason, there are instances where a piece of evidence must be excluded, whereas in other cases the decision on whether to admit the evidence in question is up to the trial

---

[922] Art. 232, sole paragraph, CPP.

[923] Art. 237 CPP.

[924] Art. 235 CPP.

[925] *Tucci*, Direitos e Garantias, p. 70.

[926] Some scholars state that a proffered piece of evidence may not violate nor offend "best practices". In this sense see *Nicolitt*, Manual de Processo Penal, p. 701; *Nucci*, CPP Comentado, p. 416. I address the problem with abstract legal terms, which have no concrete definitions in Ch. 6 B. I. 1.

judge. However, in the latter instances, the probative value given to a piece of evidence will vary according to its reliability (*grau de convencimento*).[927]

2. Statutory and Constitutional Rules for Excluding or Limiting Evidence

a) Nemo Tenetur Se Ipsum Detegere

A constitutional and statutory reason to exclude or limit the admissibility of evidence at trial is the *nemo tenetur se detegere* principle, which is provided by Art. 8 para. 2 lit. g ACHR and Art. 14, III lit. g of the International Covenant on Civil and Political Rights (ICCPR). This far-reaching principle has many dimensions that have both a constitutional and statutory basis.

The first dimension is the *in dubio pro reo* principle, which applies after the procedure of evidence taking has finished, i. e., whenever the trial judge has doubts as to whether the defendant is guilt, she must find the defendant not guilty.[928]

The second dimension – which stems from the aforementioned dimension – is the constitutionally protected presumption of innocence (*presunção de inocência*).[929] Due to this right, the defendant is to be presumed innocent during all phases of the criminal procedure, i. e., from the investigatory phase until *res judicata*.[930] This is to ensure the possibility that even if the defendant is found to be innocent at the end of the trial, his rights were not unduly or disproportionately infringed by the criminal case (*persecução penal*).

The third dimension is a consequence of the defendant's right to a full defense. As previously examined, this right encompasses both the defendant's right to defend himself and the right to legal counsel. While the right to the latter is mandatory regardless of the circumstances, the right to the former is only mandatory with respect to the judge, as the defendant may waive her right to self-defense whenever she so wishes. The right to self-defense usually reaches its full extent when the trial judge examines the defendant at trial, and it is divided into the right of active self-defense (*autodefesa positiva*) and of negative self-defense (*autodefesa negativa*).[931] Active self-defense is the defendant's right to actively seek to resist the prosecution's case, as for example, the defendant's right to clarify the facts of the case to prove his

---

[927] *Pacelli*, Curso de Processo Penal, p. 352.

[928] *Nicolitt*, Manual de Processo Penal, p. 697.

[929] Art. 5 LVII CF and Art. 8 para. 2 ACHR.

[930] However, although Art. 5 LVII CF states that the presumption of innocence prevails until the issue of a final and unappealable sentence, the STF (in HC 126292/SP) ruled that after a tribunal of second instance confirms the conviction of the defendant, the provisory execution of the sentence may be initiated.

[931] *Lopes Jr.*, Direito Processual Penal, 15th ed., pp. 101 et seq.

innocence during his examination at trial.[932] In contrast, the negative self-defense is the defendant's right to omit information, to refuse to make statements, to refuse to participate in the re-enactment of the crime, or yet, to participate in any activity that could incriminate her or harm her defense.[933]

I will presently examine two facets of the rights of negative self-defense, namely the right to silence and not to be compelled to do something except by force of law.

aa) Right to Silence

Pursuant to constitutional and statutory provisions, as well as to the ACHR,[934] the accused has the right to remain silent (*direito ao silêncio*) in both the investigatory and adjudicatory phases.[935] This right has several implications.

First, as previously seen, the examination of the defendant entails two steps: his identification, and the examination itself, which comprise questions on both the defendant's life and the merits of the case. Pursuant to Art. 186, chapeau, CPP, the right to silence only encompasses the latter step, since it sets out that after the defendant has been identified, she shall be informed of her right to silence.[936] This is owing to the first part of the defendant's examination merely seeking to ascertain whether the person taking the stand is in fact the person accused of having committed the crime in question.

Second, it is the defendant's prerogative to decide how much information she wishes to provide, i.e., the extent of her testimony. Thus, it is up to the defendant whether she will remain silent throughout the whole examination, or only with regard to some individual questions.[937]

Third, since the defendant is not a witness, she has no obligation to tell the truth,[938] and, therefore, she is not liable for perjury.[939] However, there are two limitations to the defendant's lack of duty in telling the truth; the defendant may not deliberately

---

[932] *Lopes Jr./Gloeckner*, Investigação Preliminar, p. 479.

[933] *Lopes Jr./Gloeckner*, Investigação Preliminar, p. 486.

[934] Art. 5 LXIII CF, Art. 186, chapeau CPP and Art. 8 para. 2 lit. g ACHR, respectively.

[935] *Nucci*, CPP Comentado, p. 515. However, there are scholars who believe that if the judge fails to inform the defendant of his right to silence, this is merely a relative grounds for nullity, i.e., the defense, must prove that their case was harmed by the failure to inform the defendant of this right. In this sense, see *Choukr*, CPP Comentado, vol. 1, pp. 510 et seq.

[936] *Távora/Alencar*, Curso de Direito Processual Penal, p. 97; *Tourinho Filho*, Manual, p. 600.

[937] *Nicolitt*, Manual de Processo Penal, pp. 738, 739; *Nucci*, CPP Comentado, p. 525.

[938] Some scholars openly say the defendant has a right to lie, in this sense, see *Choukr*, CPP Comentado, vol. 1, p. 515; *Nicolitt*, Manual de Processo Penal, p. 738; *Nucci*, CPP Comentado, p. 523. In contrast, other scholars believe that the defendant does not have the right to lie, but rather than he cannot be criminally liable for not telling the truth, see *Tourinho Filho*, Manual, pp. 601, 602.

[939] *Nicolitt*, Manual de Processo Penal, p. 249.

falsely incriminate another person for a crime, nor may she make false self-incriminating admissions.[940] If the defendant incurs in any of these actions, the CP sets out that she is respectively liable for slander (*denunciação caluniosa*) and false self-incrimination (*auto-acusação falsa*).[941]

Lastly, the right to silence cannot be detrimental to the defendant's case, due to it being a constitutional guarantee that seeks to further his procedural rights.[942] In this regard, Art. 186, sole paragraph, CPP expressly states that the defendant's right to silence cannot be construed as a confession nor may it be used against him.[943] A consequence of this is that during the closing statements, the prosecution may not take advantage of the fact that the defendant chose to remain silent as an indication that the defendant is guilty of the crime, nor can the trial judge use the defendant's silence as evidence in which to support a conviction.

bb) Right Not to Be Compelled to do Something Except by Virtue of Law

Pursuant to Art. 5 II CF, "no one shall be obliged to do or refrain from doing something except by virtue of law" (*obrigação de fazer e não fazer, somente em virtude de lei*). Accordingly, the defendant cannot be compelled by the government to produce evidence against herself. This is pertinent regarding the gathering of biological material (*material biológico*) to perform genetic investigations (*investigação genética*).[944] If biological material is found either at the scene of the crime, inside or on the victim's body or clothing, this evidence may be collected without any restrictions. This is also the case when the police has a search warrant (*busca e*

---

[940] *Choukr*, CPP Comentado, vol. 1, p. 515.

[941] Arts. 339 and 341 CP, respectively.

[942] *Grilo*, Defesa Técnica, p. 49; STF held this in HC 68.742/DF. This also applies to the Jury trial, as set out by Art. 478 II CPP, in which the lay jury may not construct the defendant's silence in her detriment, under penalty of the jury's decision being annulled.

[943] It is interesting to point out that this is one of the subjects that illustrate the lack of systemic coherence of the CPP. On the one hand, Art. 186, sole paragraph, states that the defendant's right to silence cannot be construed as a confession. On the other hand, Art. 198 CPP sets out that "the silence of the accused cannot be equated to a confession, but it may constitute an element in the formation of the judge's conviction". This is because the latter legal provision is a result of the incoherent cross references resulting from the many reforms made to the CPP. Due to this legal provision dating from 1941, it is not in accordance with the constitutional right to remail silent, as per Art. 5, LXIII CF and, as a result, is not part of the Brazilian normative framework. In this sense, see *Nucci*, CPP Comentado, p. 542. There are scholars who believe that Art. 198 CPP is unconstitutional; however, this is not an accurate assessment as this legal provision predates the Constitution. Further, since Art. 186 sole paragraph CPP was enacted in 2003, due to the principle of anteriority (*princípio da anterioridade*), it must prevail over Art. 198 CPP. In this sense, see *Lopes Jr./Gloeckner* Investigação Preliminar, p. 484; *Grilo*, Defesa Técnica, p. 49; *Pacelli*, Curso de Processo Penal, pp. 45, 46.

[944] *Lopes Jr./Gloeckner*, Investigação Preliminar, p. 489.

apreensão domiciliar e/ou pessoal),[945] and find biological material in the accused or defendant's home.

The problem lies, however, when evidence is found on the defendant's body. In such instances, the possibility of collecting evidence is dependent on whether the procedure is considered to be invasive (*prova invasiva*) or non-invasive (*prova evasiva*). Non-invasive evidence is that which can be found outside of the defendant's body, such as hair, saliva, or taking voice and writing samples. In contrast, invasive evidence is that which involves either collecting evidence from human cavities or the need to extract biological material from the defendant by injecting him, e. g., taking blood and marrow samples.[946] If invasive evidence could be gathered without the defendant's consent, this would reduce him to an object, rather than a person subject to constitutional and procedural rights, such as the right to human dignity.[947]

The defendant's right not to be compelled to produce evidence against himself was affected by the changes brought by L. 12.037/09.[948] Art. 5 LVIII CF sets out that no one who has undergone civil identification shall be submitted to criminal identification, save in the cases provided by law. These instances are laid out by Art. 3 IV L. 12.037/09 which state that the judge may order a criminal identification if it is essential to the police investigation. Art. 5, sole paragraph, L. 12.037/09 sets out that it is possible to capture the biological material of the accused, to obtain his genetic profile. In this context, most Brazilian scholars believe that *non-invasive* evidence may be obtained without the accused's express consent since in such instances, the accused only needs to tolerate the examination in question. A further reason is owing to the claim that the biological material is solely taken for the purpose of criminally identifying a person accused of having committed a criminal offense. Thus, seeing that the non-invasive evidence is taken in the investigatory phase – which has an administrative nature – it cannot be used at trial as a means of evidence. Consequently, as a rule, most scholars believe that these provisions are not contrary to the *nemo tenetur* principle.[949]

---

[945] *Lopes Jr./Gloeckner*, Investigação Preliminar, p. 489.

[946] *Queijo*, O Direito, pp. 245 et seq.

[947] Art. 1 III CF.

[948] L. 12.654/12 changed several provisions of L. 12.037/09.

[949] Nonetheless, there are scholars who believe that regardless of whether the evidence is invasive or non-invasive, it may only be obtained with the defendant's consent, otherwise her presumption of innocence would be void. Further, the defendant cannot be compelled to provide the state with written or voice samples as it is within the defendant's prerogative whether he wishes to help the state in any way which is harmful to his case, and in proving his guilt. In this sense, see *Lopes Jr./Gloeckner*, Investigação Preliminar, p. 494; *Nicolitt*, Manual de Processo Penal, p. 180.

b) Inadmissibility of Illegally Obtained Evidence

The inadmissibility of illegally obtained evidence (*inadmissibilidade das provas ilícitas*) has both a constitutional and statutory origin.[950] Although neither constitutional nor statutory provisions expressly define the term "illicit" (in the broad sense), most scholars understand it to encompass both evidence that was obtained in violation of legal provisions regarding matters of substantive criminal law (*prova ilícita stricto sensu*) and matters of criminal procedure (*prova ilegitíma*).[951] There is an important distinction between them; evidence obtained in violation to the former are always inadmissible at trial. In contrast, evidence gathered in violation to the latter are only inadmissible if the party affected by the presentation of illegal evidence proves that the admissibility of the evidence in question was harmful to its case.[952]

I will now briefly analyze the main provisions setting out the inadmissibility of illegally obtained evidence in the CPP. Art. 157 para. 3 CPP provides that evidence obtained in violation to either constitutional or statutory provisions are inadmissible and must be removed from the case file. The aim of this provision is to both hinder future violations of these norms and to discourage and deter the police from obtaining evidence in an illegal manner.[953] This aim is furthered by Art. 157 para. 5 CPP, which sets out that the judge "who knows the content of the evidence declared inadmissible may not pronounce the sentence or judgment". This paragraph was added to the CPP by the recently enacted L. 13.964/19 and was intended as an effective means in which to further the integrity of both the police and the parties in gathering evidence during the investigatory and the adjudicatory procedural phases. Regrettably, this provision has also been the object of four motions questioning its constitutionality and requests for injunctive relief were made.[954]

In addition to the former provisions, Art. 157, chapeau, CPP provides that evidence derived from illegally obtained evidence is also inadmissible.[955] However, this

---

[950] Art. 5 LVI CF and Art. 157, chapeau, CPP, respectively.

[951] *Lopes Jr.*, Direito Processual Penal, 11th ed., p. 394; *Capez*, Curso de Processo Penal, pp. 372, 373; *Nicolitt*, Manual de Processo Penal, p. 169.

[952] Pursuant to Art. 563 CPP no act shall be declared void if it does not adversely affect either of the parties' case. This is usually referred to in Brazilian criminal procedure as *pas de nullité sans grief*. See *Pacelli*, Curso de Processo Penal, p. 352.

[953] *Grilo*, Defesa Técnica, p. 44; *Távora/Alencar*, Curso de Direito Processual Penal, p. 628.

[954] As of this writing, the four motions in question are ADI n. 6.298, ADI n. 6.299, ADI n. 6.300, and ADI n. 6.305. Ever since 1999, the Reform Committee – who authored the bills which resulted in the reforms of 2008 – sought to establish that the judge who knows the content of the evidence declared inadmissible is precluded from rendering the sentence. However, this provision was rejected due to it being considered too "venturesome". In this sense, see *Choukr*, CPP Comentado, vol. 1, p. 453.

[955] Before the enactment of this provision, in the instances in which evidence that was derived from illegally obtained evidence were solved by application of Art. 573 para. 1 CPP,

provision's two subsequent paragraphs lay out the two exceptions to the inadmissibility of evidence, which stem from the influence of the US-American's Fruit of the Poisonous Tree Doctrine (*Teoria do Fruto da Árvore Envenenada*).[956]

The first exception is the Independent Source Theory (*Teoria da Fonte Independente*), which states that evidence derived from that which was illegally obtained may be admissible, when no causal link between them is apparent, or when the derived evidence could be legally obtained from an independent source. Thus – in cases where the evidence is legally obtained through an investigation which was parallel to that where the illegal evidence was obtained – the said evidence is admissible. For many Brazilian scholars, the Independent Source exception to the Fruit of the Poisonous Tree as applied in the Brazilian legal system is superfluous. The reasoning for this is that there is no causal link between the evidence obtained illegally and that which was legally obtained. Thus, if the latter is not derived from the former, it is not a fruit of the poisonous tree, and for this reason, there was never a reason for the evidence in question to be considered inadmissible.[957]

The second exception is the Inevitable Discovery (*Descoberta Inevitável ou curso hipotético da investigação*), which states that evidence derived from that which was illegally obtained may be admissible, when the derived evidence that is yet to be found could eventually be obtained from an independent source. In this case, if two investigations are taking place, if the investigation parallel to the one where evidence was illegally obtained is prone to find admissible evidence independently of the illegally obtained evidence, the said evidence is considered to be legal.[958]

The third and last exception to the inadmissibility of illegally obtained evidence is not expressly provided by the CPP. Although evidence favoring the prosecution is not permissible at trial, according to most Brazilian scholars, illegally obtained evidence that seek to prove the defendant's innocence is admissible at trial.[959] This is owing to the belief that although it is important to hinder the state's agents, such as the chief of police or public prosecution, from obtaining evidence in an illegal manner, this aim must give way to significantly more important aims, i.e., finding the truth and not convicting innocent people.

---

which provides that the once the nullity of an act is declared, the acts which directly depend on it or are a consequence thereof and shall also be declared void.

[956] *Queijo*, O Tratamento da Prova Ilícita, p. 19. Some scholars do not admit any exceptions to the Fruit of the Poisonous Tree Doctrine. In this sense, see *Capez*, Curso de Processo Penal, p. 374.

[957] *Capez*, Curso de Processo Penal, p. 382; *Nicolitt*, Manual de Processo Penal, p. 715.

[958] *Capez*, Curso de Processo Penal, p. 383. *Silva Júnior*, Reforma Tópica, p. 151.

[959] *Nicolitt*, Manual de Processo Penal, p. 709; *Choukr*, CPP Comentado, vol. 1, p. 457; *Pacelli*, Curso de Processo Penal, p. 340; *Silva Júnior*, Reforma Tópica, pp. 153, 154.

c) The Witnesses' Rights and Duties to Refuse Testimony

The CPP lays out two instances where witnesses are excused from testifying to protect public interests at stake (*recusa justificada de depor*). The first instance is set out in Art. 206 CPP, which provides witnesses the right to refuse testimony on personal grounds. Thus, whenever a witness is the defendant's ascendant, descendant, sibling, adopted parent, or adopted sibling or child, or yet, current, or former spouse or partner in a civil union. This extensive list has the aim of fostering familial relationships and feelings of trust within a family, which persists even after the ending of a marriage or civil union. To further this aim, before the parties examine the witnesses, the trial judge must instruct them of their right to refuse testimony, and if she fails to do so, either the prosecution or the defense may request the judge to instruct the witnesses in question. If, however, the trial judge fails to instruct a witness of this right and neither party requests him to do so, the witness's testimony must be considered as "information" (*informações*), and not as evidence sensu stricto.[960]

There is one exception to the right set out in Art. 206 CPP, which takes place when due to the specific circumstances of a case, the trial judge deems that the testimony of one of the aforementioned people are the only way to obtain or to complement relevant facts or circumstances of the case. This is true when a defendant's relative or spouse are the only witnesses in the commission of a criminal offense. In such cases, the witness in question must testify, although due to the circumstances, he does not have to make a solemn promise to tell the truth and is not liable to false testimony.[961] Consequently, this person's testimony will be considered as that of an informant, and its probative value will be inferior to the testimony of a witness sensu stricto, i.e., that of a person who has the duty to tell the truth.

The second instance a witness may refuse to testify is on professional grounds, as set out in Art. 53 para. 6 CF. As per this provision, deputies and senators have the right to refuse testimony whenever the object of their statements is information, which they acquired by virtue of the exercise of their mandate.

There is a further instance where a witness is excused from testifying; however, this right is not laid out in the CPP. Many scholars believe that witnesses have the right not to incriminate themselves; in such cases, although a witness is not exempt of her duty to testify, she is permitted to abstain from answering a question whenever the answer might incriminate her.[962] For this reason, these scholars contend that witnesses must be informed of their right to silence whenever the answer to a question may incriminate them. However, just as is the case regarding the examination of the defendant, the witness's right to silence does not apply to questions which have the aim of identifying them.[963]

---

[960] *Nucci*, CPP Comentado, p. 576.
[961] Art. 208 CPP, CPP Comentado, vol. 1, p. 552; *Nucci*, CPP Comentado, p. 578; *Choukr*.
[962] *Choukr*, CPP Comentado, vol. 1, p. 558; *Tourinho Filho*, Manual, p. 626.
[963] *Távora/Alencar*, Curso de Direito Processual Penal, p. 97.

In contrast to the witness's rights in refusing to testify, there are instances where they are prohibited from giving testimony due to their profession or ministry. This is because if the witness in question could freely testify, there would be serious implications to this testimony owing to the public having access to confidential evidence (*proibição de depor em razão de profissão*). The professionals who are prohibited from testifying are not provided in the CPP,[964] but rather in an infra-constitutional legislation, a contract, or in judicial decisions, such is the case regarding lawyers.[965] However, if any of the people listed in Art. 207 CPP are released from their obligation to confidentiality by the interested party, it is within the witness's discretion whether they wish to testify as they cannot be compelled to do so.

As to the possibility of judges and prosecutors testifying as witnesses, they may do so regarding the facts they have witnessed *outside of court*. However, if the facts in question relate to the case, which they are currently presiding or involved in, the judge or prosecutor may testify, but must subsequently declare themselves challenged (*impedidos*) and must remove themselves from the case.[966] In contrast, this does not apply when judges and prosecutors are called to testify regarding what they have witnessed *at trial* while they were exercising their role as a judge or a prosecutor. In these cases, these professionals are prohibited from testifying by force of Art. 207 CPP.

d) Hearsay

Neither the CF nor the CPP implicitly or explicitly restrict the use of hearsay evidence (*testemunhas de "ouvir dizer"*). Most scholars believe that this type of evidence is admissible provided that the witness who is testifying at court and who heard the out-of-court statement, names the declarant who perceived these facts with one of their senses.[967] For these scholars, hearsay evidence is not a matter of admissibility, but rather a matter of the amount of probative value to be given to the evidence in question.

I believe there are two considerations that must be made regarding this type of evidence, as they are seldom discussed in the Brazilian criminal procedure. First, there are many Brazilian scholars who believe that hearsay evidence should not be admissible at trial. The main argument adduced is that other legal systems – the most cited of which is the US-American – find this type of evidence inadmissible. This is imprecise, as FRE 802 states that "hearsay is not admissible *unless* any of the following provide otherwise: a federal statute; these rules; or other rules prescribed by the Supreme Court". The FRE subsequently provides several exceptions to the rule

---

[964] *Tourinho Filho*, Manual, p. 620; *Nicolitt*, Manual de Processo Penal, p. 745.

[965] As per Art. 7 XIX, L. 8.906/94, lawyers have a right to refuse to testify despite their clients having released them from their obligation to confidentiality.

[966] Arts. 252 II and 258 CPP.

[967] *Nucci*, CPP Comentado, pp. 567, 568.

against hearsay (FRE 803–807).[968] Thus, the claim that hearsay evidence should not be admissible in the Brazilian criminal procedure because it is not admissible in the US-American evidence law is inaccurate, and should not be used as a valid argument in which to argue against the admissibility of this type of evidence.[969]

Second, I believe that a clarification must be made with regard to the terminology used to refer to hearsay evidence in the context of the Brazilian criminal procedure. Considering that an out-of-court statement is believed to not have the same probative value of an in-court-statement, this type of evidence refers to evidence in the broad sense which also includes informants, rather than evidence in the strict sense (*prova testemunhal*). For this reason, the terminology "*testemunhas de ouvir dizer*" may be misleading, as it may lead the reader to infer that it has the same probative value as testimonial evidence in sensu stricto.

D. Evidentiary Principles

In the Brazilian trial setting, there are evidentiary principles, which are believed to further the features of officialized factfinding (I.) or to further the features of a party-controlled presentation of evidence (II.). I will now examine the main principles adduced by Brazilian scholars.

I. Principles Associated to the Officialized Factfinding

The main principle that shapes the trial setting as an officialized factfinding is the principle of ascertainment of the truth (princípio da verdade real ou material).[970] This principle sets out that the trial judge is the procedural actor responsible for finding out the historical events of a criminal offense.[971] A direct consequence of this task is that the trial judge is also responsible for presiding over trial and for conducting evidence

---

[968] See supra Ch. 2 C. IV. 2. e).

[969] I address the damaging effects of the lack of tradition of conducting studies on foreign legal systems and comparative law in Ch. 4 A., Ch. 4 C. I., Ch. 5 A., and Ch. 6 A.

[970] In this sense, see *Marques*, Elementos de Direito, vol. 2, pp. 351 et seq.; *Jardim/Amorim*, Direito Processual Penal, pp. 81, 310; *Capez*, Curso de Processo Penal, pp. 65, 71; *Tourinho Filho*, 59 et seq.; *Nucci*, CPP Comentado, pp. 584. Despite the latter scholar believing that the trial judge should strive to find the material truth, he concedes that in practice, this is not always possible due to human fallibility, and thus that in such cases, the formal truth is found rather than the material truth. In contrast to the scholars cited above who believe that the trial judge should seek to find the objective facts of the case, there is a growing number of Brazilian many scholars who criticize the aim of finding the material truth. They contend that since the material truth cannot be found, the aim of the criminal procedure should be of ascertaining the formal truth. For the reasons behind Brazilian scholars criticizing the principle of ascertainment of truth, see footnote 104 (Part 3).

[971] *Silva Júnior*, Reforma Tópica, p. 133.

taking. In achieving these goals, the trial judge has a vast amount of judicial discretion, which can be illustrated by Art. 400, para. 1 CPP. This provision sets out that the trial judge may dismiss evidence which he considers to be irrelevant (*irrelevante*), cumbersome or troublesome to produce (*inconveniente*) or yet, which has the aim of protracting the proceedings (*protelatórias*).

Although this principle shapes the current Brazilian trial setting, its general acceptance is very contested. On the one hand, various scholars consider it to be an important and valid principle which establishes the judge's role in shaping the trial setting (*poderes instrutórios do juiz*).[972] On the other hand, scholars who have a more "pro-defendant" stance highly criticize this principle and equate it to the (from a historical standpoint) "inquisitorial system".[973] According to these scholars, this principle is damaging to the defendant's procedural rights, and believe that a trial setting where the parties are the sole procedural actors responsible for the presentation of evidence is both preferable and desirable.[974]

The second principle is the principle of free evaluation of evidence[975] (*princípio do livre convencimento motivado*). This principle has two facets; on the one hand, Art. 155, chapeau, CPP,[976] sets out that the trial judge shall form her conviction by freely evaluating the evidence produced in a contradictory court proceeding. Due to the wording of this provision, the trial judge cannot base her decision *exclusively* on the informative elements collected in the investigatory phase.[977] Therefore, provided that the facts and circumstances of the case were presented at the procedure of evidence taking (and consequently are included in the case file), the trial judge has complete freedom to base her decision on these elements.[978]

On the other hand, as per Art. 93 IX CF, the principle of free evaluation of evidence also restricts judicial discretion in reaching a decision as it dictates that the trial judge must substantiate her decision in writing. That is, she must clearly state the concrete means of evidence that led her to convict or acquit the defendant.[979] This duty has many purposes. First, it enables both parties to have access to the trial judge's reasoning. Second, if the defense so wishes, it may appeal from the decision based on the written arguments. Third, it enables the judges at the appellate court

---

[972] See Ch. 4 C. II., Ch. 6 A. I., and Ch. 6 B. I. 3.

[973] *Lopes Jr.*, Direito Processual Penal, 11th ed., pp. 579 et seq. I address this reasoning in Ch. 4 A., whereas I examine the damaging consequences of Brazilian scholars examining the inquisitorial procedural model solely from the historical viewpoint in Ch. 4 C. I.

[974] In this sense, see infra Ch. 6 A. I.

[975] *Damaška*, Evidence Law Adrift, p. 21.

[976] Regarding the jury trial, due to the system of personal conviction/*conviction intime* (*íntima convicção*), the jury need not and cannot state the reasoning behind its decision, as Art. 5 XXXVIII CF sets out that the secrecy of voting is ensured in the institution of the jury.

[977] Concerning the possibility of the trial judge basing her decision on informative elements (*indícios*), see Ch. 6 B. II.

[978] *Capez*, Curso de Processo Penal, p. 411.

[979] *Gomes Filho*, in: Prado/Malan, Processo Penal e Democracia, p. 59.

(*desembargadores*) to examine the trial judge's reasoning, and lastly, it provides the public a means in which to control judicial factfinding.[980]

As to the content of the trial judge's reasoning, the introduction of Art. 315 para. 2, I-IV to the CPP by the newly enacted L. 13.964/19 specifies the instances the trial judge fails to provide a proper reasoning for its verdict. Simply put, it solely sets out the instances where the grounds for a conviction or an acquittal were not in conformity to this principle. Consequently, in these instances, the verdict will not be considered as substantiated when the trial judge incurs in any one of the instances set out in this provision.

The first set of instances concern issues of clarity or specificity, as the trial judge may not limit himself to merely indicating, reproducing, or paraphrasing a legal provision without demonstrating its causality to the issue in question, nor may he employ undetermined legal concepts (*conceitos legal indeterminados*) without the respective reasoning for its use.[981] Further yet, the trial judge may not invoke arguments that could be applicable to a variety of cases.[982]

The second instance is whenever the trial judge fails to address all arguments that could in theory weaken the strength of the arguments adduced by him in reaching his decision. Lastly are the set of instances which concern precedent, i.e., a trial judge may not limit himself to invoke a biding precedent (SV) without identifying his reasons for doing so. Further, when an SV is adduced, the judge must apply its reasoning to the concrete case. Therefore, if the trial judge chooses not to follow the "binding summary" in question, he must clearly specify the reasons which led him to disregard the SV.

II. Principles Associated to the Party-Controlled Presentation of Evidence

1. Principles of Audiatur et Altera Pars and (the Right) to a Full Defense

The two most cited principles in furthering and safeguarding the defendant's rights are the principle of audiatur et altera pars[983] (*princípio do contraditório*) and the principle of full defense (*princípio da ampla defesa*). As examined supra, both principles have a rather limited scope during the pretrial phase, and have their full reach at trial, as they must be observed by the trial judge. Both these principles are provided in Art. 5 LV CF and, at times, they are examined and referred to as being one single principle. However, this is not strictly accurate, as the principle of full defense

---

[980] *Grilo*, Defesa Técnica, p. 57.
[981] I will address the undetermined legal concepts in Ch. 6 B. I. 1.
[982] *Gomes Filho*, in: Prado/Malan, Processo Penal e Democracia, p. 61.
[983] *Mossin*, *Compêndio* de Processo Penal, p. 33.

only seeks to protect the defendant's rights, whereas the principle of audiatur at altera pars furthers both parties' interests.[984] Nonetheless, these principles are indeed very similar to one another and there is a certain degree of interrelatedness between them.

The principle of audiatur at altera pars provides both the prosecution and the defense the right to (i) be informed of the procedural steps the trial judge takes and the right to (ii) participate in them (*o binômio de ciência e participação*). As per the first aspect of this principle, the state has a duty to inform the defendant and her defense counsel of the allegations against her, its reasoning, and the evidence against the defendant in order to safeguard the full defense principle.[985] To this end "the evidence [must] be taken in the presence of the defense who is entitled to offer counterproof and counterarguments".[986] Owing to the second aspect of this principle, the parties have the right to influence the judge's decision-making at trial.[987] To this end, the parties may present evidence that is favorable to their respective side, request the judge to summon a witness as that of the court,[988] and make their closing arguments.

In contrast, the principle of full defense comprises both the defendant's right to defend herself (*autodefesa*) and the right to have assistance of legal counsel present in all parts of the proceedings (*defesa técnica*).[989] It is owing to the principle of full defense being implemented by the first aspect of the principle of audiatur at altera pars,[990] that some scholars examine these principles as being one single principle.

2. Principle of Equality of Arms

The principle of equality of arms (*princípio da paridade de armas*) has been increasingly mentioned by Brazilian scholars as a means in which to further the rights of the defense in advancing the party-controlled presentation of evidence. Additionally, it is the chief argument adduced by scholars for the need of providing the defense effective means in which to conduct its own investigations in the investigatory phase (*investigação defensiva*).[991]

As of this writing, neither the CF nor the CPP implicitly or explicitly provide for the principle of equality of arms. Nonetheless, this principle is furthered by Art. 8 para. 2 lit. c ACHR, which provides that every person accused of a criminal offense is

---

[984] *Távora/Alencar*, Curso de Direito Processual Penal, p. 77.

[985] *Grilo*, Defesa Técnica, pp. 34, 35.

[986] *Grande*, Italian Criminal Justice, p. 228. See also *Nicolitti*, in: Prado/Malan, Processo Penal e Democracia, p. 50.

[987] *Távora/Alencar*, Curso de Direito Processual Penal, p. 77; *Karam*, in: Prado/Malan, Processo Penal e Democracia, p. 401; *Nicolitt*, Manual de Processo Penal, pp. 140, 141.

[988] See supra Ch. 3 C. III. 2. a).

[989] *Grilo*, Defesa Técnica, p. 39; *Pacelli*, Curso de Processo Penal, p. 339.

[990] *Malan*, in: Prado/Malan, Processo Penal e Democracia, p. 155

[991] *Vieira*, in: Ambos (ed.), Polícia e Investigação, p. 338; *Badaró*, Processo Penal, pp. 160, 161.

D. Evidentiary Principles

entitled to an "adequate time and means for the preparation of his defense". The importance of this principle is that if the defense had the means in which to gather exculpatory evidence prior to trial, this would better safeguard the defendant's right to a full defense throughout the procedural phases, namely:

(i) in seeking to influence the prosecution's decision-making before it decides to indict the accused,

(ii) once the prosecution files a bill of indictment, the defense could then seek to present enough evidence in the written reply to the indictment for the judge to summarily acquit the defendant, as per Art. 397 I to IV CPP,

(iii) should the court accept the bill of indictment and the case go to trial, the defense could then seek to effectively demonstrate to the court the defendant's innocence.[992]

Thus, the need for the defense to have effective mechanisms in which to gather evidence is not only essential in fulfilling its role in presenting evidence at trial, but also in *effectively* safeguarding the defendant's right to a full defense. From the standpoint of the principle of equality of arms, the particular importance of this principle is highlighted by the necessity of finding evidence seeing as the defendant is in a vulnerable position. This is owing to the defendant having to defend himself from the charges brought against him by the state, which has a vastly superior amount of resources at its disposal. Nonetheless, the CPP provides the defense with very little means in which to have access to evidence.[993]

---

[992] *Azevedo/Baldan*, A Preservação do Devido Processo Legal, p. 7; *Andrade/Ávila*, Sherlock Holmes, p. 9.

[993] I will address this topic in more detail in Ch. 6 B. I. 2. a).

Part 3

Key Concepts of Comparative Law, Comparative Study, and (Possible) Solutions to the Brazilian Criminal Procedure

As a rule, Brazilian scholars do not have a tradition of systematically conducting studies on foreign legal systems or in comparative law. There are three main consequences to this.

First, comparative studies usually lack the necessary methodology and understanding of introductory concepts of comparative law. This is highly problematic due to this field of law being an effective means to better understand a country's domestic legal system and to pinpoint its main deficiencies. Moreover, comparative law is an important tool in which to find possible solutions to a legal system's shortcomings.[1]

Second, the few systematic studies on both foreign legal systems and comparative law lead to a misapprehension of underlying terms such as "accusatorial", "inquisitorial", and "adversarial".[2] The terms accusatorial and adversarial are at times used interchangeably and incorrectly,[3] which in the *specific* context of legal comparison leads at best to confusion, and at worst to faulty generalizations and incorrect premises.[4]

Third, the comparative studies conducted by Brazilian scholars are performed using the same rationale applied in analyzing their domestic legal system. The problem of scholars conducting research in comparative law in the same manner as in

---

[1] *Pizzi*, Understanding Prosecutorial Discretion, p. 1326; *Watson*, Legal Transplants, p. 17; *Langbein*, The Influence of Comparative Procedure, p. 545.

[2] Among the very few Brazilian scholars who employ the terminology used in comparative law (from the Anglo-American perspective) are *Zilli*, Iniciativa Instrutória do Juiz, pp. 25 et seq.; *Grinover*, Iniciativa Instrutória do Juiz, pp. 16 et seq.; *Vieira*, Paridade de Armas, pp. 116 et seq.; *Vasconcellos*, Barganha e Justiça Criminal Negocial, pp. 94 et seq.

[3] In the context of legal comparison, these terms are also used synonymously. However, they are used to describe the adversarial legal system in its analytical sense, see *Damaška*, Evidentiary Barriers to Conviction, pp. 554, 561, 569, 570; *Bohlander*, Principles, pp. 6, 7.

[4] I would like to point out that false premises and generalizations are by no means limited to the Brazilian Scholarship. Up until recently, the negative connotation associated with the inquisitorial evidentiary arrangement was also present in the US-American law. The following scholars examine this prejudice: *Bradley*, Convergence of the Continental and the Common Law, pp. 472, 477 et seq.; *Sklansky*, Anti-Inquisitorialism; *Bohlander*, Principles, p. 6; *Jimeno-Bulnes*, American Criminal Procedure, pp. 410, 413, 416, 420; *Whitebread/Slobogin*, Criminal Procedure, p. 826.

their domestic legal systems is that a "legal projection" is bound to take place. Simply put, when scholars examine the evidentiary arrangements and the roles of the different procedural actors of a foreign legal system, they do so from their own standpoint, i.e., from the perspective of both their domestic legal system's normative framework and legal culture. This is problematic, as it fails to account for various elements, namely the targeted legal system's normative framework, legal culture, and the country's social, economic, geographical, and political features.

Thus, before I address the problematic features of the Brazilian criminal procedure and offer possible suggestions to its improvement, I would like to address some fundamental concepts of comparative law, which I believe are vital to this study. To this end, I will present two introductory chapters to clarify common misconceptions in this field. In Chapter 4, I will address the key legal definitions in comparative law as their correct apprehension is vital in fully understanding the work of international scholars in this area and in conducting comparative studies. In Chapter 5, I will examine the topic of legal transplants, of legal translations, and the importance of understanding the receiving country's institutional context before importing legal provisions or ideas from a foreign legal system. The concepts I will address in these chapters will set the stage for the comparative study and suggestions of improvement of selected features of the Brazilian criminal procedure in Chapter 6.

Chapter 4

Terminology in Comparative Law

A. Introduction: Misapprehension of Legal Definitions

When conducting studies in criminal procedure, Brazilian scholars exclusively use the terms accusatorial and inquisitorial in their historical denotation.[5] The problem with this practice is that by only taking into consideration the historical approach of the latter procedural model, this fails to account for various features in modern inquisitorial systems and how they function in practice.[6] Further, by using the terms *adversarial* and *accusatorial* interchangeably and by defining them in-

---

[5] *Tornaghi*, Curso de Processo, pp. 8 et seq.; *Mirabete*, Processo Penal, pp. 41, 42; *Marques*, Elementos de Direito, vol. 1, pp. 64 et seq.; *Prado*, Sistema Acusatório, pp. 80 et seq.; *Bastos*, Investigação, pp. 1 et seq., 11 et seq.; *Mossin*, Compêndio de Processo Penal, pp. 1 et seq.; *Rangel*, Direito Processual Penal, pp. 47 et seq.; *Brasileiro de Lima*, Manual de Processo Penal, pp. 38 et seq.; *Capez*, Curso de Processo Penal, pp. 81, 82; *Távora/Alencar*, Curso de Direito Processual Penal, pp. 54 et seq., 101; *Tourinho Filho*, Manual, pp. 82, 83; *Badaró*, Processo Penal, pp. 101, 102; *Lopes Jr.*, Direito Processual Penal, 15th ed., pp. 40 et seq., 93, 94; *Pacelli*, Curso de Processo Penal, pp. 9 et seq.

[6] Regarding the pitfalls of only taking the historical approach into consideration, see *Damaška*, Evidence Law Adrift, p. 3; *Damaška*, Models of Criminal Procedure, p. 481.

correctly,[7] this fails to explain how legal systems with predominantly inquisitorial evidentiary arrangements grant defendants a panoply of procedural rights at trial. Such is the case in the German criminal procedure which safeguards the accusatorial principle[8] and the principles of publicity, orality, immediacy,[9] as well as important procedural rights, such as the presumption of innocence, the defendant's right to silence, and to a fair trial.[10]

There are two further consequences to the lack of the correct apprehension of this terminology. First, when these scholars attempt to conduct comparative studies, they make assertions based on false premises concerning the outline and the evidentiary arrangements of foreign legal systems. Second, this leads to the complete unawareness that both the adversarial and the inquisitorial evidentiary arrangements need procedural safeguards to counter their respective structural deficiencies.[11]

I will now address these legal definitions as their correct comprehension is essential to the study of comparative law and to the field of comparative criminal procedure in a consequential manner. The definition of the terminology below (B.) sets the theoretical framework by which I will define the predominant evidentiary arrangement of the Brazilian criminal procedure in the concluding subitem (C.).

B. Theoretical Framework: Procedural Models

I. Definitions

Adversarial and *Inquisitorial* are terms used to classify legal systems into two procedural models based on the outline of their procedural phases and, especially on their evidentiary arrangements at the trial setting. These elements take into consideration features such as the key roles of the procedural actors and who has the main responsibility over gathering, sifting, and presenting evidence.

---

[7] The use of incorrect terminology in the field of comparative law by Brazilian scholars is both regarding the term "inquisitorial" and "adversarial". The harmful aspect of this complete lack of clarity regarding these different evidentiary arrangements can be illustrated by a well-known Brazilian scholar which stated that the term "adversarial" evokes an "extreme form" of an "accusatorial system". In this sense, see *Jardim/Amorim*, Direito Processual Penal, p. 80.

[8] In the German Criminal procedure, the accusatorial principle is called *Akkusationsprinzip* or *Anklagegrundsatz* and is provided in §§ 151, 155 (1), 264 (1) StPO. In this sense, see *Kindhäuser/Schumann*, Strafprozessrecht, § 4 Rn. 16.

[9] These principles are respectively *Öffentlichkeitsprinzip* (§ 169 (1) GVG, Art 6 para. 1 ECHR), *Mündlichkeitsprinzip* (§ 261 StPO) and *Unmittelbarkeitsprinzip* (§§ 226, 250, 261 StPO).

[10] The presumption of innocence (*Unschuldsvermutung*) is provided in § 261 StPO and Art. 6 para. 2 ECHR, the defendant's right to silence (*Recht des Beschuldigten zum Schweigen*) is set out in §§ 136 (1) sent. 2, 243 (5) sent. 1 StPO, whereas the right to a fair trial (*Recht auf ein faires Verfahren*) is set out in Art. 20 (3) GG and Art. 6 para. 1 ECHR.

[11] I will address this topic in Ch. 6 A. II. 1.

These terms are often used in connection to the "common law" and "civil law" legal traditions.[12] These two legal traditions have many distinguishable features, the most important of which concerns their respective primary legal sources. In its inception, the common law tradition was predominantly case law centered, i.e., based on precedent, whereas the civil law tradition has codified statutes as its primary legal source. The second most important feature of each legal tradition is that throughout their development, common law countries developed an adversarial trial setting, whereas civil law countries developed an inquisitorial trial setting.[13] Thus, the main features of the adversarial procedural model stem from the Anglo-American common law system, whereas the features of the inquisitorial procedural model originate from the continental European civil law system. For this reason, several scholars interchangeably use the terms *adversarial* and *common law* on the one side, and *inquisitorial* and *civil law* on the other side.[14]

Nonetheless, nowadays the lines between the two legal traditions and the two procedural models are somewhat blurred, as their features no longer fully overlap. This could be due to a variety of reasons, such as the influence of the US-American law in other legal systems and due to the increasing exchange of legal ideas and institutions between different legal systems all over the world.[15] This phenomenon can be seen in many continental European countries which currently have an increasing number of adversarial features, such as the Italian and Spanish criminal procedures. Consequently, although these countries come from civil law traditions, their trial setting also include many features of the adversarial evidentiary arrangement.

When examining these two procedural models, there is no uniform definition of the terms "inquisitorial" and "adversarial". For this reason, there are slight variations concerning how to refer to them and how to classify them, e.g., whether they fall into a bipartite or a tripartite division. As to how these terms are referred, the terms inquisitorial and adversarial, are often cited as "procedural models", "evidentiary arrangements",[16] "systems", "criminal justice models", "theoretical categories" and "principles". In this work, I will chiefly employ the two former terms merely for reasons of uniformity and clarity, as no one term is more precise than the other.

Regardless of the terminology employed, the classification of legal systems into different groups are used by scholars to categorize different evidentiary arrangements. Whether these groups fall into two or three categories is contingent on the country analyzing them. Usually, Anglo-American countries use a bipartite division – "inquisitorial" and "adversarial" – whereas Continental European Countries employ both a bipartite and a tripartite division, i.e., "inquisitorial", "adversarial" and

---

[12] *Langer*, in: Ross/Thaman, Comparative Criminal Procedure, p. 532.
[13] See infra Ch. 4 B. II. 1. a) and Ch. 4 B. II. 2. a).
[14] *Damaška*, Evidentiary Barriers to Conviction, p. 510.
[15] *Jimeno-Bulnes*, American Criminal Procedure, p. 410.
[16] *Damaška*, Presentation of Evidence and Factfinding Precision, p. 1099.

the so-called "mixed model".[17] In this work, I will follow the bipartite division for three main reasons:

(i) it is the prevalent means to classify the evidentiary arrangements in the field of legal comparison,

(ii) to avoid that Brazilian readers interpret the term "mixed model" used in the tripartite division and believe it to be synonymous as to how Brazilian scholars employ this term, and

(iii) I believe that except when analyzing it in its historical denotation, the creation of a third category, i.e., the mixed model, is counterproductive in categorizing procedural models. This is because nowadays it is rare for a country to have a pure inquisitorial or a pure adversarial system.[18] Hence, if this criterion were to be strictly applied, it is possible that most Anglo-American and Continental European countries would be considered to have mixed legal systems.[19]

When examining the different procedural models, a word of warning is in order. Despite the grouping of legal systems into these two procedural models not being flawless[20] nor it being the only way in which to classify legal systems,[21] it persists in being enormously helpful in the field of comparative law for a variety of reasons.

First, it contains the key features a legal system's criminal procedure possesses and informs the reader of its rough outline and evidentiary arrangement prior to having any information regarding the specificities of the concrete legal system in question.

Second, it helps to "describe and explain persisting cultural and power-distribution differences among different actors and institutions across several contemporary criminal processes".[22] Moreover, it aids "researchers to generate hypotheses to explain or account for differences between procedural regulations across jurisdictions".[23] For this reason, it enables scholars to examine the main features and evidentiary arrangements of various legal systems at once.

---

[17] *Jimeno-Bulnes*, American Criminal Procedure, pp. 416 et seq.

[18] *Bradley*, Convergence of the Continental and the Common Law, p. 473; *Jimeno-Bulnes*, American Criminal Procedure, p. 411; *Damaška*, Evidentiary Barriers to Conviction, p. 577; *Pizzi*, the American "Adversary System"?, pp. 847, 848; *Bradley*, Criminal Procedure: A Worldwide Study, p. xxi; *Findley*, Adversarial Inquisitions, p. 935; *Lempert*, in: Jackson et al., Crime, procedure and evidence, p. 411; *Weigend*, Should we Search, pp. 398 et seq., and particularly, pp. 401 et seq.; *Weigend*, in: Bernsmann/Fischer, Festschrift, pp. 755 et seq.

[19] *Jimeno-Bulnes*, American Criminal Procedure, pp. 416, 417.

[20] Máximo Langer illustrates the blurring effects of categorizing legal systems into these two categories, see *Langer*, in: Ross/Thaman, Comparative Criminal Procedure, pp. 526 et seq.

[21] Examples of different ways in which to categorize legal systems are: (i) between crime control and due process model, see *Packer*, Two Models of the Criminal Process, and (ii) between hierarchical and coordinate models, see *Damaška*, The Faces of Justice, pp. 16 et seq.

[22] *Langer*, in: Ross/Thaman, Comparative Criminal Procedure, p. 525.

[23] *Langer*, in: Ross/Thaman, Comparative Criminal Procedure, p. 525.

As to the main characteristics of each procedural model, there are specific differences in the role the procedural actors play throughout the criminal procedure, specifically during the trial phase. Therefore, the procedural models are tools in which to explain several elements of a legal system, e. g., the key courtrooms actors responsible for presenting evidence, the aims and priorities of the criminal procedure, and its procedural culture. Additionally, a legal system's predominant features will directly influence the types of safeguards that must be in place to foster a fair trial and protect defendants against both system's inherent weaknesses.

II. Main Features

When examining these two evidentiary arrangements, there are two parameters of analysis which Damaška refers to as the *historical* and the *analytical* approach.[24] The former approach seeks to identify the key traits of each system, by way of explaining how each model developed throughout the centuries until it reached its current outline. Although this approach is useful in understanding the historical development of each procedural model, it is deficient in explaining the concrete structure and features of modern legal systems.

For this reason, scholars created a framework in which to classify these systems based on its *overarching characteristics*.[25] This approach is termed the analytical approach and "involves the search for ideas capable of linking procedural arrangements into recognizable patterns".[26] To this end, Damaška coined the term "party-controlled contest" to refer to the adversarial evidentiary arrangement, and "officially-controlled inquest" to refer to the inquisitorial evidentiary arrangement.[27] According to him, despite the analytical approach creating "fictitious creatures, seldom if ever found in reality",[28] it is very useful in examining the key features of each procedural model. He illustrates this by comparing these features to a particular building that can be identified as belonging to a particular architectural style. Hence, even if not all features of a determined architectural style are present, it is still possible to categorize a building into one predominant style based on its main characteristics.[29]

---

[24] *Damaška*, The Faces of Justice, pp. 4, 5.

[25] *Damaška*, Evidentiary Barriers to Conviction, pp. 561 et seq.

[26] *Damaška*, Models of Criminal Procedure, p. 482. Although the analytical approach has been studied for the past several decades by legal scholars worldwide, this approach is virtually unheard of by Brazilian scholars.

[27] See *Damaška*, Evidence Law Adrift.

[28] *Damaška*, The Faces of Justice, p. 5.

[29] *Damaška*, The Faces of Justice, p. 5.

I will now analyze each procedural model in both their historical and analytical approaches as to subsequently highlight how these systems view the concept of truth and justice (III.) and to examine their main structural strengths and weaknesses (IV.).

1. Inquisitorial System

a) Historical Approach

The term inquisitorial persists to evoke a certain level of unease due to its frequent association to the Inquisition during the Middle Ages, or yet, to the practice of torture during the same historical period.[30] However, these associations are inaccurate for two reasons. First, the Inquisition took place by applying canon law rather than secular law; and it is the latter that I will now examine. Second, the practice of torture was not as widespread as the images conjured in people's minds. Nevertheless, it is undeniable that the inquisitorial system – in its historical sense – did not grant defendants a wide berth of procedural rights.

In its origin, once a criminal offense was committed, an investigator would start an investigation to determine whether an offense was in fact committed and to identify its perpetrator. If the latter element were identified, the suspect would usually be incarcerated and would remain imprisoned during the whole criminal process. The investigator would then proceed to question both the suspect and the witnesses and would register all responses in a file. Once the investigation was concluded, the investigator would send the file containing all written evidence to a court. It would then reach a decision regarding the accused's guilt solely on the basis of this written file.[31] Due to the lack of division between the accusatory and adjudicating activities, prosecutors were not needed and, as a rule, the accused did not have the right to legal counsel.

During this time, the evidentiary standard of formal law of proof prevailed,[32] i.e., for a person to be convicted of a crime, a specific type of evidence had to be present. In cases of severe crimes, this standard of proof mandated that a person could only be convicted if there were "two unimpeachable witnesses"[33] claiming this person to be guilty. In the instances where the suspect's guilt was overwhelming, but the threshold necessary for a conviction was not met and the accused would not confess to the crimes attributed to him, a confession could be obtained by means of torture. The practice of torture was a result of the inadmissibility of circumstantial

---

[30] *Jimeno-Bulnes*, American Criminal Procedure, pp. 420, 427.

[31] *Damaška*, Evidentiary Barriers to Conviction, p. 557.

[32] In the German and Brazilian law, this standard of proof are respectively termed *Beweisregeln* and *prova tarifada*.

[33] *Langbein*, Plea Bargaining and Torture, p. 4.

evidence and in seeking to safeguard the accused's right of only being convicted if the minimum evidentiary threshold was met.[34]

In the 19th century, changes to the criminal system were sought owing to the population's dissatisfaction with the criminal proceedings, which were marked by "a trial without parties, dominated by the principle of inquisition and conducted by the judge in a solely responsible and authoritarian manner (…) in written and secret proceedings".[35]

In Germany, for example, these changes took place during Napoleon's occupation of the German territory on the left bank of the Rhine when the French code of criminal procedure (*Code d'Instruction Criminelle*) of 1808 was applied. Because of this code's popularity due to granting defendants various procedural rights in the criminal proceedings, French law continued to be applied in this area even after the French occupation ended. Among the innovations brought to the criminal proceedings were: publicity and oral proceedings, a separate prosecution authority (*le procureur*), the separation of the procedural phases into preliminary and main proceedings, and the abolition of the strict rules of evidence.[36]

b) Analytical Approach

Naturally, after the several and steady modifications made to the inquisitorial procedural model in the past two centuries,[37] the features of the legal systems of several continental European countries[38] have a very different outline and set of procedural rights than those described above. Accordingly, the features of the inquisitorial evidentiary arrangement in its analytical approach are vastly different from that of the historical approach.

By virtue of trying to detach the negative features mentioned above – i.e., the system which prevailed in Continental European countries from the 13th to the first half of the 19th century[39] – from the procedural model itself, the inquisitorial system is also referred to as a *non-adversary* system, *modified inquisitorial* system, and *reformed continental European model*. In the German criminal procedure, this evidentiary arrangement is referred to as "*Amtsermittlungsverfahren*" (roughly trans-

---

[34] Langbein, Plea Bargaining and Torture, pp. 4, 5, 8.

[35] See original text in *Henkel*, Strafverfahrensrecht, p. 37, "ein parteiloses, vom Inquisitionsprinzip beherrschtes und vom Richter alleinverantwortlich und autoritär geführtes (…) schriftliches und geheimes Verfahren".

[36] *Löhr*, Der Grundsatz der Unmittelbarkeit, p. 32; *Stüber*, Die Entwicklung des Prinzips der Unmittelbarkeit, p. 36.

[37] *Grande*, in: Jackson et al., Crime, Procedure and evidence, p. 153.

[38] The European legal systems with predominant features of the inquisitorial procedural model include Germany, the Netherlands, Portugal, Austria, and France. In this sense, see *Perron*, in: Perron (ed.), Die Beweisaufnahme im Strafverfahrensrecht, pp. 569 et seq.

[39] *Damaška*, Evidentiary Barriers to Conviction, p. 556.

lated as official investigation procedure),[40] which is akin to Damaška's term "officially controlled inquest".

In its analytical approach, the procedural phases of the inquisitorial system are usually conducted by means of an official inquiry; that is to say, the responsibility in conducting the different procedural phases is "mainly concentrated in one single organ".[41] In the investigatory phase, the investigation is usually conducted by the police under the orders of either an investigative judge[42] or an impartial public prosecutor, who is responsible for overseeing the police's investigation in finding both incriminating and exculpatory evidence against a suspect. The procedural steps taken during the investigatory phase are written down in a so-called written dossier or investigative file. After the investigation is concluded, this file is handed down to the adjudicating body, which is usually either a trial judge standing alone or a mixed court, i.e., a court composed of both professional and lay judges. From this point forward, the responsibility in finding the truth shifts from the investigative judge or public prosecution to the court.

The trial setting is that of a (mostly) unilateral factfinding enterprise where the court or the presiding judge is responsible in finding out the historical facts of the case, i.e., it has the task to "reconstruct the whole story".[43] To this end, the court must extend its factfinding abilities to all means of proof and the evidence presented at trial is considered to be that of the court. As a rule, it is up to the court to determine the order in which to examine the evidence at trial. In fulfilling this task, it is necessary for the professional judges and more specifically, for the presiding judge to have possession of the investigative file as she must thoroughly study it, to verify at trial whether the evidence contained in the investigative file can be confirmed in an oral and public trial setting.[44]

Regarding the examination of the defendant, he is usually examined by the court, and as a rule, does not have a say on whether he wishes to be questioned. However, he has the right to silence and once on the stand, the defendant may fully exercise that right regarding the merits of the case. In contrast to the adversarial system, as a rule, whenever the defendant choses to answer to the questions posed by the court rather than to remain silent, she is usually not obliged to tell the truth and – if she fails to do so – is not criminally liable for perjury.

Regarding the admissibility of evidence, as criminal cases are adjudicated by professional judges or by a mixed court, although there are many "rules rejecting

---

[40] *Perron*, in: Burkhardt (ed.), Scripta amicitiae, p. 413; *Schäuble*, Strafverfahren und Prozessverantwortung, p. 48.

[41] *Perron*, in: Eser/Rabenstein, Criminal Justice, p. 313.

[42] The investigative judge is not to be confused with the pretrial judge; see footnotes 44 (Part 2) and 95 (Part 3).

[43] *Damaška*, Presentation of Evidence and Factfinding Precision, p. 1090.

[44] *Hodgson*, in: Duff et al., The Trial on Trial: vol. 2, p. 225.

probative information for the sake of values unrelated to the pursuit of justice",[45] there are much fewer *exclusionary rules* than in the adversarial evidentiary arrangement. This is because in the latter procedural model, the rejection of probative material "is on the ground that it may be disused",[46] while in the inquisitorial evidentiary arrangement, it is up to the trial judge to decide the probative value to be given to a determined piece of evidence.

As to the prosecution, it usually has a much more objective and neutral stance than its counterpart in the adversarial system, particularly concerning the trial phase, where it has a much less proactive stance than in the investigatory phase. This is on account of the prosecutor's role of supporting and helping the judge in finding the objective truth, rather than it being the main procedural actor responsible for presenting evidence, as is the case in the adversarial trial setting. Consequently, in inquisitorial systems, prosecutors do not coach witnesses prior to trial – as is the case in some adversarial jurisdictions – because this is deemed to be contrary to the truth finding enterprise.[47]

Although the trial setting is characterized by officialized factfinding, both the public prosecutor and the defense may co-shape the procedure of evidence taking *to a certain extent*.[48] Thus, the presentation of evidence may also stem from these procedural actors, provided that "the adjudicators were at least subsidiarily authorized to raise new issues, examine proof sua sponte, and hear evidence themselves whenever necessary to advance the official inquiry".[49] One such example can be found in the German criminal procedure, where the StPO accords criminal defendants procedural rights in which to at least partly co-shape the trial setting.[50]

2. Adversarial System

a) Historical Approach

The adversarial system, also termed "adversary" or "accusatorial system"[51] has its origin in the 12th century, when common law emerged in England during the reign of

---

[45] *Damaška*, Evidence Law Adrift, p. 12. For examples of the admissibility and exclusion of evidence in the German criminal procedure, see Ch. 1 C. IV.

[46] *Damaška*, Evidence Law Adrift, p. 17.

[47] *Damaška*, Presentation of Evidence and Factfinding Precision, pp. 1088, 1089; *Pizzi/Perron*, Crime Victims in German Courtrooms, p. 43.

[48] In this sense, see *Perron*, in: Perron (ed.), Die Beweisaufnahme im Strafverfahrensrecht, pp. 574 et seq., 591.

[49] *Damaška*, Evidentiary Barriers to Conviction, p. 564.

[50] See supra Ch. 1. C. I. 2. b) and Ch. 1 D. II.

[51] In the context of legal comparison, the terminology "accusatorial" is used as a synonym for the adversarial procedural model, see infra Ch. 4 B. V. In contrast, I examine how Brazilian scholars employ the term "accusatorial" in Ch. 4 C. I.

Henry II.[52] During this period, when a criminal offense was committed, it was the community's responsibility to identify the culprit and to accuse him of having committed the crime, under penalty of the whole community suffering retribution if it failed to do so. This evolved to become the grand jury, "an institution to settle private disputes"[53] which had the main task to gather evidence and examine the evidence against the guilty party. If the grand jury found that there was enough evidence against the suspect, a trial would take place. The adversarial nature of the trial setting probably originated from the original grand jury, as it was responsible for charging the suspect, and for gathering and presenting evidence.[54]

In England, despite the defense and prosecution being present at trial in cases of treason, in the overwhelming majority of cases, the parties were absent in criminal proceedings. As a rule, it was up to the trial judges to play both these roles and for this reason, trial judges had an active role at trial until the beginning of the 18th century. It was only toward the end of the 18th century that the presence of both the prosecution and the defense counsel at trial became more common, and as a result, the trial judge became "a passive state official who was given virtually no involvement in the investigation of the actual facts".[55] The judge's more passive stance in Anglo-American law is also explained due to a "deep mistrust of any tendency to invest power in one state-appointed individual or authority".[56] For this reason, "any intervention of the judge in shaping the proceeding (…) was perceived as an unacceptable invasion of individual freedom by the state".[57]

b) Analytical Approach

In this procedural model, the parties are responsible for *gathering, sifting,* and *presenting* evidence as best they can to further each side's case and secure the best possible outcome for each respective side. This partisan stance is also reflected in the investigatory phase, as the parties have the responsibility of *gathering* evidence in preparation for a potential trial. On the one hand, it is usually the police's responsibility – either exclusively or with the participation of the prosecution – to gather evidence against a suspect, and if applicable, to gather evidence for a future criminal case. On the other hand, the defense is also responsible for gathering evidence favorable to the defendant due to three main reasons. These are to either (i) have enough evidence to neutralize the prosecution's efforts in indicting the accused, (ii) to have more leverage when making plea negotiations and should this fail and the case go to trial, (iii) to secure a strong case to present at trial.

---

[52] *Jimeno-Bulnes*, American Criminal Procedure, p. 417.
[53] *Jimeno-Bulnes*, American Criminal Procedure, p. 419.
[54] *Jimeno-Bulnes*, American Criminal Procedure, pp. 419, 420.
[55] *Grande*, in: Jackson et al., Crime, Procedure and evidence, p. 152.
[56] *Perron*, in: Eser/Rabenstein, Criminal Justice, p. 303.
[57] *Grande*, in: Jackson et al., Crime, Procedure and evidence, p. 152.

As to *preparing* and *sifting* evidence, the parties must thoroughly prepare their respective cases ahead of trial. The extent of this preparation varies between jurisdictions; as a rule, in the US-American jurisdictions this also entails extensively coaching witnesses to achieve the best possible outcome,[58] whereas in the English legal system, this practice is frowned upon.[59]

As to the trial setting, owing to the parties having the responsibility of *presenting* evidence, the procedure of evidence taking is divided into two different cases, i.e., the prosecution's case-in-chief followed by that of the defense. After the prosecution's case-in-chief, the defendant can choose whether he wishes to take the stand. However, contrary to its inquisitorial counterparts, if the defendant chooses to testify, he must take an oath and tell the truth. If he fails to do the latter, he might be liable to being prosecuted for perjury.

In this setting, the trial judge usually acts as a passive umpire that has very little prior knowledge of the case being adjudicated.[60] At trial, he has the responsibility of deciding on the admissibility of evidence, and in the US-American trial, the trial judge is responsible to make rulings only "upon the objection of the side adversely affected".[61] However, this feature is also subject to a certain amount of variation, as the amount of judicial passivity differs from jurisdiction to jurisdiction. As a rule, in US-American jurisdictions, trial judges tend to be more passive than their English counterparts.[62]

III. Differences in the Concept of Truth and Justice

In each procedural model, there are some key differences between both the concept of truth and how it is sought in the trial phase. In turn, these variants affect other elements,[63] such as the interrelation between truth and justice and the role ascribed to the trial judge and the prosecution in both the truth finding enterprise and in furthering justice.

In the inquisitorial procedural model, justice is thought to be achieved when a neutral party – usually the trial judge – ascertains the material or substantive truth. Grande coined this the "ontological truth", as it is "based on the belief that an objective reconstruction of reality is possible".[64] In contrast, the adversarial model is

---

[58] *Findley*, Adversarial Inquisitions, p. 916.
[59] *Pizzi/Perron*, Crime Victims in German Courtrooms, p. 44; *Damaška*, Evidence Law Adrift, p. 77 (footnote 5).
[60] *Damaška*, Evidentiary Barriers to Conviction, p. 510.
[61] *Damaška*, Evidentiary Barriers to Conviction, p. 564.
[62] *Pizzi*, Trials without Truth, p. 117.
[63] *Damaška*, Presentation of Evidence and Factfinding Precision, p. 1085.
[64] *Grande*, in: Jackson et al., Crime, procedure and evidence, p. 147.

structured as a dispute as the procedural actors have "independent and conflicting"[65] roles. It is believed that through the clash of both parties, the formal truth will come out. This is due to the conviction that it is impossible for a third party to be completely unbiased as to be able to find the objective truth. Although finding the truth and discovering what happened is an important objective, the main aim is that the rules of the contest – the evidentiary rules – are respected and upheld. Owing to the formal truth being ascertained by means of two interpretations of reality, Grande calls it the "interpretive truth".[66]

However, the generalized views set above on how each procedural model perceives the truth are not unitary as some scholars offer a different perspective to the strict claim that the Anglo-American factfinding enterprise only seeks to find the formal truth.[67] It is also disputed whether the inquisitorial setting is always capable of reconstructing the historical facts of the case and thus, of finding the material truth.[68] Nevertheless, in broad terms, the *concept of justice* in the adversarial system is linked to the concept of procedural fairness, whereas in the inquisitorial system, it is linked to finding an objective reconstruction of reality.

The perceived differences on how justice is achieved also influences the role of the courtroom players. As to the role of the trial judge, in the adversarial trial setting *judicial neutrality* is linked to the concept of passivity,[69] whereas in the inquisitorial trial setting, it is linked to judicial impartiality.[70] Accordingly, the trial judge's proactive stance in an officially controlled inquest is seen in inquisitorial systems in a positive light, as he is considered an objective courtroom player who is responsible for finding the truth. This mentality is reinforced by the fact that law is seen as a legal

---

[65] *Damaška*, Evidentiary Barriers to Conviction, p. 563.

[66] *Grande*, in: Jackson et al., Crime, procedure and evidence, p. 148.

[67] The perception that the US-American procedure solely seeks to find the formal or procedural truth is challenged by some scholars who believe this to be an inaccurate portrayal of this system's truth finding enterprise. In the pretrial phase, when prosecutors decide whether to indict a suspect, they must thoroughly examine the objective facts of the case, i.e., they seek to find the historical facts of the case and thus, the material truth. This stems from their responsibility in representing the state and being as accurate and thorough as possible when verifying whether there is probable cause for a case to go to trial. Consequently, the fact that the US-American trial phase is structured in a setting where the parties are the sole procedural actors responsible for the presentation of evidence does not in itself negate the fact that at least in theory, one of the parties is attempting to find the material truth. In this sense, see *Weigend*, Should we Search, pp. 398, 399; *Billis*, Die Rolle des Richters, pp. 95 et seq.; *Schäuble*, Strafverfahren und Prozessverantwortung, pp. 302, 303.

[68] In reality, despite the inquisitorial trial setting being structured in a way that confers the court prerogatives which are conducive in finding the material truth, it is unlikely that it will always be able to reconstruct the historical facts of the case. For this reason, at times, both the adversarial and inquisitorial trial setting will ascertain the formal or procedural truth. See *Schäuble*, Strafverfahren und Prozessverantwortung, pp. 302, 303.

[69] *Pizzi*, Trials Without Truth, p. 142.

[70] *Grande*, in: Jackson et al., Crime, procedure and evidence, p. 156.

science[71] and law students are taught at university to think in an objective manner, much like that of a judge.[72] In this context, if the trial judge were to be a passive umpire in the trial setting – akin to the role played by their US-American adversarial counterparts – they would be viewed to fail in their duty to conduct the criminal case akin to a scientific investigation, and in finding the historical facts of the case.

Contrary to the inquisitorial evidentiary arrangement, in the adversarial trial setting the presentation of evidence is a party-controlled contest. This mentality is underpinned by US-American law students being taught in law school to "think like a lawyer".[73] Thus, if the trial judge were to have prior knowledge of the case ahead of trial, this would be seen as judicial bias owing to the facts of the case stemming from an impartial third party rather than from the dialectic process itself.[74] For this reason, it is believed that "prior knowledge of the case on the part of the judge is more readily associated with bias".[75]

The structural differences between both procedural models also affect the *prosecution's role* in the proceedings. As the adversarial system is a party driven contest, prosecutorial discretion is inherent in this model, and particularly, in the US-legal system. Since the prosecution is a party to the proceedings, it has discretion to decide whether to pursue a case and if it decides the case is not worth pursuing, it has full discretionary powers not to bring charges against the accused.[76]

In contrast, their German inquisitorial counterparts are responsible for finding the material truth in the investigatory phase and for this reason, the prosecution cannot dismiss a case unless it is either proven that no crime was committed or that the accused did not commit it.[77] This is the reasoning why – as a rule – there is very little

---

[71] This can be illustrated in the German criminal procedure, where the Committee that authored the StPO – which dates from 1877 – had the aim to create a procedure that legal theorists could study as scientific data. This was intended as a means to protect German citizens from the arbitrary actions of the state. In this sense, see *Boyne*, The German Prosecution Service, p. 25.

[72] In Germany, judicial objectivity is further imprinted by the apprenticeship law graduates go through once they enter the judicial service. See supra Ch. 1 B. III.

[73] *Lempert*, in: Jackson et al., Crime, procedure and evidence, p. 396.

[74] *Perron*, Beweisantragsrecht, pp. 386, 396; *Bradley*, Convergence of the Continental and the Common Law, p. 471.

[75] *Damaška*, Presentation of Evidence and Factfinding Precision, p. 1105. In the US-American law, there are two further means in which the adversarial system seeks to advance the factfinders' neutrality. First, because of the strict separation of powers, voir dire is believed to be an effective means to vet those considered to be biased for or against a specific party. Second, the manner in which judges are appointed are considered effective in guaranteeing unbiased factfinders, and thus, judicial neutrality. In this sense, see *Lempert*, in: Jackson et al., Crime, procedure and evidence, p. 401.

[76] *Langer*, Legal Transplants to Legal Translations, p. 21.

[77] *Langer*, Legal Transplants to Legal Translations, p. 22.

prosecutorial discretion in this system,[78] and the reason why prosecutors must follow the principle of mandatory prosecution regarding criminal offenses of medium or serious severity.[79] Even in the jurisdictions where prosecutors have a certain amount of discretion whether to dismiss a case or to dispose of a criminal case by abbreviated proceedings – usually in criminal offenses of minor severity – they must follow the principle of discretionary prosecution, which has a normative basis and may only be applied in specific circumstances.[80]

A further difference between both evidentiary arrangements that stem from the differences in the concept of truth is concerning the *thoroughness of the evidentiary material*. In the inquisitorial procedural model, the trial judge must "ensure that the evidentiary material is as complete as possible".[81] In contrast, in the adversarial setting due to each parties' interest in furthering their respective cases, the parties may choose to not disclose evidence to the factfinder, which is not beneficial or yet, which is actively damaging to their case. For this reason, it is not uncommon for the factfinder to not have access to the whole factual basis when reaching a decision.[82] Because in the adversarial trial setting the truth is often equated to fairness, provided that the procedural and evidentiary rules are strictly adhered to, the presentation of two opposing cases by the parties should govern the trial setting. In the US-American legal system, for example, the trial judge should only interfere if and whenever the parties invoke the judge to make a ruling on a specific evidentiary matter under dispute.

IV. Structural Strengths and Weaknesses

In both the inquisitorial and the adversarial procedural models, their respective strengths and weaknesses are closely related to one another.

1. Inquisitorial System

The inquisitorial system's greatest strength is that a neutral and objective court is in charge of finding the historical events of the case, as this is one of the system's most important procedural aims. Thus, owing to the trial judge thoroughly having to examine all evidence that might be of relevance in finding the truth regardless of the

---

[78] However, this is not applicable to all systems with predominantly inquisitorial evidentiary arrangements as some countries have the principle of opportunity as its guiding principle, as is the case in France, as per Arts. 40–1 of the French Code of Criminal Procedure (*Code de procédure pénale*).

[79] See supra Ch. 1 B. IV. 1. a).

[80] For an example in the German criminal procedure, see supra Ch. 1 B. IV. 1. a).

[81] *Grande*, in: Jackson et al., Crime, procedure and evidence, p. 156.

[82] *Schäuble*, Strafverfahren und Prozessverantwortung, pp. 303, 304.

participation of the parties, the defendant's procedural rights are better safeguarded "irrespective of the adequacy of defense counsel".[83] It is also believed that "material justice is best served when the investigation and examination of evidence lies in the hands of an objective, neutral body, obliged to establish the truth, independent of particular interests, and not dependent on the actions of the other parties to the proceedings".[84]

However, the drawback of this system is that the official inquiry must truly remain neutral as "both the legitimacy of criminal justice and the fate of the individual (...) depend to a large extent on the integrity of state officials and their visible commitment to nonpartisan truth finding".[85] This is a tall order, as the trial judge has to thoroughly study the investigative file prior to trial to enable him to conduct the procedure of evidence taking.[86] Accordingly, it is inevitable for the presiding judge to "at least unconsciously develop a picture of the course of events"[87] and thus, to form preconceived ideas concerning the defendant's innocence or guilt. For this reason, there is the risk of a confirmation bias, where "new information is always processed in relation to a previously formed hypothesis or belief".[88] Thus, "confirming circumstances are unconsciously overestimated, while conflicting circumstances tend to be underestimated, so that the hypothesis is in a sense self-confirming".[89]

The risk of judicial bias is reduced by the fact that judges in inquisitorial systems are usually trained to think in an objective manner and to conduct a criminal case akin to how one would conduct a scientific investigation. Further, trial judges are aware that their prior access to information may bring with it an inherent risk to their impartiality. Nonetheless, even if the aforementioned elements are in place to reduce the risk of judicial bias, the "distorting psychological mechanism"[90] of these evidentiary arrangements cannot be completely neutralized. For this reason, there must be mechanisms in place to counter this system's inherent shortcomings. In other words, there must be mechanisms to limit judicial bias by, for example, controlling judicial discretion.

---

[83] *Perron*, in: Eser/Rabenstein, Criminal Justice, p. 313.

[84] *Perron*, in: Eser/Rabenstein, Criminal Justice, p. 313.

[85] *Findley*, Adversarial Inquisitions, p. 930. See also *Perron*, in: Alexander Bruns (ed.), p. 877.

[86] As to the risk of judicial bias in the German system, see *Perron*, Beweisantragsrecht, pp. 116, 125 et seq., 147.

[87] See original text in *Schäuble*, Strafverfahren und Prozessverantwortung, p. 67, Das Gericht durch das Studium der Ermittlungsakten "zumindest unbewusst ein Bild vom Tathergang entwickelt".

[88] See original text in *Schäuble*, Strafverfahren und Prozessverantwortung, p. 67, Danach werden "neue Informationen stets in Bezug auf eine bereits zuvor gebildete Hypothese oder Überzeugung verarbeitet".

[89] See original text in *Schäuble*, Strafverfahren und Prozessverantwortung, p. 67, "Bestätigende Umstände werden unbewusst über-, entgegenstehende Umstände dagegen eher unterschätzt, so dass sich die Hypothese in gewisser Weise selbst bestätigt".

[90] *Damaška*, Presentation of Evidence and Factfinding Precision, p. 1092.

2. Adversarial System

On the other side of the divide, in the adversarial system owing to each party being devotedly committed to their respective side, they have the duty to "search out all favorable evidence, to seek, neutralize or destroy all unfavorable evidence, and to press the most favorable interpretation of the law".[91] For this reason, its main strength is that the clash between these two parallel cases guards "against tunnel vision and confirmation biases",[92] as both positions are constantly being thwarted by each other. A further benefit is that due to the trial judge having almost no prior information of the case ahead of trial, they do not have the risk of judicial bias as is the case with their inquisitorial counterparts.[93]

Nonetheless, this procedural model has a major structural weakness. Owing to the parties being responsible for presenting evidence, inherent imbalances between the parties – i.e., considerable differences in either financial or time resources – could greatly impair the odds of the contest.[94] Considering the amount of power and resources that the state has in investigating and prosecuting criminal cases, the balance between the prosecution and the defense is usually heavily tilted towards the former. To counter this inherent weakness, it is vital for both parties to be evenly matched and have similar time and financial resources. In the absence of these conditions, the truth finding process will be skewed in favor of the strongest party. For this reason, the defendant's chances at trial are completely dependent on the quality of his legal counsel and the resources it has at its disposal.

In view of the states' advantageous position in gathering evidence during the pretrial phase and the vital importance this evidence has at trial, guaranteeing the defendant equality of arms is no easy task. Therefore, in the adversarial setting, it is *vital* for there to be procedural safeguards in place to provide the defense with equivalent rights as those afforded to the prosecution, to further the balance between both parties.

V. Definition of "Accusatorial"

Now that the terms adversarial and inquisitorial have been defined and their main characteristics identified, I will now address a common practice in the field of comparative law regarding the term "accusatorial". At times, international scholars employ the terms "accusatorial" and "adversarial" interchangeably, i.e., the term accusatorial is used to describe the adversarial evidentiary arrangement. Nonetheless, this is not entirely correct as the term accusatorial in its *literal* meaning is used to

---

[91] *Walpin*, America's Adversarial and Jury Systems, p. 177.
[92] *Findley*, Adversarial Inquisitions, p. 941.
[93] *Schäuble*, Strafverfahren und Prozessverantwortung, p. 300.
[94] *Perron*, in: Eser/Rabenstein, Criminal Justice, p. 312.

indicate that a legal system's accusatory and adjudicating functions lie in different procedural actors.[95] Thus, the term accusatorial in its main sense does not set any distinctive feature in the trial setting.[96] For this reason, the feature of being "accusatorial" is found in both modern inquisitorial and adversarial procedural models as it is not incompatible to either evidentiary arrangement.[97] This feature can be seen in all legal systems examined in this work, as all of them have a division between who is the ultimate procedural actor responsible for filing an indictment and who is responsible for adjudicating the criminal case.

Additionally, the term "accusatorial" is deficient and inadequate in examining the evidentiary arrangement of a specific legal system in comparative law for two further reasons. First, since its scope is limited to the division between the accusatory and adjudicating functions, it is completely devoid of features describing the general outline of a legal system's procedural phases, and particularly of the trial setting. Second, the term accusatorial has no explanatory power regarding the reasoning behind the roles played by each key courtroom actor, their corresponding mindset, and the varying degrees of responsibility and level of proactiveness allocated to each of them.

C. Legal Definitions in the Brazilian Criminal Procedure

I. Misdiagnosis of its Features as a Hinderance in Finding Effective Solutions

As examined in the beginning of this chapter, when conducting comparative studies, many Brazilian scholars use imprecise and vague terminology, which can lead to inaccurate premises. This is harmful *in the context* of comparative criminal procedure, as the terminology used by them differs from that which is employed by international scholars in this field.[98] As seen, most Brazilian scholars use the term "inquisitorial" as referring to the inquisitorial model purely in its historical ap-

---

[95] *Damaška*, Evidentiary Barriers to Conviction, p. 561. In this respect, Germany and Italy abolished the figure of the investigating judge as a means to separate the investigative from the adjudicatory functions. However, the figure of the investigating judge should not be confused with that of the pretrial judge. The former is responsible for presiding and conducting the criminal investigation with the help of the police. On the other hand, pretrial judges are competent to make decisions in matters concerning investigative measures that affect the accused's liberty, physical integrity, or her rights to privacy, such as arrest warrants and physical examinations. In this sense, see *Jimeno-Bulnes*, American Criminal Procedure, pp. 438, 439.

[96] *Jimeno-Bulnes*, American Criminal Procedure, pp. 429, 430; *Billis*, Die Rolle des Richters, p. 78; *Schäuble*, Strafverfahren und Prozessverantwortung, pp. 47, 48.

[97] *Zilli*, Iniciativa Instrutória do Juiz, p. 27.

[98] In this sense, see *Zilli*, Iniciativa Instrutória do Juiz, p. 25.

proach.[99] Further, the term "accusatorial" is neither used exclusively in its literal sense, nor is it used as synonymous with the adversarial procedural model in its analytical sense, as done by some international scholars. Rather, one single term is (at times) used to comprise three different features, namely:

(i) a system where different procedural actors are responsible for the accusatory and the adjudicative functions,

(ii) a mixed model, i.e., a legal system that has features of both inquisitorial and adversarial evidentiary arrangements, and

(iii) the adversarial model in its analytical approach, particularly to convey that the presentation of evidence is party-controlled.[100]

As already examined, the first two features are imprecise as they are unable to describe any distinctive characteristics of a legal system's evidentiary arrangements, and thus, are not conducive in describing the features of the Brazilian trial setting. This is because; first, most if not all modern democratic legal systems have specific procedural actors who are respectively responsible for the investigatory and the adjudicative role.[101] Second, if all the elements of a legal system were meticulously analyzed, in all probability most legal systems would have mixed models, as it is uncommon to find a country with pure adversarial or pure inquisitorial features.

A further misconception is that Brazilian scholars quite often state that the Brazilian criminal procedure has a "mixed model" due to having a secretive and written investigatory phase on the one side, and an oral and public trial setting on the other.[102] This definition is of very little descriptive value considering that most legal systems have a secretive and written investigatory phase to secure the effectiveness of the criminal investigation and in gathering evidence against the person suspected of having committed the criminal offense. For this reason, apart from a few exceptions, the general outline of the different procedural phases is very similar in all legal systems regardless of whether their trial setting has a predominantly adversarial or a predominantly inquisitorial evidentiary arrangement.

The widespread unfamiliarity and/or misconception of the terminology applied in comparative law and the consequential misdiagnosis of the features of the Brazilian legal system is not only unhelpful, but also harmful for two main reasons.

The first damaging consequence is that whenever Brazilian scholars conduct research in the field of comparative law, they frequently do so from the "historical

---

[99] See footnote 5 (Part 3).

[100] This can be observed when Brazilian scholars state that Art. 212, chapeau, CPP – which sets out that the parties are the main procedural actors responsible for witness examination – furthers the "accusatory system" (*sistema acusatório*).

[101] *Jimeno-Bulnes*, American Criminal Procedure, p. 429.

[102] *Pitombo*, Consideraçoes Iniciais, p. 20; *Mossin*, Compêndio de Processo Penal, p. 4; *Capez*, Curso de Processo Penal, p. 82; *Távora/Alencar*, Curso de Direito Processual Penal, p. 57; *Pacelli*, Curso de Processo Penal, pp. 13, 14.

approach-lens" described above. Hence, many intricacies of modern adversarial and inquisitorial procedural models are *lost in translation*, as the full scope of what these systems entail is not fully grasped due to the lack of the correct apprehension of these terms. Consequently, even though there are many Brazilian researchers, who read a vast amount of literature in the field of comparative law written by well-known international scholars from Anglo-American and Continental European backgrounds, its full meaning and scope are often not fully comprehended.

The second and perhaps the most damaging consequence is that it hinders scholars in correctly identifying the main problematic features of the Brazilian legal system. As a result, in the worst case, the solutions offered in countering the perceived failings of this legal system (at times) completely miss the mark, as the perceived reasons for the system's shortcomings do not overlap with the actual reasons.[103] In the best case, the suggestions of improving the system's failings are conducive in effecting positive changes to the Brazilian criminal procedure but fall short of reaching their full potential. Thus, the misdiagnosis of the features of the Brazilian legal system leads many brilliant and very hardworking Brazilian scholars in seeing limitations to the solution of problematic features in the Brazilian criminal procedure, where in reality no such limitations exist.

II. Defining the Predominant Evidentiary Arrangement of the Brazilian Criminal Procedure

Based on the theoretical framework set above, I will now identify the predominant procedural model of the Brazilian Criminal Procedure by examining its main features. The importance of this exercise is that only by defining these features in their current layout, rather than in their "abstract idealized form", will this lead to clarity regarding the evidentiary arrangements of the trial setting. This is a crucial step to later propose effective concrete solutions to the Brazilian criminal procedure.

Despite the trial setting having features of both inquisitorial and adversarial procedural models, it is undeniable that the former features prevail. This is owing to the reasons that follow.

(i) Because of the evidentiary principle of ascertainment of the truth, the trial judge is the procedural actor responsible for ensuring the completeness of the probative material and of finding the material truth. Regardless of several Brazilian scholars criticizing this principle and the procedural aim of finding the objective truth,[104] the fact remains that the Brazilian trial setting is char-

---

[103] I will address this matter in Ch. 6 A.

[104] The principle of ascertainment of the truth is often criticized by Brazilian scholars as it shapes the inquisitorial trial setting and/or due to scholars contending that the material truth cannot be found, owing to the impossibility of reconstructing the historical facts of the case. In this sense, see *Santos/Santos*, in: Giacomolli/Vasconcellos, Processo Penal, p. 111; *Khaled Jr*,

acterized by an officialized fact-finding. The trial judge is the main procedural actor responsible for presiding and conducting evidence taking at trial, and – except in the instances provided by the CPP – he decides the order in which to take evidence. Thus, apart from a few exceptions, he must find out what happened, regardless of and beyond any presentation of evidence by the parties.

(ii) In performing this role, the trial judge must have prior knowledge of the case, which he gains from the investigative file (*relatório*) that was compiled by the chief of police. As examined, the investigative file is a feature of inquisitorial systems. This feature contrasts with the adversarial procedural model, where the trial judge has little to no prior knowledge of the case, owing to it going against the dialectical process.

(iii) The trial judge is the only procedural actor who may examine the defendant. Although the parties may formulate the questions they wish to ask the defendant, they must direct them to the trial judge, who will then relay them to the defendant if he deems the questions to be relevant to the case.[105]

(iv) As is the case in legal systems with predominantly inquisitorial features, the defendant must take the stand. He has the full prerogative to remain silent regarding the merits of the case, and if he wishes to answer to the trial judge's questions, he is not obliged to tell the truth, nor is he liable to perjury for lying.

(v) The trial judge is responsible for selecting court-appointed experts, and evidence taking is, as a rule, to be considered the court's responsibility, rather than that of the parties. The fact that the parties may ask questions to court-appointed experts and to the privately-retained experts (*assistente técnico*) is not inconsistent with the inquisitorial procedural model.[106]

(vi) The prosecution and the defense must name the oral witnesses they wish to present at trial in the bill of indictment and in the written response to the indictment, respectively. If they fail to do this, their right to present oral witnesses precludes, and the only way they may question them is if they request the judge to produce the witness as that of the court's.[107] If this occurs, it is within the trial judge's discretion whether to admit the witness in question owing to him having the final say on the matter. Thus, although the parties are the main procedural actors responsible for examining the witnesses sensu lato at trial, in the specific instances above, if the trial judge denies the request of

---

A produção analógica da verdade, pp. 167 et seq.; *Távora/Alencar*, Curso de Direito Processual Penal, pp. 79, 80; *Badaró*, Processo Penal, p. 387; *Lopes Jr.*, Direito Processual Penal, 15th ed., p. 372; *Pacelli*, Curso de Processo Penal, pp. 342 et seq.

[105] See supra Ch. 3 C. III. 1 a).

[106] For an example of this in the German criminal procedure, see supra Ch. 1 C. III. 3.

[107] See supra Ch. 3 C. III. 2. a).

C. Legal Definitions in the Brazilian Criminal Procedure

the prosecution or of the defense to call a witness as that of the court's, this can considerably hamper the case of the party in question.

(vii) Whenever the trial judge deems necessary, she may summon and hear additional witnesses, regardless of any request by the parties to this end. Further, she may arrange for the presentation of documents, which she considers relevant to the case to be attached to the case file.[108]

(viii) Apart from a few exceptions, as a rule, there are no strict rules of evidence in the Brazilian legal procedure. Thus, the vast array of exclusionary rules provided in the adversarial setting are not in place, as it is usually up to the trial judge to decide the probative value to be given to a determined piece of evidence.[109]

(ix) A further principle in the Brazilian criminal procedure is the principle of free evaluation of evidence, which states that the trial judge shall form his conviction by the free evaluation of the evidence produced in a contradictory court proceeding. According to this principle, the trial judge must substantiate her decision to acquit or convict the defendant. If the *necessary* objective criteria is in place, this principle is very effective in countering the weaknesses inherent to the inquisitorial evidentiary arrangement as it serves as a procedural safeguard in which to counter the risk of judicial bias and in which to circumscribe judicial discretion.

(x) Although heralded as the bulwark of the Brazilian "accusatorial" system, the principles of audiatur et altera pars (*princípio do contraditório*) and the principle to a full defense[110] (*princípio da ampla defesa*) are not exclusive to a trial setting with an adversarial evidentiary arrangement. This is illustrated by the fact that both the German inquisitorial system and the US-American adversarial system provide the defendant with very similar if not identical procedural rights.[111]

Although the Brazilian trial setting has a predominantly inquisitorial evidentiary arrangement, this does not invalidate the fact that there is an ever-increasing introduction of elements of partisan control of evidence in this trial setting. This is not surprising, however, as many systems with prevailing inquisitorial or adversarial models have a certain number of features of the other procedural model. As seen, this

---

[108] See supra Ch. 3 C. I. 2. a).

[109] See supra Ch. 3 C. IV. 1.

[110] *Nicolitti*, in: Prado/Malan, Processo Penal e Democracia, pp. 48, 49.

[111] I addressed the right akin to the principle of full defense in the German criminal procedure in Ch. 1 B. III. 3., and the right akin to audiatur et altera pars in Ch. 1 C. III. 2. b). I examined the right akin to the principle of full defense in the US-American criminal procedure in Ch. 2 B. III. 3. and the right akin to the principle audiatur et altera pars in Ch. 2 C. III. 1. b) and Ch. 2 D. I. 3.

is a natural consequence of the exchange of legal ideas and thoughts between different legal systems.[112]

Among the features of the adversarial procedural model in the Brazilian trial setting are (i) the prosecution's mentality and stance at trial and (ii) the increasing amount of responsibility given to the parties in presenting evidence.

(i) Although there are some Brazilian scholars who purport that the prosecution is an "impartial party" to the proceedings, most modern scholars agree that this is not an accurate assessment. Brazilian prosecutors are far from being objective and impartial procedural actors[113] who have as their main responsibility the duty to support the court in finding the material truth, as is the case in Germany. Although Brazilian prosecutors are parties to the proceedings who want to ensure justice, once they believe the minimum evidentiary threshold of *justa causa* is present and they file a bill of indictment against a suspect, prosecutors have an aggressive stance at trial and perceive the defendant's conviction as winning, and his acquittal as losing. Thus, in the trial phase, the mentality of Brazilian prosecutors is much more similar to their US-American adversarial counterparts than their German inquisitorial counterparts.[114]

(ii) The increase in the amount of responsibility being accorded to the parties by the Brazilian legislation can be observed in them – at least in theory – becoming responsible for examining the victim, the informants, and the witnesses at trial. Further, the parties may present documentary evidence at any stage of the proceedings and may also request the court to present their respective privately-retained experts at trial. However, this latter feature in itself does not conflict with the features of the inquisitorial model.[115] This is because although the inquisitorial evidentiary arrangement is mostly characterized by officialized factfinding, both the public prosecutor and the defense may co-shape the procedure of evidence taking to a certain extent. This can be illustrated in the German criminal procedure where the parties have the right to ask questions and have the right to request the court to take additional evidence. The former right affords the defendant the possibility to ask witnesses and experts questions. This is in accordance with Art. 6, para. 3 (d) ECHR, which states that the defendant has the right to examine the witnesses against her and on her behalf. In contrast, by virtue of the motion to take evidence, defendants have an effective mechanism in which to force the court to take additional evidence and co-shape trial.

---

[112] See supra Ch. 4 B. I.

[113] See infra Ch. 5 C. II.

[114] The fact that Brazilian prosecutors are parties to the proceedings, while trial judges are responsible for finding the material truth, combined with the lack of effective procedural safeguards counteracting these weaknesses is highly problematic. In this sense, see Ch. 5 C. II.

[115] I addressed this in Ch. 4 B. II. 1. b). For an example in the German criminal procedure, see supra Ch. 1 C. III. 3.

A. Introduction

For all of the above, although the changes to the CPP have gradually afforded the parties a larger role in the presentation of evidence, the fact remains that the Brazilian criminal procedure has a predominantly inquisitorial evidentiary arrangement. This is illustrated by the various prerogatives and responsibilities the trial judge has at trial. Also, regardless of the several reforms made to the CPP with the aim of it becoming more "accusatorial", the trial judge persists to be the procedural actor who has the highest amount of discretion and power at trial.

Chapter 5

The Importance of Identifying both a Country's Normative Framework and its Legal Culture in Comparative Law

A. Introduction

I will now address the topic of legal transplants and especially of legal translations, as they are often overlooked by both Brazilian and international scholars in the context of comparative law. As the standpoint of the former is of relevance to this work, I will analyze this topic by addressing the Brazilian context.[116]

Brazilian jurists have a great interest in reading works by international legal scholars and have an overall interest in foreign legal systems, particularly the US-American, Italian, Portuguese, and German criminal procedures. Thus, it is not uncommon for Brazilian scholars to discuss how certain legal ideas and provisions should be transplanted from their legal system of origin into the Brazilian legal system. In theory, this could be a fruitful practice as comparative law is an effective means to better understand one's own legal system, pinpoint its respective deficiencies, and find possible solutions to its problematic issues. Yet, in practice, when these jurists conduct comparative studies, virtually little to no thought is given to the evidentiary arrangements of the foreign legal systems under analysis, nor to the roles that the key courtroom players play throughout the procedural phases.

One such example took place a few years ago, when Brazilian scholars discussed the possibility of Brazilian prosecutors conducting criminal investigations in the investigatory phase. During these discussions, it was a common practice for scholars to search for ideas and solutions in other legal systems. To this end, they would often allude to the roles of German, Italian, and US-American prosecutors to validate their respective positions and standpoints.[117] However, this was conducted while neither

---

[116] For examples of disregard concerning this topic in the German and Italian context, see infra Ch. 5 B. III. 1. and footnote 141 (Part 3), respectively.

[117] *Bastos*, Investigação, pp. 47 et seq., and especially, pp. 161 et seq.; *Lopes Jr.*, Direito Processual Penal, 11th ed., pp. 265 et seq.; *Nicolitt*, Manual de Processo Penal, p. 193.

taking into consideration the legal framework nor the legal culture of each country under examination.

On the one hand, this practice is understandable as public prosecutors have similar functions, e. g., they have the responsibility to file a bill of indictment when a specific evidentiary threshold is reached. On the other hand, not taking the legal framework or the legal culture of a legal system into consideration is very problematic as these procedural actors may have a different training, as well as different prerogatives, responsibilities, and roles in the trial setting. As a result, the prosecutorial mindset may be vastly different in each legal system under analysis.[118]

In addition to these elements, the evidentiary arrangements and the trial setting in these legal systems may greatly differ from one another. Consequently, as a rule, when Brazilian scholars analyze, for example, the role of German and US-American prosecutors, no afterthought is given to how these actors interact within their concrete (domestic) settings. Absent this analysis, scholars make what I would term a "legal projection", where these procedural actors are viewed as having similar roles and responsibilities as that of Brazilian prosecutors. There are two consequences to this. First, very little attention is given on how legal ideas and provisions function in their system of origin. Second, they overlook how foreign legal ideas and institutions would interact with the receiving legal system, i. e., once they are introduced into the Brazilian normative framework and legal culture.

This is why before I make suggestions of improvement to the Brazilian criminal procedure in the following chapter, I will first examine important premises on this topic. First, I will briefly analyze the definition of legal transplants and legal translations (B.). To this end, I will examine the definition of procedural culture (I.) and highlight the importance of understanding the receiving legal system's institutional context before proposing a transfer of legal ideas and institutions from one legal system into another (II.). Following this analysis, I will illustrate how introducing legal ideas to a country without taking the receiving legal system's institutional context into consideration is not conducive to changing the features of the target legal system which could benefit from improvement (III.).

Subsequently, the normative framework and the legal culture themselves must be addressed. In regard to the former, it is essential to understand both the normative framework of a legal idea or provision in their legal system of origin and that of the receiving legal system. In applying this premise to the present study, I have respectively examined in Chapters 1 and 2 the normative framework of the (potential) legal systems of origin, whereas in Chapter 3, I examined the receiving country's normative framework. Therefore, the second and last step is to address the Brazilian legal culture (C.). This has the aim to maximize the likelihood of a legal idea or provision being suited to the targeted legal system; simply put, so that it does not clash with the Brazilian normative framework and its legal culture.

---

[118] *Weigend*, Continental Cures, p. 395; *Pizzi*, Understanding Prosecutorial Discretion, pp. 1327, 1333.

B. Legal Translations

Before I address the concept of legal translations and the importance of understanding the receiving country's institutional context, I would like to first address the topic of *legal transplants*. Watson coined this term to refer to the act of transplanting institutes or arrangements from one legal system to another. According to him "a successful legal transplant – like that of a human organ – will grow in its new body and become part of that body just as the rule or institution would have continued to develop in its parent system".[119] This concept was groundbreaking as it provided an innovative view of how legal ideas and institutions were introduced from one legal system to another.

Despite it being a brilliant analogy, according to Langer, there are deficiencies to this expression as it "fails to account for the transformations that legal ideas and institutions may undergo when they are transferred between legal systems".[120] In explaining his thesis, Langer conveys that the adversarial and inquisitorial evidentiary arrangements are not only terms used to classify legal systems into two procedural models based on their evidentiary arrangements at the trial setting and on the roles played by the procedural actors.[121] In addition to these features, Langer states that these two systems are two different *procedural cultures* and for this reason, they are "two different sets of basic understandings of how criminal cases should be tried and prosecuted".[122]

I. Procedural Culture

Procedural culture is how the "law is understood, thought of, and practiced",[123] and it has three main dimensions:[124] (i) structures of interpretation and meaning, (ii) individual dispositions, and (iii) procedural powers.

(i) Langer states that owing to both the adversarial and the inquisitorial evidentiary arrangements being two different procedural cultures, they can be understood as two different "*structures of interpretation and meaning or procedural languages*".[125] For this reason, as is the case with languages, "the same terms or signifiers often have different meanings".[126] As seen in the previous chapter, this can be illustrated by

---

[119] *Watson*, Legal transplants, p. 27.
[120] *Langer*, Legal Transplants to Legal Translations, p. 5.
[121] In this sense, see supra Ch. 4 B. I.
[122] *Langer*, Legal Transplants to Legal Translations, p. 4.
[123] *Langer*, Legal Transplants to Legal Translations, p. 64.
[124] *Langer*, Legal Transplants to Legal Translations, pp. 9 et seq.
[125] *Langer*, Legal Transplants to Legal Translations, p. 10.
[126] *Langer*, Legal Transplants to Legal Translations, p. 10.

observing how the concepts of *truth*, *justice*, and *judicial neutrality* are different between the adversarial and the inquisitorial procedural models.[127]

The concept of *truth* in the inquisitorial system is "based on the belief that an objective reconstruction of reality is possible".[128] Differently, in the adversarial system owing to the belief that achieving the objective truth is an elusive enterprise, the focus is that the evidentiary rules are upheld, and, in this way, the formal or interpretive truth is achieved. As to the concept of *justice*, because the adversarial trial setting is structured as a dispute where the procedural actors have independent and conflicting roles, justice is linked to the concept of procedural fairness. In contrast, in the inquisitorial procedural model, the concept of justice is linked to a neutral party (usually the trial judge) being responsible for finding an objective reconstruction of reality. In turn, these variants affect other elements, such as the role ascribed to the trial judge. In the adversarial trial setting *judicial neutrality* is linked to the concept of passivity, whereas in the inquisitorial trial setting, judicial neutrality is linked to judicial impartiality.

In view of these examples, it is clear that although the terminology used is at times identical, – e.g., truth, justice, and judicial neutrality – these words have different meanings in each of the two evidentiary arrangements. For this reason, Langer states that the key courtroom actors "constantly make use of adversarial and inquisitorial structures of interpretation and meaning in conscious and unconscious ways".[129] This in turn, makes it possible to identify whether a legal system under analysis has a predominantly adversarial or a predominantly inquisitorial evidentiary arrangement.

(ii) Regarding the second dimension of a procedural culture, when addressing the *individual dispositions*, Langer states that they "are acquired by the internationalization of the procedural structures of interpretation and meaning, through a number of socialization processes".[130] An example of the said process is the education that students receive at law school and how they later influence the role of the procedural actors at trial. As previously seen,[131] in systems with a predominantly inquisitorial evidentiary arrangement, such as in Germany, law is seen as a legal science and law students are taught at university to think in an objective manner, much like that of a judge. In contrast, in countries with a predominantly adversarial evidentiary arrangement, such as the United States, law students are taught to "think like a lawyer".[132]

Consequently, Langer states that procedural actors "are predisposed to understand criminal procedure and the various roles within it in a particular way, and these

---

[127] See supra Ch. 4 B. III.
[128] *Grande*, in: Jackson et al., Crime, procedure and evidence, p. 147.
[129] *Langer*, Legal Transplants to Legal Translations, p. 11.
[130] *Langer*, Legal Transplants to Legal Translations, p. 12.
[131] See supra Ch. 4 B. III.
[132] *Lempert*, in: Jackson et al., Crime, procedure and evidence, p. 396.

dispositions become durable over time".[133] This dimension of the procedural culture is key when it comes to legal transplants and translations. This is because the transfer of a legal provision or idea from one legal system to another involves the interaction and struggles between both "abstract systems of meaning", as well as "between a concrete set of individual dispositions".[134] Thus, it is within the context of the individual dispositions that an imported legal idea or thought will be applied in practice.

(iii) As to the third dimension of a procedural culture, the *procedural powers* between the two procedural models also differ from one another, as the amount of "power" that the key courtroom players possess can be considerably different. In the adversarial evidentiary arrangement, the parties have a significantly higher "allocation of responsibility for procedural action"[135] at the trial setting than their inquisitorial counterparts. In contrast, the trial judge has a correspondingly weaker amount of discretionary powers than judges in the inquisitorial trial setting.

For this reason, when examining the amount of discretionary powers that judges possess in the inquisitorial evidentiary arrangement, Langer explains that this is the reason why "any attempt to change this structure of interpretation and meaning will usually generate a reaction by the judges who protest against being disempowered through a new procedural structure of meaning".[136]

Finally, Langer states that these three dimensions are not static, and they interact among themselves. These interactions account for the changes that may take place within each procedural model once a legal idea or thought is transferred from one legal system into another.[137]

II. Importance of Understanding the Receiving Country's Institutional Context

When legal ideas and institutions are transplanted from a legal system with features of an adversarial procedural model to that of an inquisitorial procedural model (or vice versa), it is particularly important to be aware of the differences in these two procedural cultures. In this regard, it is vital to have a grasp of the main features of the targeted legal system's trial setting, i.e. the procedural outline, the roles the key courtroom actors play and who is the main responsible for presenting evidence at trial. Absent the comprehension of these elements, it is especially difficult to analyze whether and to what extent a legal idea or institution could be successfully transplanted from one legal system into another. Thus, depending on the

---

[133] *Langer*, Legal Transplants to Legal Translations, p. 12.
[134] *Langer*, Legal Transplants to Legal Translations, p. 12.
[135] *Damaška*, The Uncertain Fate of Evidentiary Transplants, p. 841.
[136] *Langer*, Legal Transplants to Legal Translations, p. 14.
[137] *Langer*, Legal Transplants to Legal Translations, p. 16.

circumstances at play, an attempt to transplant a legal idea into the Brazilian criminal procedure may fail due to it not being compatible to the countries' institutional context, i.e., both its *legal framework* and its *legal culture.*

Damaška states that "the success of most procedural innovation depends less than lawyers like to think on the excellence of rules" but rather "on the institutional context in which justice is administered in a particular country".[138] He further states that when a doctrine or practice is introduced into another legal system, they will suffer alterations in this new environment. This is because "even textually identical rules acquire a different meaning and produce different consequences in the changed institutional setting. The music of the law changes, so to speak, when the musical instruments and the players are no longer the same".[139]

In describing the changes that occur to a legal system when a legal transplant occurs, Langer offers an alternative term to this phenomenon, that of *legal translation.* The advantage of this term is that it accounts for the changes that may occur to a legal institutions or a legal idea once a "legal text" is translated from its language of origin to the target language, i.e., once a legal institution is transferred from its legal system of origin into a receiving system's legal framework and culture. Langer states that when this takes place, the possible changes that might take place to the translated "text" is that it might be neutralized, by either "ostracism" or "censorship". In other words, the legal idea may either come into disuse or be considered to be unconstitutional.[140]

The changes that occur to a legal idea once it is imported may occur regardless of the system of origin and the receiving legal system having predominantly adversarial or inquisitorial features. To better understand the changes that a legal institution or a legal idea may undergo once imported to a new legal system, I will now offer examples of these interactions in the German and Brazilian criminal procedures.

III. The Introduction of Legal Ideas Conducted in Disregard to a Country's Normative Framework and Procedural Culture

I will now provide examples of legal ideas stemming from features of an adversarial evidentiary arrangement being transferred to countries with a predominantly inquisitorial trial setting.[141] In these examples, the "legal text" went through

---

[138] *Damaška*, The Uncertain Fate of Evidentiary Transplants, p. 839.

[139] *Damaška*, The Uncertain Fate of Evidentiary Transplants, p. 840.

[140] *Langer*, Legal Transplants to Legal Translations, p. 34.

[141] An illustration of an attempt to completely change the evidentiary arrangements from a country's legal system can be seen in the Italian criminal procedure. See *Pizzi/Marafioti*, The New Italian Code of Criminal Procedure: The Difficulties of Building an Adversarial Trial System on a Civil Law Foundation; *Grande*, Italian Criminal Justice: Borrowing and Resist-

transformations after it was translated from its "language of origin" – the US-American evidence law – to its "target languages", i.e., to the German and Brazilian criminal procedures, respectively. In the first example, the "legal text" introduced to the German criminal procedure came into disuse, whereas in the second example, the "legal text" was initially ostracized due to it being counter to the Brazilian legal culture.

1. Example in the German Criminal Procedure

As seen in Ch. 1, § 239 StPO introduced the institute of cross-examination (*Kreuzverhör*) into the German normative framework.[142] This legal provision sets out that both the prosecution and the defense may concurringly request the presiding judge for them to examine witnesses and experts who were named by them. In these instances, after either the prosecution or the defense examines their respective witnesses and experts, the "opposing party" may do so followed by the presiding judge who may address his questions if he finds them necessary to further clarify the case.[143]

Although this provision was initially introduced as a means to complement the court's truth finding activities, it is currently in disuse as it is incompatible with the German inquisitorial trial setting.[144] The parties' active stance in cross-examining oral testimony both clashes with the principle of ascertainment of the truth and the presiding judge's responsibility in presiding the main hearing and the examination of evidence.[145]

Additionally, there are two ancillary reasons for this provision's inapplicability. The first is due to the lack of the defense's and particularly of the prosecution's ability and interest in conducting cross-examination, due to the extraneous character of this kind of examination.[146] Although if needed, the defense can very heavily try to impeach witnesses, as a rule – unlike their US-American counterparts – the highly adversarial dialectical process between prosecution and defense is not a feature of the German trial setting. Second, the defense and the prosecution have the concern that if it cross-examines witnesses and experts, this may be construed by the court as a criticism to its fact-finding abilities.[147] For these reasons, even though this legal

---

ance; *Pizzi/Montagna*, The Battle to Establish an Adversarial Trial System in Italy; *Marafioti*, in: Jackson et al., Crime, Procedure and Evidence, pp. 81 et seq.

[142] See supra Ch. 1 C. I. 2. b).

[143] § 239 (2) StPO.

[144] *Frase/Weigend*, German Criminal Justice, pp. 357, 358; *Gaede*, in: MüKo-StPO, § 239 Rn. 1; *Roxin/Schünemann*, Strafverfahrensrecht, § 44 Rn. 24.

[145] *Jescheck*, Principles of German Criminal Procedure, pp. 248, 249.

[146] *Frase/Weigend*, German Criminal Justice, p. 358; *Findley*, Adversarial Inquisitions, p. 933; *Schäuble*, Strafverfahren und Prozessverantwortung, p. 89.

[147] *Gaede*, in: MüKo-StPO, § 239 Rn. 2.

provision was introduced as an "experimentation clause" (*Experimentierklausel*) in the 19th century,[148] it remains to be a "foreign object" (*Fremdkörper*) in the German trial setting.[149]

2. Example in the Brazilian Criminal Procedure

In the Brazilian criminal procedure, there is a clear instance where a legal idea went through transformations after its introduction to the Brazilian normative framework, and as a result, was initially ostracized. This took place with the enactment of L. 11.690/08, which both changed the original wording of Art. 212, chapeau and introduced Art. 212 para. 1 to the CPP.[150] The first part of the original wording of Art. 212 CPP sets out that "The parties' questions shall be requested to the judge, who shall relay them to the witness".[151] Thus, until the enactment of L. 11.690/08, the *sistema presidencialista* prevailed, i.e., the trial judge was the main procedural actor responsible for examining the witnesses sensu lato, and only after he concluded this examination, were the parties allowed to ask the witnesses questions through the judge.

The changes to this Article's wording sought to give the parties more control over the taking of evidence. The new wording of Art. 212, chapeau, CPP provides that "questions shall be put directly by the parties to the witness, and the judge shall not admit those that may induce (lead) the answer, have no connection with the cause, or are repetitive." Further, the newly introduced para. 1 sets out that the judge may *supplement* the inquiry regarding the matters which were not clarified.

There is no contention that the heading of Art. 212 CPP provides that the parties shall directly examine the witnesses. If the parties fail to address an issue which is relevant to the case, the trial judge may – in a supplementary capacity – ask the witnesses questions. Nonetheless, in the first decade after this legislative change, many trial judges refused to apply these legal provisions and despite their clear wording, various discussions were conducted on how to interpret them.[152]

---

[148] *Roxin/Schünemann*, Strafverfahrensrecht, § 44 Rn. 24.

[149] *Schneider*, in: KK-StPO, § 239 Rn. 1.

[150] See supra Ch. 3 C. III. 2. b).

[151] The original wording of Art. 212, chapeau, CPP "As perguntas das partes serão requeridas ao juiz, que as formulará à testemunha".

[152] Most scholars and the CPP mandate that the parties should control the examination of witnesses and victims, whereas the trial judge only has a supplementary role. However, there are scholars and legal practitioners that believe that the trial judge should remain responsible for initiating the witness's examination followed by the parties. The arguments adduced are that (i) the CPP still mandates that the judge conducts the defendant's examination in the ordinary and summary procedural outlines, as laid out by Arts. 188, 473 and 201, chapeau, CPP, and that (ii) trial judges remain to conduct both the defendant's examination and those of oral witnesses in the jury trial. In this sense, see *Nucci*, CPP Comentado, pp. 521, 529.

During several years, trial judges either ignored these legal provisions and remained to be the sole procedural actors responsible for conducting the examination of witnesses, or they construed this legal provision as to suggest that they could first examine the witnesses, and only once they concluded their examination, the parties could initiate their direct examination. Thus, even though these provisions became part of the Brazilian legal framework, owing to the Brazilian (inquisitorial) procedural culture, and more specifically to its legal culture, the application of Arts. 212, chapeau and 212 para. 1 CPP faced a massive amount of resistance by the trial judges. The reason for this is that these provisions went against the trial judges' role and their standing at trial.

It was only after several decisions of the STF and STJ (which at times annulled the entire procedure of evidence taking of trials that were conducted against the new wording of Arts. 212, chapeau and para. 1 CPP), that the parties were allowed to also examine the witnesses. The Fifth Senate (5th T.) of the STJ held that the inversion in the order of examining the witnesses are a relative ground for annulling the trial (*nulidade relativa*).[153] According to this position, the trial must be annulled if the defense can demonstrate to the court that the fact that the trial judge started the witness's examination was detrimental to the defendant's case.[154] However, in April 2020, the First Senate (1st T.) of the STF held that the inversion of the order in inquiring the witnesses is not a reason to annul the procedure of evidence taking.[155] The argument adduced was that the aim of the changes in the wording of Art. 212, chapeau, CPP was to avoid the trial judge from being the sole procedural actor responsible for examining the witnesses. Thus, provided that the parties have the opportunity to examine the witnesses, the inversion in the order of this examination is permitted.

C. Identifying the Brazilian Legal Culture

As demonstrated above, for a legal system to effectively change its legal framework, jurists must first analyze whether a legal idea or provision of a foreign legal system is prone to fit within not only the receiving legal system's normative framework, but also within its procedural culture. As I illustrated with examples in the German and Brazilian criminal procedures, absent this specific piece of the puzzle, the introduction of legal ideas or provisions will at best fail to achieve its full scope or intended potential, and at worst, it will simply be ignored and subsequently discarded.

---

[153] Resp. 1259482/RS.
[154] As per Art. 563 CPP.
[155] HC 175.048/SP.

I have previously presented an overview of the historical backdrop in describing the development of the normative framework and the context in which the CPP was enacted in Part 1.[156] Additionally, I have analyzed the main features of the Brazilian normative framework (Ch. 3) and its predominant procedural model, and by extent, its predominant procedural culture (Ch. 4). Thus, the last step is to examine Brazil's legal culture. Differently than the procedural culture, which coincides with a legal system's predominant procedural model, a country's *legal culture* is the result of a legal system's predominant procedural culture which co-exists with a country's specific characteristics, such as its social, economic, and historical features.[157] The importance of defining the Brazilian legal culture is that at times, it is very different from the inquisitorial procedural culture. This, is turn, will explain and help to correctly identify the problematic features of the Brazilian criminal procedure in the following chapter.

I. The Influence of the Historical Background

As seen in Part 1, Portuguese law was applied during most of the Portuguese colonization in Brazil from the beginning of the 16th century until the country's independence in 1822. The law which was applied in the colony during this period was based on both Roman and Canon law and was very repressive. In its more recent history, due to the urge to reunify the criminal procedure, the CPP was enacted in 1941. As this code was enacted during a dictatorship, the CPP was based on Mussolini's fascist ideology and as a result, the original framework of the CPP did not have many provisions safeguarding the accused's rights. Further, owing to this code's punitive ideology, judges had a vast amount of unchecked discretionary powers, and those accused of having committed crimes were regarded as an object and a means in which to help the state in finding them guilty.

In Brazil's more recent history, the enactment of the Federal Constitution in 1988 set out various constitutional rights and guarantees that are of great importance to the criminal procedure. Despite the CPP having gone through various changes in order to be in conformity to the Constitution, the corresponding changes to the Brazilian legal culture have not kept pace with the reforms in its normative framework. The Brazilian legal culture remains to be (predominantly) authoritarian, repressive, rigid, and highly formalistic[158] and this is reflected in the manner in which the normative framework is applied by the courts.[159]

---

[156] For the importance of the historical backdrop, see *Woischnik*, Juez de Instrucción, p. 49.

[157] *Langer*, Legal Transplants to Legal Translations, pp. 16, 17.

[158] Examples of this excessive formalism are namely, the CPP provides sets out (i) the maximum number of days the procedure of evidence taking may last (art. 400, chapeau, CPP), (ii) the maximum number of witnesses the parties may examine at trial (art. 401, chapeau, CPP), (iii) the procedural moment in which both the prosecution and the defense may list the witnesses

II. The Role of the Procedural Actors: The Gap Between the Normative Framework and the Legal Culture

As a rule, Brazilian scholars tend to assign blame of its repressive legal culture to the inquisitorial procedural culture.[160] This is imprecise and highly problematic, as various solutions to the most problematic features of the Brazilian criminal procedure could be found by analyzing the procedural safeguards that modern democratic countries with a predominantly inquisitorial evidentiary arrangement have in place in countering this system's inherent weaknesses.

The rigidity of the Brazilian legal culture can be observed by the large number of conservative scholars and practitioners who have been unwilling to change their views regarding the defendants' position at trial and remain to perceive defendants as objects in the proceedings. However, this scenario is gradually changing as an ever-growing number of Brazilian scholars are favorable to changes in the legal culture and in effectively providing the defendant with effective procedural rights. Nonetheless, a gap remains between the latter position and the legal practice, i. e., the ever-growing number of scholars who outcry for the defendant's procedural rights on the one hand, and how the legal framework is applied in practice by the main procedural actors, who as a rule, persist to conduct their daily activities in accordance with the aforementioned legal culture.

The problem with this clash between "law on the books" and "law in action" is that, at times, it leads to a high level of rigidity and to a complete lack of coherence which is not conducive to positive changes to the problematic features of the Brazilian criminal procedure. These features are clearly observed in regard to the roles played by judges (i), prosecutors (ii) and by the defense at trial (iii).

(i) As seen, the Brazilian trial setting predominantly has features of an officialized factfinding with elements of partisan control of evidence. In the legal practice, the trial judge is by far the procedural actor who has the most amount of power over the proceedings and, as seen in this chapter, has been reluctant to adapt to the changes brought by the CPP which go against this role.[161] However, this reluctant stance is not completely inconsistent with the legal system's predominantly inquisitorial evidentiary arrangement where the trial judge is responsible for finding the material truth and for conducting the procedure of evidence taking, as set out by the principle of ascertainment of the truth. Thus, despite a few inconsistencies between the role

---

they wish to present at trial under penalty of preclusion (arts. 41 and 396-A, respectively), and (iv) setting a time limit to the duration of the closing arguments (Art. 403, chapeau, CPP).

[159] In this sense, see Part 1 B. II. 2. and Part 1 B. II. 3.
[160] In this sense, see Ch. 6 A. I.
[161] In this sense, see supra Ch. 5 B. III. 2.

prescribed to the trial judge in the legal framework and the role effectively played at trial, the divide between the "law on the books" and "law in action" is not major.[162]

However, there is a large divide between the role played by the prosecution and defense *in theory* (as set out by the normative framework) and the role played *in practice* (which is largely influenced by the legal culture).

(ii) In regard to the role played by prosecutors at the trial setting, many scholars still purport that public prosecutors are "impartial parties" ("*partes imparciais*"), who act in a detached and highly objective manner. A reason which is often adduced to support this position is that a prosecutor cannot file a bill of indictment against a suspect whenever she verifies that the minimum evidentiary standard of justa causa has not been met. However, the reasoning for this is not due to the prosecutor having an objective stance, but rather, due to them having to adhere to the legal provisions set out by the CPP.[163]

Contrary to the aforementioned position, many scholars believe that Brazilian prosecutors clearly have a partisan stance at trial, particularly during the procedure of evidence taking.[164] This stems from the fact that the parties – while not being the primary procedural actors responsible for presenting evidence – are afforded a steadily increasing amount of control over evidence taking. These scholars also contend that the perception that prosecutors are an "impartial party" is both damaging and inaccurate. The reason for this is that prosecutors are often perceived by trial judges and by society in general as having a superior standpoint in the trial setting due to them being "more reliable" and trustworthy than the defendant. This mentality is further ingrained by the prosecution's position in the courtroom, where, as a rule, they remain immediately to the right of the judge, while the defense remains positioned towards the back of the courtroom and further away from the judge.[165]

(iii) As to the defense's role at trial, there is also a divide between the role played by the defense in theory and in practice. On the one hand, the Brazilian normative framework is steadily seeking to – albeit failing to do so effectively – allocate to the defense a larger amount of responsibility in presenting evidence at trial. On the other hand, in the legal practice, there is a belief that the defendant and his defense counsel are seen as those who are standing in the state's way in seeking and achieving justice.[166]

In view of the above, there is a clash between the normative framework and the legal culture. The problem with this is that prosecutors cannot have it both ways. It is

---

[162] However, this does not negate the fact that both the current "law on the books" and "law in practice" are faulty and that the Brazilian criminal procedure needs effective procedural safeguards. In this sense, see infra Ch. 6 B.

[163] *Karam*, in: Prado/Malan, Processo Penal e Democracia, pp. 402, 403.

[164] See footnote 746 (Part 2).

[165] *Karam*, in: Prado/Malan, Processo Penal e Democracia, p. 403.

[166] *Saad*, in: Santoro/Malan/Maduro, Crise no Processo Penal, p. 325.

incompatible for them to act as both an "impartial party" who only wish to achieve justice and is considered to have no interest in the case's outcome, while concomitantly having an aggressive stance at trial and seeking a criminal conviction. These two positions in their current format are contradictory and cannot coexist.

The conflict between the legal framework and the legal culture regarding the roles played by the defense and the prosecution is made more apparent as the CPP afforded the parties more responsibilities in the presentation of evidence. These changes have engendered a shift in the normative framework regarding the roles played by both the parties and the trial judge at trial. However, due to the legal culture these changes did not have the expected results, as these procedural actors have not yet fully adapted to their prescribed roles.

This further demonstrates that regardless of the changes made to the Brazilian legal framework, for them to be successfully implemented in this legal system, there must be a concomitant change in the repressive and highly formalistic Brazilian legal culture. Thus, regardless of the suggestions made to the Brazilian criminal procedure, i.e., to either remain having a predominantly inquisitorial evidentiary arrangement or to shift to a predominantly adversarial evidentiary arrangement, the current legal culture must change. Absent the corresponding changes, any attempt to change the Brazilian criminal procedure in either direction will be neutralized.

This can be illustrated in the latest change made to the CPP through the enactment of L. 13.964/19. As seen in Part 1,[167] Arts 3-B to 3-F introduced the figure of the pretrial judge, who is solely competent to make decisions in the investigatory phase. Accordingly, if the Judiciary were to be reorganized for these provisions to be correctly implemented, this would reduce the reach of judicial competence and discretion. Unsurprisingly, immediately after this law was enacted, associations of Brazilian judges and members of the public prosecutor's office presented motions questioning the constitutionality of these legal provisions.

The main reason for this is that, as seen in this Chapter, Langer states that "any attempt to change this structure of interpretation and meaning will usually generate a reaction by the judges who protest against being disempowered through a new procedural structure of meaning".[168] For this reason, the initial "censorship"[169] of these provisions is (regrettably) in accordance with the repressive Brazilian legal culture, where judges have vast and almost unchecked discretionary powers throughout the procedural phases, and especially, at trial.

---

[167] See supra Part 1 B. II. 3.

[168] *Langer*, Legal Transplants to Legal Translations, p. 14.

[169] I borrowed the term used by *Langer* in his article Legal Transplants to Legal Translations (p. 34) to indicate that once this legal idea was introduced into the Brazilian criminal procedure it was censored and its constitutionality was questioned.

Chapter 6

Comparative Study and (Possible) Solutions to the Brazilian Criminal Procedure

A. Identifying the Main Problematic Features

Before addressing the main problematic features of the Brazilian criminal procedure, I would like to address the difficulties Brazilian scholars have been facing in pinpointing its failings. I believe a possible reason for this might be due to the lack of comparative studies, which may lead to missed opportunities in better understanding the Brazilian legal system, and consequently, in correctly defining the reasons for its main deficiencies. Also, there is the missed opportunity of learning from the experiences and lessons other countries have learned from analyzing, reforming, and/or importing legal ideas and provisions from foreign legal systems into their respective domestic legal systems. This, in turn, hinders to a certain extent the proposal of possible and of effective solutions to the shortcomings of the Brazilian criminal procedure, particularly regarding the defendant's vulnerable position at trial.

For these reasons, although several scholars offer a massive number of suggestions for the improvement of the CPP, the extent of the suitability and effectivity of these suggestions could be greatly increased if the real reasons behind the problematic features of the CPP were correctly identified and assessed. As previously mentioned, this is not due to a lack of will or effort, but rather, on account of scholars looking for answers in places that are not the most conducive in finding effective solutions.

I will now analyze the reasons that led to the current standstill in finding solutions to the perceived failings of the Brazilian criminal procedure by first examining the main reason adduced by Brazilian scholars for these failings (I.). Subsequently, I will offer two alternative explanations, which I believe are the actual reasons for its most problematic features (II.). By identifying these latter reasons, this will enable the identification of the CPP's main problematic features. This, in in turn, will clarify where possible solutions in countering these features may be found. Also, I hope that the analysis of the actual reasons for the most problematic features of the CPP may highlight the dangers which may result from the misidentification of these features.

I. Alleged Reason: "Inquisitorial" Features

As repeatedly seen, the CPP currently has a predominantly inquisitorial procedural model with various elements of the adversarial system.[170] The mixture of both

---

[170] See supra Ch. 4 C. II.

these evidentiary arrangements has been the object of criticism by several Brazilian scholars, particularly in the context of the position of perceived vulnerability of the defendant at trial. This is owing to most scholars allocating blame of the procedural failings of the Brazilian criminal procedure to what they deem to be the "inquisitorial" features of the CPP.[171]

The reasoning for this is that these scholars inaccurately equate vast unchecked judicial powers and the repressive traits of both the Brazilian normative framework and of the legal culture to the inquisitorial evidentiary arrangement and, by extension, to the inquisitorial procedural culture. As seen, this faulty perception is heightened by the depiction of the adversarial and mainly of the inquisitorial procedural model in a highly abstract manner,[172] and by only taking into consideration the latter's historical features. A further reason for this perception is that most Brazilian scholars and practitioners are unaware that many modern continental European countries have predominantly inquisitorial evidentiary arrangements and that the normative framework of many of these legal systems provide defendants with several rights and principles throughout the procedural phases and safeguard their procedural rights at trial.[173]

For these reasons, the vast majority of suggestions offered to counter the failings of the Brazilian criminal procedure are to remove all "inquisitorial features" from the CPP. Thus, although the reforms that began in 2008 partly changed the trial setting to allow for a larger amount of party-controlled presentation of evidence, the widespread criticism against the current structure of the CPP remains as the procedure of evidence taking persists to be a predominantly officialized factfinding enterprise.[174]

---

[171] *Coutinho*, As Reformas Parciais do CPP, pp. 11 et seq.; *Cruz*, Com a Palavra, As Partes, p. 17; *Polastri/Ambos*, O Processo Acusatório, pp. 63 et seq.; *Coutinho*, in: Prado/Malan, Processo Penal e Democracia, pp. 252 et seq.; *Giacomolli*, Algumas Marcas Inquisitoriais do CPP, pp. 147 et seq.; *Jardim/Amorim*, Direito Processual Penal, p. 485; *Capez*, Curso de Processo Penal, pp. 72, 73; *Tourinho Filho*, Manual, p. 84; *Choukr*, in: Santoro/Malan/Maduro, Crise no Processo Penal, pp. 135 et seq.; *Lopes Jr.*, Direito Processual Penal, 15th ed., pp. 93, 94; *Melchior*, in: Santoro/Malan/Maduro, Crise no Processo Penal, pp. 39 et seq.; *Silva Júnior*, Reforma Tópica, pp. 76 et seq.

[172] The inquisitorial system and "mixed model" are analyzed in their historical sense, whereas the adversarial system is mostly ignored by Brazilian scholars in both its historical and analytical sense. Further, the fact that many developed democracies have an inquisitorial evidentiary arrangement is almost entirely absent from the legal discussions taking place in the country.

[173] In this sense see also *Perron*, in: Perron (ed.), Die Beweisaufnahme im Strafverfahrensrecht, pp. 569 et seq.

[174] Termed *gestão probatória do juiz* and/or *poderes instrutórios do juiz*.

II. Possible Reasons

1. Unawareness of the Indispensability of Procedural Safeguards

The current structure of the trial setting and the judge's role in the truth-finding enterprise are not *in themselves* the sources of the problematic features in the Brazilian criminal procedure as many scholars claim.

Also, contrary to the prevailing criticism, the fact that the Brazilian criminal procedure has elements of both inquisitorial and adversarial systems is not in itself problematic, because as repeatedly mentioned, it is rare for a country to have a pure inquisitorial or a pure adversarial procedural model.[175] On the contrary, it is not uncommon for legal systems to have certain features that start converging with one another.[176] There are many countries that have a mixture of both these evidentiary arrangements and yet, they have effective safeguards to neutralize the deficiencies which are bound to occur in this setting. Further yet, in the context of the Brazilian criminal procedure, the features of both procedural models may be beneficial to the finding of truth and in protecting the defendants' position at trial.[177]

I believe the real reason for the many problematic issues in the defendant's procedural rights not being effectively safeguarded lies in the overall lack of awareness that regardless of the evidentiary arrangement in question, safeguards must be in place to counter their inherent structural deficiencies. It is likely that this lack of awareness stems from the lack of clarity regarding the characteristics of the different procedural models and their structural weaknesses. Absent these concepts, it is plausible that when Brazilian scholars analyze the Brazilian trial setting, they trace the failings of this legal system to its predominant evidentiary arrangement.

A further reason is because absent the key concepts of comparative law, scholars tend to make "legal projections" when conducting comparative studies.[178] Thus, the premise resulting from this legal projection is that if the Brazilian trial setting is an officialized factfinding, where judges have a virtually unchecked amount of discretion at trial, consequently, all inquisitorial procedural models have this feature. This skewed belief is further validated by the analysis of this evidentiary arrangement solely from its historical perspective (i.e., solely from one aspect of an abstract perspective) and the virtual lack of studies on how legal systems with inquisitorial evidentiary arrangements function in practice (concrete perspective).

In contrast, once the structural strengths and weaknesses of each procedural model are clearly defined, it is possible to trace the failings of the Brazilian trial setting in a more informed manner. In reality, the reason behind the vast amount of judicial discretion present in the Brazilian criminal procedure does not lie on the inquisitorial

---

[175] See supra Ch. 4 B. I.
[176] *Frase/Weigend*, German Criminal Justice, pp. 359, 360.
[177] In this sense, see *Weigend*, Should We Search, p. 408.
[178] See supra Ch. 5 A.

evidentiary arrangement. Instead, it is because the normative framework does not set any concrete and effective limits to judicial factfinding, and as a consequence, does not provide any effective safeguards against the risk of judicial bias, which is an inherent weakness of this evidentiary arrangement.

It is not by choosing a procedural model over another that a legal system's shortcomings will disappear. This belief is not only guileless, but also dangerous, since it may convey the false impression that once a country changes its legal system from a predominantly inquisitorial to a predominantly adversarial procedural model (or vice versa), its problems are solved, and the defendant's procedural rights are automatically safeguarded. This belief is flawed because without the *corresponding safeguards* in place, a country will trade one evidentiary arrangement for another creating a whole set of problems it is unfamiliar with and unprepared to address.[179] Thus, legal systems with predominantly inquisitorial features and those with predominantly adversarial features need mechanisms in which to counter deficiencies that are bound to exist regardless of the evidentiary arrangement in question.

I do not contend that countries such as Germany and the United States do not have various problems in their respective legal systems,[180] nor are they completely immune from the "one procedural model is better than the other" discourse.[181] This can be illustrated by Perron who after briefly describing the historical aspects of each procedural models states that "due to their deep historical roots, there is still little inclination on either side to doubt the superiority of their own system".[182] None-

---

[179] *Elisabetta Grande* examines how this took place in her native legal system. In 1988, Italy enacted a new code of criminal procedure which sought to change its inquisitorial trial setting to an adversarial trial setting. However, only some features of the adversarial model were transplanted to the Italian system, which currently has both adversarial and inquisitorial features. Furthermore, due to effective safeguards not being in place, this new model "does not appear to protect the rights of the defendant any more than did the previous one". See *Grande*, Italian Criminal Justice, pp. 230, 232, 256 et seq.

[180] For criticisms regarding the US-American criminal procedure and evidence law, see: *Weigend*, Continental Cures for American Ailments: European Criminal Procedure as a Model for Law Reform; *Bradley*, Reforming the Criminal Trial; *Kassin/Wrightsman*, The American Jury on Trial: Psychological Perspectives; *Langbein*, The Influence of Comparative Procedure in the United States, pp. 546 et seq.; *Krey*, Characteristic Features of German Criminal Proceedings – An Alternative to the Criminal Procedure Law of the United States; *Pizzi*, Trials Without Truth. Why Our System of Criminal Trials Has Become an Expensive Failure and What We Need to Do to Rebuild It; *Kagan*, Adversarial Legalism: The American Way of Law. For criticisms regarding the German criminal procedure, see: *Perron*, Das Beweisantragsrecht des Beschuldigten im deutschen Strafprozess; *Schäuble*, Strafverfahren und Prozessverantwortung: neue prozessuale Obliegenheit des Beschuldigten in Deutschland im Vergleich mit dem US-amerikanischen Recht.

[181] In this sense, see *Damaška*, Evidentiary Barriers to Conviction, pp. 588, 589; *Bradley*, Convergence of the Continental and the Common Law, p. 473; *Weigend*, Should we Search, pp. 398 et seq., and particularly, pp. 406, 407.

[182] *Perron*, Beweisantragsrecht, p. 124, "Entsprechend der tiefen historischen Verwurzelung besteht auf beiden Seiten vielerorts auch heute noch wenig Neigung, an der Überlegenheit des eigenen Systems zu zweifeln".

theless, both these countries have a long tradition of conducting legal studies, and the study of comparative criminal procedure is conducted in an exceedingly more comprehensive and systematic manner. Consequently, when US-American and German scholars examine their respective legal systems, they do so far more often from a "searching for effective procedural safeguards" standpoint[183] than from a "which procedural model is superior" analysis, which alas is the prevailing stance among Brazilian scholars.[184]

Thus, the crux of when examining whether a legal system is efficient while also safeguarding the defendant's procedural rights is not whether the system in question predominantly has adversarial or inquisitorial features, but rather, whether the specific safeguards it has in place to counter the inherent deficiencies found in each procedural model are effective.

a) Sample of Lack of Procedural Safeguards in a Setting of Party-Controlled Presentation of Evidence

To drive this point home, I would like to illustrate the abovementioned risks of the lack of effective procedural safeguards irrespective of the predominant evidentiary arrangement by examining a very recent development in the Brazilian criminal procedure. This illustration is by no means a criticism to changing the Brazilian trial setting to a predominantly adversarial procedural model itself, but rather to the complete lack of accompanying discussions as to the creation of procedural safeguards that must be in place should this ensue.

As previously seen, the enactment of L. 13.964/19 introduced many legal provisions to the CPP.[185] Among the many changes to the CPP, Art. 3-C, paras. 3 and 4 set out that the investigative file shall be kept at the registry of the pretrial judge (*Secretaria do juiz das garantias*). While the parties will be given broad access to this file, the trial judge will have no access to the investigative file, as it will no longer be appended to the case file. If this occurs, the only pretrial evidence that trial judges will have contact to are those collected due to an unsurmountable reason that prevents the evidence from being presented at trial.[186]

---

[183] *Bradley*, Reforming the Criminal Trial; *Frase/Weigend*, German Criminal Justice as a Guide to American Law Reform, particularly, pp. 356 et seq.; *Krey*, Characteristics Features of German Criminal Proceedings.

[184] In this sense, Langer states that in lieu of questioning which evidentiary arrangement "is normatively superior, we should start by asking which principles and goals we value in the criminal process and then we should discuss the best ways to implement those principles and goals in specific jurisdictions". In this sense, see also *Langer*, in: Ross/Thaman, Comparative Criminal Procedure, p. 532.

[185] See supra Part 1 B. II. 3. and Ch. 6 A. II. 1. a).

[186] Among these instances are the witness' unavailability in testifying at court for an uncertain period of time, due to reasons of infirmity, due to the great amount of distance involved, or in cases of expert evidence.

Should the STF find paras. 3 and 4 of Art. 3-C L. 13.964/19 to be constitutional,[187] and should trial judges correctly apply these legal provisions, a corresponding shift in the control of the presentation of evidence from a predominantly officialized fact-finding to a predominantly party-controlled presentation of evidence would follow. This is further underpinned by Art. 3-A which sets out that "the criminal procedure shall have an accusatory structure", which in this specific context is meant to refer to a party-controlled presentation of evidence at trial.[188]

Thus, if these provisions come into force and are properly applied by judges, once the trial judge no longer has access to the investigation file, this will completely hinder her ability in conducting evidence taking at trial and in finding the material truth. If this were to ensue, this would not be problematic provided that procedural safeguards were in place to counter the structural weaknesses that would occur due to the corresponding shift in the evidentiary arrangement.[189] However, the ensuing changes that would take place should these provisions be found constitutional were not addressed by either the committee which authored this reform, nor by the scholars and practitioners who were in favor of these changes in the Brazilian trial setting. As a result, the procedural safeguards that must be in place to hinder the inevitable weaknesses that will arise from this shift in the evidentiary arrangement were neither weighed nor considered.

Further yet, the sheer need for accompanying safeguards were not even mentioned in the aftermath of the enactment of this law. As it will become apparent after the comparative study below, the problematic issues that will arise from the lack of necessary accompanying safeguards, will very likely lead to a whole new set of problems. Among these problematic features are the lack of equality of arms, and the resulting inefficiency in safeguarding the defendant's procedural rights owing to the lack of provisions setting out mechanisms in which the defense may fulfill its roles at trial. Consequently, after yet another legal reform, we are going back to square one.

b) Consequences of the Lack of Procedural Safeguards in a Setting of Officialized Factfinding

In allocating blame of the procedural failings of the Brazilian criminal procedure to its "inquisitorial" features, the baby is thrown away with the bath water. Simply put, instead of tracing the main failings of the Brazilian trial setting to the lack of effective procedural safeguards in countering the inquisitorial evidentiary arrangement's inherent weaknesses, most scholars deem that this evidentiary arrangement as a whole must be rejected. The problem with this practice is that it is much easier to remedy the shortcomings of an existing predominant procedural model by setting

---

[187] See supra Part 1 B. II. 3.

[188] The Brazilian scholarship equates the term accusatorial to three features, one of which is the party-controlled presentation of evidence at trial, see supra Ch. 4 C. I.

[189] In this sense, see *Langer*, Legal Transplants to Legal Translations, p. 15.

appropriate procedural safeguards, than entirely changing the predominant evidentiary arrangement.

This is particularly important in a context where the reasoning behind the need and existence of procedural safeguards (*garantias processuais*) are hardly, if ever, considered by Brazilian scholars. As seen in the previous subitem, the complete shift in evidentiary arrangements without the corresponding safeguards in place will very likely lead to future defendants being in an even more vulnerable situation than the one that defendants currently find themselves in.

As of this writing, the fact remains that the Brazilian trial setting has a predominantly inquisitorial evidentiary arrangement, and that specific procedural safeguards must be in place to counter its inherent structural weakness. As seen in Ch. 4, the inquisitorial procedural model has as its main inherent structural weakness the risk of judicial bias. This stems from the fact that because the trial judge is the main procedural actor responsible for conducting evidence taking and in finding the material truth, she must have access to the investigative file prior to trial to fulfill her tasks.[190] By having access to this file, it is inevitable for the judge to "at least unconsciously develop a picture of the course of events"[191] and consequently, to form preconceived ideas concerning the defendant's innocence or guilt. For this reason, there is the risk of a confirmation bias, where "new information is always processed in relation to a previously formed hypothesis or belief".[192] As seen in Ch. 4, "confirming circumstances are unconsciously overestimated, while conflicting circumstances tend to be underestimated, so that the hypothesis is in a sense self-confirming".[193]

Hence, it is inherent to this system that there must be safeguards in place to circumscribe judicial discretion in order to neutralize judicial bias. These effective safeguards are completely lacking in the Brazilian criminal procedure,[194] and as a result, judges have a virtually unchecked amount of discretion, particularly at trial. Interestingly, contrary to German professional judges who are aware that their prior access to information may bring with it an inherent risk to their impartiality, the risk of judicial bias is hardly ever discussed by Brazilian scholars and practitioners. I believe the reason for this lies in the Brazilian legal culture, where despite the huge amount of progress that has been made to change the perception on how the defendant

---

[190] See supra Ch. 4 B. II. 1. b).

[191] See original text in *Schäuble*, Strafverfahren und Prozessverantwortung, p. 67, Das Gericht durch das Studium der Ermittlungsakten "zumindest unbewusst ein Bild vom Tathergang entwickelt".

[192] See original text in *Schäuble*, Strafverfahren und Prozessverantwortung, p. 67, Danach werden "neue Informationen stets in Bezug auf eine bereits zuvor gebildete Hypothese oder Überzeugung verarbeitet".

[193] See original text in *Schäuble*, Strafverfahren und Prozessverantwortung, p. 67, "Bestätigende Umstände werden unbewusst über-, entgegenstehende Umstände dagegen eher unterschätzt, so dass sich die Hypothese in gewisser Weise selbst bestätigt".

[194] In this sense, see Ch. 6 A. II. 1. and Ch. 6 B. I.

and his rights are perceived at trial, the repressive legal culture is still predominant in the legal practice.

2. Features Unrelated to the Inquisitorial Evidentiary Arrangement that Increase the Risk of Judicial Bias

As seen above, the virtually unchecked amount of judicial discretion and the consequential risk of judicial bias mostly stem from the lack of procedural safeguards in counteracting the inherent structural weaknesses of the inquisitorial procedural model. However, there are two features of the Brazilian criminal procedure – which are completely unrelated to the inquisitorial evidentiary arrangement – that considerably heighten the risk of judicial bias. These are the partisan character of the criminal investigation (a)) and the lack of division of judicial roles throughout the procedural phases (b)).

a) Mostly Partisan Character of the Criminal Investigation

As seen in Ch. 3. the chief of police and the public prosecutor's office are the two main procedural actors, who have the legitimacy to conduct criminal investigations. In practice, once a crime is committed, there is a police investigation (*inquérito policial*), presided by the chief of police. This investigation is conducted in a partisan manner,[195] where the police mostly focus on searching for inculpatory evidence.[196] This is because the chief of police has the task to gather enough evidence to prove that a crime was in fact committed (*prova da materialidade*) and to identify the suspect believed to having committed it (*autoria do crime*). For reasons of celerity and pragmatism, once these two elements termed the "minimum evidentiary standard" (*lastro mínimo probatório*) are met, the chief of police concludes the criminal investigation and finishes compiling the investigation file. The reason for this is that the CPP sets out strict deadlines for the chief of police to conclude the criminal investigation, which he must meet.[197]

---

[195] I borrowed the term "partisan" in relation to the police from *Bradley*, Convergence of the Continental and the Common Law, p. 481.

[196] *Rascovski*, Investigação Criminal Defensiva, p. 14; *Vieira*, in: Ambos (ed.), Polícia e Investigação, pp. 355 et seq.

[197] The procedural deadlines the chief of police has in concluding a criminal investigation depend on various factors, such as whether the accused is in pretrial detention, or whether the criminal offense is of state or federal competence. In regard to the latter feature, Art. 10, chapeau, CPP and Art. 66 L. 5.010/66 sets out the number of days the chief of police has in concluding a criminal investigation regarding non-federal and federal crimes, respectively. There are other factors that may influence this deadline, such as the type of the criminal offense committed. An example of this can be observed in crimes involving narcotics, where Art. 51 L. 11.343/06 sets out the number of days the chief of police has to conclude the criminal investigation.

Consequently, the Brazilian trial judge is in possession of an investigative file which mostly contains evidence against the defendant. This increased risk of judicial bias does not stem from the inquisitorial evidentiary arrangement. This is because in this procedural model, the investigation is usually conducted by the police under the orders of either an investigative judge or an impartial public prosecutor, who are responsible for overseeing the police's investigation in finding both incriminating and exculpatory evidence against a suspect. As seen in Ch. 1, in the German criminal procedure, it is up to prosecutors to seek *both incriminating and exonerating evidence*.[198] Thus, although the risk of judicial bias is still present, at the very least, the trial judge receives a more balanced view of the facts of the case.

Thus, the weaknesses of the inquisitorial evidentiary arrangement are aggravated in the Brazilian trial setting, as the risk of judicial bias stemming from the trial judge's prior knowledge of the investigative file is increased, as the judge does not receive a balanced view of the case.

b) Lack of Division of Judicial Roles

As of this writing, there is only one procedural actor (*juiz*) who combines both the roles of the pretrial judge and that of the trial judge. This is a highly problematic feature of the Brazilian criminal procedure seeing that depending on the city where a criminal offense is being adjudicated, this may lead to the disregard of the defendant's procedural right to an impartial trial. This is because a single judge may be competent to decide – in the same criminal case – on matters of both an investigatory and an adjudicatory nature. Thus, the same person that ordered an arrest warrant to be issued against the accused, will also decide whether the evidentiary standard of *justa causa* for a criminal case to go to trial is met, and will be responsible for having the final say on whether the defendant is guilty of the charges laid against him.

The need for *both* a pretrial and trial judge is especially important in a legal system with an inquisitorial procedural model, due to its inherent risk of judicial bias. As seen in Ch. 1, there is a division of judicial competence between different types of judges in the German criminal procedure, where the roles of the pretrial judges (*Ermittlungsrichter*) clearly differ from those of the (professional) trial judges (*Prozessrichter*). By clearly stating the competences of each type of judge, the chances of judicial bias are highly reduced, as despite German professional judges having access to the investigation file, they did not actively participate in the investigative proceedings.

The division of judicial roles is absolutely vital in safeguarding the defendant's right to an impartial judge, and thus in guaranteeing him a fair trial. This is why it is critical for there to be two different types of judges, who have specific judicial roles and may only make decisions in their defined sphere of competency. In this sense, I believe that Art. 3-B of. L. 13.964/19, which introduced the figure of a pretrial judge

---

[198] § 160 (2) StPO.

(*juiz das garantias*) was conducive in achieving this goal. Should the STF find this legal provision to be constitutional, the CPP will set out one type of judge who is only competent to make decisions during the investigatory phase (*juiz das garantias*) and one who is solely competent to act in the adjudicatory phase (*juiz do processo*).

Additionally, it is necessary for there to be a provision that states that if a judge makes a decision in the investigatory phase of the procedure, she is automatically barred from adjudicating the same case, regardless of the legal instance in question. In this sense, the newly enacted Art. 3-C CPP would also further this end, as it states that pretrial judges are only competent to make rulings on matters that involve the investigation of felonies and are thus precluded from adjudicating criminal cases.

B. (Possible) Solutions to Selected Features of the Brazilian Criminal Procedure

After having identified the main reasons for the failings in the Brazilian criminal procedure, I will now analyze two features of this legal system, which I believe that if addressed would lead to considerably advancing the defendant's position at trial. First, I will assess the existing procedural safeguards and make suggestions to their improvement (I.). Second, I will address a topic that for past decades has been the point of contention among Brazilian legal scholars, which is the possibility of the trial judge alluding to information gathered in the investigatory phase when stating the reasons for finding the defendant guilty of the charges laid against her (II.).

The suggestions I will set out below can only be effective in countering the most problematic features of the Brazilian criminal procedure *if* the basic requirement of there being both a pretrial judge and a trial judge – as set in the subitem above (b)) – is met. Only by there being two different types of judges, who have specific judicial roles and may only make decisions in their defined sphere of competency, will the defendant's right to an impartial judge and, consequently, to an impartial trial be safeguarded.

I. Lack of Effective Procedural Safeguards

Interestingly, despite the topic of procedural safeguards (*garantias processuais*) often being debated by Brazilian scholars, the reasoning for its existence is hardly, if ever, considered. Furthermore, the fact that procedural safeguards are necessary to counter the structural weaknesses inherent in each evidentiary arrangement has been virtually absent from the legal discussions taking place in the country.

I will now briefly address the general reasons why the current principles in the Brazilian criminal procedure are not effective procedural safeguards (1.) as to subsequently assess the specific safeguards in place to counter the deficiencies of the adversarial and of the inquisitorial features of the Brazilian trial setting. For this purpose, I will assess these safeguards by examining the main safeguards the US-American (2.) and the German (3.) legal systems have in place to counter the structural deficiencies in their respective evidentiary arrangements. This is important to illustrate how despite of both these countries having very different trial settings and evidentiary arrangements, they both have mechanisms in place to further the defendant's position at trial. Nonetheless, the means in which each legal system achieves this aim is directly linked in accommodating for the differences in their trial setting.

After concluding each respective analysis in (2.) and (3.), I will offer suggestions of improvement to the Brazilian criminal procedure *within* the context of its legal framework and – when possible – of its legal culture.

1. Initial Assessment

Owing to the Brazilian trial setting having both aspects of officialized factfinding and of partisan control of evidence, there must be procedural safeguards in place to counter the unavoidable weaknesses which stem from the features of each respective evidentiary arrangement.

As examined, there are five main principles that shape the trial setting and/or seek to further the defendant's procedural rights at trial.[199] The two principles which relate to the inquisitorial trial setting are the principle of ascertainment of the truth and the principle of free evaluation of evidence. Although Brazilian scholars view the latter principle as a procedural safeguard, the former principle is often the object of criticism by many scholars, owing to it furthering the inquisitorial trial setting. For this reason, there is a disproportionate overreliance on the principles of audiatur et altera pars and of full defense. These principles are deemed by most Brazilian scholars to further the "accusatorial system" (*sistema acusatório*) and are considered to be important procedural safeguards (*garantias processuais*). As such, these principles are usually considered to be important in guaranteeing a democratic society (*Estado Democrático de Direito*) and of furthering the features of party-controlled presentation of evidence at trial.

Contrary to this belief, although these principles are indeed important, they are by no means adequate in countering the failings of the adversarial features of the Brazilian trial setting. The same is true regarding the lack of efficiency of the procedural safeguards in place to counter the shortcomings of the inquisitorial features of the Brazilian trial setting. I will now indicate the two *general reasons* for the inefficiency of these principles, as to subsequently specify in the following subitems why they are deficient in countering both the failings that are inherent to the offi-

---

[199] See supra Ch. 3 D.

cialized factfinding and those inherent to the features of a party-controlled presentation of evidence.

The first general reason for the lack of effectivity of the current procedural safeguards is that the Brazilian criminal procedure is very (and solely) reliant on principles that do not have the corresponding constitutional or statutory provisions circumscribing them and/or ensuring their enforceability. Thus, there are no provisions setting out the limits to a principle's scope whenever it limits the defendant's procedural rights. This can be illustrated by the principle of ascertainment of truth, where the trial judge may reject a parties' request to present additional oral evidence, without having to provide any objective reasons for doing so, nor are there any objective parameters in which to circumscribe judicial discretion. The reasoning for this is that some Brazilian scholars equate this principle mandating that the trial judge is responsible for presiding and conducting evidence taking, with the trial judge having complete judicial discretion to fulfill these tasks. As a result, trial judges are given a vast amount of discretion in basing their decisions on subjective criteria without there being any corresponding means in which to circumscribe these powers.

The second reason for the lack of effectivity of these principles as procedural safeguards is that it is not uncommon for principles and provisions to include terminology that have an abstract meaning (*conceitos jurídicos indeterminados*). Hence, certain terminology are set out in the Constitution and in the CPP without there being any uniform definition of these terms, of what they entail and how they should be applied. This can be illustrated by the terms "best practices" (*bons costumes*) and "public order" (*ordem pública*),[200] which are vague and open-ended. Without the corresponding development of their concrete definitions by either Brazilian scholars or by the higher courts, trial judges have carte blanche to make rulings based on their own subjectivity.

The combination of legal provisions containing vague terminology and the lack of objective criteria regulating the main constitutional and statutory principles is highly problematic and leads to a gross abuse of judicial discretionary powers and consequential lack of enforceability in protecting the defendants' procedural rights.

I will now examine the *specific reasons* for the inefficiency of the current principles as effective means in which to counter each procedural model's inherent weaknesses. For reasons of clarity, I will assess them separately. First, I will address the main evidentiary principles adduced by Brazilian scholars as those which further the defendant's rights in an adversarial trial setting, i.e., the principles of audiatur altera pars and to a full defense, and the principle of equality of arms. Subsequently, I will examine the effectivity of the principles that respectively shape the trial setting

---

[200] The term "public order" is frequently used as a rationale by the trial judge in limiting the defendant's procedural rights, e.g., in ordering pretrial detention (Art. 312, chapeau, CPP) and in determining that the defendant must be examined by means of videoconference rather than at court (Art. 185 para. 2 IV CPP).

and limit the features of judicial discretion, i. e., the principles of ascertainment of the truth and of free evaluation of evidence.

2. Countering the Structural Weaknesses Stemming from the Features of the Adversarial Evidentiary Arrangement

As seen, in the US trial setting, each party has the duty to collect, evaluate and present evidence as best they can to secure the best possible outcome for each respective side. The weakness of this setting is that the defendants' chances at trial are closely linked to the quality of their defense counsel, and to the time and financial resources it has to prepare the defense's case. To counter the adversarial procedural model's inherent failings, the US-American system developed procedural safeguards to further the defendant's rights from the standpoint of gathering evidence on the one side, and from the standpoint of presenting evidence on the other side.[201] These safeguards seek to both counter the state's vast superiority of resources in preparing its criminal case against the defendant, and in furthering the equality of arms between the parties.

As seen, the Brazilian trial setting is gradually shifting from the judge being the main procedural actor responsible for evidence taking to a trial setting with more elements of a party-controlled presentation of evidence. For this reason, there must be effective procedural safeguards in place to protect the defendant from the structural weaknesses which are inherent in this evidentiary arrangement.

In this sense, Brazilian scholars often cite the principle of audiatur et altera pars and the principle of (the right to) a full defense as the bulwarks in protecting the procedural rights of the defendant. The widespread overreliance on these principles is very problematic, because although the aforementioned principles are indeed important, they should by no means be deemed as the ultimate strongholds in furthering the defendant's procedural rights at trial. This widespread mentality leads many scholars to believe that, if these principles are upheld, the defendant's stance at trial will be safeguarded. This is a risky stance, as without the specific accompanying safeguards, these principles are not enough in effectively safeguarding the defendant's right to equality of arms.

This can be illustrated by the fact that despite the various reforms to the CPP that aimed to afford the parties means in which to participate in the co-shaping of the trial setting, they failed to provide the defense with concrete mechanisms in which to effectively gather evidence prior to trial. This, in turn, directly hinders the defense's ability in sifting and especially in presenting evidence at trial. Thus, although in theory, the CPP grants the parties the right to present evidence at trial, it fails to effectively guarantee the enforceability of this right.

---

[201] See supra Ch. 2 D. I.

B. Solutions to Selected Features of the Brazilian Criminal Procedure   235

I will now examine the extent of the inefficacy of these principles as procedural safeguards by comparing them to the procedural safeguards found in the US-American criminal procedure and evidence law. To this end, I will analyze these safeguards separately by dividing them into those that provide the defense with means or mechanisms in which to *gather* evidence prior to trial (a)) and in which to *present* evidence at trial (b)). Lastly, I will make a few suggestions to remedy the failings in achieving the equality of arms in the Brazilian criminal procedure (c)).

a) Rights Afforded to the Defense in Gathering Evidence Prior to Trial

As seen in Ch. 2, the main US-American safeguards afforded to defendants to this end are the right to discovery and the right to deposition.

(i) The *right to discovery* enables the defendant to have access to information which is under either possession or control of the prosecution. The Brazilian criminal procedure has no legal provision setting a right akin to that of discovery, as this right does not fit within the Brazilian criminal procedure's procedural outline. As seen, during the investigatory phase, the chief of police compiles an investigative file, which must contain enough evidence to prove that a crime was in fact committed and to identify its suspect.[202] Once the criminal investigation is concluded, the investigative file is sent to the judge who then forwards it to the public prosecutor's office, who will then verify if the minimum evidentiary standard of *justa causa* has been met to file a bill of indictment.

As seen in Ch. 3, pursuant to SV 14 "It is the right of the defense, in the interest of the defendant, to have broad access to evidence that has already been documented in the investigative proceedings carried out by the judicial police, which concerns the exercise of the right of defense".[203] Thus, apart from information stemming from ongoing investigations, the defendant's defense counsel (and not the defendant himself) has access to all information collected by the chief of police. As a result, both parties are in possession of the information contained in the investigative file, and for this reason, a safeguard akin to the right to discovery would be rendered unnecessary in the Brazilian criminal procedure.

(ii) The second main mechanism the defense has in which to gather evidence prior to trial is the *right to deposition*, whereby a party may preserve evidence ahead of trial. In these instances, the party must request the court to take a deposition and state the reasoning for believing that there is a risk that the witness in question or that the document or object sought may not be available for examination at trial. There is no right akin to the right to deposition in the Brazilian criminal procedure as the CPP does not provide the defense with the possibility of requesting the court to preserve

---

[202] See supra Ch. 3 B. IV. 2. a).
[203] Original wording of SV 14, "É direito do defensor, no interesse do representado, ter acesso amplo aos elementos de prova que, já documentados em procedimento investigatório por órgão com competencia de polícia judiciário, digam respeito ao exercício do direito de defesa".

evidence ahead of trial. Instead, as per Art. 156 I CPP, the judge is the only procedural actor who decides whether to take anticipated evidence.

Apart from SV 14, there are two other instances, which theoretically afford the defense the right to gather evidence prior to trial. The first instance is set out in Art. 14, chapeau, CPP which states that the defense may request the police to carry out "tasks" or investigations (*diligências*). However, neither the constitution nor the infra-constitutional legislation provide the defense with concrete means in which to enforce this latter right as it is fully within the police's discretion whether to carry out these investigations.[204] The second instance which sought to further the defendant's right to gather evidence in the investigatory phase is set out in Provision 188 of the OAB.[205] However, as this provision was not enacted by the National Congress, it has no power in which to change the CPP. As such, this resolution "is far from establishing a legal prerogative of the lawyer to investigate"[206] and "at most it establishes guidelines for the lawyer's performance".[207]

Thus, apart from SV 14, the Brazilian normative framework does not set out any concrete means in which the defense may effectively gather evidence during the pretrial phase. For these reasons, it is vital for the defense to gather evidence by its own initiative. This should include finding witnesses that may offer exculpatory evidence or that may prove the defendant's alibi, reconstructing the crime scene, and hiring private experts (*assistente técnicos*) to aid in matters that need technical expertise, which include finding technical errors or omissions in the prosecution's case.[208] For this purpose, the defense must either conduct these investigations themselves or hire a private detective to this end.[209] Regarding the latter, L. 13.432/17 sets out that private detectives are professionals who collect data and information

---

[204] *Mossin, Compêndio* de Processo Penal, p. 92.

[205] See supra Ch. 3 B. IV. 1. b).

[206] See original text in *Choukr*, CPP Comentado, vol. 1, p.181, "está longe e estabelecer uma prerrogativa legal do advogado investigar".

[207] See original text in *Choukr*, CPP Comentado, vol. 1, p. 181, "Quando muito, estabelece diretrizes disciplinares da atuacao do advogado".

[208] *Rascovski*, Investigação Criminal Defensiva, p. 14; *Dias*, A Investigação Defensiva, p. 163.

[209] In an attempt to grant the defense concrete means in which to gather evidence akin to that set out in the current Art. 14, chapeau, CPP PL 156/09 provides a legal provision to this end. As per the alternative wording given to Art 14, "The investigated person, through his lawyer (…) is allowed to take the initiative to identify sources of evidence in furthering his defense and may even interview persons". Also, Art. 14 sole paragraph states that "Interviews conducted in the form of the heading of this article should be preceded by clarification of their objectives and the consent of the people heard". However, as seen in Part 1, although PL 156/09 is an attempt to enact a new code of criminal procedure, as of this writing, it is not yet foreseeable whether the National Congress will pass this bill. The original wording of Art. 14 PL 156/09 "É facultado ao investigado, por meio de seu advogado (…), tomar a iniciativa de identificar fontes de prova em favor de sua defesa, podendo inclusive entrevistar pessoas". Art 14, sole paragraph, PL 156/09 "As entrevistas realizadas na forma do caput deste artigo deverão ser precedidas de esclarecimentos sobre seus objetivos e do consentimento das pessoas ouvidas".

with "technical knowledge and using the resources and technological means allowed, aiming at clarifying matters of private interest of the contracting party".[210] As per Art. 5 L. 13.432/17, private detectives may "collaborate with an ongoing police investigation" provided that they were expressly asked to do so by the person who hired their services.

In the absence of provisions affording the defense concrete means in which to gather evidence, the quality of the defendant's legal defense is almost entirely contingent on the quality and resourcefulness of his legal counsel, which, in turn, is exclusively contingent on the defendant's financial means. Considering that only a small percentage of Brazilian defendants have the financial means to retain a lawyer, the vast majority of them are represented by public defenders.[211] The problem with this lies that although public defenders are usually well paid and very competent professionals, depending on the state or city in question, the public defender's office may be (grossly) understaffed and underfinanced. In these instances, these professionals are overworked and do not have the time nor the resources to dedicate themselves fully to all of their cases.

The defense's lack of prerogatives in this respect contrasts to the rights conferred to the public prosecutor's office which have more prerogatives in gathering evidence against the accused[212] and a vastly superior number of resources than that of defendants.

Among the first set of prerogatives are the right of prosecutors in the Federal Public Prosecutor's Office and the State Public Prosecutor's Offices to order the police to conduct "inspections and investigative tasks"[213] (*inspeções e diligências investigatórias*) and the right to summon people to their offices to give depositions.[214]

The second set of prerogatives given to the state in gaining access to evidence largely differs to those granted to the defense. Contrary to the latter, present the legal requisites to do so, the prosecution may gather evidence, which is protected by constitutional and statutory provisions,[215] such as having access to private data and telephone communications.[216] In contrast to the first set of prerogatives, these constitutionally protected rights must be protected from its access by private citizens, and the state should only continue to have access to them if the strict legal requisites

---

[210] Art. 2 L. 13.432/17.

[211] Although, the public defender's office in the state of Rio de Janeiro is very well staffed and possibly has the best organization and distribution of public defenders in the country, this is far from being representative. For more information on the topic, see *Castro* et al., Access to Justice in Brazil, pp. 111 et. seq.

[212] *Vieira*, in: Ambos (ed.), Polícia e Investigação, pp. 348, 349.

[213] Art. 13 II CPP.

[214] As per Art. 8 V and Art. 8 VII LC 75/93 and Art. 26 I "e" and Art. 26 I "a" L. 8625/93, respectively.

[215] *Dias*, A Investigação Defensiva, p. 160.

[216] Art. 5 XII CF.

to do so are present. However, both sets of prerogatives illustrate the great divide between the prerogatives afforded to the state in gathering evidence from those provided to the defense.

The complete absence of legal provisions affording the defense rights akin to the first set of prerogatives provided to the prosecution is partly explained by the repressive Brazilian legal culture, in which the defendant is perceived as being "in the way" of the state achieving justice for the commission of a criminal offense.[217] This can be exemplified by a very well-known Brazilian scholar who stated that "the police investigation should not be disturbed by the defendant's intrusion".[218]

For these reasons, many Brazilian scholars believe that the equality of arms is neither promoted nor safeguarded.[219] The various prerogatives afforded to the chief of police[220] and the prosecution in gathering evidence starkly contrasts with the defense's virtual lack of the corresponding rights. As per *Vieira*, the prerogatives given to the defense are neither proportional nor even comparable to those afforded to the public prosecutor's office.[221] Consequently, owing to the defense being impaired in gathering evidence prior to trial, the presentation of evidence at trial is also heavily skewed in favor of the state.

b) Rights Afforded to the Defense in Presenting Evidence at Trial

The main US-American safeguards afforded to defendants to this end are the constitutional rights set out in the Compulsory Process Clause (aa)) and in the Confrontation Clause (bb)).

aa) The Extent of the Right to Subpoena

As seen in Ch. 2, the Compulsory Process Clause is a mechanism for the defense to obtain witnesses in his favor. This constitutional right is concretized in the statutory level by means of the right to subpoena, whereby the defense may request the court for a person to present an object or a document, or yet to testify at trial at a specific place and time. The right to subpoena is not conferred to Brazilian de-

---

[217] *Vieira*, in: Ambos (ed.), Polícia e Investigação, p. 360.

[218] See original text in *Marques*, Elementos de Direito, vol. 1, p. 168, "A investigação policial não pode ser tumultuada com a intromissão do indiciado".

[219] In this sense, see *Karam*, in: Prado/Malan, Processo Penal e Democracia; *Machado*, Investigação Criminal Defensiva; *Rascovski*, Investigação Criminal Defensiva; *Saad*, in: Santoro/Malan/Maduro, Crise no Processo Penal; *Vieira*, Paridade de Armas no Processo Penal: Do Conceito à Aplicação no Direito Processual Penal Brasileiro; *Vieira*, in: Ambos (ed.), Polícia e Investigação; *Andrade/Ávila*, Sherlock Holmes; *Silva*, Investigação Criminal Direta pela Defesa.

[220] Art. 6 I to X CPP.

[221] *Vieira*, in: Ambos (ed.), Polícia e Investigação, pp. 348, 349.

B. Solutions to Selected Features of the Brazilian Criminal Procedure 239

fendants in the same extent as it is conferred to their US-American counterparts for two reasons.

First, in the US-American system, it is up to the defense to request the court to subpoena the witnesses it wishes to examine at trial. For this purpose, FRCP 17 provides that the defendant may use the "court's subpoena power to compel persons to appear as witnesses (...) at trial".[222] In contrast, in the Brazilian criminal procedure, the defense has two possibilities in which to summon witnesses and request their attendance at trial; it can either directly summon the witnesses or expressly request the court to summon them. In the latter case, for the court to grant the request, the defense must state the need for the court to summon the witnesses rather than the defense summoning them itself.[223] If a witness does not attend trial on the assigned date and time, the court may only impose legal sanctions – such as ordering the witness in question to be coercively conducted to trial[224] – to the witnesses who were summoned by the court. In contrast, if the defense fails to expressly request the court to summon the listed witnesses or the court rejects the defense's request for it to summon them, there is no means in which the defense may enforce the witnesses' attendance at trial.[225]

Second, there is a significant difference between the right to subpoena in these two legal systems, as the defense in the US-American legal system may also request the court to use its "subpoena power to compel persons (...) to produce designated documents and objects at trial".[226] In contrast, Brazilian defendants have no corresponding right in which to request the court to summon a person to produce the said pieces of evidence at trial. This is very damaging to the defense, as apart from the instances where a person willingly agrees to produce the designated document or object at trial, the defense has no means in which to compel someone to present a determined piece of evidence at trial. Consequently, in this respect Brazilian defendants are also in a weaker position than the state, which has the power to gather evidence by means of search and seizure (*busca e apreensão*)[227] and may later present them at trial.

---

[222] *LaFave* et al., Criminal Procedure, p. 1382.

[223] *Brasileiro de Lima*, Manual de Processo Penal, p. 1315; *Nucci*, CPP Comentado, p. 1000.

[224] Art. 218 CPP. As per Art. 219 CPP, the trial judge may also impose the absent witness a fine (*multa*). This witness may also be liable for the crime of disobedience (crime de desobediência) and the trial judge may also sentence the witness to pay for the costs of his failure to attend trial.

[225] *Rangel*, Direito Processual Penal, p. 541; *Nucci*, CPP Comentado, pp. 1000, 1001.

[226] *LaFave* et al., Criminal Procedure, p. 1382.

[227] The requisites for the state to conduct search and seizure are set out in Arts. 240 to 250 CPP.

bb) As to the Desirability of Employing Cross-Examination in Examining Witnesses

The US-American defendants' constitutional right to the Confrontation Clause is almost synonymous to the right of cross-examination. This is an effective means in which the defense can unravel the weaknesses and inconsistencies in the opposing parties' case by examining the testimony and credibility of the witnesses against him by means of leading questions or by impeaching them. Consequently, this is a procedural safeguard which is essential in furthering both parties' case. This procedural safeguard is considered of such a vital importance that *Wigmore* stated that "cross-examination is beyond any doubt the greatest legal engine ever invented for the discovery of truth".[228]

In the Brazilian trial setting, although the defense may examine the prosecution's witnesses, due to the still predominant features of officialized factfinding, the parties may only do so by means of direct questions. As seen in Ch. 3, cross-examination is expressly discouraged as Art. 212, chapeau, CPP *explicitly* states that the trial judge should not allow the parties to ask witnesses questions that may induce them to give a specific answer (leading questions).[229]

For this reason, the Brazilian trial setting is not characterized by a level of polarization and incisiveness in examining the opposing party' witnesses as is the case in the US-American trial setting. As a result, in comparison to its US-American counterparts, the manner in which the parties examine witnesses is less conducive to unearthing and showing the inconsistencies and omissions of the testimony of the opposing party's witness.

Nonetheless, considering the current Brazilian evidentiary arrangement and the main roles played by the key courtroom actors at trial, I do not believe that cross-examination is a feature that would "fit" within the Brazilian trial setting for three main reasons.

First, this reason is very similar to those adduced when addressing why this form of witness examination is currently in disuse in the German criminal procedure. As is the case in its German counterpart, the parties' active stance in cross-examining oral testimony would clash with the presiding judge's responsibility in presiding trial and conducting evidence taking. Further, due to the feature of leading questions being extraneous to the Brazilian trial setting, I believe that even if the prosecution and the defense were to attempt to ask the witnesses leading questions, the trial judge would not allow them to do so, owing to it going against the Brazilian normative framework and its procedural and legal culture.

Second, it is important to highlight that contrary to the Brazilian and German criminal procedures, in the US-American evidentiary law, the term "witness" en-

---

[228] *Wigmore*, A Treatise on the Anglo-American System, § 1367, at 29.
[229] See supra Ch. 3 C. III. 2. b) and Ch. 5 B. III. 2.

compasses (i) *witnesses* sensu stricto, (ii) *expert witnesses* – which in the Brazilian and German criminal procedure correspond to both court-appointed and privately-appointed experts – and (iii) the *defendant*.

Thus, if cross-examination were applied in the Brazilian context in the same extent as it is applied in the US-American trial setting, it would be very likely that this would be construed by the court as leaving the defendant in a vulnerable position at trial. This is owing to the fact that in the Brazilian criminal procedure, some scholars and practitioners view judicial examination as a means in which to protect the defendant from aggressive questioning by the prosecution in seeking to obtain a confession and in protecting the defendant from misguided questions made by the defense.[230] For this reason, the defendant's examination by means of cross-examination could be construed by the judge as an undue harassment of the defendant.

Third, I believe that the use of cross-examination in questioning defendants would be extremely harmful in the Brazilian context due to its legal culture. As seen, the vast majority of defendants are people who do not have the financial means to retain an attorney and are usually in a vulnerable position not only from an economic standpoint, but also from a social standpoint. This is because law is seen by the Brazilian society at large as highly complex, cumbersome, and elitist. This perception of law coupled with the complex judicial organization and the high degree of formalism present in Brazilian trials is made even more apparent for a large segment of Brazilians that are marginalized from society and which view the state – in the context of the repression of criminality – as a highly biased and intimidating entity.

Moreover, the fact that Brazilian courts (as a rule) mirror the repressive and elitist Brazilian legal culture on the one side, and that public defender's offices are (as a rule) overworked and understaffed on the other side, is a problematic combination. In this context, I believe that the right to examine defendants by means of cross-examination would result in an undue burden and in the risk of defendants being treated as an object to the proceedings. This would go against the predominant view of the examination of defendants as a means of defense and in it being an opportunity for them to present evidence furthering their innocence.

c) Suggestions

From the comparative study above, it is apparent that US-American defendants are afforded more procedural rights than their Brazilian counterparts in both gathering evidence in the pretrial phase and in presenting evidence at trial. Regardless of whether the Brazilian trial setting remains predominantly inquisitorial or shifts to a predominantly adversarial evidentiary arrangement, the normative gap in affording the defendant effective means in which to gather evidence at trial on the one side, and the state's prerogatives in doing so must be balanced.

---

[230] See supra Ch. 3 C. III. 1. a).

Nonetheless, it is undeniable that the procedural failings stemming from the lack of procedural safeguards in furthering equality of arms will highly increase if the STF find paras. 3 and 4 of Art. 3-C L. 13.964/19 constitutional. If this occurs, and the trial setting shifts from a predominantly officialized fact-finding to a predominantly party-controlled presentation of evidence, it is imperative for corresponding safeguards to be introduced to the Brazilian criminal procedure. Absent these safeguards, Brazilian defendants may find themselves in an even more vulnerable position than the one in which they currently find themselves.

For this reason, it is vital for the CPP to afford the defense with rights that are similar to those provided to the prosecution. To this end, I will offer two suggestions of modifications to the CPP to further the defense's rights in gathering evidence prior to trial and one suggestion to further the defense's right in presenting evidence at trial.

First, the CPP must provide the defense with concrete investigatory measures in which to gather evidence akin to those of the prosecution.[231] To this end, the current wording of Art. 14, chapeau, CPP must be altered. It currently states that that the defense may request the police to conduct investigations "inspections and investigative tasks" (*inspeções e diligências investigatórias*). The CPP must provide objective and concrete criteria, in which to circumscribe the chief of police's discretion is denying this request. According to *Saad*, a possible solution in this sense is that the only factor that should be taken into consideration by the police in assessing whether to comply with the defense's request is its importance and its correlation to the clarification of the facts in furthering the defense's case.[232]

In order to guarantee the enforceability of the right set out in Art. 14, chapeau, CPP, for the chief of police to deny said request, two requisites must be present (i) she must state in a written reasoning the circumstances which led her to reject this request, and why she believes it is it is not conducive in furthering the defendant's case, and (ii) these written statements must be verified by a pretrial judge. Because the investigatory phase is not the main procedural phase where the rights of the accused are safeguarded, it is necessary to strike a balance between allowing the state to have enough leeway to secure evidence against the defendant while effectively affording the defense the means in which to gather evidence prior to trial.[233]

Second, the CPP must provide the defense with the possibility of requesting the pretrial judge (*juiz das garantias*) to examine witnesses or objects that could be beneficial to its case. For this purpose, the CPP must estipulate the formal and material requisites for the defense to request the trial judge to conduct anticipated evidence taking. This could take shape in a manner similar to the instances provided by FRCP 15 regarding the right to deposition, i. e., whenever the defense fears that the evidence might otherwise be lost. A further instance is when the defense believes that

---

[231] *Vieira*, in: Ambos (ed.), Polícia e Investigação, pp. 348, 349.

[232] *Saad*, in: Santoro/Malan/Maduro, Crise no Processo Penal, p. 318.

[233] *Weigend*, Should we Search, pp. 412, 413.

B. Solutions to Selected Features of the Brazilian Criminal Procedure   243

a person is in possession of an object or a document that may be essential to its case and in advancing the defendant's innocence. In these two instances, the defendant's lawyer must have the right to be present at this person's examination by the pretrial judge, thus having the right "to participate and to obtain access to the results of the investigation."[234]

Third, the CPP should afford the defense a means in which to guarantee the enforceability of the witnesses' attendance at trial. In this sense, I believe that the defense should be set out a right akin to the right to subpoena. That is, instead of the defense having to summon the witnesses' themselves, the court should summon the witnesses listed by the defense within the maximum number provided by the CPP, i.e., up to eight witnesses in the ordinary procedural outline and five witnesses in the summary procedural outline.[235] Thus, if a witness fails to attend trial, the court may impose them the legal sanctions set out in the CPP, which include coercively bringing the witness in question to court.[236]

3. Countering the Structural Weaknesses Stemming from the Features of the Inquisitorial Evidentiary Arrangement

The two principles that respectively establish the trial judge's main responsibility in finding the truth at trial and that seek to limit and circumscribe judicial discretion on reaching a verdict are the principle of ascertainment of the truth (*princípio da verdade material ou real*) and the principle of free evaluation of evidence (*princípio do livre convencimento motivado*). Despite the terminology being slightly different, these principles are also found in the German criminal procedure, i.e., *Aufklärungspflicht des Richters* and *der Grundsatz der freien richterlichen Beweiswürdigung*, respectively. Although they present similar premises and features, there are decisive differences between both these principles in each respective legal system.

The German principle of ascertainment of the truth establishes that the court is responsible in finding the (material) truth. To this end, it is the court's task to thoroughly examine all evidence that might be of relevance in finding out what happened, regardless of and beyond any motion to take evidence that the parties may present to the court. In this setting, evidence is not considered as that of the prosecution or of the defense, but of the court. As seen in Ch. 1, the principle of ascertainment of the truth is an unsuitable means in which to remedy possible judicial bias as it is devoid of an objective criterion in which to guide the trial judge's subjectivity.

To counter the risk of judicial bias, the StPO provides the prosecution and defense the possibility to present to the court a motion to take evidence as an efficient way in which to force it to examine additional evidence that is relevant both to the question

---

[234] *Weigend*, Should we Search, pp. 413, 414.
[235] Arts. 401, chapeau, and Art. 532 CPP, respectively.
[236] See footnote 224 (Part 3).

of guilt and to the legal consequences.[237] The motion to take evidence at trial is an important instrument in which to neutralize possible judicial bias and to provide for a certain degree of polarity in the trial setting.[238] This is because it enables the defense the right to request the court to take evidence favorable to their client's case and "push for alternative understandings of the facts that might reveal the truth".[239] The resulting introduction of new evidence and new arguments in favor of the defendant co-shapes the trial setting in a manner that deviates from the mere confirmation or rebuttal of the contents of the investigative file.

The efficacy and more importantly, the *enforceability* of this motion is secured by §§ 244 (3) to (5) and 245 StPO. As seen in Ch. 1, these provisions set out that the court may only reject the motion to take evidence if one of the strict objective criteria listed in these provisions is present. Simply put, absent one of the specific grounds to refuse the motion, the court must take the evidence in question, even if it deems the requested evidence to be unnecessary. This motion is an important mechanism in which to limit judicial discretion, as the court is completely barred from rejecting a motion to take evidence based on subjective criteria.

Different than its German counterpart, there is no corresponding mechanism in the Brazilian criminal procedure in which to limit judicial discretion. Simply put, the parties are not afforded any rights to present a motion to take or present evidence, nor is there any objective criteria to guide and/or circumscribe judicial discretion in fulfilling its responsibility of finding the truth. There are two main instances, which illustrate the lack of objective criteria in which to circumscribe judicial discretion in the Brazilian trial setting.

First, both the prosecution and the defense must indicate the witnesses they wish to summon when filing the bill of indictment and the written response to the indictment, respectively.[240] If a party fails to do this, its right to present witnesses precludes, and the only way it may call and examine these witnesses at trial is if the party requests the judge to call the witness in question as a witness of the court. However, in these instances, Brazilian judges have complete discretion in deciding whether to accept a party's request for them to summon and call a witness. This is because in these specific instances, there are no concrete means for a party to co-shape evidence taking in a meaningful way, as the CPP does not provide the defense any effective mechanisms in which to force the trial judge to summon and call additional witnesses.

Second, the lack of objective criteria in which to circumscribe judicial discretion not only applies in the latter context, but also regarding other types of evidence. This is because Art. 400 para. 1 CPP provides that the trial judge may dismiss evidence

---

[237] See supra Ch. 1 D. II.

[238] *Schäuble*, Strafverfahren und Prozessverantwortung, pp. 101, 102.

[239] *Findley*, Adversarial Inquisitions, p. 934.

[240] See supra Ch. 3 C. III. 2. a).

which he considers to be irrelevant (*irrelevante*), cumbersome or troublesome to produce (*inconveniente*) or yet, which has the aim of protracting the proceedings (*protelatórias*). On the one side, the concept of "*irrelevante*" and "*inconveniente*" have an open-ended definition, and neither Brazilian scholars nor the higher courts clearly define and limit these terms.[241] On the other side, the term for protracting the proceedings "*protelatórias*" is not in itself problematic, as both the German and US-American criminal procedures set out this requisite as a means in which the trial judge may decide on the admissibility of the motion to take evidence and on the admissibility of a proffered piece of evidence, respectively.[242] However, in contrast to the terms set out in § 244 (3) StPO and FRE 403, which were extensively developed by both scholars and higher courts of the respective legal systems, the term "*protelatórias*" lacks a concrete definition and was neither extensively developed nor minimally defined by the higher courts and by Brazilian scholars. Thus, the decision on how to interpret and apply the terms set out in Art. 400 para. 1 CPP is completely left to the trial judges' discretion.

In theory, the shortcomings of the lack of objective criteria limiting judicial discretion in presiding the trial and conducting evidence taking could be mitigated by the principle of free evaluation of evidence. This is because – in theory – this principle is a means in which to circumscribe and control to a certain extent the trial judge's decision-making, by mandating that she must state her exact reasoning for finding the defendant to be guilty or innocent.

This is the case in the German trial setting, where this principle effectively sets limitations to the court's discretionary powers. § 261 StPO explicitly mandates that the court "shall decide on the result of its discretion and conviction based on the entire content of the hearing". Consequently, on the one hand, this legal provision states that the decision is based on the court's "conviction and discretion", that is, it clearly concedes that the reasoning behind a decision is subjective. On the other hand, this principle concurrently mandates that the presiding judge must state the rational-objective factual basis that led the court to its decision. Accordingly, the presiding judge must write a thorough written foundation where the subjective certainty must stem from a high objective probability that the defendant is guilty.

---

[241] This instance is a further example of the general reasons why the principles of the Brazilian criminal procedural are not effective safeguards. In mandating that the trial judge has the responsibility of finding the material truth at trial, the CPP does not set out any limits to the principle of ascertainment of the truth. Further, the only legal provision which theoretically seeks to circumscribe judicial discretion includes terminology that is vague and open ended, and which in practice, does not fulfill its task of circumscribing judicial discretion.

[242] § 244 (3) StPO also provides that "an application to take evidence may be rejected only if (…) the application is made to protract the proceedings" as one of the instances in which the trial judge may reject the motion to take evidence. Also, FRE 403 provides the instances in which "the court may exclude relevant evidence if its probative value is substantially outweighed by a danger of one or more of the following" prejudicial effects.

Further requisites mandated by this principle is that the court's reasoning must be free from logical errors and contradictions, and it must respect scientific knowledge, i.e., expert evidence. Hence, the objective factual basis is met by the court having to analyze "all trial findings and assessing each piece of evidence exhaustively".[243] These guidelines control the subjectivity that is inherent in a judicial decision, and if this decision reaches to the appellate level, the criteria for examining the decision's validity is based on whether the presiding judge's judgment was based on the elements set above. Absent this foundation, the conviction will be overturned.

Contrary to its German counterparts, Brazilian judges are not bound to expert evidence, as they have complete discretion to reject it either in part or in its entirety.[244] Further, the Brazilian principle of free evaluation of evidence does not set any specific criteria circumscribing the trial judge's inherently subjective decision making. This is owing to CPP not setting out any corresponding objective criteria to guide the trial judges in reaching their decisions. This can be illustrated by Art. 315 para. 2, I-IV which was introduced to the CPP by the newly enacted L. 13.964/19. This provision set out the bare minimum requirements the trial judge must follow in stating the reasons for reaching his decision. Although it would have been desirable (and necessary) for these newly introduced requirements to set objective criteria in circumscribing judicial discretion, in practice these "subitems" (*incisos*) merely provide examples of instances where the trial judge (grossly) fails to provide a proper reasoning for her verdict.[245]

In summary, the defense has no means in which to co-shape the trial setting regarding oral evidence (in the specific instances set above) and the trial judge may reject the admissibility of evidence on subjective reasons owing to Art. 400, para. 1 CPP failing to set out objective criteria circumscribing judicial decisions. These features exemplify the absolute lack of mechanisms in which to circumscribe judicial discretion. Further yet, the principle of free evaluation of evidence fails to provide trial judges a framework in substantiating their written reasons for reaching a verdict. As a result, the problematic features of the inquisitorial evidentiary arrangement are not due to the procedural model itself. Rather, the vast amount of virtually unchecked judicial discretion stem from the complete lack of mechanisms in which to limit judicial discretion and consequently, in which to counter judicial bias. To counter this situation, I believe three modifications must be made to the CPP.

First, the current criteria allowing judges to deny the presentation of evidence by the parties (Art. 400 para. 1 CPP) are too open-ended and lack the necessary spe-

---

[243] *Eisenberg*, Beweisrecht, Rn. 100.

[244] See footnote 839 (Part 2). Despite the presentation of the *corpus delicti* exam being mandatory, this evidence does not have absolute probative value. Consequently, the trial judge may order expert evidence to be reconducted by other court-appointed experts, and may partly or totally disregard expert evidence, when the totality of the evidence produced at trial (*conjunto probatório*) proves otherwise (art. 182 CPP).

[245] See supra Ch. 3 D. I.

B. Solutions to Selected Features of the Brazilian Criminal Procedure 247

cificity to allow for an effective control over judicial discretion. To counter this, there must be mechanisms in which the parties may compel the trial judge to allow them to present additional evidence at trial. To this end, the CPP must state the precise and objective instances in which the judge may deny a party from presenting a proffered piece of evidence. Thus, in the absence of one of these specific instances, the trial judge must allow the evidence in question to be presented. This would restrict the principle of ascertainment of the truth and allow the parties to effectively co-shape the procedure of evidence taking. This provision would slightly differ from the motion to take evidence, as the trial judge will not take the evidence himself as is the case in the German criminal procedure.

The CPP must set out objective criteria to limit judicial discretion. This would be an important procedural safeguard to protect the defendant's rights as – in the absence of a reason to reject the presentation of a determined evidence – it would enforce the court to hear evidence presented by the defense. As is the case in its German counterpart, the resulting introduction of new evidence and new arguments in favor of the defendant's case would co-shape the trial setting in a manner that deviates from the mere confirmation or rebuttal of the contents of the investigative file. This is especially important in the Brazilian context owing to the investigative file mostly containing inculpatory evidence. Thus, the need to also introduce exculpatory evidence in the investigative file is vital for there to be a balance of the evidence contained in the said file.

Second, a further safeguard necessary to control judicial bias is by setting out objective criteria which the trial judge must follow when stating the specific reasons that led her to reach the verdict. Hence, although the decision is based on a subjective certainty, the court must state the rational-objective factual basis that led it to its decision. This limitation should in theory circumscribe and control the trial judge's decision-making, as it mandates the trial judge to state her exact reasoning for finding the defendant to be guilty or innocent. For this to be effectively enforced, there must be objective guidelines which the trial judge must strictly follow. Furthermore, the CPP must provide that if the trial judge fails to comply with these requirements, the verdict must be overturned in the appellate level.

Third, there must be a limitation to the scope of the evidence that may be alluded by the trial judge in his written reasoning for reaching a verdict. As of this writing, trial judges may allude to information gathered in the investigatory phase in their written reasons for finding the defendant guilty. In the past decades, both the admissibility of making reference to evidence gathered in the pretrial phase and the extent of its use in the written reasoning of a verdict has been the bone of contention among Brazilian legal scholars. As this topic must be addressed in more detail, I will now examine this matter separately (II.).

II. The Trial Judge's Access to Information that was Gathered in the Investigatory Phase and its Use in Basing a Conviction

In the past decades, Brazilian legal scholars have often debated regarding the possibility of the trial judge alluding to information gathered in the investigatory phase when basing a conviction. While some scholars criticize the fact that the trial judge has access to information gathered in the investigatory phase, others criticize the use of this information in basing a criminal conviction.[246]

As of this writing, after the investigatory phase is concluded and the prosecution indicts a suspect, it must subsequently send the bill of indictment to the trial judge. Additionally, whenever the prosecution bases the bill of indictment on the investigation file – which occurs in the vast majority of criminal cases – this document must also be sent to the trial judge.[247] Therefore, as a rule, the trial judge has access to all steps partaken in the criminal investigation and to all evidence provided in the bill of indictment, as they are necessary for her to verify whether the minimum evidentiary standard of *justa causa* is present. Additionally, if this evidentiary standard is met, the trial judge will need the investigative file to conduct the trial and to verify whether the information it contains can be confirmed during evidence taking.

For most Brazilian scholars and as per Art. 155, chapeau, CPP, the trial judge may allude to evidence produced during the investigatory phase.[248] This provision states that "the judge will form his conviction by freely assessing the evidence produced in a contradictory setting and may not base his decision *exclusively* on the information gathered in the investigation, with the exception of anticipated evidence taking".

As a rule, the second part of this legal provision is not contested by most Brazilian scholars, i.e., regarding anticipated evidence basing a criminal conviction. As previously seen, there are two instances when a judge may order the anticipated production of evidence.[249] First, when there is reason to believe that there is an unsurmountable reason that prevents a witness or the victim to attend trial for a long or uncertain period.[250] These instances are namely, due to an infirmity, old age, or due to a witness or the victim moving to a country which has no extradition laws with Brazil. In these instances, the court must notify both parties when the taking of anticipated

---

[246] Nicolitti, in: Prado/Malan, Processo Penal e Democracia, pp. 51 et seq.; *Lopes Jr.*, Direito Processual Penal, 11th ed., p. 323.

[247] Art. 12 CPP.

[248] STF (2nd T.), RE-AgR 425.734/MG; STF (1st T.), RE 287.658/MG, STF (1st T.), HC 83.348/SP. See *Brasileiro de Lima*, Manual de Processo Penal, pp. 107, 108; *Capez*, Curso de Processo Penal, pp. 120, 121, 406; *Távora/Alencar*, Curso de Direito Processual Penal, pp. 159 et seq.; *Badaró*, in: Ambos (ed.), Polícia e Investigação, pp. 269 et seq.

[249] See supra Ch. 3 C. I. 2. a).

[250] If the STF finds Art. 3-B VII CPP to be constitutional, it will be the pretrial judge's (*juiz das garantias*) responsibility to decide whether to take anticipated evidence. If this is the case, the taking of the said evidence will take place in a public and oral hearing, where both the principle of *audiatur et altera pars* and full defense must be safeguarded.

B. Solutions to Selected Features of the Brazilian Criminal Procedure 249

evidence will ensue, as to ensure that the production of the evidence in question is conducted while safeguarding the defendant's procedural rights.[251] The second instance in which the judge may order an anticipated taking of evidence is when evidence of a perishable nature (*prova perecível*) must be taken immediately, as is the case of certain types of expert evidence.

As both types of evidence taken prior to trial are considered to be evidence sensu stricto,[252] virtually all Brazilian scholars believe that they may be alluded by the trial judge in basing a criminal conviction. This is because the examination of the oral testimony is produced in accordance with the defendant's constitutional right to a full defense and to a contradictory hearing. Regarding expert evidence, despite it being collected during the investigatory phase, it will be later presented at trial where all the defendant's procedural rights are safeguarded.[253] Thus, although these specific pieces of information were collected during the investigation phase, they are also considered to be evidence sensu stricto and not informative elements.

The problematic aspect of Art. 155, chapeau, CPP is regarding its first part, i.e., the fact that this provision merely prohibits the trial judge from using informative elements as the sole source on to base a conviction. To most scholars, the judge may allude to evidence sensu lato that was not presented at trial, only to the extent to reinforce the validity of the evidence sensu stricto and of the arguments that were in fact presented at trial.[254]

Contrary to the majority position, a significant part of Brazilian scholars hold that whenever the trial judge states the reasoning for a conviction, she should be completely barred from alluding to evidence that has not been previously presented at trial.[255] Thus, according to this position, the pieces of information (*elementos informativos*) collected by the police during the investigatory phase may only be used to base a bill of indictment and some precautionary measures (e.g., arrest warrant), and for the judge to verify whether the minimum evidentiary standard for a case to go to trial is met.[256] The three main reasons adduced by these scholars are the following.

First, the investigative file is produced in a procedural phase, where most of the procedural rights that are inherent to the trial phase are not present, i.e., the principle

---

[251] Arts. 155, chapeau, and 156 I CPP.

[252] *Lopes Jr.*, Direito Processual Penal, 11th ed., p. 328; *Brasileiro de Lima*, Manual de Processo Penal, p. 107; *Távora/Alencar*, Curso de Direito Processual Penal, pp. 159 et seq.; *Badaró*, Processo Penal, pp. 428 et seq.; *Nicolitt*, Manual de Processo Penal, pp. 698 et seq.; *Nucci*, CPP Comentado, pp. 415, 416.

[253] A further argument adduced by Brazilian scholars is that expert evidence is conducted by court-appointed experts, who are considered to be impartial procedural actors, as per Arts. 275 and 280 CPP.

[254] *Choukr*, CPP Comentado, vol. 1, pp. 439, 445, 446.

[255] *Lopes Jr.*, Bom para que(m)?, pp. 9–10; *Scaranse Fernandes*, Processo Penal Constitucional, pp. 65, 74; *Lopes Jr./Gloeckner*, Investigação Preliminar, p. 323; *Nicolitt*, Manual de Processo Penal, pp. 209, 699; *Nucci*, CPP Comentado, pp. 412 et seq.

[256] *Badaró*, in: Ambos (ed.), Polícia e Investigação, p. 261.

of publicity, orality, audiatur et altera pars, the right to a full defense and to an impartial and competent judge (*juiz natural*).[257] For this reason, only information that was produced at trial – i.e., where all of the defendant's procedural rights are fully effective – should be adduced in the trial judge's written reasoning.

Second, the first part of the original wording proposed by the bill[258] to reform Art. 155 chapeau CPP stated that "the judge will form his conviction by the free assessment of the evidence produced in accordance to a contradictory hearing (*contraditório judicial*), and may not base his decision on the informative elements, which were gathered in the investigation".[259] As such, it was the Reform Committee's intention that information gathered in the investigatory phase which was not later presented at trial was prohibited from being adduced by the trial judge in reasoning a conviction.[260] However, during the debates that took place in the National Congress on whether to transform this bill into a law, this provision's intended wording was modified to its current wording, which considerably increased the scope of judicial discretion in writing the reasoning of a conviction, and consequently, in basing a conviction.[261]

Third, the investigation file contains the findings of the investigatory phase presided by the head of police and contains all steps she partook in finding incriminating evidence against the defendant. As seen in this chapter, differently than in the German criminal procedure, the investigative file reflects a partisan preliminary investigation. As a result, this file almost exclusively contains elements of who the presumable author of the criminal offense is and its materiality. Consequently, the risk of judicial bias is intensified as the trial judge not only has knowledge of the case prior to trial, but also because this knowledge is based on an investigative file which does not provide the judge a balanced view of the facts of the case.

The three criticisms adduced above led scholars to make suggestions on how to reduce judicial bias stemming from the judge having access to evidence gathered in the investigatory phase. The two following suggestions were offered.

First, due to the trial judge needing the investigative file to verify whether the minimum evidentiary standard of justa causa is present to bind the case to trial, a possible solution is that after the trial judge makes a decision in this sense, the

---

[257] *Lopes Jr./Gloeckner*, Investigação Preliminar, p. 468.

[258] PL 4205/01 later became L. 11.690/08, which altered various provisions of the CPP. See supra Part 1 B. II. 1.

[259] The original wording for Art. 155, chapeau, CPP of PL 4205/01 was "O juiz formará sua convicção pela livre apreciação da prova produzida em contraditório judicial, não podendo fundamentar a sua decisão nos elementos informativos colhidos na investigação (...)".

[260] *Zilli*, O Pomar e as Pragas, p. 2; *Pitombo*, Considerações Iniciais, p. 20; *Badaró*, in: Ambos (ed.), Polícia e Investigação, pp. 268, 269.

[261] *Choukr*, CPP Comentado, vol. 1, p. 439.

investigation file should be removed from the case file.²⁶² However, the problem with this solution is that owing to the trial judge still being the main procedural actor responsible for taking evidence, the removal of the investigative file would seriously hinder his ability to fulfill this role. This, in turn, would seriously damage one of the main objectives of the criminal procedure, i.e., finding the truth. A further reason this solution is faulty is that even if the investigative file were to be taken from the trial judge, she would have already read its contents and thus, the risk of judicial bias would have already taken place.

The second solution offered is that an intermediate proceeding ("*etapa intermedia*") should be created, where a judge other than the sentencing judge decides whether the evidentiary standard of justified cause is present, thus preventing judicial bias.²⁶³ This solution is similar to that provided by L. 13.964/19, which I will analyze below. Before I offer (possible) solutions to this issue, I will first examine whether and to what extent the factfinders in the German and US-American trial setting have access to information that was gathered in the investigatory phase and whether they may use this information in basing a conviction.

1. Comparative Study

a) Germany

In Germany – akin to what takes place in Brazilian criminal trials – after the prosecution indicts a suspect, the court's professional judges will then receive both the bill of indictment and the investigation file. However, the main difference between both legal systems is that as per § 160 (2) StPO, the latter document must contain both incriminating and exonerating evidence. The reason for this is that the chief responsible for the criminal investigation is the public prosecutor's office; and as seen, German prosecutors are not parties to the proceedings and are bound by the need of being objective.²⁶⁴ Further, regardless of whether the prosecution requests the police for their assistance in investigating crimes, the investigation file must contain both incriminating and exonerating circumstances and must contain all steps taken during the investigatory phase.

As is the case regarding its Brazilian counterparts, the German professional judge's access to the investigation file in the intermediate proceedings is necessary to determine whether the evidentiary standard of *hinreichender Tatverdacht* is met to open the main proceedings. Further, the investigation file is necessary for the presiding judge to analyze the evidence that was gathered during the investigatory

---

²⁶² *Lopes Jr.*, Bom para que(m)?, p. 10; *Lopes Jr./Gloeckner*, Investigação Preliminar, pp. 317, 330.
²⁶³ *Melchior*, in Santoro: Homenagem aos 30 anos da Constituição de 1988, p. 56.
²⁶⁴ See supra Ch. 1 B. III. 2.

phase, thus enabling enable him in presiding the trial and verifying whether the evidence contained in the investigative file is correct and can be sustained at trial.

Nonetheless, owing to the principle of free evaluation of evidence, the court shall decide "at its discretion and conviction"[265] based on the entire content of the procedure of evidence taking. Thus, differently than their Brazilian counterparts, whenever German trial judges state their reasons for reaching a verdict, they are barred from alluding to any evidence that was gathered during the investigatory phase and was not later presented at trial. Additionally, the investigatory phase is merely a preparatory phase for the trial, which is the central part (*Kernstück*) of the German criminal proceeding.[266] It is only in the main proceeding where the whole scope of the defendant's procedural rights is safeguarded, i.a., principles of publicity, orality, immediacy, and the full scope of the motion to take evidence. Thus, in this setting, if the court were to base a conviction on elements gathered during the investigatory phase, this would go counter to § 261 StPO and would inevitably be overturned at the appellate level.

b) The United States

In examining the judge's access to evidence gathered in the investigatory phase and its use in basing a conviction, I will solely focus on the trial phase (finding of guilt). This is because the sentencing phase (finding of punishment) takes place in a different procedural moment and with a completely different set of rules.[267]

As seen in Ch. 2, prior to the trial phase, a probable cause hearing takes place either at the preliminary hearing or by a grand jury.[268] The preliminary hearing is conducted by the magistrate judge, whereas in the grand jury, there are – as a rule – no judges present,[269] owing to the grand jurors being the ones responsible for screening the indictment and verifying whether probable cause is present for a case to go to trial. Therefore, when the case goes to trial by means of indictment, the trial judge will not have contact to the evidence prior to trial.[270] For this reason, as a rule, the trial judge's first contact with the case itself will only take place at arraignment.

At trial, the parties must present their evidence to the factfinder. As seen in Ch. 4, the factfinder does not have access to information regarding the case prior to trial. If they were to have access to the police's findings in the investigatory phase,

---

[265] § 261 StPO.

[266] *Schäuble*, Strafverfahren und Prozessverantwortung, pp. 62, 63.

[267] Differently than in the trial phase, in the sentencing phase the trial judge may base the defendant's punishment on evidence that was collected prior to trial. In this sense, see footnote 471 (Part 2).

[268] See supra Ch. 2 B. IV. 2. b).

[269] However, at times a judge may be called to decide on certain matters, e.g., granting a witness immunity. In this sense, see *Saltzburg/Capra*, American Criminal Procedure, p. 1004.

[270] *Perron*, Beweisantragsrecht, p. 391.

B. Solutions to Selected Features of the Brazilian Criminal Procedure   253

this could be very harmful to a case, particularly in jury trials. Hence, differently than their German and Brazilian counterparts, US-American trial judges have little to no knowledge of the case prior to trial and only have access to information which was presented by the parties at trial. This rationale applies to both bench and jury trials.[271]

2. Suggestions

In regard to the trial judge's access to evidence gathered in the investigatory phase and its use in basing a decision, I would like to propose two sets of suggestions to the Brazilian trial setting, which are contingent on whether and to what extent the changes to the CPP by L. 13.964/19 will ensue.

(i) Suggestions to the current setting: if the Brazilian trial setting remains as it currently is, i.e., the trial judge's responsibility of presiding over the trial and conducting the evidence taking persists, there is a corresponding need for him to have access to the investigative file. However, it is *indispensable* that an effective procedural safeguard is introduced to the Brazilian criminal procedure to counter the inherent failings of the trial judge having access to evidence gathered prior to trial. The trial judge must be completely barred from adducing evidence which was gathered in the investigatory phase in the written reasoning of a verdict.

To enforce this, the trial judge must – at the very least – state the reasons that led him to reach the verdict, which must follow strict guidelines. However, owing to the Brazilian legal culture, a change in the normative framework might not suffice in guaranteeing that these legal provisions are correctly followed. As seen in Ch. 5, if a legal idea or provision goes against what a procedural actor believes its roles and prerogatives to be, the legal provision in question may simply be ignored. For this reason, the thoroughness of the trial judge's written reasoning of a criminal decision will in great part depend on the higher courts enforcing its correct application.

(ii) Suggestions to the trial setting should a shift in the evidentiary arrangement ensue: as previously seen, the enactment of L. 13.964/19 introduced many legal provisions to the CPP,[272] which would – in principle – considerably change the trial setting from a predominantly officialized factfinding to a (mostly) party-controlled enterprise. Should the STF find these provisions to be constitutional, the fear of the trial judge basing a conviction on the investigation file would (in theory) be neutralized. This is owing to two reasons.

First, according to Art. 3-C para. 3 CPP, the investigatory file shall be kept at the registry of the pretrial judge. As a result, while the parties would be given broad access to this file, the trial judge would have no corresponding access to it, as the

---

[271] *Grande*, Italian Criminal Justice, p. 230.
[272] See Part 1 B. II. 3. and Ch. 6 A. II. 1. a).

investigatory file will no longer be appended to the case file. If this occurs, anticipated evidence would be the only pretrial evidence that trial judges will have access to. Second, Art. 3-B chapeau CPP sets out the figure of a pretrial judge, who is responsible for both overseeing the legality of the criminal investigation and for safeguarding the suspect's individual rights. Further, Art. 3-D chapeau CPP states that the judge who takes decisions during the pretrial phase cannot be a trial judge, i.e., the pretrial judge is barred from being a trial judge in the same criminal case. Consequently, if these three articles are considered to be constitutional by the STF, the trial judge will not have access to evidence gathered in the pretrial phase. As such, the risk of him adducing to this type of evidence in his written reasoning for convicting a defendant will cease to exist.

Against this background, I believe it would be highly detrimental to the Brazilian criminal procedure for the CPP to remain in its current setting as the need of mechanisms to confine judicial bias would not have been minimally addressed. It is for this reason that I believe that it is vital for the provisions of L. 13.964/19 – that are currently suspended by the STF – to be introduced to the CPP. In addition to the reasons examined above, I would like to highlight once more the fact that the figure of a pretrial judge is a powerful means in which to counter the risk of judicial bias. This is because – regardless of a legal system being predominantly inquisitorial or adversarial – the existence of a pretrial judge is a very basic requirement in a legal system's criminal procedure. And as repeatedly seen, it is only by there being two different types of judges, who have specific judicial roles and may only make decisions in their defined sphere of competency, that the defendant's right to an impartial judge and to an impartial trial will be safeguarded.

C. Silver Lining: A Case for the Benefits of a Trial Setting with Both Inquisitorial and Adversarial Elements

According to Perron "in countries where democracy is young or where the criminal procedure is viewed as being in need of reform due to its rigid, authoritarian structure, (…) the Anglo-Saxon model has been met with significantly more interest than the reformed continental European model."[273] He states that the interest in the latter model is owing to the features of the adversarial trial setting being desirable as they provide for a "distinct separation of functions among various bodies."[274]

The observation above is applicable to the Brazilian context and certainly explains the desire of many Brazilian scholars and practitioners to change the trial setting to allow the parties to have control over the presentation of evidence. This is a reasonable reaction as many scholars, who seek to further the defendants' rights at trial

---

[273] *Perron*, in: Eser/Rabenstein, Criminal Justice, p. 314.

[274] *Perron*, in: Eser/Rabenstein, Criminal Justice, p. 314.

wish to break free from the repressive and rigid legal culture and from the vast amount of judicial discretion in the trial setting. Nonetheless, I believe it to be unlikely that the Brazilian trial setting will shift from the current predominant evidentiary arrangement to a setting where the parties are the main procedural actors responsible for evidence taking. Additionally, I am not convinced whether this complete shift in the trial setting is attainable or desirable for two reasons.

On the one hand, the rigidity of the Brazilian legal culture is consistently being illustrated by the unwillingness of scholars and, particularly, of legal practitioners in embracing the minor changes sought in allocating more power to the parties in presenting evidence at trial.[275] On the other hand, the current CPP lacks safeguards affording the defense the means in which to gather evidence prior to trial. Further, the majority of the defendants either lack the resources to retain legal counsel or are represented by public defenders, who lack the time and the financial resources to fully represent all of their clients to the best of their abilities.[276] Accordingly, there is an utter lack of equality of arms in the Brazilian trial setting.

In view of this situation, I would like to address the possibility of a middle way, i.e., of considering the benefits of the Brazilian trial setting having (a balanced amount of) features of both officialized factfinding and of party-controlled presentation of evidence. When considering which procedural actor(s) should be responsible for finding the truth at trial, Weigend states that "to provide double control, the person(s) responsible for collecting and presenting evidence and the judge(s) who hear(s) the case and ultimately render judgment should be independent of each other."[277] He contends that if the defendant is found guilty by these two different agents, it is likely that the defendant is indeed guilty. He further states that "if the criminal process is organized in the manner described above, the question of who is responsible for presenting the evidence at the trial is of secondary importance."[278] Finally, Weigend states that "there are strong indications for a convergence of the two models toward shared responsibility, with judges becoming more active in adversarial systems and parties obtaining greater participation rights in inquisitorial systems."[279]

Considering that the Brazilian trial setting has a predominantly inquisitorial evidentiary arrangement, effective procedural safeguards must be introduced to this system to counter the risk of judicial bias stemming from the inherent weakness of this predominant evidentiary arrangement and those whose origin is completely unrelated to this procedural model.

---

[275] For an example of the sheer amount of resistance – of both the legal practitioners and the higher courts – in accepting the changes made to the CPP, see supra Ch. 5 B. III. 2.

[276] See supra Ch. 6 B. I. 2. a).

[277] *Weigend*, Should we Search, p. 409.

[278] *Weigend*, Should we Search, p. 409.

[279] *Weigend*, Should we Search, p. 414.

Provided that these safeguards are present, I believe that judicial discretion will be greatly circumscribed and, as a consequence, the risk of judicial bias will decrease. Concurrently, for there to be a balance between the features of both procedural arrangements, the CPP must afford the parties the option of having a larger amount of responsibilities in presenting evidence at trial. For this purpose, the CPP must provide the defense with effective mechanisms in which to both gather evidence prior to trial and to provide the parties a higher degree of participation in presenting evidence at trial. I believe that the result of the combination of these two features in the Brazilian trial setting would considerably further the defendants' rights at trial. Also, by gradually shifting the trial setting to allow for a higher amount of participation of the parties, the Brazilian legal culture will have time to catch up with the changes to its legal framework.

Conclusion

The Brazilian legal framework developed from the Portuguese law as applied in that country during the Middle Ages. Consequently, since its inception the Brazilian criminal procedure had a very repressive nature which – although at times lessened – persisted throughout the centuries. In its more recent history, the Brazilian legal culture's authoritarian and repressive mentality was reinforced in 1941, as the Code of Criminal Procedure was enacted under a fascist ideology. As a result, although this code has considerably changed in the past two decades due to many procedural reforms, the lack of the corresponding shift in the repressive and highly formalistic legal culture remains pervasive in the legal practice. This can be observed by the many features of the Code of Criminal Procedure which reflect its authoritarian nature, such as the almost unchecked amount of judicial discretion.

Brazilian scholars and practitioners have been facing difficulties in identifying the main problematic features of the Brazilian criminal procedure, and consequently, in finding effective solutions to its main failings. The solutions to these questions must be searched outside of this legal system. To this end, I examined the German and the US-American criminal procedure and evidence law. By examining the trial setting of each of these foreign legal systems, concrete examples of a predominantly inquisitorial and of an adversarial procedural model were provided. This, in turn, illustrated how the concrete roles prescribed to the procedural actors, the rules regarding admissibility and exclusion of evidence, and the procedural safeguards needed in furthering the defendant's rights at trial starkly differ in these two different evidentiary arrangements.

In the German trial setting, the court is responsible for finding the objective facts of the case and deciding on both matters of fact and of law, and the prosecution is an objective procedural actor who has the role to support the court in fulfilling its tasks at trial. In contrast, in the US-American trial setting, the parties are the sole procedural actors responsible for presenting evidence, whereas the trial judge is a passive umpire who only makes ruling on matters of evidence when invoked by one of the parties. Considering that the Brazilian criminal procedure has features of both these evidentiary arrangements, the examination of the aforementioned legal systems was very valuable for the purpose of better understanding this legal system and the nature of its main problematic features.

After having concluded the very first step necessary in conducting a study in comparative law, i.e., examining how concrete foreign legal systems function in practice, I addressed the fundamental topics of comparative law as to fill the gap stemming from the Brazil's lack of tradition in conducting systematic research in this field. For this purpose, I examined the key legal definitions employed in comparative procedure as there is a widespread misunderstanding in the country regarding the definition, characteristics, and the scope of the different evidentiary arrangements.

I examined the theoretical framework of the adversarial and inquisitorial procedural models and based on this framework: I defined the main evidentiary arrangement of the Brazilian trial setting. Subsequently, I examined the topic of legal translations and the importance of understanding both the receiving country's normative framework and its legal culture before importing legal provisions or ideas from a foreign legal system. I also illustrated the deleterious effects of introducing legal ideas or provisions into a receiving legal system without taking these elements into consideration. Accordingly, I examined the normative framework of the three legal systems and the Brazilian legal culture, as at times, it starkly differs from the inquisitorial procedural culture. This step was necessary in order to offer suggestions to improve the Brazilian criminal procedure within the context of its legal framework and legal culture.

Finally, I addressed the reasons behind the difficulties in pinpointing the main problematic features of the Brazilian criminal procedure, by first analyzing the main reason alluded by Brazilian scholars, as to subsequently provide two explanations which I believe are the true reasons for the main problematic issues of this legal system.

The first reason is that owing to the lack of clarity regarding the different procedural models, most scholars perceive that the main reason for the failings of the Brazilian criminal procedure are what they deem to be the "inquisitorial" features of the CPP. In turn, I contend that the biggest reason for the defendant's vulnerability in the Brazilian trial setting does not stem from the features of officialized factfinding. Rather, they stem from a lack of effective procedural safeguards to counter the risk of judicial bias which is an inherent weakness of the inquisitorial trial setting.

The second reason I adduced is that the lack of procedural safeguards were not the only factors which contributed to the high risk of judicial bias in the Brazilian criminal procedure. This risk also stems from two features, which are completely unrelated to the inquisitorial evidentiary arrangement namely, the partisan character of the criminal investigation and the lack of division of judicial roles throughout the procedural phases. This latter feature is highly damaging to the defendant's right to an impartial judge and, consequently, to a fair trial. For this reason, regardless of the suggestions I offered for the improvement of the Brazilian criminal procedure, the first crucial step is for there to be both pretrial and trial judges who have specific roles and may only make decisions in their defined sphere of competency.

Following the identification of the reasons for the failings in the Brazilian criminal procedure, I addressed its most problematic features. By addressing the lack of procedural safeguards in the Brazilian legal system, the two main consequences of the widespread misconception that the inquisitorial features are to blame for the failings of this legal system became more clear.

On the one hand, it led Brazilian scholars to idealize a party-controlled presentation of evidence as a model that could automatically solve most failings of the Brazilian criminal procedure and led them to over rely on the principles of audiatur altera pars and (the right to a) full defense. This, in turn, led scholars to completely ignore the shortcomings of the adversarial system and the need for specific procedural safeguards to be in place to protect the defendant from the inherent weaknesses of this evidentiary arrangement. Absent the introduction of specific safeguards, if the Brazilian trial setting shifts from a predominantly officialized factfinding to a predominantly party-controlled presentation of evidence, Brazilian defendants might find themselves in an even more vulnerable position that the one in which they currently find themselves.

On the other hand, the fact that the real reason behind the procedural failings were not addressed, i.e., the introduction of the necessary safeguards to counter the weaknesses of the inquisitorial trial setting, caused an almost unchecked amount of judicial discretion at trial. As a result, the vulnerable position of the defendant at trial is owing to both the lack of procedural safeguards in countering the inherent weaknesses stemming from the inquisitorial and of the adversarial features of the Brazilian trial setting.

Considering the vastness of this subject and owing to both time and space constraints, I had to heavily circumscribe this topic, and consequently, I was not able to examine the three legal systems under analysis in depth. I hope that despite having to considerably limit the scope of this work, it still has the potential to make a contribution in two ways. First, by examining the key concepts of legal comparison, I hope that this research may aid Brazilian scholars to better apprehend the contents of international literature on comparative studies. Further, I hope it will be a helping tool for them to communicate effectively, i.e., in the same language as that spoken by international researchers in the field of comparative law, and that it will encourage scholars to meaningfully participate and to make positive contributions in this field.

Second, as I stated in the introduction, the main purpose of this work was to attempt to shed some light on some of the blind spots that have led Brazilian scholars and practitioners to be unable to identify the reasons behind the main problematic features of the Brazilian criminal procedure and to find effective solutions for these failings. For this purpose, I addressed the inquisitorial and the adversarial evidentiary arrangements both from a theoretical (Ch. 4) and from a concrete perspective (Chapters 1 to 3). By identifying the reasons for the problematic features of the Brazilian criminal procedure and by addressing the most problematic features themselves, I hope I have contributed to dispel the widespread prejudice regarding the inquisitorial evidentiary arrangement. My hope is that this will encourage Brazilian researchers to avail of the massive amount of sources and material written by international scholars of legal systems of both adversarial and predominantly inquisitorial trial settings.

As I have only scratched the surface, further study on the problematic features of the Code of Criminal Procedure addressed in this research is needed. Also, the future developments of the Brazilian criminal procedure are contingent on whether the Constitutional Court will hold the many legal provisions which were introduced to the Code of Criminal Procedure by L. 13.964/19 to be constitutional. If this is the case, in principle, the Brazilian trial setting may shift from a predominantly officialized factfinding to a (mostly) party-controlled presentation of evidence. However, these changes will depend on various factors, such as whether and to what extent these legal provisions will be accepted by the Brazilian legal culture, and whether and to what extent the higher courts will enforce its compliance. Irrespective of these changes, I hope this work will in some measure shed some light as to what types of safeguards are necessary in countering the trial setting's main failings.

Finally, I hope that the findings presented in this research may be a stepping-stone to equip the many talented and determined Brazilian scholars and practitioners with the tools necessary in further developing and implementing effective solutions to the Brazilian criminal procedure, thus safeguarding and promoting the defendant's rights at trial.

Bibliography

Allen, Rolland J./*Alexakis*, Georgia N., Utility and Truth in the Scholarship of Mirjan Damaška, in: John D. Jackson/John Howard Jackson/Mirjan Damaška/Máximo Langer/Peter Tillers (eds.), Crime, Procedure and Evidence in a Comparative and International context. Essays in Honour of Professor Damaška. Portland 2008, 329–350.

Almeida Jr., João Mendes, O Processo Criminal Brasileiro. Vol. 1. 4th ed. Rio de Janeiro 1959.

Alschuler, Albert W., The Prosecutor's Role in Plea Bargaining. 36 U. Chi. L. Rev. (1968), 50–112.

Ambos, Kai, Internationales Strafrecht. Strafanwendungsrecht, Völkerstrafrecht, europäisches Strafrecht, Rechtshilfe; ein Studienbuch. 4th ed. Munich 2014.

Andrade, Andressa Paula de/*Ávila*, Gustavo Noronha, Sherlock Holmes no Processo Penal Brasileiro? Lineamentos sobre a Lei 13.432 de 11 de abril de 2017 e a Investigação Criminal Defensiva, Boletim do IBCCrim, ano 25, n. 296, julho/2017, 8–9.

Azevedo, André Boiani/*Baldan*, Édson Luís, A Preservação do Devido Processo Legal Pela Investigação Defensiva (ou do direito de defender-se provando). Boletim do IBCCrim, ano 11, n. 137, abril/2004, 6–8.

Badaró, Gustavo Henrique Righi Ivahy, Tribunal do Júri, in: Moura, Maria Thereza Rocha de Assis, As Reformas no Processo Penal. As Novas Leis de 2008 e os Projetos de Reforma. Revista dos Tribunais, São Paulo 2009, 50–245.

Badaró, Gustavo Henrique Righi Ivahy, O Valor Probatório do Inquérito Policial, in: Kai Ambos/Ezequiel Malarino/Eneas Romero de Vasconcellos (eds.), Polícia e Investigação no Brasil, Brasília 2016, 255–282.

Badaró, Gustavo Henrique Righi Ivahy, Processo Penal. 6th ed. São Paulo 2018.

Barros, Romeu Pires de Campos, Lineamentos do Direito Processual Penal Brasileiro. Ação Penal: Atos Processuais, dos Atos de Provas. Vol. 1. Goiania 1967.

Bastos, Marcelo Lessa, Investigação nos Crimes de Ação Penal de Iniciativa Pública. Papel do Ministério Público. Uma Abordagem à Luz do Sistema Acusatório e do Garantismo. Rio de Janeiro 2004.

Belknap, Michael R., The Supreme Court and the Criminal Procedure: The Warren Court Revolution. Washington, DC 2011.

Beulke, Werner/*Swoboda*, Sabine, Strafprozessrecht. 14th ed. Heidelberg 2018.

Billis, Emmanouil, Die Rolle des Richters im adversatorischen und im inquisitorischen Beweisverfahren. Berlin 2015.

Bittencourt, Cesar Roberto, Tratado de Direito Penal: Parte Geral 1. 21st ed. São Paulo 2015.

Bohlander, Michael, Principles of German Criminal Procedure. Oxford 2012.

Boyne, Shawn Marie, The German Prosecution Service: Guardians of the law? Berlin/Heidelberg 2014.

Bradley, Craig M., Reforming the Criminal Trial. 68 Ind. L. J. (1993), 659–664.

Bradley, Craig M., The Convergence of the Continental, and the Common Law Model of Criminal Procedure. 7 Crim. Law Forum (1996), 471–484.

Bradley, Craig M., Criminal Procedure: A Worldwide Study. Durham 2007.

Brasileiro de Lima, Renato, Manual de Processo Penal. 5th ed. Salvador 2017.

Britz, Marjie T., Criminal Evidence. 2nd ed. Boston 2016.

Broun, Kenneth S., Giving Codification a Second Chance – Testimonial Privileges and the Federal Rules of Evidence. 53 Hastings L. J. (2002), 769–815.

Burnham, William, Introduction to the Law and Legal System of the United States. 5th ed. St. Paul, MN 2011.

Caianiello, Michele/*Hodgson*, Jacqueline S., Discretionary Criminal Justice in a Comparative Context. Durham 2015.

Capez, Fernando, Curso de Processo Penal. 24th ed. São Paulo 2017.

Castro, André Luis Machado de/*Alves*, Cleber Francisco/*Esteves*, Diogo/*Silva*, Franklyn Roger Alves, Access to Justice in Brazil: The Brazilian Legal Aid Model. Rio de Janeiro 2017.

Chemerinsky, Erwin/*Levenson*, Laurie, Criminal Procedure: adjudication. Wolters Kluwer, 3rd ed. New York 2018.

Choukr, Fauzi Hassan, Permanências Inquisitivas no Processo Penal brasileiro – Aspectos determinantes nos 30 anos de vigência da CR/1988, in: Antonio Eduardo Ramires Santoro/Diogo Rudge Malan/Flávio Mirza Maduro, Crise no Processo Penal Contemporaneo: escritos em homenagem aos 30 anos da Constituição de 1988. Belo Horizonte 2018, 135–150.

Choukr, Fauzi Hassan, Código de Processo Penal Comentado: Comentários Consolidados e Crítica Jurisprudencial, Vol. 1. 9th ed. Belo Horizonte 2019.

Choukr, Fauzi Hassan, Código de Processo Penal Comentado: Comentários Consolidados e Crítica Jurisprudencial, Vol. 2. 9th ed. Belo Horizonte 2019.

Cooper, Laura, Voir Dire in Federal Criminal Trials: Protecting the Defendant's Right to an Impartial Jury, 48 Ind. L. J. (1973), 269–280.

Coutinho, Jacinto Nelson de Miranda, As Reformas Parciais do CPP e a Gestão da Prova: Segue o Princípio Inquisitivo. Boletim do IBCCrim, n. 188, p. 11, jul. 2008, 11–13.

Coutinho, Jacinto Nelson de Miranda, Um Devido Processo Legal (Constitucional) é Incompatível com o Sistema do CPP, de Todo Inquisitorial, in: Geraldo Prado/Diogo Malan, Processo Penal e Democracia: Estudos em Homenagem aos 20 anos da Constituição da República de 1988. Rio de Janeiro 2009, pp. 253–262.

Cruz, Rogério Schietti Machado, Com a Palavra, As Partes. Boletim do IBCCrim, n. 188, jul. 2008, 17.

Damaška, Mirjan, Evidentiary Barriers to Conviction and Two Models of Criminal Procedure: A Comparative Study, 121 U. Pa. L. Rev. (1973), 506–589.

Damaška, Mirjan, Presentation of Evidence and Factfinding Precision. 123 U. Pa. L. Rev. (1975), 1083–1106.

Damaška, Mirjan, The Faces of Justice and State Authority: A Comparative Approach to the Legal Process. New Haven 1986.

Damaška, Mirjan, Evidence Law Adrift. New Heaven 1997.

Damaška, Mirjan, The Uncertain Fate of Evidentiary Transplants: Anglo-American and Continental Experiments. 45 Am. J. Comp. L. (1997), 839–852.

Damaška, Mirjan, Models of Criminal Procedure. 51 Zbornik PFZ (2001), 477–516.

Davis, Angela J., Arbitrary Justice: The Power of the American Prosecutor. New York 2007.

Dias, Gabriel Bulhões Nóbrega, A Advocacia Criminal, A Investigação Defensiva e a Luta pela Paridade de Armas. RBCCrim, Vol. 150 ano 26, 145–187.

Dressler, Joshua/*Michaels*, Alan C., Understanding Criminal Procedure. Newark 2002.

Eberle, Edward J., The Method and Role of Comparative Law. 8 Wash. U. Global Stud. L. Rev. (2209), 451–486.

Eisenberg, Ulrich, Beweisrecht der StPO. Spezialkommentar. 9th ed. Munich 2015.

Engländer, Armin, Examens Repetitorium Strafprozessrecht. 7th ed. Heidelberg 2015.

Findley, Keith A., Adversarial Inquisitions: Rethinking the Search for the Truth. 56 N.Y.L. Sch. L. Rev. (2011–2012), 911–941.

Frankel, Marvin. E., The Search for Truth: An Umpireal View. 123 U. Pa. L. Rev. (1975), 1031–1059.

Frase, Richard S./*Weigend*, Thomas, German Criminal Justice as a Guide to American Law Reform: Similar Problems, Better Solutions? 18 B.C. Int'l & Comp. L. Rev. (1995), 317–360.

Friedman, Lawrence M./*Hayden*, Grant M., American Law: An Introduction. 3rd ed. New York 2017.

Gardner, Thomas J./*Anderson*, Terry M., Criminal Evidence: Principles and Cases. 9th ed. Boston 2016.

Gercke, Björn/*Julius*, Karl-Peter/*Temming*, Dieter/*Zöller*, Mark A./*Ahlbrecht*, Heiko/*Bär*, Wolfgang, Heidelberger Kommentar: StPO. 6th ed. Heidelberg 2019.

Giacomolli, Nereu José, Algumas marcas inquisitoriais do Código de Processo Penal brasileiro e a resistência às reformas. Revista Brasileira de Direito Processual Penal, Porto Alegre, Vol. 1, n. 1 (2015), 143–165.

Gilliéron, Gwladys, Public Prosecutors in the United States and Europe: A Comparative Analysis with special Focus on Switzerland, France, and Germany. Heidelberg 2014.

Gold, Victor J., Federal Rule of Evidence 403: Observations on the Nature of Unfairly Prejudicial Evidence. 58 Wash. L. Rev. (1983), 497–533.

Gomes Filho, Antonio Magalhães, Provas – Lei 11.960/08, de 09.06.2008, in: Moura, Maria Thereza Rocha de Assis, As Reformas no Processo Penal. As Novas Leis de 2008 e os Projetos de Reforma. Revista dos Tribunais, São Paulo 2009, 246–297.

Gomes Filho, Antonio Magalhães, A Garantia das Motivações Judiciais na Constituição de 1988, in: Geraldo Prado/Diogo Malan, Processo Penal e Democracia: Estudos em Homenagem aos 20 anos da Constituição da República de 1988. Rio de Janeiro 2009, pp. 59–84.

Graham, Michael H., Evidence, A Problem, Lecture and Discussion Approach. 4th ed. St. Paul 2015.

Graham, Michael H., Federal Rules of Evidence in a Nutshell. 10th ed. St. Paul 2018.

Grande, Elisabetta, Italian Criminal Justice: Borrowing and Resistance. 48 Am. J. Comp. L. (2000), 227–259.

Grande, Elisabetta, Dances of Criminal Justice: Thoughts on Systemic Differences and the Search for the Truth, in: John D. Jackson/John Howard Jackson/Mirjan Damaška/Máximo Langer/Peter Tillers (eds.), Crime, Procedure and Evidence in a Comparative and International context. Essays in Honour of Professor Damaška. Portland 2008, pp. 145–164.

Greco, Filho, Manual de Processo Penal. São Paulo 1991.

Grilo, Fabiano Franklin Santiago, Defesa Técnica, Eficiencia e Garantismo: Paridade de Oportunidades no Processo Penal. Saarbrücken 2015.

Grinover, Ada Pellegrini, O Processo em Evolução. Rio de Janeiro 1996.

Grinover, Ada Pellegrini, A iniciativa instrutória do juiz no processo penal acusatório. Revista do Conselho Nacional de Política Criminal e Penitenciária, Brasília, 1(18), pp. 15–26, jan./jul. 2005.

Hannich, Rolf/*Appl*, Ekkehard/*Bartel*, Louisa/*Barthe*, Cristoph/*Bruns*, Michael/*Diemer*, Herbert, Karlsruher Kommentar zur Strafprozessordnung mit GVG, EGGVG und EMRK. 8th ed. Munich 2019.

Heger, Martin/*Pohlreich*, Erol Rudolf/*Kütterer-Lang*, Hannah, Strafprozessrecht. 2nd ed. Stuttgart 2018.

Henkel, Heinrich, Strafverfahrensrecht: ein Lehrbuch. Stuttgart u. a. 1968.

Hodgson, Jacqueline, Conceptions of the Trial in Inquisitorial and Adversarial Procedure, in: Antony Duff, Lindsay Farmer, Sandra Marshall, and Victor Tadros, The Trial on Trial Volume 2: Judgement and Calling to Account. Oxford 2006, pp. 223–242.

Ingram, Jefferson, Criminal Evidence. 13th ed. New York 2018.

Jardim, Afrânio Souza/*Amorim*, Pierre Souto Maior Coutinho de, Direito Processual Penal. Estudos e Pareceres. 14th ed. Salvador 2016.

Jescheck, Hans-Heinrich, Principles of German Criminal Procedure in Comparison with American Law. 56 Va. L. Rev. (1970), 239–253.

Jimeno-Bulnes, Mar, American Criminal Procedure in an European Context. 21 Cardozo J. Int'l & Comp. L. (2013), 409–459.

Juy-Birmann, Rudolphe, The German System, in: Mireille Delmas-Marty/John R. Spencer (eds.), European Criminal Procedures. Cambridge 2006, pp. 292–437

Kagan, Robert. A. Adversarial Legalism: The American Way of Law. Cambridge et al. 2003.

Karam, Maria Lucia, O Direito à Defesa e a Paridade de Armas, in: Geraldo Prado/Diogo Malan, Processo Penal e Democracia: Estudos em Homenagem aos 20 anos da Constituição da República de 1988. Rio de Janeiro 2009, pp. 395–406.

Kassin, Saul M./*Wrightsman*, Lawrence S., The American Jury on Trial. Psychological Perspectives. New York 1988.

Kaye, David H./*Broun*, Kenneth S./*Dix*, George E./*Imwinkelried*, Edward J./*Mosteller*, Robert P./*Roberts*, E. F./*Swift*, Eleanor, McCormick on Evidence. Vol. 1. 7th ed. St. Paul 2013.

Khaled Jr., Salah H. A produção analógica da verdade no processo penal. Revista Brasileira de Direito Processual Penal, Porto Alegre, Vol. 1, n. 1, pp. 166–184, 2015.

Kindhäuser, Urs/*Schumann*, Kay H., Strafprozessrecht. 5th ed. Baden-Baden 2019.

Klein, Jennifer Sawyer, "I'm Your Therapist, You Can Tell Me Anything": The Supreme Court Confirms the Psychotherapist-Patient Privilege in Jaffee v. Redmond. 47 DePaul L. Rev. (1998), 701–742.

Knauer, Christoph/*Kudlich*, Hans/*Schneider*, Hartmut (eds.), Münchener Kommentar zur Strafprozessordnung. Vol. 2: §§ 151–332 StPO. Munich 2016.

Krey, Volker, Characteristic Features of German Criminal Proceedings – An Alternative to the Criminal Procedure Law of the United States. 21 Loy. L.A. Int'l & Comp. L. Rev. 591 (1999), 591–605.

Krey, Volker/*Heinrich* Manfred, Deutsches Strafverfahrensrecht: Studienbuch in systematisch-induktiver Darstellung. 2nd ed. Stuttgart 2019.

Kühne, Hans-Heiner, Strafprozessrecht. Eine systematische Darstellung des deutschen und europäischen Strafverfahrensrechts. 9th ed. Heidelberg 2015.

LaFave, Wayne R./*Israel*, Jerold H./*King*, Nancy J./*Kerr*, Orin S., Criminal Procedure. 6th ed. St. Paul Minn. 2017.

Langbein, John H., Torture and Plea Bargaining. 46 U. Chi. L. Rev. (1978), 3–22.

Langbein, John H., The Influence of Comparative Procedure in the United States, 43 Am. J. Comp. L. (1995), 545–554.

Langbein, John H., Historical Foundations of the Law of Evidence: A View from the Ryder Sources. 96 Colum. L. Rev. (1996), 1168–1202.

Langbein, John H., The Origins of Adversary Criminal Trial. Oxford 2003.

Langer, Máximo, From Legal Transplants to Legal Translations: The Globalization of Plea Bargaining and the Americanization Thesis in Criminal Procedure. 45 Harv. Int'l L. J. (2004), 1–64.

Langer, Máximo, Revolution in Latin American Criminal Procedure: Diffusion of Legal Ideas from the Periphery. 55 Am. J. Comp. L. (2007), 617–676.

Langer, Máximo, Strength, Weaknesses or Both?, in: Jaqueline E. Ross/Stephen C. Thaman, Comparative Criminal Procedure. Northampton 2016, 519–536.

Lempert, Richard O., Anglo–American and Continental Systems: Marsupials and Mammals of the Law, in: John D. Jackson/John Howard Jackson/Mirjan Damaška/Máximo Langer/Peter Tillers (eds.), Crime, Procedure and Evidence in a Comparative and International context. Essays in Honour of Professor Damaška. Portland 2008, 395–413.

Löhr, Holle Eva, Der Grundsatz der Unmittelbarkeit im deutschen Strafprozess. Berlin 1972.

Lopes Jr., Aury, Bom para que(m)?. Boletim do IBCCrim, n. 188, p. 9, jul. 2008, 9–10.

Lopes Jr., Aury, Direito Processual Penal. 11th ed. São Paulo 2014.

Lopes Jr., Aury, Direito Processual Penal. 15th ed. São Paulo 2018.

Lopes Jr., Aury/*Jacobsen Gloeckner*, Ricardo, Investigação Preliminar no Processo Penal. 6th ed. São Paulo 2014.

Machado, André Augusto Mendes, Investigação Criminal Defensiva. 2009. Dissertação de Mestrado – Faculdade de Direito, Universidade Federal de São Paulo, São Paulo.

Malan, Diogo, Defesa Técnica e seus Consectários Lógicos na Carta Política de 1988, in: Geraldo Prado/Diogo Malan, Processo Penal e Democracia: Estudos em Homenagem aos 20 anos da Constituição da República de 1988. Rio de Janeiro 2009, pp. 143–186.

Marafioti, Luca, Italian Criminal Procedure: A System Caught Between Two Traditions, in: John D. Jackson/John Howard Jackson/Mirjan Damaška/Máximo Langer/Peter Tillers (eds.), Crime, Procedure and Evidence in a Comparative and International context. Essays in Honour of Professor Damaška. Portland 2008, pp. 81–98.

Marcus, Paul/*Moreno*, Joelle Anne/*Miller*, Tommy E./*Duncan*, David K., The Rights of the Accused Under the Sixth Amendment: Trials, Presentation of Evidence and Confrontation. 2nd ed. Chicago 2016.

Marques, José Frederico, Elementos de Direito Processual Penal. Vol. 1. 2nd ed. Campinas 2000.

Marques, José Frederico, Elementos de Direito Processual Penal. Vol. 2. 2nd ed. Campinas 2000.

Mc Gabe, Peter G., A Guide to the Federal Magistrate Judges System: A White Paper Prepared at the Request of the Federal Bar Association. August 2014.

Melchior, Antonio Pedro, O projeto de Código de Processo Penal trinta anos após a Constituição da República: um novo entulho inquisitivo?, in: Antonio Eduardo Ramires Santoro/Diogo Rudge Malan/Flávio Mirza Maduro, Crise no Processo Penal Contemporaneo: escritos em homenagem aos 30 anos da Constituição de 1988. Belo Horizonte 2018, pp. 39–60.

Mendes, Gilmar Ferreira/*Branco*, Paulo Gustavo Gonet, Curso de Direito Constitucional. 10th ed. São Paulo 2015.

Meyer-Goßner, Lutz/*Schmitt*, Bertram, Strafprozessordnung. Gerichtsverfassungsgesetz, Nebengesetze und ergänzende Bestimmungen. 62nd ed. Munich 2019.

Mirabete, Júlio Fabbrini, Processo Penal. 2nd ed. São Paulo 1993.

Mossin, Hieráclito, Antonio, *Compêndio* de Processo Penal: Curso Completo. Barueri 2010.

Nance, Dale A., Understanding Responses to Hearsay: An Extension of the Comparative Analysis (1992). 76 Minn. L. Rev. (1992), 459–472.

Newton, Samuel P./*Welch*, Teresa L., Understanding Criminal Evidence. A Case Method Approach. New York 2013.

Nicolitti, André Luiz, A Garantia do Contraditório: Consagrada na Constituição de 1988 e Olvidada na Reforma do Código de Processo Penal de 2008, in: Geraldo Prado/Diogo Malan,

Processo Penal e Democracia: Estudos em Homenagem aos 20 anos da Constituição da República de 1988. Rio de Janeiro 2009, pp. 47–58.

Nicolitti, André Luiz, Manual de Processo Penal. 7th ed. Belo Horizonte 2018.

Nijboer, J. F., Common Law Tradition in Evidence Scholarship Observed from a Continental Perspective. 41 Am. J. Comp. L. (1993), 299–338.

Nucci, Guilherme de Souza, Código de Processo Penal Comentado. 18th ed. Rio de Janeiro 2019.

Pacelli, Eugenio, Curso de Processo Penal. 32nd ed. São Paulo 2019.

Pacelli, Eugenio/*Fischer*, Douglas, Comentários ao Código de Processo Penal e sua Jurisprudencia. 7th ed. São Paulo 2015.

Packer, Herbert, Two Models of the Criminal Process. 113 U. Pa. L. Rev. (1964), 1–68.

Perron, Walter, Das Beweisantragsrecht des Beschuldigten im deutschen Strafprozess: eine Untersuchung der verfassungsrechtlichen und verfahrensstrukturellen Grundlagen, gesetzlichen Regelungen und rechtstatsächlichen Auswirkungen sowie eine Erörterung der Reformperspektiven unter rechtsvergleichender Berücksichtigung des adversatorischen Prozessmodells. Berlin 1995.

Perron, Walter, Rechtsvergleichender Querschnitt und rechtspolitische Bewertung, in: Walter Perron (ed.), Die Beweisaufnahme im Strafverfahrensrecht des Auslands. Freiburg im Breisgau 1995, pp. 549–608.

Perron, Walter, Function and Composition of the Court during the Preliminary Investigation and the Trial, in: Albin Eser/Christiane Rabenstein (eds.), Criminal Justice between Crime Control and Due Process. Convergence and Divergence in Criminal Procedure Systems. Berlin 2004, pp. 303–314.

Perron, Walter, Adversatorisches Parteienverfahren oder Amtsermittlungsprinzip im Strafprozess?, in: Alexander Bruns (ed.), Festschrift für Rolf Stürner. Tübingen 2013, pp. 875–889.

Perron, Walter, Menschengerechter Strafprozess – Beweisverfahren und Bürgerinteressen im deutschamerikanischen Vergleich, in: Björn Burkhardt u.a. (ed.), Scripta amicitiae. Freundschaftsgabe für Albin Eser zum 80. Geburtstag am 26.1.2015. Berlin 2015, pp. 413–430.

Pierangelli, José Henrique, Processo penal: Evolução histórica e fontes legislativas. Bauru 1983.

Pieroth, Bodo/*Schlink*, Bernhard, Grundrechte, Staatsrecht II. 35th ed. Heidelberg 2019.

Pitombo, Cleunice Valentim Bastos, Considerações Iniciais sobre a Lei 11.690/08. Boletim do IBCCrim, n. 188, jul. 2008, 20–22.

Pizzi, William, Understanding Prosecutorial Discretion in the United States: The Limits of Comparative Criminal Procedure as an Instrument of Reform. 54 Ohio St. L. J. (1993), 1325–1373.

Pizzi, William, Soccer, Football and Trial Systems. 1 Colum. J. Eur. L. (1995), 369–377.

Pizzi, William, The American "Adversary System"? 100 W. Va. L. Rev. (1997–1998), 847–852.

Pizzi, William, Trials Without Truth. Why Our System of Criminal Trials Has Become an Expensive Failure and What We Need to Do to Rebuild It. New York 1999.

Pizzi, William, Sentencing in the US: An Inquisitorial Soul in an Adversarial Body?, in: John D. Jackson/John Howard Jackson/Mirjan Damaška/Máximo Langer/Peter Tillers (eds.), Crime, Procedure and Evidence in a Comparative and International context. Essays in Honour of Professor Damaška. Portland 2008, pp. 65–79.

Pizzi, William T./*Marafioti*, Luca, The New Italian Code of Criminal Procedure: The Difficulties of Building an Adversarial Trial System on a Civil Law Foundation. 17 Yale J. Int'l L. (1992), 1–40.

Pizzi, William T./*Montagna*, Mariangela, The Battle to Establish an Adversarial Trial System in Italy. 25 Mich. J. Int'l L. (2004), 429–466.

Pizzi, William T./*Perron*, Walter, Crime Victims in German Courtrooms: A Comparative Perspective on American Problems. 32 Stan. J. Int'l L. (1996), 37–64.

Podgor, Ellen S., Prosecution Guidelines in the United States, in: Erik Luna/Marianne L. Wade, The Prosecutor in Transnational Perspective. New York 2012, pp. 9–19.

Polastri, Marcellus/*Ambos*, Kai, O Processo Acusatório e a Vedação Probatória: Perante as Realidades Alemã a e Brasileira com a Perspectiva Brasileira já de Acordo com a Reforma Processual Penal de 2008; leis 11.689, 11.690 e 11.719. Porto Alegre 2009.

Prado, Geraldo, Sistema Acusatório. A Conformidade Constitucional das Leis Processuais Penais. 2nd ed. Rio de Janeiro 2001.

Queijo, Maria Elizabeth, O Direito de Não Produzir Prova Contra Si Mesmo. São Paulo 2003.

Queijo, Maria Elizabeth, O Tratamento da Prova Ilícita na Reforma Processual Penal. Boletim do IBCCrim, n. 188 (18 jul. 2008), 18–19.

Rangel, Paulo, Direito Processual Penal. 23rd ed. São Paulo 2015.

Rascovski, Luiz, Investigação Criminal Defensiva: Uma Luz no Fim do Túnel Com Sua Previsão no Novo Código de Processo Penal (Projeto 156/09). Boletim do IBCCrim, ano 18, n. 219, fevereiro/2011, 14–15.

Rauxloh, Regina, Plea-Bargaining in National and International Law. A Comparative Study. London 2012.

Roberson, Cliff/*Winters*, Robert, Evidence for Criminal Justice. Durham 2016.

Roberts, Paul, Faces of Justice Adrift? Damaška's Comparative Method and the Future of Common Law Evidence, in: John D. Jackson/John Howard Jackson/Mirjan Damaška/Máximo Langer/Peter Tillers (eds.), Crime, Procedure and Evidence in a Comparative and International context. Essays in Honour of Professor Damaška. Oxford 2014, pp. 295–328.

Rodrigues, Maria Stella Villela Souto Lopes, ABC do Processo Penal. 9th ed. Rio de Janeiro 1996.

Roxin, Claus/*Schünemann*, Bernd, Strafverfahrensrecht. Ein Studienbuch. 29th ed. Munich 2017.

Rudolphi, Hans-Joachim (Begr.), Systematischer Kommentar zur Strafprozessordnung. Vol. 2: §§ 94–136a StPO. 5th ed. Köln 2016.

Rudolphi, Hans-Joachim (Begr.), Systematischer Kommentar zur Strafprozessordnung. Vol. 4: §§ 198–246 StPO. 5th ed. Köln 2015.

Saad, Marta, Direito de defesa no processo penal: novos desafios, velhos dilemas, in: Antonio Eduardo Ramires Santoro/Diogo Rudge Malan/Flávio Mirza Maduro, Crise no Processo Penal Contemporaneo: Escritos em homenagem aos 30 anos da Constituição de 1988. Belo Horizonte 2018, pp. 311–330.

Saltzburg, Stephen/*Capra*, Daniel J., American Criminal Procedure. Cases and Commentary. 11th ed. St. Paul, MN 2018.

Saltzburg, Stephen A./*Martin*, Michael M./*Capra*, Daniel J., Federal Rules of Evidence Manual. Vol. 1. 11th edition. San Francisco 2015.

Santos, Daniel Leonhardt dos/*Santos*, Lívia Limas, Nemo Tenetur se Detegere e Verdade no Processo Penal, in: Nereu José Giacomolli/Vinicius Gomes de Vasconcellos (eds.), Processo Penal e Garantias Constitucionais: Estudos para um Processo Penal Democrático. Rio de Janeiro 2014, pp. 109–133.

Satzger, Helmut, Internationales und Europäisches Strafrecht. Strafanwendungsrecht, europäisches Straf- und Strafverfahrensrecht, Völkerstrafrecht. 9th ed. Baden-Baden 2020.

Satzger, Helmut/*Schluckerbier*, Wilhelm/*Andrä*, Markus/*Eschelbach*, Ralf/*Franke*, Ulrich/ *Grube*, Andreas, Strafprozessordnung mit GVG und EMRK: Kommentar. 4th ed. Cologne 2020.

Scaranse Fernandes, Antonio, Processo Penal Constitutional. 6th ed. São Paulo 2010.

Scaranse Fernandes, Antonio, Vinte Anos de Constituição e o Processo Penal, in: Geraldo Prado/Diogo Malan, Processo Penal e Democracia: Estudos em Homenagem aos 20 anos da Constituição da República de 1988. Rio de Janeiro 2009, pp. 85–104.

Schäuble, Johannes, Strafverfahren und Prozessverantwortung: neue prozessuale Obliegenheit des Beschuldigten in Deutschland im Vergleich mit dem US-amerikanischen Recht. Berlin 2017.

Scheb, John M./*Sharma*, Hemant, An Introduction to the American Legal System. 4th ed. New York 2015.

Silva, Franklyn Roger Alves, Investigação Criminal Direta pela Defesa. Salvador 2019.

Silva Júnior, Walter Nunes da, Reforma Tópica do Processo Penal: Inovações aos Procedimentos Ordinário e Sumário, com o Novo Regime das Provas, Principais Modificações do Júri e as Medidas Cautelares Pessoais. 3rd ed. Natal 2019.

Sklansky, David Alan, Anti-Inquisitorialism. 122 Harv. L. Rev. (2008), 1634–1704.

Souza, José Barcelos, Novas Leis de Processo. Inquirição Direta de Testemunhas. Identidade Física do Juiz. Boletim do IBCCrim, n. 188, jul. 2008, 14–15.

Stüber, Michael, Die Entwicklung des Prinzips der Unmittelbarkeit im deutschen Strafverfahren. Frankfurt am Main 2005.

Távora, Nestor/*Alencar*, Rosmar Rodrigues, Curso de Direito Processual Penal. 12th ed. Salvador 2017.

Thaman, Stephen, Landesbericht USA, in: Walter Perron (ed.), Die Beweisaufnahme im Strafverfahrensrecht des Auslands. Freiburg im Breisgau 1995, pp. 489–547.

Thaman, Stephen, World Plea Bargaining: Consensual Procedures and the Avoidance of the Full Criminal trial. Durham, NC. 2010.

Thompson, Alan R./*Nored*, Lisa S./*Worrall*, John/*Hemmens*, Craig, An Introduction to Criminal Evidence: Cases and Concepts. New York 2008.

Tornaghi, Helio, Curso de Processo Penal. Vol. 1. 2nd ed. Belo Horizonte 1981.

Tourinho Filho, Fernando da Costa, Manual de Processo Penal. 17th ed. São Paulo 2017.

Tucci, Rogério Lauria, Direitos e Garantias Individuais no Processo Penal Brasileiro. 2nd ed. São Paulo 2014.

Vasconcellos, Vinicius Gomes de, Barganha e Justiça Criminal Negocial: tendências de expansão dos espaços de consenso no processo penal brasileiro. 2014. Dissertação (Mestrado em Ciências Criminais) – Faculdade de Direito, Pontifícia Universidade Católica do Rio Grande do Sul, Porto Alegre.

Vieira, Renato Stanziola, Paridade de Armas no Processo Penal: Do Conceito à Aplicação no Direito Processual Penal Brasileiro. Dissertação (Mestrado em Direito) – Faculdade de Direito da Universidade de São Paulo. São Paulo 2013.

Vieira, Renato Stanziola, Investigação Defensiva: diagnóstico e possibilidades no processo penal brasileiro, in: Kai Ambos/Ezequiel Malarino/Eneas Romero de Vasconcellos (eds.), Polícia e Investigação no Brasil, Brasília 2016, pp. 337–372.

Volk, Klaus/*Engländer*, Armin, Grundkurs StPO. 9th ed. Munich 2018.

Walpin, Gerald, America's Adversarial and Jury Systems: More Likely to Do Justice, 26 Harv. J. L. & Pub. Pol'y (2003), 175–188.

Watson, Alan, Legal Transplants: An Approach to Comparative Law. 2nd ed. Athens, Ga 1993.

Weigend, Thomas, Continental Cures for American Ailments: European Criminal Procedure as a Model for Law Reform, in: N. Morris/M. Tonry, Crime and Justice: A Review of Research, Vol. 2. Chicago 1980, pp. 381–428.

Weigend, Thomas, Should We Search for the Truth, and Who Should Do It? 36 N.C. J. Int'l L. & Com. Reg. (2010–2011), 389–415.

Weigend, Thomas, Rechtsvergleichende Bemerkungen zur Wahrheitssuche im Strafverfahren, in: Klaus Bernsmann/Thomas Fischer (eds.), Festschrift für Ruth Rissing-van Saan zum 65. Geburtstag am 25.1.2011. Berlin 2011, pp. 749–766.

Weinstein, Jack B./*Berger*, Margaret A., Student Edition of Weinstein's Evidence Manual: A Guide to the Federal Rules of Evidence, Based on Weinstein's Federal Evidence. 9th ed. Newark 2011.

Westen, Peter, Compulsory Process II. 74 Mich. L. Rev. (1975), 191–306.

Whitebread, Charles H./*Slobogin*, Christopher, Criminal Procedure: An Analysis of Cases and Concepts. 6th ed. St. Paul 2015.

Wigmore, John Henry, A Treatise on the Anglo-American System of Evidence in Trials at Common Law: Including the Statutes and Judicial Decisions of All Jurisdictions of the United States and Canada, Vol. 5. 3rd ed. Indiana 1940.

Woischnik, Jan, Juez de Instrucción y derechos humanos en Argentina: un analisis critico del codigo procesal penal de la Nación. Buenos Aires 2003.

Zilli, Marcos Alexandre Coelho, A Iniciativa Instrutória do Juiz no Processo Penal. São Paulo 2003.

Zilli, Marcos Alexandre Coelho, O Pomar e as Pragas. Boletim do IBCCrim, n. 188, p. 2, jul. 2008, 2–3.

Subject Index

accusatorial (comparative law)   196, 203
accused   21, 24, 27, 30, 31, 35, 36, 46, 48, 50, 52, 53, 63, 76–79, 81, 84, 89, 92, 93, 95, 97, 98, 121, 132, 133, 135, 138, 148–150, 160, 161, 174, 176, 185, 192, 193, 197, 199, 200, 218, 230, 237, 243
acusatório/accusatorial (Brazilian criminal procedure)   21, 32, 34–37, 186–188, 203, 204, 207, 209, 232
adjudication proceedings   40
admissibility of evidence   35, 74, 88, 120, 121, 172, 178, 195, 197, 247
adversarial evidentiary arrangement   21, 22, 26, 32, 189, 191, 195, 203, 204, 207, 213, 215, 221, 234, 242
adversarial features   189, 204, 214, 225, 226, 232, 233, 259
adversarial model   32, 88, 198, 204
adversarial procedural model   21, 189, 200, 203, 204, 206, 208, 214, 223–226, 257
adversarial system   23, 88, 190, 194–196, 198, 199, 202, 207, 212, 223, 224, 255, 259
adversarial (terminology)   21, 186, 188–190, 196, 197, 202, 203
adversarial trial setting   93, 106, 109, 120, 129, 168, 189, 195, 196, 198, 200, 212, 234, 254
adversary system *see under* 'adversarial (terminology)'
Afonsinas Ordinances   27, 28
Akteneinsichtsrecht *see under* 'right to request the inspection of the investigation file'
alternatives to formal proof   111, 112
American Convention on Human Rights (ACHR)   33, 140, 145, 173, 174, 185
Amtsermittlungsgrundsatz *see under* 'officialized-controlled inquest'
analytical approach   32, 191, 193, 194, 196, 204

Anfangsverdacht   50, 78
arraignment   92, 97, 99, 253
assistente de acusação *see under* 'private accessory prosecutor (Brazilian criminal procedure)'
associate judge   57–59, 68
attorney-client privilege   126
audiatur et altera pars   31, 145, 156, 157, 161, 183, 184, 207, 232, 234, 250, 259
Aufklärungspflicht des Richters   83, 243 *see also* 'principle of ascertainment of the truth'
Augenscheinsbeweis *see under* 'inspection evidence'
Auskunftsverweigerungsrecht   80
authentication   118, 119, 121
autodefesa   145, 173, 184

bench trial   100, 103, 105, 106, 136
best evidence rule   118, 119
Beweisantragsrecht *see under* 'motion to take evidence'
Beweiserhebungsverbot (prohibition in obtaining evidence)   75
Beweisgrundsätze *see under* 'evidentiary principles'
Beweisverbote   75, 87 *see also under* 'prohibition of evidence'
Beweisverwertungsverbot (prohibition in exploiting a piece of evidence)   75
bill of indictment   38, 49, 52, 93, 144, 149–151, 154–156, 185, 207, 208, 210, 220, 235, 245, 248, 250, 252
binding precedent/ binding summary   141, 183 *see also* 'súmulas vinculantes (SV)'

case file   38, 150, 155, 172, 177, 182, 207, 227, 251
case-in-chief   101, 102, 130, 131, 197
case law   24, 25, 88, 89, 104, 189
challenges for cause   101

Subject Index

character witness 117
charging document 55, 96, 99, 149–151
circumstantial evidence 110, 112, 121, 136, 158, 193
civil law 172, 189
closing arguments 55, 100–103, 137, 152, 153, 184
co-defendant 60, 64, 68, 71, 152, 165
common law 88, 113, 189, 196
comparative law 21, 22, 26, 149, 186–188, 190, 203, 205, 209, 224, 257, 259
complaint 96, 98, 99, 109, 147
completeness of the investigative file 51
compulsory process clause 132, 239
confrontation clause 46, 115, 129, 132–135, 239, 240
confusing the issues 122
court-appointed counsel 48, 94, 145
court-appointed expert 69, 74, 158, 170–172, 206
criminal case 24, 35, 40, 43, 50, 57, 87, 88, 93, 98, 99, 123, 125, 132, 138, 139, 142–146, 153, 195, 199–203, 211, 230, 231, 234, 248
criminal justice system 31, 57, 87, 135, 139, 149
criminal offense 24, 27, 40, 43, 44, 47–50, 64, 76, 77, 93, 94, 103, 113, 118, 130, 137–140, 143, 147, 149, 160, 162, 164, 165, 172, 176, 179, 181, 185, 192, 196, 200, 205, 230, 238, 251
criminal record 64, 130
cross-examination 114–116, 128, 129, 133–135, 168, 215, 240, 241
cross-examination (German criminal procedure) 59, 215, 216 *see also* 'Kreuzverhör'

das allgemeine Persönlichkeitsrecht *see under* 'right of personality'
declarant 127–129, 134, 135, 180
defendant's examination 34, 54, 55, 58, 62, 63, 76, 78, 79, 112, 124, 152, 154, 159–163, 167, 174, 194, 241
defendant's right to have the last word 55, 83, 86

defense counsel 46–48, 51, 53, 54, 59, 60, 64–66, 70, 73, 78, 81, 84, 93, 94, 97, 145, 148, 161, 167, 196, 201, 234, 235
defensor 145 *see also* 'public defender'
defesa técnica *see under* 'right to defense counsel'
demonstrative evidence 118, 119, 122
deposition *see under* 'right to deposition'
direct evidence 110, 158
direct examination 114, 115, 131, 168, 217
discovery 94, 95, 100, 129–131, 133, 148, 235, 236
discretionary forms of proof 61, 71
diversion 41
documentary evidence 62, 70–73, 118, 119, 159, 171, 172, 208
duty to attend trial 66, 67, 163, 169
duty to testify truthfully 66, 67, 113

Eidespflicht 66 *see also* 'oath'
equality of arms 129, 184, 185, 202, 227, 234, 235, 238, 242, 255
Erkenntnisverfahren *see under* 'adjudication proceedings'
Erklärungsrecht 59 *see under* 'right to make statements during evidence taking'
Erscheinenspflicht 66, 67 *see also* 'duty to attend trial'
Estado democrático de direito *see under* 'principle of a democratic society'
European Convention on Human Rights (ECHR) 24, 41–43, 48, 60, 209
European Court of Human Rights (ECtHR) 42, 43
evidentiary arrangement 21–23, 26, 32, 35, 187–191, 193–195, 199, 200, 202–205, 207, 209–213, 215, 219–221, 223–225, 227–230, 232, 234, 240, 242, 243, 247, 254, 255, 257–259
evidentiary principles 62, 82, 181, 234
examination of the defendant *see under* 'defendant's examination'
examination of victims *see under* 'victim's examination'
examination of witnesses *see under* 'witness examination'
exclusion of evidence 26, 102, 107, 120, 122, 136, 257

exclusionary rules 107, 195, 207
ex officio 49, 83, 141, 162, 163
expert 53, 54, 59, 60, 62, 69–74, 77, 79, 85, 155, 159, 170, 171, 209, 215, 216
expert evidence 74, 87, 158, 171, 246, 249
expert witness 57, 112, 130, 131, 241

factfinder *see under* 'finder of fact'
fair trial 42, 48, 64, 78, 93, 109, 140, 188, 191, 231, 258
federal constitutional court 40, 43, 75
federal court of justice 40, 44
federal jurisdiction 24, 87–91, 132
felony 41, 88, 91, 97, 98, 105, 135, 139, 142, 144, 231
finder of fact 57, 93, 100–103, 105–107, 115, 118, 120, 121, 123, 136, 153, 200, 251, 253
first state exam 45
formal truth 106, 198, 212
formalistic (normative framework and legal culture) 219, 221, 257
Fragerecht 42, 59 *see also* 'right to ask questions'

grand jury 91, 93, 97–99, 131, 196, 253
Grundsatz der Aktenvollständigkeit *see under* 'completeness of the investigative file'
Grundsatz der freien richterlichen Beweiswürdigung 86 *see also* 'principle of free evaluation of evidence'
Grundsatz der persönlichen Vernehmung *see under* 'principle of examination in person'
Grundsatz des rechtlichen Gehörs *see under* 'right to a fair hearing'

hearsay 108, 121, 127–129, 180, 181
higher regional court 44, 45
highly summarized procedural outline 138, 140
hinreichender Tatverdacht *see under* 'standard of adequate suspicion'
historical approach 192, 193, 196, 204, 205

illegally obtained evidence 177, 178
impeach witnesses *see under* 'impeachment of witnesses'

impeachment of witnesses 60, 94, 102, 115–118, 129, 135, 193, 216, 240
in dubio pro reo 173
inferences 110, 112
informantes *see under* 'informants'
informants 155, 156, 164–166, 181, 208
initial suspicion 78 *see also* 'Anfangsverdacht'
inquisitorial (terminology) 21, 32, 186–190, 192, 203, 204 *see also* 'inquisitorial trial setting', 'inquisitorial procedural model', 'officialized-controlled inquest' and 'officialized factfinding'
inquisitorial evidentiary arrangement 22, 26, 32, 188, 191, 193, 195, 199, 205, 207, 209, 211–213, 219–221, 223, 225, 228–230, 243, 247, 258, 259
inquisitorial features 204, 206, 214, 223, 225, 226, 232, 233, 259
inquisitorial model 204, 208
inquisitorial procedural model 23, 58, 189, 198, 200, 205, 206, 212, 214, 223, 224, 228, 230, 258
inquisitorial system 23, 32, 182, 188, 192, 194, 198, 199, 201, 207, 212, 255
inquisitorial trial setting 82, 189, 212, 213, 215, 232, 258–260
inspection evidence 54, 62, 73, 74
intermediate proceedings 46, 52, 84, 252
invasive evidence 176
investigation phase *see under* 'investigatory phase'
investigative file 38, 49, 51, 58, 70, 83, 84, 86, 147, 155, 194, 201, 206, 227, 228, 230, 235, 244, 247, 248, 250–254
investigatory phase 37, 38, 47, 49, 51, 69, 77, 84, 92, 94, 95, 146, 147, 157, 164, 173, 176, 182, 184, 194–196, 200, 204, 205, 210, 221, 231, 235, 236, 243, 248–253

judicial bias 144, 199, 201, 202, 207, 225, 228–231, 244, 247, 251, 255, 258
judicial discretion 109, 182, 202, 207, 229, 233, 234, 243–247, 254, 255, 257, 259
judicial examination 71, 72, 241
judicial neutrality 109, 199, 212
judicial notice 111
jury deliberation 103, 105, 136

Subject Index

jury instructions 103, 136
jury trial 34, 36, 57, 100, 105, 106, 135, 136, 140, 142, 153, 253
justa causa 147, 149, 220, 235, 248, 251 *see also* 'standard of justified cause'

Kreuzverhör 59, 215 *see also* 'cross-examination'

lay judge 43, 54–59, 63, 65, 68, 194
legal certainty 141
legal counsel 42, 48, 49, 51, 66, 77, 123, 145, 148, 160, 161, 173, 184, 237, 255
legal projection 187, 210, 224
legal tradition 189
legal translation 187, 209, 211, 214
legal transplant 26, 187, 209–211, 213, 214
Legalitätsprinzip 50 *see also* 'principle of mandatory prosecution'
local court 43–45, 57

magistrate (judge) 91, 92, 96–99, 253
main hearing 52–56, 61, 64, 68, 71, 73, 84, 215
main procedural actor(s) 33, 45, 91, 140–143, 154, 195, 207, 208, 216, 228, 229, 234, 251, 255
marital privilege 127
material truth 21, 33, 47, 55, 59, 62, 74, 83, 154, 156, 198, 200, 206, 208, 228
Ministério Público *see under* 'public prosecutor's office (Brazilian criminal procedure)'
Miranda warnings 123
misconception 23, 168, 187, 204, 205, 259
misdemeanor 91, 98, 138, 140
misleading the jury 122, 123
mixed court 41, 43, 56, 57, 195
mixed model 32, 190, 204
modified inquisitorial system 194 *see also* 'inquisitorial (terminology)'
motion to take evidence 58–61, 82–86, 244, 245, 247, 252
Mündlichkeitsprinzip *see under* 'principle of orality'

Nebenkläger *see under* 'private accessory prosecutor (German criminal procedure)'
needlessly presenting cumulative evidence 122
nemo tenetur 76, 173, 176
nemo-tenetur-Grundsatz *see under* 'nemo tenetur'
non-adversary system 194 *see also* 'inquisitorial (terminology)'
non-invasive evidence 176

oath 66, 67, 113, 114, 124, 128, 197
officialized-controlled inquest 194, 199 *see also* 'officialized factfinding'
officialized factfinding 58, 154, 181, 195, 208, 224, 227, 228, 232, 233, 240, 254, 255, 258–260 *see also* 'inquisitorial trial setting' and 'inquisitorial evidentiary arrangement'
opening statements 100–102
Opportunitätsprinzip 50 *see also* 'principle of discretionary prosecution'
ordinary procedural outline 138–140, 149, 165, 243
out-of-court statement 127–129, 180, 181

party-controlled contest 110, 191, 199 *see also* 'party-controlled presentation of evidence'
party-controlled presentation of evidence 21, 106, 156, 183, 184, 224, 226, 227, 233, 234, 242, 255, 259, 260
peremptory challenges 101
plea bargaining 88
pleading guilty 99
pleading nolo contendere 99
pleading not guilty 99
prejudicial effects 117, 121–123, 129
preliminary hearing 91, 96–99, 134, 135, 253
preparation for the main hearing 53
presiding judge 46, 52–60, 62–64, 68, 81, 83, 86, 194, 201, 215, 241, 246, 252
presumption of innocence 30, 42, 111, 136, 173, 188
presumptions 110–112
pretrial detention 33, 52

Subject Index

pretrial judge 37, 38, 46, 51, 66, 143, 144, 221, 227, 230, 231, 242, 243
pretrial motion 99, 133
princípio da ampla defesa *see under* 'principle of full defense'
princípio da comunhão da prova *see under* 'principle of evidence sharing'
princípio da duração razoável do processo *see under* 'principle of reasonable length to all judicial and administrative proceedings'
princípio da legalidade *see under* 'principle of discretionary prosecution'
princípio da liberdade probatória *see under* 'principle of probative freedom'
princípio da obrigatoriedade 144 *see also* 'principle of mandatory prosecution'
princípio da paridade de armas *see under* 'equality of arms'
princípio da verdade material ou real 154 *see also* 'principle of ascertainment of the truth'
princípio do contraditório *see under* 'audiatur et altera pars'
princípio do impulso oficial *see under* 'principle of official impulse'
princípio do livre convencimento motivado 182, 243 *see also* 'principle of free evaluation of evidence'
principle of a democratic society 31, 233
principle of ascertainment of the truth 58, 61, 62, 82–84, 154, 181, 206, 215, 220, 232, 233, 234, 243, 244, 247
principle of discretionary prosecution 50, 200
principle of equality of arms *see under* 'equality of arms'
principle of evidence sharing 154
principle of examination in person 71, 72
principle of free evaluation of evidence 82, 86, 182, 207, 232, 234, 243, 246, 247, 252
principle of full defense 31, 145, 148, 156, 157, 160, 173, 183–185, 207, 232, 234, 250, 259
principle of immediacy 62, 86, 188, 252
principle of official impulse 155
principle of orality 62, 64, 86, 188, 250, 252
principle of publicity 62, 86, 188, 193, 250, 252
principle of probative freedom 172
principle of mandatory prosecution 50, 144, 200 *see also* footnotes 747, 767
principle of reasonable length to all judicial and administrative proceedings 33
principle of the rule of law 74
private accessory prosecutor (Brazilian criminal procedure) 151, 170
private accessory prosecutor (German criminal procedure) 59
private plaintiff 59, 65, 68, 69 *see also* 'Privatkläger'
privately retained expert 69, 156, 170, 171, 206, 208
Privatkläger *see under* 'private plaintiff'
privilege 95, 98, 108, 121, 123–127, 131, 132
pro bono 94
probable cause 92, 93, 95–99, 124, 153, 253
probative value 106–108, 117, 120–123, 126, 128, 129, 157, 158, 160, 164, 171–173, 179–181, 195, 207
procedimento comum (common procedure) 35, 138
procedimento especial (special procedure) 35, 138
procedural culture 191, 210–215, 217–219, 223, 258
procedural phase 25, 38, 49, 51, 63, 66, 76, 89, 94, 100, 138, 146, 148, 157, 177, 185, 189, 193, 194, 203, 205, 209, 222, 223, 229, 243, 250, 258
procedural safeguards 21, 25, 26, 31, 41, 60, 82, 88, 129, 188, 202, 219, 224, 226–229, 231–235, 240, 242, 247, 253, 255, 257, 258
(procedure of) evidence taking 25, 33, 34, 55, 59–63, 73, 91, 101, 102, 104, 105, 107, 135, 136, 143, 151, 152, 154–156, 159, 160, 166, 169, 173, 181, 182, 195, 197, 201, 206, 208, 217, 220, 224, 227, 228, 233, 234, 241, 243, 245, 247–249, 252, 253, 255
pro-defendant 182
professional judge 43, 44, 46, 52, 55–57, 84, 106, 142, 153, 194, 195, 229, 231, 251

Subject Index

prohibition in exploiting evidence   38, 75, 79, 86, 87, 107
prohibition in obtaining evidence   75, 79, 121, 123, 124, 132, 172
prohibition of anticipation of evidence   85
prohibition of evidence   75, 78, 87 *see also* 'Beweisverbote'
pronouncement of judgement *see under* 'announcement of the verdict'
prosecutor(s)   45–47, 49–51, 54, 63, 65, 66, 68, 69, 73, 79, 83, 91–93, 96–99, 141, 142, 144, 147, 156, 180, 192, 194, 195, 200, 208, 210, 219–221, 230, 237, 252
prosecutorial discretion   50, 92, 199, 200
psychotherapist-patient privilege   126
public defender(s)   48, 91, 93, 141, 142, 145, 161, 237, 255
public defender's office   145, 148, 237, 241
public prosecutor's office (Brazilian criminal procedure)   38, 146, 147, 221, 229, 235, 237, 238
public prosecutor's office (German criminal procedure)   41, 45, 47, 49, 54, 69, 252

question of guilt   71, 84 *see also* 'Schuldfrage'

real evidence   118, 121
reasonable doubt   93, 94, 102, 103, 111, 131, 135, 136
Recht auf die freie Entfaltung seiner Persönlichkeit *see under* 'right to free development of one's personality'
Rechtsstaatsprinzip *see under* 'principle of the rule of law'
record   71, 73, 94, 122
reformed continental European model   194, 254 *see also* 'inquisitorial (terminology)'
regional court   43–45, 57
residual exception   128
right against self-incrimination   112, 123, 124, 131, 132
right to a full defense *see under* 'principle to full defense'
right to free development of one's personality   75
right to request the inspection of the investigation file   51

right of personality   75, 76
right to ask questions   60, 70, 208 *see also* 'Fragerecht'
right to make statements during evidence taking   59, 60
right to a fair hearing   61, 62
right to defense counsel   48, 145
right to deposition   52, 95, 96, 235, 236, 237, 243
right to human dignity   75, 76, 176
right to silence   55, 76–78, 112, 161, 174, 175, 179, 194
right to refuse to testify   66, 67, 74, 80, 81, 125, 179
right to refuse testimony *see under* 'right to refuse to testify'
rito ordinário *see under* 'ordinary procedural outline'
rito sumário *see under* 'summary procedural outline'
rito sumaríssimo *see under* 'highly summarized procedural outline'

Schuldfrage   53, 56, 61, 84
Schutz der Menschenwürde *see under* 'right to human dignity'
search and seizure   124
second state exam   45
segurança jurídica *see under* 'legal certainty'
self-reading procedure   70
sentencing phase   100, 103, 253
sistema acusatório *see under* 'acusatório/accusatorial (Brazilian criminal procedure)'
sistema presidencialista   155, 167, 216
Staatsanwaltschaft *see under* 'public prosecutor's office (German criminal procedure)'
standard of adequate suspicion   50, 52, 53, 84, 252
standard of justified cause   147, 149, 150, 251 *see also* 'justa causa'
standard of proof   86, 98, 149, 192
stare decisis   89
state jurisdiction   24
strict forms of proof   61, 62
structural weaknesses   224, 227, 229, 232, 234, 243
subpoena   95, 96, 132, 133, 239, 243

summary procedural outline 138–140, 149, 165, 243
súmulas vinculantes (SV) 141, 148, 183, 235, 236 *see also* 'binding summary'
supra-legality theory 140
Superior Court of Justice 142 *see also* 'Superior Tribunal de Justica (STJ)'
Superior Tribunal de Justiça (STJ) 142, 217
Supreme Court (US-American legal system) 89, 90, 104, 120, 123, 125, 127, 130–132, 134, 135, 180
Supreme Federal Court 38, 140–142 *see also* 'Supremo Tribunal Federal (STF)'
Supremo Tribunal Federal (STF) 140, 142, 147, 217, 227, 231, 242, 254 *see also* 'Supreme Federal Court'

testimonial evidence 112, 118, 124, 127
testimonial privilege 127
trial setting 21, 23, 26, 36, 45, 57, 58, 60, 82–84, 93, 95, 103, 106, 109, 115, 120, 129, 135, 154, 168, 170, 181, 182, 189, 194–200, 203–208, 210–216, 220, 224, 225, 227, 228, 230, 232–234, 240–242, 244, 246, 247, 253–260

undue delay 122, 123
unfair prejudice 122

varas criminais (criminal courts) 142, 143
varas federais (federal courts) 142
verdict 32, 102, 103, 105, 106, 136, 183, 243, 246–248, 252–254
victim's examination 155, 156, 166, 169, 208
victim's statements 151, 152
voir dire 100, 136
Völkerrechtsfreundlichkeit 42

Wahrheitspflicht 66, 76 *see under* 'duty to testify truthfully'
wasting time 122
witness competency 113, 121, 127, 163
witness credibility 108, 113–115, 117, 121, 133, 240
witness examination 35, 46, 68, 71, 77, 79, 109, 114, 152, 166–168, 241
witnesses for the prosecution 94, 97, 102, 130, 135
written dossier *see under* 'investigative file'

Zeugenbeweis 62
Zeugnisverweigerungsrecht 80, 81